More Praise for Bob Ba
THE BOURBON K

• • •

"Death and deception! Money and mayhem! Murder in broad daylight! The trial of the century! With *The Bourbon King*, Bob Batchelor brings us a story that seems ripped from the tabloids, except it all happens to be true. Batchelor tells the story of George Remus, one of the world's most notorious bootleggers, with verve and pizzazz worthy of the gangster movies of Hollywood's Golden Era."

—BRIAN JAY JONES,
New York Times bestselling author of
Becoming Dr. Seuss and *Jim Henson: The Biography*

"Batchelor covers Remus' entire life, from his days in Chicago as a pharmacist and showboating attorney to his meteoric rise as 'the king of the bootleggers' to his final days in obscurity in Covington. And he meticulously traces how Remus built—and lost—his empire." —CINCINNATI ENQUIRER

"Guns, ghosts, graft (and even Goethe) are all present in Bob Batchelor's meticulous account of the life and times of the notorious George Remus. Brimming with liquor and lust, greed, and revenge, this entertaining book might make you reach for a good, stiff drink when you're done." —ROSIE SCHAAP,
author of *Drinking with Men*

"*The Bourbon King* is a much-needed addition to the American mobster nonfiction bookshelf. For too long, George Remus has taken a backseat to his Prohibition-era gangster peers like Lucky Luciano and Al Capone. Read here about a man who intoxicated the nation with a near-endless supply of top-shelf Kentucky bourbon, and then got away with murder." —JAMES HIGDON,
author of *The Cornbread Mafia: A Homegrown Syndicate's
Code of Silence and the Biggest Marijuana Bust in American History*

"Al Capone had nothing on George Remus, the true king of Prohibition. His life journey is fascinating, a Jazz Age cocktail that Bob Batchelor mixes for readers within these pages. Remus went from pharmacist to high-profile defense attorney to bourbon king to murderer." —TOM STANTON,
author of *Terror in the City of Champions: Murder, Baseball,
and the Secret Society That Shocked Depression-Era Detroit*

"An aggressive, ambitious foray into the brutal life and times of George Remus, an archetypal figure emerging from the sordid tapestry of life and crime in the Prohibition Era. This historical portrait is presented not in traditional, dry prose exposition, but rather in lucid, hard-hitting, tight writing interlaced with striking dialogue—a form of storytelling that is effective, efficient, and transporting."

—**PHILLIP SIPIORA,**
editor of *Mind of an Outlaw: Selected Essays of Norman Mailer*

"A captivating portrayal of the Roaring Twenties, *The Bourbon King* shows how George Remus built and lost a bootleg empire, only to be entangled in a love triangle that led to murder. Bob Batchelor brings the seedy underworld of the 1920s fully to life."

—**RICHARD STEIGMANN-GALL,**
author of *The Holy Reich*

"Bob Batchelor is at the top of his game in this fascinating study, which combines the thrilling and often disturbing story of George Remus's life with penetrating insights into the history of Prohibition, corruption, law enforcement, and the business of American bootlegging. A pleasure to read for historians and bourbon aficionados alike."

—**THOMAS HEINRICH,**
author of *Ships for the Seven Seas:*
Philadelphia Shipbuilding in the Age of Industrial Capitalism

"This is another contribution from a leading scholar of popular culture. He brings to life a colorful character from the Prohibition era in a style worthy of his subject."

—**LAWRENCE S. KAPLAN,**
University Professor Emeritus, Kent State University

"[A] comprehensive look at Remus's life . . . Recommended primarily for readers already interested in nonfiction accounts of organized crime or Prohibition."

—**LIBRARY JOURNAL**

"Impressively researched . . . Batchelor charts the growth of Remus's liquor empire and his spectacular downfall in astounding detail, and brings plenty of local knowledge to his version of the story." —**ELLERY QUEEN MYSTERY MAGAZINE**

"Strongly recommend . . . Very entertaining and a good read that provides an excellent look at the life and crimes of George Remus." —**BOURBONFOOL.COM**

"Batchelor delves into the story of a man whose name, strangely, has faded into the mist while that of Al Capone remains the archetype of the 1920s booze peddler."

—*AKRON BEACON JOURNAL*

"The book provides great insight into a brilliant man who was greatly troubled."

—*COLLECTED MISCELLANY*

"Wonderfully researched and entertaining." —*BROOKLYN DIGEST*

"A splashy story about a character as colorful as any born in Hollywood."

—*MILWAUKEE SHEPHERD EXPRESS*

"Historians and connoisseurs alike will love reading *The Bourbon King* by Bob Batchelor. It's the story of George Remus, his crimes, and his totally illegal prohibition-era empire." —*THE BOOKWORM SEZ*

"Bob Batchelor breathes life into the tale of George Remus . . . A lens into the dark heart of Prohibition." —*ENTERTAINMENT REPORT*

"Outlines the fascinating rise and fall of the hoodlum bon vivant, who built an empire on hooch." —*SOPHISTICATED LIVING*

Also by Bob Batchelor

Stan Lee: The Man Behind Marvel

Mad Men: A Cultural History

*Gatsby: The Cultural History of
the Great American Novel*

Bob Dylan: A Biography

The Bourbon King

THE LIFE AND CRIMES OF GEORGE REMUS, *Prohibition's Evil Genius*

BOB BATCHELOR

DIVERSION
BOOKS

For more information, email info@diversionbooks.com

Diversion Books
A division of Diversion Publishing Corp.
www.diversionbooks.com

Book design by Aubrey Khan, Neuwirth & Associates
Cover design by Tom Lau

First Diversion Books edition September 2019
First Diversion Books trade paperback edition December 2020
Paperback ISBN: 978-1-63576-738-4
eBook ISBN: 978-1-63576-585-4

Library of Congress cataloging in-publication data is available on file.

For Suzette, Kas, and Sophie—I love our team!

Contents

· · · · ·

PROLOGUE
Awash in Red

* * * * * *

"Lock me up. I've just shot my wife."

Emmet Kirgan, chief of detectives, looked back at the man in disbelief. George Remus bounced back and forth in front of the desk, then sank into a chair and surrendered. At one time rich, famous, powerful, and feared, he had been King of the Bootleggers; and Kirgan recognized him right away. Frank McNeal, another Cincinnati police officer in the room, stopped for a moment, unsure how to proceed. Kirgan stood quickly, grasping what Remus had admitted. Murderers usually had to be caught…

Earlier that day, George felt the blood slick on his hand and looked down in horror. His white silk shirt—crisp and unsoiled only several minutes before—was now awash in red. The pearl-handled pistol heavy in his grip, Remus glanced up, turning toward the street. Cars careened to a halt and bystanders cried out in disbelief. He scanned the area for the dark blue Buick and his driver.

The car was gone.

Just then, Remus heard the women's screams and the cries of children who had been playing nearby. He searched for an escape, his eyes darting left and right in the morning sunlight that washed over Eden Park. Turning away from the red and white rotunda at the heart of the park, Remus disappeared into the thick trees lining the area. He could still hear shrieks echoing in the air.

Emerging from the woods minutes later, Remus surfaced on Gilbert Avenue. He wandered south toward downtown. He continued to look back over his shoulder. A local Studebaker dealer named William Hulvershorn spotted him. He pulled over, offering a lift. Swinging open the dark green coupe door, Remus poked his head inside and then took a seat next to the man, thanking him profusely. George kept up a constant patter.

At times the driver struggled to follow his passenger's stream of thought. The stranger spoke in bursts with a German accent quite strong at times.

"Take me to the central station," he repetitively muttered between flurries of conversation. At first, Hulvershorn thought Remus was a traveling salesman, so he drove off toward the Pennsylvania Station train depot at the corner of Pearl and Butler Streets, Cincinnati's downtown hub.

When they arrived, Hulvershorn pulled the car up to the curb. He wished the man well. George popped open the door, stepped out, and realized he was at the train depot downtown.

"Why, you don't know who I am, do you?" Remus asked the car salesman.

"No sir, I don't," he replied.

"Well, my name is George E. Remus."

"Mr. Remus of fame? Well, I am glad to meet you."

"Then is when he told me he had done some shooting in the park," Hulvershorn would remember later.

With the confession, Remus closed the door. As the Studebaker pulled away, George turned. He saw a group of cabs and hailed one over, frustrated because he thought he'd told Hulvershorn to take him to the police station.

Still, it was only thirty minutes after he had fled Eden Park when Remus calmly walked into Cincinnati's First District Police Headquarters. Within that time, law enforcement across Cincinnati and northern Kentucky had been alerted to the heinous crime. As Remus approached Kirgan, the station's officer on duty, police were combing the area for the former bootleg baron.

"I will never forget the expression on her face when I was pulling her to me and she realized I had gotten her. She turned that hypocritical face to me and said, 'Oh, don't hurt me, Daddy, you know I love you,'" George said, exhausted.

PART ONE

· · · · ·

Birth of a Bootlegger

1

Napoleon of the Bar

George Remus leaned in close to his client, whispering into his ear. He glanced over at the jury, turned away, then took a longer look. The attorney noted their faces, the slightest reactions. He stared ahead, stopping on each juror for a split second. They saw his steel-blue eyes home in on them. Then, swinging up from the table, he bounded to his feet. George tugged at his shirtsleeves and smoothed out the thin wrinkles in his jacket. Ready to pounce, he pushed toward the jury box.

Remus stopped short. He smiled, letting them see his confidence, letting it wash over them—a singular moment to plead for his client's life.

Behind him, the accused man sat stone-faced. Another in a long succession of defendants who faced the gallows. The murderer felt the weight of the proceedings push down on his shoulders and chest. His wife was dead!

Doomed, observers thought. The prosecution had built a thorough case proving that he had poisoned her. It was a sinister thing, killing one's spouse. A guilty conviction meant sure death. Investigators had even found the bottle he used in the plot. Thoughts of the electric chair hung in everyone's minds.

Doomed! Everyone could see it.

After a momentary pause, George turned fast and snatched the bottle from the table. He spun the container around so all the jurors clearly caught a glimpse of the label. He raised it to them, as if toasting them at the end of a raucous night out on the town. Each person determining the fate of this wife-killer saw the familiar, dark skull-and-crossbones that adorned those types of toxins.

"There has been a lot of talk about poison in this case," Remus exclaimed. "But it is a lot of piffle. Look!"

Before anyone in the courtroom even had a chance to gasp, George dropped the deadly bottle to his lips. He gulped down the remaining liquid.

Empty!

The jurors reacted in unison. They were spellbound, but horrified. Did they really just see that? Did he drink it? Certainly, the jurors expected Remus to collapse, dead on the spot.

George stood there motionless for a moment longer, then turned and placed the bottle back on the table. He made sure that the skull-and-crossbones faced the jurors. Rather than falling over, he continued on with his closing argument. Once again looking at each in turn, the attorney demanded that they return a "not guilty" verdict.

Remus finished, spinning on his heels, and casually walked back to the defense table where he stood at his client's side. After the judge gave final instructions, the jurors quietly shuffled out of the courtroom, each one glancing over at the lawyer. He'd swallowed the poison. They expected it to be the last time they saw him alive.

Fifteen minutes later, they filed back into the packed room. After a tense few moments...

"Not guilty," the foreman announced.

He looked over at the judge. Immediately, catcalls reverberated around the room. Spectators gasped, some covered their mouths with their hands. Stunned.

In the front of the room, George beamed and nodded toward the jury box. Remus, "the Napoleon of the Bar," they called him.

Another win.

The famous attorney had not only downed the poison, but his precarious gambit kept his client from the gallows. The jurors must have thought: "Well, if the poison isn't actually poison, then there is no way it was murder." They barely had time to hash out the details. The "not guilty" verdict seemed the only possibility.

What no one in the courtroom seemed to know that day was that George Remus had been a successful pharmacist for more than a decade before making the odd career leap to lawyer. Putting his extensive pharmaceutical background to work, he knew exactly what antidote counteracted the poison in the bottle on the table.

Trusting his deep knowledge and experience, he mixed and drank the potion before entering the courtroom. George knew that the toxin would be rendered harmless. Another Remus trick.

Whether or not his client had murdered his wife did not mean much to Remus. His triumph—one of many he had threaded together recently—meant keeping the man from death row.

George would do anything to keep a client from that barbaric end. He had watched too many people go to the electric chair. In his mind, if the justice system created loopholes that only he were willing or intelligent enough to exploit, then he should not be criticized or sanctioned for taking those risks.

No emotion, no shame, just victory.

"I could have lasted two hours longer," George asserted, nearly breathless and waterlogged after five hours in the chilly Lake Michigan water.

At thirty years old, Remus was older than most competitive swimmers, perhaps considered by most as too old to compete—but the pharmacist-turned-lawyer had mouths to feed and a full-time career, so he remained a true amateur. He relied on toughness to make up for the gap between his age and that of his rivals.

George had entered the Chicago Athletic Association's ten-mile swimming marathon, a grueling course that ran from the Chicago Yacht Club to the South Shore Country Club. Although it was August, temperatures had dropped the morning of the race. A lilting wind turned steady, which created choppy conditions. The weather, always a wildcard in the Windy City, turned what swimmers thought was an achievable distance race into an endurance test.

Even in perfect conditions, these contests were exhilarating, but brutal, for the combatants. A ten-mile water race, like a marathon on land, demanded a combination of stamina and mental resolve. Unlike their counterparts on foot, though, swimmers faced extreme dangers. Battling waves and near hypothermia took a toll. Physical breakdown could happen in an instant, obliging race officials to watch from lifeboats to constantly oversee the competitors.

Life and death hung in the balance.

E. P. Swatek, the contestant pulled out of the water just before Remus, reportedly faced "imminent danger." He survived because two men from shore had jumped in to save him. According to a reporter on the scene, the heroes "helped keep him above water" until a boat fished him out. Swatek lived but came out of the water "delirious" and "in a weak condition." Several others had to be treated by medical personnel after being hoisted out of frigid Lake Michigan.

Remus had been the last one of the swimmers pulled from the drink—urged actually—by race officials. Endurance swimming was George's specialty. Like he had done in so many of his pursuits, Remus outlasted the competition, exhibiting extraordinary toughness and determination.

A sports reporter who covered the race wrote, "The big fellow, although making little progress, was still in first-class condition."

George himself said afterward, "I would not have given up the race if it were not for the judges calling me in and taking me into their boat." Contending that he was ready for two or three more hours, he explained that the owner of a launch "brought some sandwiches...which I ate in the water."

Athletic competition, particularly swimming and water polo, was a centerpiece of George's life. He joined a series of sporting associations, including the Chicago Athletic Association, which gave him standing and reputation on the local and national athletic scenes.

Remus traveled the country participating in events, even as his professional life flourished and his personal life became more complicated. In September 1907, a month after the Chicago swim, he qualified for the open water swimming national championship in St. Louis. The Windy City sent a strong contingent, driven by civic pride and the desire to prove that they were tougher than men from other locales.

Spectators were attracted to the novelty of these long-distance swimming races—this was the era of Theodore Roosevelt's "Strenuous Life," after all—drawn to the danger participants faced in attempting such feats. Crowds lined the banks to cheer on men from their hometowns, while more adventurous fans climbed aboard boats or skiffs to get a closer view of the action from the water. These vessels would become makeshift emergency ferries. Often, spectators helped fish besieged swimmers out of the river, essentially saving lives when rowboats could not reach contestants fast enough.

The grueling ten-mile championship race took place in a swift stretch of the Mississippi River and ended under the city's Eads Bridge. Reporters covering the event regaled readers with stories of failed attempts and daring rescues. Several men nearly lost their lives attempting to win the championship. Remus was not one of the first ten finishers, but again demonstrated his grit by entering the race and competing against athletes that were often a decade younger.

The exertion of staying in the water for hours and the determination to compete in these kinds of long-distance races were lynchpins of George's evolving physical and mental condition, both in his early life and as he grew into manhood. His life had never been easy, from growing up in a poor German immigrant family to the long hours he worked to support and care for his parents. The endurance tests seemed a perfect complement to the way his mind blossomed.

Struggle was a way of life for George when he was young, just as it had been for his parents Carl Franz Remus and Marie Louise (Karg). Carl was born in August 1849 in Friedeberg, one of two walled cities in Neumark, a region within the Electorate of Brandenburg that had become part of Prussia in 1701. His brother Johan arrived in May 1850 but both parents died later the same year, suspected casualties of a cholera outbreak. Luckily, Frank and Amelia Karg took in the orphans. The local family ran a successful wool milling operation.

As he grew up, the young orphan took on an apprenticeship with Mr. Karg. Young Carl began courting his mentor's daughter Marie, and they fell in love. The older Karg evidently accepted the boy, who everyone now called "Frank," a nickname earned out of respect for the Karg family patriarch. Marie and Frank were married in 1872 in Friedeberg, shortly after the end of the Franco-Prussian War. Frank's brother Johan also married, a local girl named Julia, but details of her life have been lost to history.

Marie and Frank started a family in Friedeberg. Some of their children, like so many millions across Europe in that era, died either in childbirth or infancy. Two daughters lived: Elizabeth, born in her parents' hometown in 1875, and Martha four years later in 1879. Between the girls, Marie and Frank welcomed their oldest son, George, on November 13, 1876. Over the ensuing decades, George played fast and loose with his birth year, usually listing it somewhere between 1874 and 1879. The date changed to fit whatever the circumstances were at the time.

Frank and Marie did not have a particularly easy life in West Prussia, despite her family's middle-class status. In many respects, the situation worsened for the five Remus family members when they reached America. They traveled to the United States aboard the *Fitlington*, a passenger ship that had departed from Kristiansand, a bucolic seaside town on the southern tip of Norway. They arrived in New York City in June 1882.

The Remus clan did not stay in New York City, unlike millions of immigrants who streamed into America. Instead, they moved south, settling for a short time in Baltimore. Soon, however, they moved halfway across the country to Milwaukee, a city rich in German and Prussian heritage. In the late 1880s, the Wisconsin city served as a haven for people arriving in America and claimed the highest percentage of foreign-born residents in the country.

The Remuses would have felt at home in Milwaukee's extensive German neighborhoods surrounded by people who spoke their language and had similar cultural norms. Frank, however, continued to struggle to find employment, and troubles continued to mount. Although family lore claimed that two American-born sons perished in infancy in Wisconsin, only one—Francis— was uncovered in official records. He died in childbirth in 1884.

Not having much luck establishing a homestead or financial footing, the Remus family left Milwaukee and moved south to Chicago when George was eight years old. While many immigrant families took advantage of the city's bustling industry and constant need for workers, the Remuses' economic challenges persisted. Frank suffered chronic unemployment in the Windy City. When he found work, the pay amounted to only about $9 to $11 per week. The money did not go far in a household with many hungry children to feed.

"It was a hardship," George said about his early years.

The Remus family grew in Chicago. Another daughter, Anna, came into the world in 1889, while Herman was born in 1891. Frank's brother Johan also immigrated to the city, arriving in 1888 with his wife Julia and son John, who had been born in Losen, a city in Prussian Poland on June 24, 1878.

With little hope that his father could earn a steady living, George interceded, explaining, "I took hold of matters from the age of about 14 years and three months [February 1890] and assisted in supporting the family." As a matter of fact, the youngster soon became "the main supporter of the family."

Although a good student, George could not continue his education while working. He dropped out, opting for a job in the pharmacy that his uncle George Karg owned. His financial burden encompassed the entire family, extending to his three sisters Elizabeth, Martha, and Anna, both before and after their later marriages. George also supported his younger brother Herman, who had suffered a mysterious head injury as a boy. George would later explain that his brother had been hit in the head by a brick, unsure whether someone threw it or the object fell on him. The traumatic brain injury and resulting complications forced Herman to be admitted to the Kankakee Hospital for the Insane. He died there in 1913 at the age of twenty-two.

The financial obligations George carried put him under enormous strain. As a result, when he took over the economic reins as a young teenager, he distanced himself from his father—whom he considered an abusive alcoholic. As the oldest male sibling, he had to take on a guardian role for his sisters and brother. He would continue to provide for their well-being but withdrew emotionally.

Remus found a substitute passion for family love by developing an intense single-mindedness about sports and health. The young man was obsessive about swimming and took to the water whenever he could, diving headlong into rivers and lakes around Chicago with his boyhood friends. He allegedly swore off alcohol during his formative years. George had seen how the excursions down to the beer garden had changed his father, quickly withering him and further weakening the man's inner resolve. Even the occasional drink ran counter to George's dedication to exercise. His inner reservoir of steadfastness became a defining trait.

Years later, a physician would describe the youngster's behavior as "hyperactivity," but also noted ominously, "he is emotionally unstable, he is devoid of normal emotional reaction." Even as a child George became relentless in chasing success and tested himself in physical activities that required toughness.

Meanwhile, the years of hardship and stress took a toll on George and his family. In the late 1880s and early 1900s, leaders in the push for state and national Prohibition attacked casual drinking by German immigrants, which was a focal point of their culture, especially in the camaraderie and fellowship exhibited at beer gardens. As Frank's employment woes continued, his drinking increased, as did his time away from home.

In 1916, Frank Remus left the world quietly, just as he had lived in his final years. The cause of death was an ailment diagnosed as heart disease. If family tales hold water, it is more likely that alcoholism was at the root of his deterioration. The German habit of drinking beer with meals was frowned upon in polite American society, so it is difficult to gauge whether the older Remus's consumption reached the threshold of alcoholism. Frank was sixty-seven years old.

Marie Remus—George's plainspoken, old-world German mother—lived for another dozen years. She passed away on December 10, 1928, in Cincinnati.

Uncle George Karg treated his nephew well. George was allowed to spend more and more time at the pharmacy, located at 952 Milwaukee Avenue in Wicker Park in the stately, red brick Christensen Building, which had been built in 1887. The robust business district around the Wicker Park location and its vast, green public park had attracted many German and Scandinavian immigrants to the neighborhood. The main thoroughfare held a mix of grocers, real estate offices, and saloons that many observers would later call a "city within a city" for its many amenities.

Young George started as a clerk, learning about people by watching how they interacted with his uncle. Gradually, he took on more complicated tasks. As his workload increased, the teenager began sleeping in the store at night, primarily as a way to live frugally, but also establishing himself apart from his family. He still turned most of his earnings over to Frank and Marie, a dutiful son providing for his parents and siblings. Learning from his uncle helped George get a strong footing, but he wanted a more substantial life.

Enrolling in pharmacy courses at night, George eventually passed the Illinois pharmacy examination when he was just nineteen years old. Still two years away from being able to legally practice as a druggist, Remus took the most pragmatic route—he lied to the licensing board about his age. He heeded no rules or regulations that seemed illogical. As he came into manhood, George developed his own opinions about rules and regulations, creating an internal scale that guided his decision-making.

Passing the examination served as a springboard. In later years, George liked to boast that although he only had $9.88 saved at the time he took the pharmacy test, due to supporting his parents and siblings, he was still able to buy the pharmacy from his uncle. Young Remus promised to pay Karg $6,000 through a series of loans that the older man helped him procure. George worked long hours to pay off the notes in little more than two years. As a trusted storeowner, Remus's stature grew in the local community. Then, he utilized this position to buy another store on credit for $4,500, just three blocks down the street.

At twenty-one years old, George had already gained broad insight into the minds of his customers and patients by running the pharmacies, doling out basic medical advice, and working directly with several physicians. Looking for additional opportunities to make money, Remus took a ten-month basic optometry service course and passed the certification exam. The license enabled him to give patients routine eye care and permitted him to call himself "Dr. Remus." George later admitted that he wanted the title to evoke respectability among his immigrant patients and among fellow business leaders.

Though his title was primarily a status symbol for the young man, George didn't much believe in what passed as contemporary medicine anyway. From his pharmacist role, he realized that many medical prescriptions doctors ordered were pure claptrap. The endless pills were more or less placebos meant to possibly fill some need, but rarely addressed what truly ailed the patient. Despite its shortcomings, the system worked profitably—doctors were viewed as authoritative community leaders, while patients received what they thought was proper treatment, even if the medications only loosely filled that definition and might be little more than a concentrated dosage of alcohol or some pain-killing or hallucinogenic powder.

Pharmacists, George realized, played a significant role as caregivers in this chaotic system, particularly in the poor immigrant neighborhoods where he operated. Families did not have money to spare for more expensive office visits. He gained the trust of his German customers. In turn, they looked to him for advice.

As a young, prosperous pharmacist, George took the path that many German immigrants would follow—he started a family. George thought that his first duty had always been building a strong financial standing for himself and his kin. He had little time for romance. Then, Lillian Kraus became George's first serious love.

After a quick courtship, Remus married Lillian, an accomplished pianist and music teacher, on July 10, 1899. He was about to turn twenty-three years old, while his new bride was two years younger. Nine months later, they welcomed a little girl to the family, naming her Romola. As she grew, Romola developed jet black hair and dark eyes, like her mother. George was already balding and had a pale complexion, though sometimes tanned to a mottled brown with all the outdoor swimming. His most defining trait was piercing blue eyes that seemed to leap from his head when he looked at someone. His thick German accent rounded out as he aged, but he still spoke fluently with his countless immigrant customers. Remus also possessed an unheard-of level of brute strength. He was physically squat and powerful.

Later, George would boast that before meeting Lillian, his love life was "like every man, but not nearly as bad as most." He viewed himself as chivalrous, and definitely not a cad, like many successful young people.

Without going into detail, Remus explained, "I could have had all kinds of women at my feet if I had wanted them, but I did not take advantage of that."

Yearning to capitalize on his intelligence and expand his business interests beyond the poor customers he served in Wicker Park, George created the Remus Pharmaceutical Company. Specializing in "proprietary medicines," he cooked up a variety of treatments for common ailments, all using his personal brand—"Remus' Pain Celery Compound, Remus' Pinkham Compound... Remus' Liver Pills and Cathartic Pills, and stomach remedies and cough drops and lozenges." The Remus Pharmaceutical Company sold these creations— modifications of more popular tonics and elixirs sold by traveling salesmen and in large stores nationwide—in the German communities of Milwaukee and Chicago. George also founded the S & S Drug Company at the corner of 59th and Halstead in Chicago. The firm sold drugs wholesale to 250–500 retail druggists.

Despite the successes he had as a business owner and pharmacist, working long hours during the day and conducting some rudimentary medical examinations, the young man dreamed of a more illustrious life. He did not lack gratitude for what the pharmacy had given him—a job at his uncle's shop when his own father could no longer support the family and the considerable wealth to buy that store as well as another to run as his own.

Remus just wanted more.

The simplest route for George may have been medical school, but he had reservations about becoming a physician. The enterprising young pharmacist simply didn't believe in how medicine was practiced at the time, viewing many physicians as charlatans.

"I saw too much from the viewpoint of where certain doctors, where you have a little pain in the head, would say it was neuralgia and have the patient come two or three times a week...I suppose I didn't like that angle of it." Medicine, for George, would have crossed that line between right and wrong he had created.

When Remus considered other options, he thought about a career in the law as a possibility. He had needed legal representation on several occasions, and his attorneys were intelligent and respected in the community. The young man also perceived law as more thrilling, whereas medicine might feel like the work he was already doing as a pharmacist. "I figured that the law practice had a larger field for future activities and I was tired of looking at the same four walls," he said.

With the same enthusiasm that had helped him attain his pharmacy license as a teenager, George plunged into the idea of studying the law. But, first he had to find a school that would enable him to continue the pharmacy operations a little longer.

Seeing a nearby program listed in the *Chicago Tribune* classified ads under "Instruction," where it promised the "best preparation for business and public life," Remus enrolled at the Illinois College of Law. The school offered classes during the day and at night, which enabled George to alternate his schedule, sometimes taking regular classes and other times doing so after the pharmacy closed.

The law school operated in a suite of classrooms headquartered above the Olympic Theater at 112 Clark Street. Rebuilt in 1896, the Olympic featured striking marble walls and a mirrored ceiling. Artists carved a flotilla of mermaids prancing among enormous waves into the balcony woodwork, while the seating areas were covered in leather. The back of the building featured large, ornate stained-glass windows. Many observers considered it the grandest vaudeville joint in the nation. This was an apt setting to study law in the early twentieth century, since law was more carnivalesque than formal and many trials were determined by a particular lawyer's theatrics.

On May 30, 1904, George took his place at the seventh annual commencement of the Illinois College of Law. Howard N. Ogden, president of the college, conferred Remus's degree along with his thirty-three classmates, including one woman—H. Helen Arnett-Castles—still a rarity among law degree awardees. Illinois College of Law graduates had achieved some local renown for having the highest percentage of successful candidates on the state bar exam, so Remus and most of his classmates would soon enter firms around the Chicago law scene. George had sped through the law work, graduating in about 18 months, cutting more than a year off the regular program.

Spring 1904 marked Remus's move from pharmacist and storeowner to attorney, but it took some time to extricate himself from the pharmacy. Shortly after graduating, he sold the first store he had purchased from his uncle for $6,500. These funds gave him the startup cash he needed to open a law practice on Wilson Avenue in a residential section of Chicago along its fashionable North Shore.

Being in the right place at the right time often adds to one's fortunes, and George's lucky streak continued. His business grew alongside Chicago's booming economy. Modernizing the nation's Midwest hub necessitated endless construction, which required countless workers, as well as people to service the flourishing marketplace. Remus plunged into this world, initially specializing in labor law. The hardscrabble world of labor and unionization efforts fit into George's self-conception of hard work and toughness. In this early period of his law career, Remus took great pride in leading men.

"I represented the Teamsters' Union; I organized them…We had 45,000 members…I became the attorney to the steamfitters," he explained. As it would be known across the country, George dubbed Chicago "the hotbed for organized labor."

The connection with organized labor also brought the young attorney into the circle of Clarence Darrow, the activist legal scholar who had gained a national following. The older man had established his reputation advocating ideas centered on equitable wages and working conditions for the countless working-class immigrants in the US, but also basic human rights for the poor. Many workers across the nation were not fluent in English, so they could not speak for themselves or protest the horrific labor conditions they were forced to endure. Darrow became their hero.

Among his many meaningful battles, Clarence stood at the fore in the clash between corporations and labor unions. He represented the United Mine Workers in the early years of the century when the vast majority of homes nationwide were heated by coal. In 1902, when mine owners in eastern Pennsylvania refused union demands to discuss wage increases, the UMW launched the great anthracite coal strike. The pitched clashes led to outright warfare between labor forces, the Pennsylvania National Guard, local police, and hired guns from private detective agencies. The violence and uproar forced President Theodore Roosevelt to intervene, eventually working with financier J. P. Morgan to establish a commission to oversee the negotiations.

In his masterful closing argument in that landmark legal case, Darrow had defended the honor of the union to strike. More importantly, he advocated for the individual integrity of the immigrant workers, which the union saw as the core of its mission. Unions must be allowed to organize, Darrow proclaimed, because unionization led directly to "the right of the individual to have a better life, a fuller life, a completer life."

Meanwhile, a combination of smarts, confidence, and hard work enabled Remus to prosper in law just as he had in the pharmacy business. Darrow became a kind of mentor. Just like the older attorney, Remus took on cases in several areas. Initially, he focused on labor law and worker's rights, but also took up cases defending criminals who faced the death penalty, just like Darrow.

Certainly Darrow, who had a growing cadre of young lawyers in his orbit, was an influential role model for Remus. They shared a Chicago office building and saw each other often. As Remus took on more of Darrow's philosophical leanings, he adopted a deep hatred for the death penalty.

Remus directed his practice toward criminal defense, particularly when capital punishment was on the line. He specialized in defending murderers and criminals while never breaking completely away from the union and corporate work. The decision to become a courtroom attorney was a wise choice. Juries found him spellbinding—like they did Darrow—even if George's over-the-top performances might draw eyerolls from opposing counsel and irritated judges. Whether viewed as a compliment or an affront, the nickname "Napoleon of the Bar" fit the stocky attorney well.

Remus solidified a partnership with two fellow attorneys that became Remus, LaBuy, and Gulano. They were part of a new breed of attorneys in the Windy City, not part of the traditional boys' club based on family connections and an Ivy League pedigree. In hopes of breaking down some of those barriers, the three established the Lawyers' Association, a kind of upstart alternative to the stuffy Chicago Bar Association. They grew the organization to 2,800 members with Remus as the first vice president. It was a taste of greater glory in the legal community and George lapped it up. Leadership suited him.

By 1915, George had helped build the practice into a thriving firm, not only defending high-profile criminals, but also mixing with some of the nation's finest legal minds. Joseph S. LaBuy, his partner for fifteen years, noted George's fine reputation during this time as an attorney and "law-abiding citizen."

He had the leadership positions and the look. And a deeper dive into how, exactly, he practiced law explains why an editorial in *The Virginia Law Register* once labeled him a "godsend" for the "elite of crime" in Chicago.

Remus did everything in his power to win. In more polite and aristocratic legal circles, his cutthroat tactics earned him a wave of detractors. Many legal aces in the Windy City suffered his blowhard ploys and bullying tactics. They derisively called him "Weeping, Pleading Remus," but only behind his back. None of his critics could risk offending him out of fear that they might some-day have to face off against Remus in the courtroom.

For opponents, Remus was all theatrics and bluster, an idea that went hand-in-hand with his growing reputation as a dandy. Onlookers gawked as he walked down the street nattily dressed or pulled up in his chauffeured limou-sine, chest puffed out and sporting a perfectly fitted suit. He liked having eyes on him.

George's association with Darrow deepened his philosophical opposition to the death penalty, but Remus would push boundaries to save his clients from execution in ways that Darrow may not have appreciated. In what his opponents would have considered particularly appalling, when it came to cases that involved a potential death penalty verdict, George stopped at nothing to stave off that verdict, even if it meant risking the sanctity of the legal establishment and the law itself.

In one high-profile case, the thirty-five-year-old attorney defended Lillian Beatrice Ryall-Conway, who faced murder charges for conspiring with her husband Charles to murder Sophia Singer on October 29, 1912. The characters involved in the Singer murder were stranger than fiction: Charles was a circus clown with a wooden left leg who sometimes performed as a high-dive acrobat, while his wife Lillian was a burlesque dancer, bareback horse rider, lion tamer, and snake charmer who worked using the alias May Monte. Singer was a Baltimore heiress and actress who had fallen in love with a man named William R. Worthen and the couple ran away to the Windy City to elope. What seemed to be hope for a new beginning for Sophia and William devolved into a gruesome tragedy that unfolded in a run-down Chicago flophouse at 3229 Indiana Avenue.

The *Chicago Tribune* and other papers across the nation made the Singer murder front-page news, a story of high-brow and low-brow society violently colliding with fatal consequences. According to newspaper reports, Worthen came home late that evening after storming out following an argument with his fiancée. He grew alarmed, seeing blood spattered in the hallway, then a trail of blood leading into the kitchen and covering the table. He rushed to Singer's room and found Sophia dead—bound and gagged, with her body wrapped in a blanket. Police later determined that the heiress had been beaten to death with a homemade billy club fashioned from an iron doorknob and handle that had been wrapped up in a handkerchief.

Worthen told police that Conway had showed them this trick of making a weapon, because his life in the circus was fraught with danger and he needed a way to protect himself. "This is what I knock 'em out with," the circus clown had told the couple.

Chicago police put out an alert and they were captured in Lima, Ohio, Charles's hometown. Under questioning, Lillian confessed that Charles had murdered Sophia in a fit of rage because she had declined his sexual advances. He beat her to death and stole her cash and jewels. The next day, Charles admitted that he'd murdered the woman.

While the evidence and confessions made the case seem cut-and-dry, lawyers were brought in and the fireworks began, fueled by the media coverage.

The Conways and their strange carnival lives titillated readers. Dozens of papers picked up the story, filling in the details of the gruesome murder, always leaving readers hungry for more intrigue.

Representing Lillian against both her husband and the conspiracy charges, George added to the spectacle by battling defense attorney Samuel Foos, who represented Charles. Reporters disclosed that Remus got into a "bitter fight" with Foos over which Conway would testify first. The heated exchange led to a fistfight. Several deputy sheriffs were forced to intervene. The notion that the lawyers threw punches took some of the focus off Lillian's role as conspirator and demonstrated that Remus would insert himself, if necessary, to divert attention away from the gruesome murder.

George built a defense strategy to demonstrate that Lillian had given a forced confession to police, who had roughed her up. He knew she was guilty, but hoped to portray her as a dutiful wife as well as a victim in the crime so that the jury would not lump her into a death penalty verdict with her husband. Instead, the *Chicago Tribune* noted, George "pictured her to the jury as an obedient wife...willing to perjure herself and take the risk of a long term in the penitentiary, or even death, to save her husband from the gallows." Lillian was a devoted wife, according to the attorney, not a coldblooded murderer.

George pulled out even more tricks at the end of the trial, painting himself as a sympathetic figure. Allegedly, he became deathly ill, but later "came to the courtroom from a sick bed." The paper reported that he "was kept going on injections of strychnine." He then delivered the typical stirring Remus argument, filled with impassioned pleas and theatrics.

It all worked.

Yes, she was guilty, but rather than hang, Remus's client received a fourteen-year prison sentence, and the jurors even recommended clemency. Members of the jury later told reporters that they believed Remus's view that the "love for her husband...caused her to commit perjury." Lillian later corroborated that she lied to police to protect her husband.

The glut of national headlines surrounding the Conway trial earned Remus another burst of fame. More murder and more headlines were to come.

Hotel manager Frank Bering and physician A. H. Waterman burst through the door and into a nightmare. In front of them, a man stood half-naked, partially covered by a flimsy lounging robe. Crimson stains were smeared across the neckline. His torso, hands, and underwear were covered in blood.

In one hand, he held a gun. In the other, a pocketknife. He stared at a photo on the nearby dresser, a picture of pretty woman posed with two small children. Barely noticing the two men, he began hacking at his own neck, drawing a wide gash that sprayed blood around the room.

After a moment to assess the carnage, Bering and Waterman dove toward him, grabbing the knife and gun before he could do more damage. In the tussle, they noticed a woman immobile on the bed. The doctor flew to her side, ready for triage. Her throat had been cut from ear to ear.

"She did it herself," the man blurted. "We decided to die. I made a failure of business. We were sick of it."

Choking back the blood in his throat and growing more frantic, he explained, "I didn't shoot her. She shot herself. Then I used the pistol. I made a bad job of it. I tried the knife. It wouldn't work."

Then they saw blood streaming from bullet holes in the man's chest and lower leg. Waterman peeled back the covers blanketing the woman and saw four bullet wounds scattered over her body, including the one that most likely killed her directly above her left ear.

"She couldn't have inflicted those wounds," Dr. Waterman yelled. "You say you stood by and saw your wife kill herself."

"She did it," the man mumbled.

The grisly events that took place on October 16, 1913, in Chicago's prestigious Hotel Sherman launched one of the decade's most scandalous true-crime stories. The ensuing trial grabbed national headlines, virtually ensuring that people across the country would soon learn the names of William Cheney Ellis, the husband/murderer; deceased socialite Eleanor Hosea Ellis; and Mr. Ellis's masterful defense attorney, George Remus.

William and Eleanor Ellis were both from wealthy and influential Cincinnati families. They grew up in luxurious settings among the elite in the Queen City. William's father dealt in leather goods and had a buggy shop. The Hosea family's renown dated back to the Civil War era when they attained their riches in the prosperous steamboat industry. Their wealth and upper-crust status immediately thrilled readers. Reporters flocked to the scene.

Ellis and Remus knew the trial was a fight to keep the defendant from the hangman's noose. He would be convicted. Period. And the double-suicide claim had no chance of saving Ellis's life. Neither—of course—did any of the known facts surrounding the actual killing.

Instead, Remus shifted the focus—away from the bloody mess and the real rationale for the murder—to temporary insanity, and how Eleanor Ellis's infidelity and its effect on her husband's state of mind stood as the true reason for the crime. If Remus could convince the jury that Eleanor's lover was the villain, then they might just spare William. Fred Cauldwell, a dry goods dealer from Brantford, Ontario, became Remus's target.

Ellis testified at trial in late February and early March. He spoke in a calm voice, nearly monotone.

"He steadfastly declared that his wife had confessed her love for another man," a reporter noted.

Ellis claimed that he begged Eleanor to return to Cincinnati, where "he was a respected and prosperous businessman" and where they had "two little children." She would not listen, he countered, causing him to enter a blackout-like state.

"The first thing I knew I–I–I found myself in bed with my arms around Mrs. Ellis. I had on her kimono. And–and–and, I saw my darling wife was dead. I held the knife and cut my throat and wrists."

Compelled to answer the ultimate question about why he would kill her, Ellis explained, "She had no wrong thoughts. She simply was infatuated with that man, Fred Cauldwell…she confessed her love for him."

Whenever the prosecution seemed to be scoring points with the jury, Ellis would faint or he and Remus would conceive of other means to distract them. Remus would have Ellis cry or lose consciousness to emphasize his own points, as well.

Eleanor's father unwittingly played into the courtroom drama, rushing to his daughter's honor when William declared her infidelity to the world. From the witness stand, prosecuting attorney Stephen Malato asked Ellis if he had told his wife before he married her that he had a venereal disease, which he categorized as "a horrible blood disease." When Ellis said, "no," his father in-law Robert Hosea jumped up, shouting: "You dog—You dog! I will kill you! I will kill you! You dog! You dog!" The older man continued yelling before finally sitting back down, gripping the arms of his chair. His wife, said a witness, "stroked the old man's arm while she bent her head forward to hide the tears."

Ellis fainted when the prosecutor—holding the actual murder weapon—asked him about killing Eleanor. Malato tried to match Remus gimmick-for-gimmick, leveling the gun at Ellis's head and pulling the trigger three times. The hammer clicks sent loud echoes through the room.

"With an inarticulate groan Ellis wilted back in the chair," a reporter described. "Remus," he explained, "rushed to the witness stand and saved Ellis from crumbling to the floor. It was five minutes before he could be revived."

Ellis passed out at least two more times during the trial. Once, he lost consciousness after a four-hour cross-examination session. The prosecution had skewered the defendant, but then he fainted, hoping to undermine those points and grasp at the jury's sympathies. The second episode took place as Remus read a telegram that Eleanor had sent the "other man," her alleged lover Fred Cauldwell.

"Holding the copy of the telegram at arm's length," an observer noted, "Remus glanced triumphantly toward his client. But Ellis was blinded with tears. 'I knew it! I knew it,' he sobbed, then slid forward in his chair, swooning."

At the end of the day, Remus took the battle public, announcing that reading the telegram into the court record constituted "a great victory for us." He then implied that nefarious forces were at work to put William Cheney Ellis to death. "Powerful interests in Cincinnati and men of influence have conspired to send my client to the gallows in order to protect the name of his wife. I believe this jury will acquit him on the plea of transitory insanity."

Three different medical experts later testified that Ellis suffered from some form of epilepsy. Arthur F. Beifeld, who examined the murderer, diagnosed Ellis with "psychic epilepsy," which "affects only the brain cells and does not harm the nerves." George pushed him for more information, and Beifeld obliged, explaining that the person would have "an absolute blank" mind during such an attack and not know the difference between right and wrong.

In his final plea for Ellis, George proved masterful, as usual, in front of the jury. Leading them away from the facts and toward the ruse he and William had created, Remus explained:

> I know you cannot believe what they have told you—that such a murder was the work of a man in his right mind; that a sane husband would so wantonly destroy the woman at whose side he had spent so many happy years; that all the kisses he gave to her were shams, masking murderous intent. You are men. Treat this unfortunate creature as such. The best that is in me is not good enough for him in his hour of need.

When Ellis was finally called in front of the jury at verdict, it was as if he were a new man. He confidently strode into the courtroom—packed with a crowd that included local government officials and dignitaries—and stood straight and tall next to Remus. Ellis fidgeted with his cufflinks, and then broke open an orange, his lone nod to the misery and fainting spell he had experienced earlier in the trial. "He carried the attentive attitude of a keen business man, preparing to face a business issue," a reporter noted. When the clerk read the decision—guilty, but with only a fifteen-year sentence, instead of death by hanging—"no change of expression came over the man's face…When the words 'fifteen years' were spoken he swallowed a segment of orange."

Turning to the newspapermen in attendance, Remus shone, declaring, "It is a complete victory. We are more than assured."

Saving William Cheney Ellis from the gallows launched George Remus's legal reputation to new heights. The Chicago press found the flashy lawyer, decked out in handmade suits and his signature silk shirts, eminently quotable. Each new story splashed across the headlines brought the Napoleon of the Bar increased attention. His celebrity status also brought a ballooning bank account.

By 1920, when the average home in America cost $4,500, the talented counselor earned $45,000 a year as a criminal defense attorney, sometimes representing big shots in the midst of hostile divorces, small-time booze peddlers, or vicious murderers.

On May 15, 1921, Illinois state officials released Ellis from the Joliet penitentiary after just seven years. A reporter from the *Chicago Tribune*, which had so closely watched the infamous trial and reported its every detail, declared Ellis was "damaged goods." Despite being a "model prisoner," spending his time laboring at the prison farm, "Ellis left prison broken in health, impoverished, friendless, unknown to his children." Remus's scheming had granted Ellis his life, but he would live that sentence out as a shell of his former self.

In stark contrast, George's ego, back account, and belly—despite his long addiction to sports and exercise—swelled. He enjoyed what his hard work delivered, lodging at luxury hotels and feasting on expensive gourmet foods.

As with athletics and the pharmacy business, George's triumphs as attorney were fueled by his relentless addiction to success. Over and over, he demonstrated resilience. He did whatever it took to score.

His personal life, however, grew increasingly disheveled. In maintaining a successful marriage, he was a failure. When it came to women, Remus's self-discipline crumbled.

2

Illicit Relations

DATELINE CHICAGO—
TWO SHOES FOR FOUR FEET, BUT FURS FOR AFFINITY

The headline shouted from the page. And the accompanying story provided a much-needed break from constant reports of World War I battlefronts in Europe and economic woes afflicting America.

The article ran in the *Philadelphia Inquirer* Sunday morning edition on September 17, 1916. Circulation had been surging in recent months, making the paper one of the three most widely read in America. Hundreds of thousands of readers in and around the City of Brotherly Love—like other readers across the nation with their own newspapers—were hungry for news, whether serious or more lighthearted. This short piece hit the spot.

The *Inquirer* called the story a "domestic tragedy." The hype and salacious details were hallmarks of these kinds of daily newsprint tales. People loved the offbeat—yarns that seemed straightforward but had alarming twists. Readers enjoyed scandalous material, not just for the shocking minutiae, but also for measuring themselves against their neighbors, a kind of collective "There but for the grace of God, go I."

In the accompanying narrative, readers quickly learned that "Mrs. Holmes" accused her husband Albert W. Holmes, a grain trader and salesman, of going "East with another woman in an automobile." Off philandering while she and her two children suffered back home.

As if an illicit affair weren't enough bait for eager newspaper readers, the daily reported that Albert had spent so much money on expensive gifts for his new lover that "his two children had but one pair of shoes."

The *Chicago Tribune* filled some gaps in the story. The hometown paper identified the adulteress as Jennie Lindner. Reports disclosed that Holmes bought the young woman "furs and a gold watch, but refused to provide for his own wife and children." Expensive gifts to woo the new paramour while his family languished.

The consequences were shocking and scandalous. According to "Mrs. Holmes," the spurned wife and mother, "When one child wanted to go out of doors, the other child had to stay in the house, thus they wore the shoes alternately."

That poor mother and her poor children! She could neither feed nor clothe the two darlings. All they wanted was to go outside and play. The travesty!

Like women all over the country, the reports implied, the maltreated wife needed a hero.

What readers didn't know was that "Mrs. Albert W. Holmes" was a kind of fabrication or substitute persona of Augusta Imogene Brown Holmes, a desperate, lonely, Evanston, Illinois, housewife who wanted to find a way out of a long marriage that she considered a dead end. And what's more, "Mrs. Holmes" had no need for an additional pair of shoes. She didn't have two children, just her lone daughter Ruth, about to turn nine years old early the next month.

The story was a ruse.

Mrs. Holmes had a history of altering her identity. At that time, she favored using her middle name "Imogene" or the shortened version, "Gene." She tried on these different aliases and the invented lives that went with them in hopes of getting in the newspapers. For the young housewife, the media attention added much needed spice to her life. "Mrs. Holmes" was a kind of role created for reporters hungry for juicy tidbits of family disarray, the stories that sold newspapers to readers who had few alternatives for getting both information and entertainment.

Imogene had always yearned for the spotlight. She enjoyed the gossip and self-created drama, being the center of attention among her family and friends. The young woman also had a more concrete rationale—in media-saturated Chicago, she knew that she could use the salacious press accounts as a weapon in divorce proceedings against her husband, regardless of how much of the story had been fabricated. Imogene would have to secure alimony and child support if she planned to leave her husband. Without other financial prospects, she was dependent on painting a picture of Albert as a womanizer and deadbeat father.

The *Tribune* piece about Windy City mother "Mrs. Albert W. Holmes" and her two children transformed Imogene's ho-hum marriage into publicity gold. Suing her husband for divorce and then announcing her woes through the papers gave Imogene the hint of fame she longed for and made her version of the marriage concrete.

True, Imogene's marriage *was* a dud.

But it wasn't what she'd reported.

Twelve years earlier in late 1904, she had married Albert W. Holmes in Milwaukee when she was only a teenager. At the time, the thirty-four-year-old Holmes was slowly establishing himself in the thriving but cutthroat grain-trading industry. He had learned the ropes bouncing around as a traveling salesman and then working as a clerk on the fringes of the business. Al probably knew Imogene's father, Frank R. Brown, a local veterinary surgeon who worked at a building on the same block as Holmes in 1898. Her mother, Julia, sometimes rented rooms in their home, earning some additional money as a landlord. Al may have at one time been one of Julia's boarders.

Holmes had seen a bit of the world and had prospects, making him a logical choice for Imogene, known simply as "Gussie" Brown when she was a young girl. Gradually, Holmes won a foothold as a grain merchant, opening the Holmes, Frost Company in Milwaukee with partners Frank S. Frost and R. M. Koppelkamm. The men pooled together $5,000 to launch the concern in the chamber of commerce building in the city. The challenge for Imogene was that life in Milwaukee did not interest her, nor did the slow-moving, buy-and-sell world of grain commissions. Al just wasn't as driven as Gussie was by an overarching desire for money and social station.

As she got older, Gussie saw what others had, the shiny new touring sedans and the kitchen gadgets in their homes, and she wanted more. She also noticed men's eyes on her when she was out in public. Their heads turned and their eyes darted toward her. The young woman basked in the attention. What could boring old Al Holmes give her, but a drab life?

Gussie had bigger dreams.

George Remus reigned over an immense workload at his law practice. He routinely took on sensational cases that taxed him mentally and physically. The unyielding pressure strained his marriage to Lillian further and further. The union had already been damaged by his long hours away from home. Remus seemed disinterested in duties as a husband and father. Instead, he holed up in area hotels, habitually working late into the night, which exacerbated his insomnia, but enabled prodigious amounts of work.

Lillian and Romola went long stretches without seeing him or receiving much in the way of financial support. George dropped off a meager weekly check, usually about twenty dollars, and then went on his way. If he stayed too long, the stress on husband and wife would erupt into screaming matches and threats. The rocky relationship continued, neither party willing to risk a divorce scandal, particularly as George's practice took on an increasing number of marriage cases. He needed to stand above the fray to represent his clients from a morally upright position.

As a crusading attorney, Remus grew in popularity and became well known as he threw sound bites at newspapermen like machine-gun fire. Not radiant like some barristers who could twirl a jury in their fingers, or brilliant, like Clarence Darrow, the attorney and human rights activist that everyone in Chicago admired, George had a different quality that drew people to him. One aspect was "good copy," which the newshounds craved. And, observers had dubbed him "the man about town with the moonlight smile." He wasn't magnetic like a silent film star, but he had charisma.

The professional successes masked the fact that things had come to a head at home. After fifteen years of marriage, Lillian filed divorce proceedings on March 6, 1915, publicly charging George with "cruelty." Privately, she told friends that Remus had repeatedly beaten her, striking her with his fists and violently pinching her, in addition to unloading extensive verbal abuse. Lillian also suspected that her husband was with other women on his many nights away.

Although no one would call the marriage "happy," George begged Lillian to reconsider. He denied that he had ever cheated on her and declared his undying fidelity. Remus also vowed that he would treat his wife and daughter better, providing a lifestyle more suited to his increasing wealth and stature. With few options for supporting herself and Romola on her own, Lillian relented. She

withdrew the divorce papers, despite her ongoing suspicions. Another victori-
ous argument for the fast-talking attorney.

Although Lillian had taken him to the brink of divorce, George did not actually change. He continued to work at a relentless pace and stay away from
home for long stretches. The money he promised his wife went toward his
growing list of expenses, from club fees and new clothes to expensive dinners
and travel. Remus had to keep up appearances, so he funneled funds toward
his growing public reputation as a big shot. Lillian and Romola would have to
again make due with a small weekly stipend.

Even more discouraging, however, were the rumors that circulated through
the tightly knit German community—George was out carousing again. According to wags, he could not steer clear of a pretty face. By 1916, within
months of their supposed reconciliation, word got back to his wife about his
repeated infidelities. Yet, Lillian had no proof to corroborate the talk, so she
made due, even as the rumors piled up. She could not have known how correct
the gossipers actually were.

George had fallen hard for Imogene Holmes, now also using the alias "Susan
Imogene." Beautiful, young, and as eager for wealth and fame as he had become, she brought him an aura of excitement and vitality.

Her wavy black hair bounced on her shoulders and shook when she spoke.
She had piercing black eyes. When she turned them on men, they staggered
away, entranced. Most found her stunning and wanted to be around her, an
exotic beauty with olive skin and dark features. For his part, George loved the
attention that followed Imogene like flies to honey. His pride swelled when he
watched men gaze at her. They desired her, but also held him in awe for winning the heart of such a beauty.

"She impressed me in the first instance," he professed.

Imogene was also a decade younger than Remus, another lure for the older
man. "One prides himself on taking out young women," George remembered
about the early stages of their relationship.

Later, when friends would ask Imogene about how they met, she spun a
romantic tale of working behind the counter in an Evanston deli and waiting
on a particular customer who came around almost daily. The grocery runs
turned into miniature dates, George whispering in a thick German accent and

Imogene holding his hand and openly flirting. Gradually, the two became a couple and then later fell in love. The starry-eyed story became part of the couple's lore. They told the yarn over and over again until it seemed genuine.

Reality would have thrown a bucket of ice-cold water on that fantasy. Truth be told, both were still married to other people. Imogene wasn't even actually as young as she claimed. Born on September 15, 1884, in Milwaukee, she made herself five years younger in a spell of self-creation while in Chicago, maintaining that she was born in 1889. The lustful, thirteen-year age difference that George took so much pride in was actually a much more pedestrian eight.

Changing her age was one more stroke of Imogene's deliberate reinvention. Rather than a dreamy love story based on a chance encounter at the deli, the story and subsequent moves were much more calculated.

Imogene filed for divorce after the affair with George began, regardless of the "one pair of shoes" storytelling. Remus was a catch—unhappy in his own marriage, wealthy, dressed in flashy clothes, and famous. She was not going to let him off the hook. Although George secretly moved in with his mistress, he did not file for divorce. Imogene, however, took a more direct path. She threw caution to the wind, publicly shaming her husband in an attempt to get out of the union. George, with much more to lose financially, reacted cautiously and with uncharacteristic slowness, dragging his feet, unwilling to take a definitive step.

No one, however, could have denied that George was smitten with Imogene. He showered his lover with expensive gifts. In turn, she gave him all that he desired sexually.

"There were illicit relations," George confessed.

When Remus realized how little money Imogene had, sometimes not even enough to feed her young daughter Ruth and keep her in decent clothes, he began paying the rent. She needed the money, she claimed, because Al Holmes had cut her off. Perhaps that single aspect of her fabricated story was actually authentic. George, however, did not question the amount of truth that lay at the heart of her accusation against her husband. Money was not his concern when it came to Imogene.

One day George visited her apartment on Sheridan Road, remembering that he "found the furniture out on the hallway step for the want of the payment of $285, which I paid."

Rumors circulated about Remus having a love nest. People claimed that he had moved in with Imogene and Ruth. Others claimed that he had hired a pretty, young beauty as a clerk at his law firm. Eventually, George took over the rent completely and gave Imogene money to buy more lavish furniture. Later, he helped her get into a larger, luxury apartment at 203 Ridge Avenue in south Evanston. The red brick building was chopped up into suites tucked in among Chicago's suburban elite. At $95 a month, the rent was not an issue for Remus. Venerable Northwestern University sat about three miles to the north with its toney, tree-lined streets and large mansions. Imogene could walk to Lake Michigan with Ruth, only a handful of blocks away. She dreamed of a more extravagant life, maybe one of those alabaster castles that seemed so far away.

When they had met, George said, Imogene "didn't have a dollar." Her beauty lured him, but he also wanted to rescue her, give her the fairytale life that she coveted. Imogene willingly reciprocated and played into the role that he created for her. She was attracted to the glamour.

"I had taken her from absolute poverty...tried to make a woman out of her," Remus claimed.

The strain of running a thriving legal practice while simultaneously maintaining two separate residences and two families was a powder keg waiting to explode. Lillian heard a new wave of rumors about George's love nest in Evanston. When he showed his face, she raged at him for the years of neglect.

According to Lillian, George gradually just stopped coming around. The distance between the married couple had grown to seem normal. She wanted to believe that he told the truth about the stresses of his career as a high-flying attorney and the long nights holed up with law books and plotting legal strategies. Later, Lillian reckoned that he had moved out on December 26, 1918, but she had seen so little of him that she did not know where he had been or where he would relocate.

George had carried on a dual life for about two years.

*   *   *

In early February 1919 a story broke that George got into a fistfight with Herbert Youngs, an Evanston plumber. The fight took place, according to the papers, at the home of "Mrs. Gene Holmes." What editor could turn down juicy details of a famous attorney, flying fists, adultery, and divorce? The mystery surrounding the escapade quickly grew into a national story.

The woman, who told the *Chicago Tribune* that she was a "widow," had advertised a reward if someone found a watch that her young daughter Ruth treasured, but somehow misplaced. In short order, however, a series of misadventures quickly ended with one man in a bloody heap, badly beaten, and needing medical attention.

When the police arrived at the Evanston flat there were conflicting accounts of what had taken place. Remus contended that he was visiting Carl Detcher, a client who lived upstairs from Mrs. Holmes, when Youngs tried to extort $15 from her as reward for her daughter's watch, which he claimed a friend had found nearby. The plumber—dazed and bleeding—countered that Remus had attacked him without provocation after the do-gooder returned the missing timepiece and attempted to collect the reward. Based in part on the severity of the beating, police charged George with assault and arrested the lawyer.

Imogene corroborated Remus's story, explaining to the *Tribune* that George was visiting her upstairs neighbors, the Detchers, and came to her rescue after Youngs announced "that he was going to stay until I gave him the $15."

"While Mr. Remus was questioning the man," she continued, "Youngs attempted to strike him. Then Mr. Remus threw him out."

Another reporter, however, noted that the thumping George gave the plumber went far beyond showing him the door.

"Assaulting, battering, smashing, disfiguring, and otherwise maltreating and messing up the classic countenance of Herbert Youngs," the reporter explained, turning the beating into poetry for willing readers.

"I throwed him out of the premises," Remus responded flatly when asked what had taken place.

Within a month, a fuller picture of the assault and its ramifications played out in the media. This was the ammunition that Lillian Remus had been waiting for. The proverbial "love triangle" unfolded in newspapers with splashy headlines and oversized photographs of George, Lillian, and Imogene. Revving up the melodrama, the photos primarily focused on the two women—the matronly, well-kept Lillian and the lascivious younger woman. The photographs of the two women heightened the intrigue with Lillian in heavy, dark makeup and the sleek mistress baring a revealing shoulder in profile.

Suspicious of her husband and sensing that something nefarious existed behind the initial account, Lillian went to see the plumber's wife at her Evanston home. Without a reason to lie, Youngs's wife reported that Remus had been in the Holmes apartment during the whole incident, not coming to the rescue from upstairs as the newspaper reported. Herbert had told her that George was in slippers and a robe when the argument broke out, hardly the clothes of an attorney visiting a client.

Knowing that George would try to talk his way out of anything she accused him of, Lillian went to see a divorce attorney. With the adultery charge cemented by the newspaper stories, she had George where she wanted him. She told him that the marriage was over. Four years earlier, the Remuses had separated, but Lillian had revoked divorce papers when he begged and pleaded. This time she wasn't backing down. Lillian realized that the long nights away from home were not spent at one of the Chicago hotels that her husband claimed he went to when he needed to prepare late into the night. Lillian now knew that her husband had actually been living with Imogene.

Lillian's final move in uncovering the truth was going to see Imogene. She wanted a confession, which would not only guarantee her divorce, but also clear her conscience. Her husband was a rising star in the Windy City and the Youngs publicity demonstrated how public their lives had become. Lillian wanted retribution for being duped for years. George's secret life with Imogene became public folly.

When Lillian Remus showed up unannounced at Imogene's Evanston apartment, the younger woman stood on the other side of the door, quaking in fear. The current Mrs. Remus cut a thick path through life and the news stories portrayed her as a little angry and bemused about her husband getting caught in such an outlandish episode. Imogene paused for several minutes, wondered if she should open the door. She believed that she was about to get a good slapping from the older woman.

"I had a long talk with her," Lillian told a reporter after the episode with Imogene. "She broke down completely. She cried as though her heart would break and offered, if I wanted my husband, to give him up."

Lillian's answer was a curt, thanks, but no thanks. As the story grew more intriguing, reporters pried from her what she had told Imogene. Lillian explained that Remus hadn't supported her and Romola properly for five years, only giving her about $20 a week to run the household. She declared, "He's just sporty, and spends all his money on women." Lillian didn't want him back and "was glad it was all over." Imogene could have him.

A reporter from the *Associated Press* news service tracked down Imogene. He got her to talk, but also editorialized a bit, clearly pinning her for lying, but also coyly noting that she answered "with a flash of pearly teeth."

Men noticed Imogene and the way she responded to them.

"Mrs. Holmes"—the "other woman"—proclaimed: "I haven't done anything that isn't nice. My life is above suspicion." Ultimately, she denied Lillian's claims, asserting, "There is no truth in her absurd statements."

The judge in the subsequent divorce case between the Remuses saw things a bit differently. Lillian portrayed George as an adulterer, as well as a slipshod husband and father. According to Lillian, he fought their battles with harsh words and by slapping her around. Remus's attention, she gathered, had been fixed on Imogene for several years. The assault charge in the Youngs fight and the hare-brained attempt at a cover-up were simply the last straws for her.

Even for a newshound like George, the heat of the divorce proceedings and bad publicity made him nervous. He attempted to outrun the negative spotlight shining down on him. "Remus, penitent and contrite, left town," one paper reported.

"There was some publicity up in Evanston as a result of my being on her premises there," George recalled. "Mrs. Remus, of course, found out about it and applied for a [divorce] bill."

Initially, Lillian attempted to take the high road, according to an observer, and "omitted all mention of infidelity." She took these measures because she didn't want Romola to hear the many undesirable details about her father. Smelling a story and hoping to increase newsstand sales, the papers were not so forgiving. Piece by piece, they pried out all the salacious elements they could uncover.

Whenever it seemed that George was going to be difficult about the divorce settlement, Lillian went to the press. Reporters eagerly printed her accusations. The defining nail in the coffin for George was hammered when Lillian revealed that her husband had "provided a home for another woman for the last three years."

When Lillian confronted him about this at his law office and demanded answers, given that he was only giving her a measly stipend each week, "He made emphatic denials and threw me out of the office."

Lillian also claimed that George "had beaten her many times."

Lillian's charge of "intolerable cruelty" on its own was enough to whet the public's interest. Remus dropped all pretensions and did not contest the divorce or her financial demands. On March 7, 1919, the judge granted the divorce, ordering that Remus pay his first wife a hefty lump sum of $50,000 and establish a $30,000 trust for his daughter Romola. He also had to pay $25 a week in alimony.

The assault mess with Herbert Youngs had forced George's hand. The divorce trial only lasted a week, but the headlines skewered him publicly and put a dent in his income. Remus also had to figure out a way to stay out of jail in the impending assault trial. Rather than stew over what he had lost, he set out to win the case by any means necessary.

• • • • •

While George juggled divorce negotiations, he concurrently maneuvered to get the assault charge adjudicated in an Evanston courtroom. He argued that based on his notoriety he wouldn't stand a chance at a fair trial anywhere else in the area. Actually, George believed that he could convince a group of simple-minded Evanston jurors that his actions were gallant rather than brutal. In his mind, after all, he was defending the sanctity of Mrs. Holmes and her home. As usual, it would be up to him to spin the jury in his direction.

During the trial, Remus represented himself and portrayed his actions as heroic. The story he told the jury and assembled crowd was that he had valiantly rescued Imogene, who conveniently played the damsel in distress. He pictured the case as the classic shakedown. Youngs, he implied, had stolen the watch and then came to ransom the timepiece for a higher reward. George, ever the upright citizen and defender of the weak, told the jury that he could not idly stand by when witnessing such deeds.

"I acted in self-defense, as any red blooded man with a spark of chivalry would have acted," Remus said.

Despite George's orations, the real star in the trial seemed to be Imogene. She became the center of attention, which she adored.

A reporter watching the proceedings spent a great deal of time noting Imogene's appearance. He claimed that she was in court "with both feet," explaining that "the jury and judge were much interested."

While Remus argued on, Imogene won the hearts of all the men in the room, "smiling archly" and "nodding pleasantly."

As she spoke about Remus coming to her rescue, the reporter noted, "Mrs. Holmes ever and anon raised a foot—ever so slightly, but enough to give a ravishing vision of a silken clad ankle that caused several of the jurors to remark later that 'twas a pity the lighting arrangements of the courtroom were not better."

All the men assembled were clearly smitten with Imogene and she drew in the attention like a breath.

No one seems to have realized that the "Mrs. Albert W. Holmes" from 1916 and the "Mrs. Gene Holmes" from 1919 were the same woman. Al Holmes had fled the two shoes fiasco by moving back to Milwaukee, throwing his work efforts into the Holmes-Frost Company in the city's famous, tri-colored Blatz Hotel, near City Hall. He clearly wasn't dead and she clearly wasn't a widow.

Facts, however, didn't matter in the little courtroom. Men's minds were elsewhere.

A pearly smile, a flash of skin, a pack of little white lies, and George's sweet orations. Imogene won George. George won acquittal. What a team.

• • •

The "Two Shoes" article helped Imogene escape her dead-end marriage and she flirted her way into George's heart, though she had to bide her time as his mistress while he fretted and sputtered in vain in the hope of ending his marriage with his fortune intact. The notoriety from the newspaper article gave her a bit of glamour. She created an imaginary world with herself—as she wanted to be seen—at the center. Without checking the facts or the details, the newspapers portrayed her as a loving mother courageously facing down financial hardship brought on by a lazy, cruel husband. Imogene got away with it.

The eager press gave Imogene a taste of celebrity that continued to fuel her for the rest of her life. The woman who at one time was simply "Gussie" Brown, from an ordinary family in mundane Milwaukee, suddenly had notoriety. People in the big city now knew her name. Gussie created her own hero. Her lucky streak continued when she met George. The Windy City insider would give boring, tied-down Gussie the ticket to the dazzling life she so desired.

Gussie Holmes might have been a neglected housewife in a cramped Evanston apartment, but if she could wrangle her way to become "Imogene Remus," well, then she would have the riches and luxury that she craved. She felt emboldened by the formal end of George's marriage and his newfound commitment to her. The attention she received at the assault trial also fueled her desire and demonstrated how she could turn men's heads.

Within two weeks of George's divorce, before the ink even seemed dry on the agreement with Lillian, Imogene was back at it, yearning to get her name in the papers, this time writing as "Gene Holmes." In the subsequent press release, she counseled "modern wives…how to keep that husband of yours from becoming a wild man." Picked up by more than two dozen papers from Vermont to Montana, her "tips" included:

"Never, never try to curb his liberty...always appear cheerful and pretty...pet him...[and] never look upon him as a mere provider—they should be treated like pets." These points were meant to "tame" one's husband and keep him happy.

"If after doing all these things, the husband does not want to stay at home," Imogene concluded, "he isn't human, that's all."

What Imogene hadn't counted on was that reporters would include a bit of their own editorializing with the list of tips. Editors divulged—tongues firmly planted in their cheeks—the details of Lillian Remus having just named her as "the other woman in Chicago's latest triangle."

Bringing all of the salacious details back into the public eye so quickly after George and Lillian's divorce was a way to prolong the story and take a shot at George. The succession of events, beginning with Lillian's 1915 divorce threat, George's infidelity, Imogene's "two shoes" debacle the following year, George moving in with her, the Youngs assault, the extensive media attention, the divorce proceedings, and Imogene's marriage tips had kept the three of them in the papers on and off for four years. Knocking local bigwigs down off their pedestals had long been a media tactic to gain readers.

For Imogene, the type of recognition was immaterial, whether it centered on celebrity or infamy. She had end goals and the notoriety fueled her desires. Becoming "Mrs. Remus" was at the center of her efforts.

"Remus is a good guy," Imogene confided to her friend A. W. Brockway, an appliance salesman at a department store on State Street in Chicago. Then she got down to business, announcing: "I'm going to roll him for his roll."

She and A. W. saw each other a dozen or more times after he sold her a washing machine while she was still technically married to Holmes, who had moved back to Milwaukee. Imogene needed to come clean. She could confess to the young salesman, guessing that he would never meet George.

"I'll get his dough even if I have to marry him, although I don't want to. I am going to nick him," she told Brockway.

Brockway knew Imogene filled her head with visions of self-aggrandizement. Talking about her plans was almost like a first step in acting them out. A. W. realized that Imogene had now targeted Remus.

"Her general attitude toward him was that she held him lightly," Brockway remembered. "But, she said she would coach him and show him how to make more."

"I've got the big boob right where I want him," Imogene told another friend.

Imogene met George at nearly the perfect time for running a con. On one hand, Remus was vulnerable, wallowing in the midst of a midlife crisis. Yet, he was also arrogant and susceptible to the charms of a younger woman. Imogene played into this idea by lying about her age and making the gap between them more than a decade.

George had taken other steps to transform his life when he was in his late thirties. He frequently reinvented himself in an effort to move beyond his humble immigrant past. Falling in love with a dark-haired, younger woman seemed part of that makeover. He needed a youthful, energetic partner that would help him shed his lowly upbringing.

Lillian Remus explained the attraction between the two in stark terms, explaining, "Mrs. Holmes satisfied the vanity of George in the early days."

Remus's desire for transformation went well beyond finding a new woman to parade around town. George developed several eccentricities that in his mind must have symbolically put distance between his current decorum and dirty past. His meticulousness regarding personal hygiene and clothing bordered on neurosis. He grew fascinated with the feeling of silk next to his skin and never wore underwear. George's obsession with washing and cleanliness nearly grew into a phobia and his commitment to dressing in the finest, tailored clothing took on greater importance.

Imogene took deliberate steps too. Hers, though, were undoubtedly more calculated and cunning than anything George had envisioned. Her confession to Brockway was an admission of her plan. She had already repeatedly demonstrated that she would lie or invent stories to fit her ever-evolving persona. Imogene was determined to attain the life she saw herself living when she imagined high society.

The next critical step in cementing their relationship would be marriage. Long before Remus made any progress to leave Lillian permanently, rumors had whipped through the German community about George's new girl. Although Imogene never admitted that she tipped off the society page and gossip reporters about their secret affair, the couple soon turned up in the newspapers.

Reporters followed them, providing Windy City readers with lurid tales of infidelity and indulgence. Rumors spread of Imogene sporting a large diamond engagement ring. Another batch of stories affirmed that the fancy automobile he had supposedly given Romola was now in Imogene's name. Newspapermen tracked the car down and saw it parked at Imogene's Evanston apartment. Readers loved a juicy tidbit about a local celebrity. The high-flying attorney and his mistress fit the bill.

Despite the media spotlight, George and Imogene stood side-by-side. She quickly became his trusted partner and confidante. When they looked to the future, they realized that their desires merged, just as their relationship had sparked something in them that neither had ever felt previously.

They had fame. That part was not difficult. George dazzled reporters. He had a knack for consistently offering great sound bites. His work as an attorney mirrored his competitive nature and desire to win over all else. Reporters followed his work, knowing that he would give them the kind of copy that their readers would devour. Behind the scenes, Imogene counseled him on how to get newspapermen interested in a story. Celebrity, however, did not provide enough. They both yearned for wealth and opulence.

Despite his law partnership, ownership stakes in several thriving businesses, and a handful of promising real estate investments, Remus sensed that he had maximized what he could do in the Windy City. The marriage to Lillian had felt like an anchor, pulling him under financially and emotionally. In contrast, Imogene envisioned having the affluence she saw all around her in Chicago's well-heeled neighborhoods. The woman felt at home in the fancy shops and growing suburbs. Imogene sent George's heart soaring. His spirit matched hers in flight.

Remus's $45,000 a year salary suddenly seemed puny when he considered what he and Imogene could get if they combined their efforts. Together, they could grow rich—fantastically rich—like the aristocrats they knew on Chicago's vaunted North Shore. Maybe more. With Imogene behind him, helping him craft a new future, George pictured himself conquering the world, becoming a titan of industry, and forging a path toward untold treasure.

The journey, however, had to launch from a new headquarters. George had an idea—they would move from Chicago and the baggage they had there from decades of building separate lives. A fresh beginning would set the tone for their immaculate life together. He would make them truly rich, but first they had to make their union official. There could be no loose ends.

Cincinnati felt the brunt of the dry laws.

Ohio, the home of the Anti-Saloon League, had gone dry on May 27, 1919, a handful of months prior to the national legislation. Prohibition shut off the taps in the city's famous Over-the-Rhine neighborhood, one of the beer-making strongholds in America. For decades prior to World War I, Cincinnati was famous for manufacturing beer, while many argued that the city was also the beer drinking capital of the nation. It seemed as if every other door led to a saloon. The German neighborhood was filled with concert halls, gambling joints, and beer gardens to keep the party going around the clock.

"Without equal in the United States," said one writer, who lamented the rollicking past, explaining that in OTR, "Beer flowed in torrents…actors were made there and politicians flourished."

Though OTR would struggle as jobs and people drifted away and the breweries dried up, George saw the Queen City of the West from a different vantage. For him, it was no longer a route west, but a gateway south. Perhaps like no other city its size in America, Cincinnati opened the path to all the illegal booze that could be siphoned from its splendor on the banks of the Ohio River and then south to the bluegrass hills of Kentucky.

George knew that within 300 miles of Cincinnati, about 80 percent of all bourbon in America was manufactured and stored. Gaining access to this liquor would create the heart of Remus's bootlegging network.

He wanted it all. Every drop.

George, Imogene, and Ruth left Chicago and settled in a fabulous suite at the Sinton Hotel in downtown Cincinnati. Money talked at the Sinton, one of the more luxurious establishments in the Midwest. George liked to flash his roll in front of Imogene. The money gave them access to the lifestyle they both craved.

The Sinton became Remus's favorite local haunt. At night, the hotel lit up the evening sky with an explosion of color emanating from the high arching windows. Inside, the ornate lobby stretched upward several stories. The ceiling was framed in handcrafted gilded designs that made it seem like a French castle. Interior hallways high above the floor enabled guests to look down on the hustle and bustle below.

George and Imogene got married on June 25, 1920, in Newport, Kentucky, the infamous red-light district across the Ohio River from Cincinnati. Licenses were easy to come by in Newport. A handful of dollars greased the path to a quickie marriage or speedy divorce. It made no difference to eager city officials. Everyone had a price in Newport.

"I married her as a matter of duty," George explained, thinking back to their early days in Cincinnati. "I thought she would appreciate the good happenings that happened to her."

As he began operations in Cincinnati, however, Remus still had unfinished business in Chicago. He was trying to outrun challenges on several fronts and the 300 miles between him and his former hometown provided a much-needed buffer.

Imogene had other reasons for keeping ties to the big city. She could not let the occasion of her wedding go by without issuing press reports back in the Windy City. She needed her friends to see that she had made it.

Subsequent articles in the *Chicago Tribune* paid tribute to Remus's legal reputation, dubbing him the "militant genius of a thousand open court battles." The couple sent the newspaper two key bits of information. First, George acknowledged that he and Imogene Holmes had wed. Second, according to the paper, "He had left Chicago forever" to establish "business connections" in his new Queen City locale.

Remus also had to tidy up loose ends at his law partnership. He had an astonishing 732 open cases on the docket. Several junior associates and his personal legal secretary took on the bulk of the work, with George overseeing their efforts. It was important that he clean up the cases as a matter of pride. The team took eighteen months to close them all.

Although George had made the flamboyant public declaration about new business relations and the splashy avowal about leaving Chicago, the truth emerged less than a month later when the *Tribune* noted that the attorney general's office issued warrants for his arrest related to conspiracy charges in a scheme to sell thirty-seven cases of Silbey liquor from a warehouse on Chicago's North Side using fraudulent whiskey permits.

In truth, the move to Cincinnati was primarily a tactic to avoid arrest. When authorities heard rumors that Imogene had been seen in her old haunts in Evanston, they immediately launched a search for her husband.

George also lied about his wedding date to avoid capture and gain valuable time to deal with the charges. According to the Chicago paper, Remus reported that he and Imogene had been married on July 8, 1920, and then set off for a honeymoon in New York City. Actually, they exchanged vows on June 25. Once they hit New York, the paper reported, they dropped from sight, with Remus "said to be somewhere in the east."

The couple could not, however, outrun the forfeiture of a cash bond for $10,000 George had deposited after his earlier run-in with the attorney general in May 1920 for forging whiskey licenses. Illinois law enforcement agents telegrammed New York officers in an attempt to get George arrested at the Pennsylvania Hotel while he was on his honeymoon with Imogene, but no one there would comply with the request.

Remus countered that the initial removal of the illicit liquor was legal. He claimed that the certificates he had furnished were legitimate. There may have been some truth in his explanation. Chicago officials were notorious for issuing whiskey certificates and then claiming later that they were stolen or forged if the right amount of bribery money wasn't accompanied with the requests.

The formal explanation was more direct. Prohibition agents explained that the justification was simply one of Remus's many deals gone awry. They planned that he would be "vigorously prosecuted" for violating national Prohibition.

Although Illinois agents could not get George extradited, the grand jury indicted him. Mysteriously, however, officials from Chicago did not make any further efforts to bring him back to the state for prosecution. Stories swirled about what Remus had done to cool the heat. Allegedly, rumors insisted, he paid at least $120,000 to various officials to suppress the charge.

"I went on the theory that every man has his price and I could afford to pay it," Remus claimed.

With Imogene by his side, George remembered these lessons in Cincinnati and Newport. With mountains of bootlegging riches ripe for the taking, George would happily buy his way in.

3

Birth of a Bootlegger

"Stick 'em up high!"

Remus had spent many hours talking with journalist Paul Anderson from the *St. Louis Post-Dispatch* about how he had built the bourbon empire. Yet, all these years later, he still felt uneasy recalling the events from early 1920, on that night he nearly lost his life.

He remembered looking down those gun barrels and remembered the scene as if it just happened…

Slowly rolling up onto the enormous steel and iron suspension bridge that spanned the murky, quick-moving Ohio River between Cincinnati and Covington, the driver prodded the truck up the incline. Loaded down with cases of Kentucky's finest bourbon, the heavy vehicle slipped into gear for the short trip over the water. Its headlights cut into the night. The glow from the Queen City across the river reflected off the windshield. A hazy spark filled the cabin, throwing shards of light onto the driver and his boss who occupied the seat next to him.

George squinted out into the darkness. He tugged at his silk shirt and tailored suit, feeling the fabric shift over his powerful, broad shoulders. They needed nightfall to get these illegal shipments from the rail yard into the city. The shadows, however, did not hide them from the police officers that guarded the bridge. Patrolmen kept regular lookout on both the Ohio and Kentucky sides of the structure. Remus sat stone-faced, eyes wide for the potential dangers that went along with carrying such treasured cargo. His man at the wheel had an automatic weapon tucked within easy reach.

Just ahead, as the truck plodded forward, the bootleggers saw an automobile stalled in the middle of the road. They attempted to maneuver around the wide touring car, but it took up too much of the road. Four men then stormed from behind the sedan. Pistols drawn, the bandits jumped from the bridge deck up onto the truck's running board and screamed out their demands.

Outmanned and outgunned, the driver panicked. He swung open his door and leapt, running madly toward the far side of the bridge. The gunmen let him bolt. They focused on commandeering the precious shipment without alerting the Ohio or Kentucky police.

Unarmed, George also reacted quickly, but he did not run. Instead, he flung the truck door open and pushed past the bandits. Even without the aid of his driver or the man's weapon, he was desperate to protect his bourbon. The easiest thing for the hijackers to do would be to shoot the lone combatant. But the sound of gunshots would alert the police, who could easily thwart their escape or call in reinforcements.

Remus lunged at the closest gunman, landing a punch to the chest that knocked him backward. The aggression left him vulnerable. The other three descended on the bootlegger. One of the thugs swung his pistol wildly from behind. The revolver smashed down on George's head. The bootleg baron fell to his knees.

Dazed and bloodied, but still hoping to scare off the hijackers, Remus got to his feet again. Fueled by adrenalin more than intelligence, he started swinging. George connected, knocking one goon back with a roundhouse punch. The exertion left him exposed. Another thug attacked him from behind, smashing George in the skull with the butt of his gun. A fresh gash opened wide, dropping him to the pavement for the second time.

Despite the pain, Remus staggered to his feet again. He advanced toward them. The bandits thought that the cargo truck would be an easy score, but now found themselves in the midst of an intense battle.

Wild with rage, Remus hurled his powerful body at the criminal who had hit him. George grabbed him with both arms and pushed him toward the railing, the only obstacle between the roadway and river below. Lifting the man off his feet, Remus carried the gunman to the side of the bridge and flung him toward the water. Remus's heave came up short and the thug crashed into the barrier, a few feet from falling over the edge. While the two had struggled, one of the others jumped into the cab of the truck. He yelled for his accomplices and they made a break for the vehicles. Another thug pulled the first assailant into the sedan and they zoomed off, leaving the truck grinding into gear and slowly moving up the grade.

With the fight a bit more fair now at two-on-one, George made one last-ditch attempt to stop the burglary. Before the truck could gain momentum, he jumped onto the running board. He reached in through the driver's side window and tried to pull the man out. The crook bashed Remus across the face to get him to release his grip. The battered bootleg baron collapsed to the pavement as the truck gained momentum and finally sped off.

Defeated, George walked the length of the bridge. Without alerting the police, he found a phone, and hailed a cab. The car dropped him off at a local doctor's office, one that could be trusted not to alert the authorities. The physician stitched up the lacerations, which had spilled blood down his thick neck and saturated his collar.

Wounded and angry, Remus made an important decision—one he'd immediately have executed by his second-in-command, George J. Conners. All future shipments would be accompanied by at least one car, chock full of armed men. This kind of business would not happen again. In other words, Remus commanded Conners to create an army.

According to the top aide, Remus even extended the offer to the next group in his distribution line—the band of rumrunners who sold his shipments of booze to speakeasies, hotel restaurants, and wealthy patrons. As a courtesy and sign of good business, bootleggers who loaded up at one of Remus's locations then received an armed escort to a pre-arranged marker about ten miles outside of whatever depot they had visited. The orders given to the gunmen were simple—at the first sign of trouble, come out shooting.

Now, years later, reassessing the events of that evening and just how close he'd come to losing his life, George shrugged off the danger, instead contemplating the scars. He rubbed his nearly bald head, reliving the attack, which had become a piece of nostalgia. He saw his role as more heroic than it was, a show of his personal resilience. By this time, the scars had mostly faded, but the marks of that night still grew visible when he got angry, seeming to swell up when he raised his voice. In these fits of rage, it looked as if his entire head puffed up several hat sizes.

These days, Remus still wore tailored suits, but sported even finer quality silk shirts. His trusty cane was always within arm's reach. When he picked the walking stick up, he felt the heft of the immaculate accessory, but more importantly, saw it as a potential weapon if he needed to thrash someone who stepped out of line. Come out swinging.

George thought he'd had it all back then, but he looked down at his little finger and saw perched there a six-carat diamond solitaire ring that Imogene had given him. She claimed that it cost her a cool $6,000. Even more ornate, he sported an $8,000 pearl stickpin that had an embedded five-carat diamond, another gift from his wife.

George chuckled at the memory of his hijacking escapade. Despite the dangers, bootlegging had made him richer than he could have imagined.

Scrambling to keep up with his caseload and direct the efforts of the junior associates that worked for his law office, George did not have time to philosophize about Prohibition. He remained steadfastly indifferent, but realized that it had caused an unnecessary national rift. From a legal standpoint, however, he considered the Eighteenth Amendment and the Volstead Act hollow. People would always drink, no matter what the Anti-Saloon League wanted the public to believe. Making booze illegal seemed unjust.

He didn't have strong personal feelings about alcohol either. Publicly, Remus had always claimed to absolve from drinking—a slave to his obsession with exercise. And while the damage alcoholism had done to his father and his immediate family was real, giving him every reason to want drinking outlawed, he just did not believe that the government should legislate these kinds of moral issues. His family's personal challenge was old news, a topic that didn't matter anymore as he plotted the next phase of his life. Contemplation took time, the one commodity Remus could not buy.

The personal decision to drink or abstain did little for George. However, what Remus did cherish were legal skirmishes. He loved wading into the minutia of arguing arcane points and interpreting ideas. The client fees that resulted weren't bad either. Fighting toe-to-toe against an adversary in a courtroom gave him the kind of rush he found in athletic competition.

When federal agents and police officers in Illinois began piling up liquor-related arrests, Remus took on case after case of bootleggers pinched trying to quench the Windy City's insatiable thirst. Chicago, like all big cities it seemed, had turned to illegal booze with gusto, as if regular law-abiding people enjoyed the walk on the other side of the law.

While Chicagoans adjusted to their new lives without legal liquor, there were also larger business implications that had to be adjudicated. Having long-standing union and corporate connections, George became an important figure in representing brewery and trucking interests. These were the organizations that faced closure as a result of the Eighteenth Amendment, a concern that many legislators seemed to forget in the morality play of dry laws. Business leaders scrambled to make sense of new statutes in a world in which their products could lead to jail sentences. It was one thing to have a little nip from a hidden bottle for John Q. Public, but another thing entirely to trade one's business attire for prison garb.

Even in the most straightforward court cases, Remus could not turn off his over-the-top personality. He defended his bootleg clients with all the vigor he could muster. The small-time thugs, he felt, deserved his finest efforts. He argued their cases as if a trip to death row hung in the balance.

George's determination that his clients get a fair hearing ran headlong into the path of Judge Kenesaw Mountain Landis in federal district court. Rising to a seat on the federal bench, Landis had become famous for his stern decisions and the intensity of his eyes. He looked like an eighteenth-century pastor with a long, narrow face and curly shock of steel-gray hair. Landis ran his courtroom as if he were being directed from the heavens above. He withered opponents and anyone he considered a nuisance, targeting them with his unyielding stare.

Kenesaw Mountain Landis would soon become even more celebrated, taking over the reins of the national pastime by serving as Major League Baseball's first commissioner. The fixing of the 1919 World Series at the hands of New York gambler and criminal mastermind Arnold Rothstein and others had left a stain on the game. The public demanded the American pastime be overhauled. The judge's impeccable record and harsh sense of justice helped the game survive the controversy, although holding his two jobs simultaneously did draw fire from some Congressmen until he resigned his judgeship in early 1922.

On the bench back in Chicago, Landis hated two things: longwinded lawyers and lengthy trials (and, yes, one often led to the other). Before long, Landis and Remus squared off in the courtroom. Although both men believed deeply in the legal profession, George's perspective was that alleged criminals needed defense from the strictures of those in power. Landis, however, wanted those same alleged wrongdoers to be brought to justice. Landis wanted swift action, while Remus demanded that his clients be given a chance to be heard. The judge and lawyer were inevitably going to butt heads. The national reform campaign against booze, which had gained momentum in the late 1880s and early twentieth century, provided the judge and barrister a battleground.

Illinois lawmakers had ratified the Eighteenth Amendment in 1919, making booze illegal in the state. While some in Chicago decided to look the other way when it came to implementing Prohibition, Judge Landis had little regard for rumrunners. He had been a lifelong prohibitionist. Ill-tempered when bootleggers were in his courtroom, he was quick to judgment. "In the Chicago of Big Bill Thompson, Big Jim Colosimo, and Al Capone," a historian later quipped, "Kenesaw Mountain Landis seemed to be one of the few public officials taking Prohibition seriously."

When Remus attempted to draw out the proceedings or get his clients free on some arcane technicality, Landis struck even faster. In September 1919, Remus worked for a trucking company owner accused of running beer between Illinois and Wisconsin. After many confrontations, and an actual admission by the defendants that they had broken the law, Landis finally had enough of Remus trying to impede the decision through a flurry of words and what he considered gibberish.

"Take that man from my courtroom," Landis boomed. "Escort him clear away. I don't want him here anymore."

In other cases during the first year of Prohibition enforcement in Illinois, Landis imposed enormous fines on George's misfit assortment of thugs, sometimes upwards of $10,000 (about $140,000 today). It was as if the judge simply pulled figures out of thin air.

To the dismay of onlookers and courtroom staff, when the judge announced a particularly outrageous fine on a convicted bootlegger, Remus's client simply shrugged at George, then walked to the judge's bench. Reaching in his pocket, he pulled out a thick wad of cash. Slowly, the man peeled one thousand dollar bills one by one off the top, dropping them on the table. Remus's eyes darted between the bootlegger and the bailiff and back again. Everyone else in the room looked on in amazement. This was the end result of federal Prohibition?

The steady stream of liquor cases and the litany of foul-mouthed, nearly illiterate criminals forced George to consider what was happening as a result of Prohibition. Few of the criminals were educated. Most had been poor prior to Prohibition, from working-class backgrounds or fresh off the farm. George knew this was why they had been caught. Many weren't smart enough to avoid capture. Their methods were shoddy. The bootleggers he defended had taken unnecessary risks with no plans for contingencies. Remus shook his head and prepared for the next case.

Dealing with thugs wasn't much of a thrill, he thought, but how could anyone discount all that money? No matter what outlandish fine Landis threw at them, they just paid as quickly as possible and went back to their business. These petty criminals had so much cash that they didn't know what to do with it.

Watching the bootleggers get nabbed in the earliest Prohibition violation cases and then quickly buy their way out of the fines played out as if it were being staged. George had an epiphany. His plan would be extreme, but the potential payoff would be staggering. He thought back to the William Cheney Ellis murder case and his visits to Ellis's hometown. Maybe he and Imogene might like living in the heart of bourbon country. Cincinnati, he thought, the thriving industrial and trade mecca founded on the banks of the mighty Ohio River.

George loved the region's vibrancy and elegance. City leaders were conservative, making the region a Republican stronghold, which aligned with his ideas of how business should operate. They had also been building its cultural base, bringing art and entertainment to the city.

George remembered window-shopping along Fourth Street downtown during a trip to conduct background interviews for the Ellis case. In a high-end studio, he saw a famous marble sculpture called "Three Graces." The proprietor alleged that the Duke of Tuscany had previously owned the piece. Almost certainly a copy of the original by Italian sculptor Antonio Canova, the three beauties depicted Zeus's daughters: Talia (beauty), Euphrosyne (mirth), and Aglaea (elegance). In the early twentieth century, owning this kind of artwork marked one's sophistication and prominence. He promised himself that someday he would be rich enough to buy it.

"I said at that time that when I became wealthy enough I would buy that statuary and have it sent to Chicago," George remembered.

Another significant asset of Cincinnati was its strong German community. The thriving Over-the-Rhine neighborhood contained a countless number of saloons and nightspots prior to Prohibition that stayed open around the clock and provided a rousing nightlife. While most of its many breweries had closed—at least a dozen operating before manufacturing beer became illegal—German heritage still flourished.

An intricate network of tunnels for transporting lager ran under OTR and enabled speakeasies to thrive. About 560 neighborhood saloons stayed open after Prohibition, though many were forced to serve refreshment within the gray area of what was legally defined as an "alcoholic beverage," ultimately selling near beer or soda as a means of survival. "A city as wet as Cincinnati didn't go truly dry overnight," claimed one writer, "but staying open during Prohibition was trickier than keeping a side door open on Sunday in violation of a law that nobody had ever taken seriously."

Although World War I and the ensuing anti-German sentiment it created in America had changed Over-the-Rhine, Remus would still be among like-minded people in the neighborhood. In time, Prohibition would hasten the area's decline, but during the early years it remained deeply German. George also had a broader objective in mind: while focusing his efforts on Cincinnati, he'd also go south, deep into the hills of Kentucky.

"After surveying the entire country, I picked Cincinnati as my headquarters because 80 percent of the bonded whiskey in the country was within 300 miles of that city," George explained.

True, Remus had built a small fortune and lived well in Chicago, but his work with bootlegger after bootlegger almost compelled him to consider a new life. If these simpletons could make untold money selling illegal liquor, then perhaps he could bring in millions using his intelligence and grasp of the legal codes related to the new amendment. Prohibition had already created untold consequences. Legislators understood that there were potential loopholes in the law when they passed it—they just didn't think criminals would be so quick to exploit its flaws.

George pored over the new legislation and court documents in an effort to find weaknesses in the law. He concluded that the Volstead Act's provisions that legalized "medicinal" alcohol for sick patients—as long as they had received government-certified whiskey certificates from their physicians and pharmacists—would enable him to legally get booze back into circulation. There were few limitations on doctors and pharmacists to write scripts for the medicinal use of alcohol, as long as the prescriptions were authorized by the state-run enforcement office. These prescriptions would serve as the supply point for the illegal liquor business he envisioned.

"I knew it [the Volstead Act] was as fragile as tissue paper," Remus concluded. "I knew it would take the government some time to catch its breath."

The whiskey certificates took care of obtaining a steady supply of alcohol. With that challenge unscrambled, George turned to the distribution system. He utilized his experience as a pharmacy and drug company owner to figure out that he could remove booze in large quantities if it looked like the alcohol were destined for a medical business or entity, rather than a private owner. From the work he had done in Chicago in the early 1900s, George had experience both buying up existing drug companies and creating them from thin air on paper. In either case, the drug companies and pharmacies would seem like thriving entities and completely legitimate (and legal) to any prying eyes.

"I read the Volstead Act," Remus explained. "I knew that these permits were available, and by being the owner of the institution we could withdraw the whiskey with a greater amount of ease…than if you were not the owner."

One of George's sizeable moneymaking enterprises in Chicago had been purchasing ownership stakes in a handful of wholesale liquor businesses. As a pharmacist and drug manufacturer, Remus knew that alleged "medicines" were often little more than a slightly diluted alcohol. He himself had written innumerable scripts for bourbon, vodka, gin, and other liquors. When his drug entities prospered in the early 1900s, he used the profits to purchase shares in Isaac Propenzano and Company and Isaac Meyer and Company, as well as minor positions in similar firms in Peoria and Aurora, Illinois.

After his own close call in Chicago, barely escaping a jail sentence, Remus knew federal enforcement officials and the overtaxed local and statewide agents could not really handle the influx of work. He took on so many bootleggers that it clogged his schedule, even though he assigned a great deal of work to junior associates.

He would strike while the feds were still trying to figure out what to do next. There would be no more slipups, like the bungled caper that nearly led to his demise. He would be smart and hire consultants to help him create a national bootlegging network.

"In defending these people, I was impressed by the remarkable profits which they were making out of petty, hip-pocket bootlegging."

To fulfill his idea of a far-reaching bourbon empire, however, Remus had to first embrace criminality. Since he had little personal feeling for the Eighteenth Amendment, he changed his mindset by envisioning his new journey as an exciting game that he controlled.

The transformation required him to devise a corrupt path that would at times seem legal but would actually necessitate wholesale law-breaking. George had always taken such pride in being an attorney, but he found the likely gains from a better organized brand of bootlegging too enticing.

"It occurred to me that this demand must be general throughout the country, and that millions could be made in supplying it," he said. "I knew there was plenty of good whiskey in the government bonded warehouses, and that the problem would be to get it out."

Grasping an opportunity to launch one of the great heists of modern America, the legal ace turned dark.

"Big money," Remus said flatly when asked why he turned to bootlegging. But that wasn't all he desired. He bragged, "I didn't care anything about money...and don't care anything about it now. I went into it mostly for thrill and excitement."

Cincinnati would serve as "the neck of the bottle" for his bourbon empire, the perfect locale for him to pour his illegal liquor out to the rest of the thirsty nation.

When Remus decided to relocate to Cincinnati, he most certainly knew this was a William Howard Taft stronghold. The ex-president and his extended family had a grip on the city and an obvious stake in keeping it clean.

Taft, the patriarch of Cincinnati's first family, had a bird's-eye view of Volstead Act enforcement from the Queen City with its heavy immigrant and brewery influences. The former president could see the consequences in the downtown Over-the-Rhine district, which had been one of the beer meccas in the nation. If that neighborhood were any indication of what people thought about Prohibition enforcement, then the public at large was not going to give up easily, if ever. The new law was particularly odious to those individuals who never dreamed that imbibing might be considered a societal evil. Many people from numerous ethnicities simply believed that drinking beer or wine was as natural as water.

Taft knew Prohibition meant trouble.

"The business of manufacturing alcohol, liquor and beer," he made clear, "will go out of the hands of law-abiding members of the community and will be transferred to the quasi-criminal classes."

Men like George Remus were the type that Taft feared most—smart men who would apply their intelligence to breaking the law. The stocky lawyer had the financial savvy, business acumen, and guts to take on the risk. Even a person with Taft's long political career and insight into the public mindset could hardly conceive how Remus and other criminal masterminds would not only grow to be pillars of their communities in dry America, but would be perceived as folk heroes.

"My personal opinion had always been that the Volstead Act was an unreasonable, sumptuary law, and that it never could be enforced," George explained.

He realized that if members at the top of the economic ladder were ignoring Prohibition, then that notion would trickle down to the masses as well. The elites set the moral agenda, just as they did in style and culture.

"I took notice of the fact that the bootleggers had for customers the so-called 'best people,' whose chief complaint was the difficulty of getting good whiskey," George said.

Scale. That's what George needed to eclipse the success of the petty thugs he had defended in Chicago. His objective centered on a combination of legal intelligence and sheer determination. The former would enable him to maneuver the intricacies of the legislation and its enforcement codes, while it took grit to set up an organization capable of achieving his aims.

Cash served as the grease allowing the machine to run efficiently. George had about $100,000 after selling his law practice, partnerships, and real estate in Chicago. As soon as he arrived, Remus took that money to Lincoln Savings Bank downtown in Cincinnati. Lincoln had been called the German National Bank prior to the sinking of the *Lusitania* in 1915 and American entry into World War I. Anti-German hysteria forced many Queen City companies—and organizations across the nation—to dissolve all ties with Germany, including the bank. If a business had a traditional German heritage, it potentially faced an angry mob that might burn it to the ground or blow it up. In the madness of war, all Germans were considered possible saboteurs. Lincoln Savings extended Remus a virtually unlimited line of credit.

With the money to begin, Remus hired people and procured machinery, from automobiles and trucks to bottling machines. He also began a far-reaching bribery network, trading cash for insider information, protection, and secrecy. He needed police officers, railroad workers, and more on his side—the day-to-day people whose prying eyes could alert state or federal enforcement officials. Finally, Remus had to buy the expertise of others who knew how to work the system to serve as mentors. This knowhow would cost a small fortune, but was essential to avoid the traps that almost landed him in jail in Chicago.

All the circumstances aligned for him. Remus knew he had made the correct decision, explaining:

Late in 1919, I made my decision to quit the law and go into the whiskey business. I closed out my practice and sold my real estate, and had a total of about $100,000 in cash. Then I went to Cincinnati to inspect the ground. I found a score of men operating in what was regarded as a large way, without interference either from the police or the Federal officers. They had various sources of supply. Some of the whiskey was fairly good, and a great deal of it was undoubtedly bad. None of them owned their own sources. We decided to have our own, and to sell nothing but the best.

With a steady supply of cash and credit, Remus launched a secret liquor ring by employing the talents of people who had already learned a great deal about circumventing Prohibition. These early maneuvers were so private that his handpicked lieutenants did not know about the partnerships. These experts helped Remus establish his organization in the early years when the mechanics of the federal government's Prohibition enforcement were still a mystery. Discussing these key figures in later years Remus would simply lump these men together into one mysterious duo he referred to as "the two Jews." He was circumspect about their identities or even how many there were in his inner circle (probably more than two) because he did not want to attract added heat to them from Prohibition Bureau investigators or snooping reporters. On one or two occasions he did offer the names "Albrecht and Kole," but given his heavy German accent the names could have been misconstrued.

When observers assessed how a single mastermind could create such an extensive bourbon empire, they usually built a fable about Remus's lone genius and how it was a manifestation of his legal training. In that version, George was the crafty lawyer who figured out a way to break Prohibition by drawing on his unique career path from pharmacist to attorney. One reporter dubbed it the "Big Idea," claiming, "He was, early in 1919, perhaps the only person in the United States who visualized accurately the farce that prohibition is today. It was his big shot and he acted." Certainly, Remus's hutzpah and ability to see the holes in the Volstead Act fostered his desire to go dark, but he needed help and found the appropriate guides.

One of the men who aided Remus—and one of the only two names he would later credit for helping him set up his network—was most likely Samuel Albrecht, a Baltimore liquor broker. In the early Prohibition era, Albrecht specialized in establishing nationwide whiskey networks from a suite in the Commodore Hotel in New York City. The Commodore had been Remus's primary residence when he traveled to New York when he was an attorney, so they may have met there prior to the implementation of Prohibition.

Albrecht helped Remus get started in bootlegging, but he took too many risks and became a victim of his own greed and conceit. In late 1921, newspapers reported that Albrecht was a "so-called ring leader" of a "bootleggers' trust" that operated in Baltimore, Louisville, Philadelphia, Cincinnati, Washington, DC, and Chicago. Considered one of the original "bootleg kings," Albrecht was arrested by federal authorities for offering a $50,000 bribe to New York State Prohibition Director E. C. Yellowley and Green Miller, one of Yellowley's staff agents. As a liquor broker, Albrecht could remain behind the scenes, but once he was arrested, details became known, certainly a deliberate attempt by Prohibition Bureau leaders to show the public that they could enforce the Volstead Act. For example, the *New York Herald* reported that Albrecht was the leader of "one of the craftiest and richest of the rum rings," and had interests in "nine distilleries and manipulated 35 percent of the traffic in illegal permits in the Eastern States."

Enforcement agent Green Miller told federal authorities that during a meeting with Albrecht, the bootleg leader offered him the initial $50,000 bribe, a bonus for each case withdrawn via a certified whiskey certificate, and "all the money in the world" thereafter. In return, Miller and Yellowley would give the whiskey ring an unlimited supply of whiskey certificates.

When asked his side of the story, Albrecht countered that local Prohi agents stole money from him at gunpoint and then charged him with bribery to cover their theft. When the case made it to trial in July 1923, the jury acquitted the bootlegger, deliberating for five minutes before declaring him "not guilty." Arguably, New York was the wettest state in America during Prohibition, so juries were loath to jail bootleggers in the early years of enforcement, particularly leaders at the top.

When their partnership began, Albrecht and Remus launched a campaign to funnel whiskey certificates through the M. E. Hunter Company, a wholesale pharmacy at 53 J Street in New York City, in the shadow of the Manhattan Bridge in Brooklyn. The wholesale outfit became one of Remus's main conduits into the lucrative Big Apple bootleg liquor marketplace.

Along with Albrecht, Remus unquestionably benefited from the skills of a small handful of secret operatives who helped build his enterprise in its nascent stage, not just the "two Jews" he later mentioned. The larger group of key figures included Mannie Kessler and Morris Sweetwood, financiers with deep ties to the underground booze market in New York City. Kessler's claim to fame—coming to this conclusion at about the same time Remus did—was determining that he could legally withdraw booze from government-sanctioned—more commonly known as "bonded"—warehouses if he had government permits that allowed it to be used for so-called "medicinal purposes."

"I mentioned my thoughts…to two men who were in the liquor business," George confessed. "We began to talk it over. They knew the ropes, and believed that with my knowledge of the law, we could find a way to evade the regulations and outwit the government." Kessler and Remus picked up on the legal loophole and knew they could exploit it to make money, but the two had distinctly different ideas about how to achieve their ends. While the financier planned to stay behind the scenes, Remus would be the face of the partnership, occupying the public space he had grown accustomed to in Chicago.

"The ideal place to operate, they said, was Cincinnati," Remus recalled. "First, because it was the center of the distillery region of Ohio, Kentucky and Indiana; and second, because bootlegging had succeeded with less interference there than elsewhere. This, notwithstanding that Ohio was the home and the headquarters of the Anti-Saloon League."

While the Queen City gave Remus access to the vaunted Kentucky bourbon industry, the location also provided less competition than other parts of the country. Most men who were jostling to corner the illegal booze market focused on importing alcohol by sea—either bringing in scotch from England; shipping in rum from Jamaica, the Bahamas, and other Caribbean ports; or smuggling a variety of liquors across the border from Canada. These import methods were favored by Arnold Rothstein, the criminal impresario who created a vast booze empire from his headquarters, his favorite table at Lindy's Restaurant in Times Square.

Mannie Kessler, Rothstein's fellow New Yorker and almost certainly a business associate, reportedly owned several ships and speedboats to bring rum into the US. He was the best kind of connection for Remus because he could help him establish distribution ties. Kessler had partnerships with William "Big Bill" Dwyer in New York, Maxie "Boo Boo" Hoff in Philadelphia, and Frankie Yale, a Brooklyn boss who operated from a cabaret he owned on Coney Island called the Harvard Inn. Yale was also a personal friend of Johnny Torrio and Al Capone in Chicago, which then gave Remus entry into that lucrative market. Despite the efforts of enforcement efforts on the federal, state, and local levels, this national network of suppliers and distribution points grew quickly as men like Rothstein, Kessler, Yale, and Remus created both formal and informal agreements to ship and supply booze across the East and Midwest. In later years, organized crime syndicates would replicate this system, but with more authoritarian leadership able to pull all the pieces under a tighter command structure.

Remus also profited from an early partnership on many secret liquor deals with Cincinnati financier Sam Friedman. Together, they orchestrated a mix of legal and illegal maneuvers meant to get more liquor onto the black market where they could charge colossal markups.

One lucrative scheme centered on Remus and Friedman purchasing the liquor rights of the John D. Parks & Co. retail and wholesale drug business. Using George's money, Friedman gained the rights to 10 percent of the company's gross business, which at the time was bringing in about $10 million annually in stores and via mail order.

According to Remus, "that gave us a chance to draw $1 million worth of liquor from distilleries at wholesale prices."

The wholesale costs were miniscule—about $17 or $18 dollars per gallon—versus the price they could charge on the black market.

George confessed, "That million dollars worth of liquor became about $70 million in bootlegging prices."

With competitors eager to service the large cities, Remus would not have the Midwest to himself. However, operating at a distance from New York and Chicago enabled him to supply the chieftains in those ever-thirsty markets without being viewed as a threat that had to be eliminated. Gaining a reputation for supplying high-quality bourbon would set Remus's operation apart from low-level rumrunners who sold rotgut—barely more than paint thinner or denatured industrial alcohol mixed with some flavoring to mask the taste.

In contrast, Remus declared, "Kentucky whiskey was always in demand."

Experts considered bourbon from Kentucky the best in the world, its taste enhanced by limestone-filtered water taken directly from the Kentucky River. Others dubbed it "Kentucky's dew," for the distilling process that seemed so natural to the state's whiskey makers.

Remus looked across the Ohio River into Kentucky and found the perfect headquarters there in Newport, the small city opposite Cincinnati. Newport, which people alternatively dubbed "Sin City" or "Little Mexico," had a reputation for lawlessness, which made it well suited for George's operations. Newport's decadence dated back to the Civil War when Union troops occupied the region. Soldiers needed entertainment and soon a glut of saloons, gambling halls, and prostitution houses dotted the city.

Rather than stem the tide of illegality in Newport, national Prohibition actually turned the area into a hotbed of iniquity, spurred by a credo that established the individual's rights over interference from government sources. Moonshine stills littered the city as formerly law-abiding establishments transformed overnight into speakeasies. Allegedly the smoke and smell from homemade alcohol left the city awash in a kind of liquor-fueled haze. Enforcement agents stayed away from Newport, either on the take or unwilling to risk getting shot. Brothels also flourished. Newport's reputation spread quickly—the nation's adult playground. Remus became a kind of king there, using it as a base of operations and reigning over the city with a team of thugs and enforcers.

People who visited the Queen City could barely escape the allure of the Newport, despite the dangers. An out-of-towner might travel across the river for a little late-night merriment, but there was a chance he would end up on some remote side street, penniless and dazed. Newport establishments had begun perfecting what was known as the "bustout joint." These places, according to investigative reporter Hank Messick, didn't allow customers to leave until they were broke. The bustout joints specialized in taking every penny—on a rigged game of chance or a dash of knockout drops surreptitiously placed in a person's drink. As one Newport religious leader told Messick, "Either way you go out busted."

Next door to Newport sat Covington, another small Kentucky town transformed by Prohibition. Remus bought a storage depot in Covington from John Marcus, a hardened criminal and murderer that everyone called "Jew John" due to his half-Jewish, half-Mexican heritage. He had built his reputation as a professional gambler in the gaming dens of Juarez and Tijuana, the kind of inveterate underworld figure that emerged in the early decades of the twentieth century. Gangland gossip credited Marcus with being the first whiskey runner in the United States, transporting liquor in from Mexico when states in the South went dry prior to national Prohibition.

Marcus possessed several particular talents, killing people being the most formidable. He had built up a thriving bootlegging business in Cincinnati prior to George's arrival. And when Remus needed muscle and early tutelage, Jew John served as an aide-de-camp and mentor.

Remus provided an organizational structure that put order to Marcus's madness. When George made so much money so quickly, Marcus started working for him full-time. The desperado ensured that liquor runs operated smoothly across the Ohio, Indiana, and Kentucky state lines. Marcus's reputation grew and people knew he pulled his gun with little provocation. A veteran newspaperman who made his living covering crime remarked, "A more sinister looking figure this writer has seldom seen."

Marcus's skillset did not extend to leadership or strategic thinking, which would never elevate him to Remus's top man. To fill this role, Remus turned to George J. Conners. Although much younger, Conners soon became Remus's chief lieutenant and partner. A one-time real estate broker, he met Remus soon after the latter arrived in Cincinnati. Still in his late twenties, Conners was a life-long Cincinnati resident, bumping from job to job, including working as a stenographer in a railroad office, engaging in small-time politics, and working for the Democratic State Committee. He was young, married, and the father of a small daughter, looking for an edge, and willing to join his uncle in his real estate practice to get close to the older man's political associates.

Prior to officially joining the Remus gang, Conners profited from his association with several area bootlegging operations. As Remus worked with partners to initially launch the network, Conners would put clients with large orders in touch with Remus, who could supply upwards of 100 cases at a time. This early order fulfillment provided Remus with some of the funds he needed to build an infrastructure. The booze was certainly later resold to an odd assortment of buyers, from petty bootleggers to wealthy socialites.

Conners grew into the role as number-two man quickly. A reporter declared that Conners exuded "wariness, coolness, courage and poise," explaining that "There is about him a suggestion of the successful gang leader…shrewd and reflective." He was quick on the draw, but more like the kid next door than a hired gun or bourbon operative. He peppered his hard talk with phrases like "Oh, boy" and called his enemies and competitors "saps."

Next, George told Conners to start hiring men. An early recruit was John Gehrum, dubbed "Rat-faced Johnny" by his enemies. He provided muscle for the fledgling outfit. Gehrum had a quick temper and was quick to settle arguments, sometimes with a pistol or shotgun.

Although Ohio outlawed alcohol six months earlier than the federal government, a general lawlessness emerged that allowed bootlegging networks to form in Cincinnati and across the river in northern Kentucky. The overwhelming demand basically established a bourbon superhighway. Out of this mayhem, men came forward who were willing to use brute force and lethal tactics if necessary to guard transport and distribution routes.

Remus's cash and early connections via his silent partners enabled him to begin selling bootleg liquor before he had much of an infrastructure. At first, they worked with a few mid-sized suppliers to get the booze into the Cincinnati market. These initial forays taught Remus lessons about what he would have to do to become a significant operation, particularly when it came to hijacking thugs. At one point, he lost 850 cases in about two and a half weeks. He suspected it was the work of a notorious murderer and small-time bootlegging thug named Ernest "Buck" Brady, from Highlands, Kentucky, about seven miles south of Cincinnati. Brady had a reputation in Covington for hard-hearted violence and mayhem.

Remus, of course, prided himself on his powerful physique. He would bash a few heads when someone lit his infamously short fuse. A confrontation was coming.

"I lost pretty nearly $250,000 there in two and a half weeks," George said later.

Even in this tense environment, though, Buck went to visit George at his operations center at the Sinton Hotel in downtown Cincinnati. He also knew about the hijacking, claimed he had no part in it, and wanted a job in the growing bootleg operation.

Glancing toward the thief, Remus warned: "You come near me, I don't care how tough you are, I will crack your head."

Brady turned on his heels, warning George that he needed the kind of protection that he could provide. That evening, another Remus truck was run off the road, with the highwaymen getting away with another 250 cases. Two of John Marcus's trucks were also stolen. Remus realized that he had to bring in outside muscle.

He relented, calling Brady and announcing, "You have got me whipped. You take charge of the outside as to the delivery and collection of funds." But, he warned, "You be honest with me."

George pledged to pay Buck $2 for each case delivered, which meant that the Kentucky man could grow incredibly wealthy if he played straight with George. In the first year of supervising Remus's transportation network and taking shipments in and out of Kentucky, Brady reportedly made $280,000. He brought in fellow Newport tough guys to work in the Remus gang: Peter Schmidt, Sam Schraeder, and Albert "Red" Masterson. With Brady, the criminal activities of these men would later dominate Newport headlines and the gossip-filled chatter of the mafia underworld.

Newport sat perched on steep slopes, jutting away from the broad, fast-moving Ohio River and the cops.

Lawless.

Prohibition had birthed countless speakeasies in the little town on the backs of the thriving brothels and illegal gambling dens. People flocked to Cincinnati to join the streams of visitors to Sin City. Around the clock, Newport earned its moniker, and Remus's booze powered its decadence.

The pressure of moving to the Queen City and launching the operation there and in Newport pressed Remus emotionally. He felt the strain of mounting responsibilities and the uneasy idea that he could be double-crossed at any moment. The move into bootlegging had nearly cost him his life, which forced him to hire muscle and protection. The stakes, as they were when he was a criminal defense attorney, were life and death. But now it was intimate. He might not be able to return to Imogene at the end of the day.

As the stress escalated, rumors swirled that George and Imogene got into a knockdown fight at the Gibson Hotel, another one of their downtown Cincinnati haunts. In the midst of an argument, George had allegedly slapped Imogene. Then, he threatened to kick her out if she continued to pester him. Supposedly, the ruckus led to them being booted from the venerable establishment.

Remus brushed off these tales, explaining that the couple "had gotten tired of the hotel life and wanted the atmosphere of country surroundings."

Imogene's daughter Ruth saw the fight from a different perspective. To her young eyes, the two had been at each other physically almost from the start after their move to Cincinnati. Ruth claimed that two days after Imogene and George wed, he had "struck mother in the nose causing the blood to flow."

According to her daughter, Imogene's screams could be heard around the hotel, causing attendants to rush to the scene. Already accustomed to bribery, George pulled out his roll and started doling out cash. The hush money kept the staff members quiet. No one alerted the police.

Ruth explained the change in her stepfather, who would soon adopt the girl, explaining that George "glorified in bending us to his will."

From Ruth's viewpoint, George started abusing and intimidating Imogene and Ruth physically and mentally. The teen said that they were "terrible years, constantly filled with fear and dread of the brute instincts that characterized George Remus in his frequent fits of temper."

George countered that he never laid a finger on his wife or stepdaughter. Instead, he focused all his efforts on the bourbon kingdom. Remus now had a team of men and muscle in place to create a nationwide bourbon empire. However, constant worry kept him on the edge mentally. Remus put safeguards in place to fend off attacks that would disrupt his bourbon empire, but whether he could keep his home life stable was a different battle.

Just as he had in Chicago when he was practicing law and living with Imogene while still married, George kept up a double-life in Cincinnati, having just as much difficulty balancing the two. Could he keep the competing demands separate or would the violence he encountered continue to be replicated at home? Would this be the downfall of the new King of the Bootleggers?

PART TWO

· · · · · ·

King of the Bootleggers

4

The Bourbon Empire

Throughout Cincinnati, Kentucky, and Indiana, brewery and distillery owners turned off the lights. Many Kentucky distillers—proud men whose families had been in the bourbon business for generations—panicked when Prohibition took hold. The Anti-Saloon League, headed by Wayne B. Wheeler, had used the strength of its organization as a voting bloc to strong-arm politicians into declaring alcohol illegal nationwide.

For these proud owners and the many thousands of people who worked for them, producing unsellable beer, whiskey, or any other kind of distilled spirit was a total loss. Hundreds of millions of dollars of alcohol and infrastructure were basically useless.

Americans, though, proved to have an insatiable thirst once Prohibition went into effect. As the economy ticked northward, people found the money for illegal booze, even if it meant that they paid a substantial markup. Remus knew that this was where the real profits could be had. Going directly to the owners and indirectly through a team of attorneys, Remus began asking around to see which distilleries could be procured. He found plenty of sellers. The whiskey men were desperate. Prohibition was a part of the Constitution; they thought it would be the law of the land forever. America had just made them public enemy number one.

The distillery owners might as well light their businesses on fire. A lightning strike or some other real or manufactured Act of God would at least bring in insurance money.

Or, Remus and his gang would be their saving grace. The chaos that developed in the uncertainty regarding illegal liquor gave George the opening he needed.

"In most instances I would pay cash," he explained. "I would pay down $25,000 or $50,000 and pay the balance in 30 or 60 days thereafter."

Remus purchased a host of distilleries outright, estimating "about eight, I owned as an individual, solely and entirely."

There were also some three to six more plants or warehouses that he bought up secretly, owning one-third to one-half interests in the operations. George acquired distilleries so quickly that he might not have known the actual figure. The Remus empire stretched out over eight states. He dropped the cash and put a team of attorneys to work to iron out the details. Like famed prospector George Hearst, one of America's first venture capitalists, Remus wanted the product. He yearned for the bourbon stored in those factories.

Americans responded to the bootleg efforts, sucking down all the booze he could tender. Although probably not realizing its full extent, by mid-1921 Remus's network supplied most of the bootleg whiskey across the entire Midwest and East Coast. Millions of bottles were leaving his distilleries and making it into the glasses of thirsty Americans, who seemed to have an insatiable desire to drink as the decade began to roar.

Remus's buying spree began with a local operation, the Fleischmann Distillery in Cincinnati. He paid $197,900 for the land, buildings, and 115 barrels of whiskey. Procuring the excess liquor stored in the warehouse was a separate transaction, but this was a critical part of the deal. At Fleischmann, there were another 3,000 barrels in storage, which Remus bought for an additional $150,000. Each barrel contained about forty-five to fifty gallons of bourbon, so this last purchase alone unleashed roughly 135,000 gallons of illegal liquor into the nation's bloodstream. The bourbon inside the barrels was siphoned into bottles, with three gallons making up a case of whiskey. The bootleggers would usually then sell alcohol by the case. In the early days of Prohibition, cases sold on a floating scale of $60 to $125 per case, so the street value of the Fleischmann haul alone might bring in $4 million to $5 million. Like any other commodity, rumrunners sold the product based on supply and demand. This often pushed the price even higher than $125 per case.

Remus took pride in selling the finest bourbons and spirits that he could acquire, but he had little control over how the independent bootleggers who bought from him might downgrade the product. Cash ruled and many bootleggers got into business for the money and excitement of outwitting enforcement, so most of them would cut the alcohol three or four times to extend its shelf life and increase profits. They added a variety of substances, some drinkable, like molasses, and some not, like antifreeze or industrial alcohol. The liquor changed hands so many times that most people had no idea where it originated.

During Prohibition, "bathtub gin" quite possibly contained many substances that one would find undrinkable at best and deadly at worst. Although his competitors would spread rumors that Remus diluted his liquor, he asserted that it remained pristine. A report from Philadelphia, for example, revealed that many people selling "Canadian" whiskey were actually peddling a liquid made "in the cellar of some alleged toilet preparation manufacturer." Tests on the supposed booze in one raid showed "much of the liquor contained a large volume of poison."

The Remus gang not only made its reputation by selling the best liquor it could procure, but also on its broad control over an industry as it adapted to national Prohibition. One prominent journalist—who made his own reputation covering bootlegging—exclaimed, "Remus was to bootlegging what in earlier years Rockefeller had been to oil and Gary to steel."

Quality and market share. There were many wealthy consumers who were willing to pay any price for unadulterated booze. The focus on selling unsullied liquor transformed Remus from one of a number of large bootlegging operatives into the leader of an elite organization. Remus's acquisitions were among Kentucky's most prized distilleries, including Pogue (Maysville), Old Lexington Club (Nicholasville), Burks Spring (Loretto), Rugby (Louisville), Hill and Hill (Owensboro), and Old 76 (Newport). He also purchased other facilities in Ohio: Clifton Springs (Cincinnati), Edgewood (Cincinnati), and Freiberg & Workum (Lynchburg). And then in Indiana: Squibb (Lawrenceburg) and Greendale (Lawrenceburg). Add to the Remus empire the other properties he kept secret, and you have what writer Paul Anderson remarked was "by far the most pretentious ever uncovered…[noted for] its brilliance and audacity."

Next came connecting Remus's astounding supply to the seemingly unquenchable demand. The genius in his scheme for dominating the bootleg network came about when he reverse-engineered the legal distribution network that had existed prior to Prohibition. His men posed as thieves to hijack his legal shipments (headed to the medicinal marketplace), thereby enabling him to claim that the goods were stolen or lost. In turn, his men transported the "stolen" liquor to centralized distribution centers where they offloaded the booze to runners from across the country. Remus owned a trifecta: quality, market share, and distribution.

George's successive moves—Chicago attorney, running from Illinois feds, transition to Cincinnati, marriage, and founding the network—happened at lightning speed, some pieces crisscrossing in a frantic pace to move liquor. Initially, he bounced back and forth between his new and old homes, still arguing cases and extricating himself from the grand jury indictment that threatened him. Federal agents were on his heels, but Remus countered that his Chicago liquor transactions were legal and that enforcement officers in the city were essentially shaking him down. As he settled in Cincinnati, he kept up a frantic travel schedule, forging deals and solidifying distribution operations.

Like a modern-day corporate raider, Remus employed a variety of tactics to secure the bourbon stored in distillery warehouses and other facilities. The most direct route, he found, was to purchase the property itself, often at a steep discount, because the family or partnership presiding panicked as Prohibition darkened first the state, then the national scene. The distillery owners were rattled, believing that the liquor business in America was shut down forever. Remus then swooped in with a large cash offer. Many took the bait.

When Remus wanted to stay out of the spotlight or did not want to risk local authorities questioning his role, he would put his close circle of henchmen to work, installing them as officers in the operation he controlled. Rather than replace the existing workforce, however, he paid them well to maintain operations. Most line workers and people who made the product did not even realize that they were working for the bootleg baron, but they appreciated the pay. George's payroll grew exponentially with each purchase, eventually including salaries for facilities across several states. Each location ran as its own fiefdom with Remus presiding over the whole, sometimes in plain sight and other times as a silent owner.

"Some of those institutions cost me, for the upkeep, many, many thousands of dollars," Remus explained. "All of those institutions had their own presidents, their own superintendents, their own managers, and their own set of employees."

"For the Hill and Hill plant at Owensboro, Kentucky, I paid $325,000," Remus said. "I invested an additional $60,000 or $90,000 there, which brought the investment up to about $400,000."

The most expensive operation was the Freiberg and Workum plant in Lynchburg, Ohio, the bootleg boss explained: "Before I got through with it, it cost me $640,000."

The cost skyrocketed because Remus's men attempted to centralize at that Lynchburg location, delivering the products of other facilities there, including what was left of the Fleischmann plant and the Greendale Distillery plant from Lawrenceburg, Indiana. In total, the combination of cash down and upkeep for all the distilleries that Remus purchased outright or might be traced to him reached $2 million.

Transactions had to be completed quickly, sometimes sight unseen, because Remus and other prominent bootleggers feared that the Prohibition Bureau enforcement officials would eventually figure out their plans.

"I never saw the Freiberg & Workum Company," Remus later claimed, but he knew the primary reason for buying it: "they had 14,000 barrels of liquor in there."

That supply translated to about 560,000 gallons of liquor, which would gross upwards of $18 million to $23 million on the open market. Given that fantastical return on investment, Remus did not have to physically occupy the space. Instead, he sent teams of men to the property to get the booze offsite by whatever means they had to employ and regardless of local law officials. Often George or one of his lieutenants would have expedited the transaction through a series of bribes. As long as his informants kept watch, he could rest assured that the money would continually accumulate.

The payroll obligations were included under the general "upkeep" tab, a necessity to keep men from gossiping about what they might see or hear down at the distillery. The cat and mouse game was never an equal playing field. The feds would bend or break the law to catch bootleggers and neither side could ever really anticipate the other, so constant double- and triple-crossing kept everyone alert and afraid.

Many buyouts, like at Freiberg & Workum, were essentially hostile takeovers. The distillery had pre-dated the Civil War and grown into one of the largest whiskey makers in the United States. Founder Julius Freiberg passed away in 1905, which disrupted operations just as state and national prohibition forces began solidifying their efforts. Julius's sons took over the business with J. Walter Freiberg as president.

George's top aides or army of attorneys approached desperate owners with large cash offers. The Ohio distillery, which had grown into one of the largest operations in the Midwest, kept its basic independence, with Remus installing former owner Thomas Darlington as president and paying him an annual salary of $12,000.

This kind of buy and pilfer routine took place at America's most venerable distilleries. For example, the Burks family had been operating in Loretto, Kentucky, since their ancestors Charles and Sarah settled on the banks of Hardin Creek in 1803. They opened a gristmill powered by damming the waterway, but local legend claims the Burkses began distilling bourbon within two years. Several distilling operations were formalized nearby by the late 1890s.

Burks Spring Distilling opened a century later in 1905 when George Burks, Charles's great grandson, sold part ownership to local banker J. Ernest Bickett and J. H. Kearns. Bickett took over ownership in 1920 when Prohibition began, bringing in Louisville businessmen Gabe Felsenthal and Sidney Hellman as partners. By that time, Bickett had been elected to the Kentucky state legislature. Without his knowledge, Felsenthal sold his interest to Remus for what the bootlegger estimated at "$115,000."

When he went to Loretto, Remus balked at paying for the bourbon, because the records had been seized and Boston businessman Fred Smith owned rights to the stored whiskey there, about 1,800 barrels. However, an unnamed "notorious bootlegger" met with Remus, guaranteeing him $90 a case.

George accepted the terms and installed his chauffeur Harry Boyd as president of Burks Spring. They then forged documents to keep Bickett on the officer list as secretary and treasurer, which they hoped would keep local officials at bay. While letters from Smith and others went unanswered, Remus "fixed" the distillery's guards. More importantly, each warehouse had a federal official installed—called a gauger—whose job consisted of checking the supply and ensuring the safety of the barrels, including tasting the product to certify that no one had replaced it with vinegar, water, or some other liquid to mask a theft.

A Louisville reporter who had covered the illegal operation explained, "Bit by bit the liquor was drained out…filched in two-gallon lots from each barrel, taken out through the back door and placed on a truck." The vehicle was driven by Remus's appointed strong-arm Buck Brady.

Prohibition created a world where the line between lawfulness and law-breaking blurred almost on a moment-by-moment basis. While Remus's gang smoothly stole the bourbon right out from under the noses of government officials overseeing Burks Spring, J. Ernest Bickett had essentially begged

George "to get this place out of the jam it is in now and realize something out of the wreck."

After years of hijacking and thievery at the distillery and others in the area, including one guard at another facility being murdered, Bickett asked Remus to provide the "protection and service they are entitled to." In other words, selling out to the king of the bootleggers made sense, rather than dying from a thousand small cuts generated at the hands of bandits and crooks. Bickett most certainly knew that he was asking Remus to break the law.

According to Remus, as the incoming owner of any new facility, he demanded "absolute control of the whiskey that was in the distillery belonging to the organization."

Then, Remus would buy up whiskey certificates that enabled him to get the liquor out of the warehouses. If he couldn't find them on the black market or bribe an official into signing off on the papers, he would have his men find forged documents or create fakes. Access stood at the center of the Remus operation. He would get the bourbon out legally, if possible, but usually turned to illegal maneuvers to funnel the booze to distribution headquarters, then out onto the black market. Regardless of the cost of the buildings or upkeep at a distillery, the willingness of the public or other bootleggers and rumrunners to pay a premium for quality bourbon kept Remus rolling in cash.

With so much alcohol moving across Kentucky and over state lines, operations like Remus's faced down officers and other bootleggers who wanted to squeeze them out. Several months after the Burks Spring operation began, Prohi agent U. G. McFarland received a tip about Brady passing through Perryville in a car loaded with liquor. McFarland sent a secret coded message to William H. Kinnaird, another agent closer to the scene. The agent spotted Brady's car and a gunfight ensued, which locals later dubbed the "Perryville Fight."

The chase ensued over twenty miles on the Bluegrass State's roughhewn back roads with Brady firing away with his big cannon of a pistol. Kinnaird, keeping his cool and not backing down, did not shoot back until he was close enough to hit the tires. A skillful shot forced Brady into a ditch along the side of the road. Out of ammo, the outlaw gave up. Kinnaird had hit pay dirt, discovering 450 gallons in the truck that had been loaded at Burks Spring.

Two other Prohis went to Loretto to investigate after they realized the scope of Remus's operations. The agents could hardly believe what they found. George's men had already stolen some 5,000 gallons from the distillery warehouses. The street value of that haul exceeded $165,000. The Prohis took

Beecher Pierce, the plant gauger, into custody, along with several of the guards who were supposed to keep thieves at bay. One confessed that he received $1,200 to look the other way while the Remus gang stocked Brady's car.

With all the illegal activity taking place, Remus simultaneously moved to procure a percentage of the liquor legally. He orchestrated this plan by purchasing whiskey certificates, which entitled the holder to sell bonded alcohol legally into the medicinal market. The challenge with this system, as with so many aspects of enforcement, was that Prohis were selling these documents under the table—a wrinkle that Mannie Kessler had introduced and that Remus understood well from his days as a pharmacist and storeowner. When the Volstead Act was passed, no one could have anticipated that enforcement agents would so brazenly sell forged or stolen documentation.

Whiskey certificates varied in price from under a dollar to $4 a gallon. Remus realized that buying the certificates and paying officials along the way just rolled into overhead, which he then made back when he sold to rumrunners or syndicates in different metropolitan areas.

Remus did not want to depend on rumrunners and others outside his control to get the illicit liquid into the bellies of thirsty Americans. Using his knowledge of the drugstore and pharmaceutical businesses, he opened a string of locations, some legitimate and others merely paper operations. The network of drug companies, drugstores, and false-front operations stretched from New York City across the East Coast and into the Midwest.

"It was a very simple procedure," Remus explained, yet no one else had figured out to combine the legal and illegal pieces.

Remus recognized that loopholes in the Volstead Act enabled a nearly unlimited amount of whiskey to be taken from the government-controlled distillery warehouses to lawfully fill prescriptions. During his own days as a pharmacist and drugstore owner on Chicago's North Side, he had filled countless prescriptions for alcohol or alcohol-infused elixirs. The medical research community simply had not caught up with the innumerable ailments that plagued Americans. Booze with a high alcohol content masquerading as medicine was the norm in homes across economic and social classes. If Remus and his men could get their hands on that part of the industry, they would essentially legitimize bootlegging by getting the bourbon into the legal reserves of the nation's drugstores.

Just across the river from Cincinnati in Covington, Kentucky, for example, he bought a retail pharmacy and transformed it into the wholesale Kentucky Drug Company. These places enabled Remus to forge fake liquor prescriptions and ship bourbon to different cities where his men waited to sell it into the black market.

This important early purchase transpired on January 8, 1921, when Remus and his attorney Maurice Galvin approached Harry Weichelman about acquiring his tiny retail pharmacy in Covington. They offered the owner $9,000, far beyond its true value, because they wanted to snatch it up quickly. The storefront setup had two significant merits. First, it occupied the corner of Fifth and Madison in Covington, the growing town that sat across the river from Cincinnati, and an important hub for Remus's activities in sister city Newport.

Second and more important, the store was bought using the name "Elizabeth Dobrats." What the current owner and none of the Kentucky officials that would have to sanction the sale knew at the time was that "Elizabeth Dobrats" was an alias used by several of the women who worked for George. It was a takeoff of the married name of George's sister Elizabeth Dobbratz. The real Elizabeth had a strong German accent, but was otherwise unremarkable, which enabled her to play the role of buyer without saying too much or arousing suspicion.

Imogene herself had applied for a Kentucky wholesale drug license just the week before as "Dobrats." At times these aliases were codenames indicating to officials on the take that this was a Remus application. Other pseudonyms were created to delay or throw off enforcement officials, since their offices were understaffed and they had challenges chasing down leads. Based on George's widespread bribery network, officials in Washington, DC immediately approved Imogene's forged application.

After the purchase, Remus and Galvin then renamed the pharmacy the Kentucky Drug Company, essentially using the locale to open the Bluegrass State to George's illicit booze trade. With "Mrs. Dobrats" no longer needed, Conners stepped in as superintendent and general manager.

"Of course," Remus said, "the permit states 'for medicinal purposes only,' but you know it was an easy matter to divert it. There was no interference either from Covington or Cincinnati."

George plowed profits back into infrastructure. He kept creating drug companies until he had inroads into many major cities, including Bronx, Imperial, and Ellkay in New York and Stratton, Tri-State, Big Sandy, and Pyrola in Cincinnati, along with others.

"I bought $50,000 worth of drugs and toilet articles to stock it, and obtained a basic permit to withdraw, purchase, and sell whiskey," Remus explained. "As soon as that company had withdrawn as much liquor as was possible without attracting undue attention, I organized another wholesale company, closed up the first one and shipped the stock of drugs off to the second one."

Conners and Remus scoped out and purchased a warehouse not far from the Kentucky Drug Company. The location enabled them to store liquor safely, regardless of whether the product was obtained legally or illegally.

Next, Remus established another pharmaceutical operation, again using the fake "Dobrats" moniker. The Dobrats Chemical Company in Cincinnati provided access to whiskey certificates that he then used to pull about 800 cases of bourbon from the Old 76 Distillery in nearby Newport.

The US District Attorney's office caught wind of the operation and filed charges against the company for failing to pay taxes on the transactions. A Supreme Court ruling later overturned the charges, but officials still revoked the Dobrats Company liquor permit.

Remus concentrated many of the real and fake drug companies near the Kentucky and Cincinnati-area distilleries that he owned. Like the Kentucky Drug Company, the other operations used generic names, such as the Central Drug Company or the S. and B. Drug Company, to confuse local or regional enforcement agents and officials that might investigate. Other false fronts were located in cities where they planned to ship liquor, including New York, Detroit, Pittsburgh, and Chicago. Remus or his men then purchased whiskey certificates as quickly as possible. This effort ranged from bribing government workers to buying them on the black market.

"I would buy twenty, thirty, or forty thousand dollars worth in the open market," Remus explained. Yet, often these transactions could not be traced directly to him.

Slowly, Prohibition Bureau agents started to investigate the rumors they heard about a large liquor ring coming out of Cincinnati. They had numerous informants, including bootleggers arrested and interrogated in other large cities, but they were not sure how extensive the Midwest network was or who led the operation.

Although Remus had been notorious in Chicago, he was virtually unknown in the Queen City. Those who took his payoffs kept their secrets to themselves, so it took the understaffed enforcement agencies time to catch up. Different Prohi outposts had no system to communicate efficiently with one another, so vital information was often overlooked or kept local to a particular office. Even leadership in Washington, DC did not have a broad handle on disparate investigations.

To keep his identity shrouded, George ordered his underlings to purchase whiskey certificates, since he did not want the distillery owners or feds to realize his full role as the mastermind of the burgeoning bourbon network. The underworld gossip mill buzzed with discussion about Remus, but he remained a mysterious figure among officers whose primary task was to get criminals like him behind bars.

●   ●   ●

"The Remus Building"—the name took on a regal flair.

As he cemented his place as America's bourbon king, Remus did nothing halfway. His playground would stretch across the country, but the headquarters would be in Cincinnati.

Whatever befit a business baron would also suit him, regardless of price. Like a corporate titan, he purchased a six-story office building at 225 Race Street in the Queen City. The building on the southwest corner of Race and Pearl Streets cost him $25,000, which seemed a pittance considering his daily intake.

Artisans created an intricate mosaic tile design in the lobby, most likely handcrafted by potters at the nearby Rookwood Studios, which also had created the immaculate installations at Remus's treasured Sinton Hotel. The tile display in the lobby spelled out "Remus" to greet visitors. Yes, he thought, this beauty demonstrated his authority. Industry giants purchased real estate and named it after themselves as a sign of deification.

The bootlegger's offices were decked out with expensive furniture, accessories, and equipment, costing him another $75,000, including a large mahogany table where he and his chief operators gathered to discuss the challenges of running the liquor network.

George hired a personal chef to work at the Remus Building. His men needed to eat at all hours of the day and night. The sun never set on his bourbon empire. For his part, George had grown fond of gourmet meals over the years.

George's wealth and influence grew. As his operations expanded, the threats from within increased as well. He had inherited some greedy, reckless men from other bootleggers or gangs. He and Conners weeded out those who proved disloyal or too inept. To excel in the Remus enterprise, workers had to have the right mix of tact, muscle, and persuasive skills.

Having grown into a loosely unified corporate structure with Remus at the top, the operation needed lieutenants to take on greater responsibility, particularly in running the parts of the business that they controlled, whether it was the trucking and automobile fleets or one of the far-flung distilleries. Remus ordered them to keep as little as possible on paper. He understood that carelessness, especially with written records, could lead to ruin. George's skittish feelings about possible paper trails that tracked back to him ran so deep that he would later have difficulty estimating the totality of his empire in either revenue or barrels sold.

The top generals in Remus's army were given prestigious roles at the companies he purchased. For example, he made Conners the owner of the Edgewood Distillery in Cincinnati, while Harry Gardewig, a longtime liquor dealer who helped Remus set up deals, became superintendent of operations.

Conners remained second in command. Despite a gambling habit that was becoming more pronounced as his personal fortune grew, he raked in about $250,000 over a two-year period. Conners was usually reserved, but when he needed to step up, he proved to be commanding and decisive—even downright frightening. His men knew Conners was handy with a pistol and had Remus's authority to use it. He approached his work logically and coldly, just like his boss.

"All I did was to buy and sell good whiskey and bribe a few crooks who would have been bribed by somebody else if I hadn't done it," Conners explained.

While Remus found men to fill leadership roles, he had trouble with large-scale transportation firms. He could not rely on freight or railway companies. There were many spying eyes around freight yards and terminals. As a counter, Remus ordered Conners and his underlings to begin buying vehicles—armored trucks and reinforced touring cars—both for making local deliveries and protecting bootleggers under his care. George built his personal collection, too, a sign of status among his underworld friends. He purchased six Marmons, several Packards, a Locomobile, a Cadillac, a Pierce-Arrow, and some Dodges.

In short order, Remus had a fleet of thirty trucks, including bulletproof armored vehicles that could deliver 325 cases each. Those beauties cost Remus $16,000 a piece. Although approaching a $500,000 outlay for the armored cars alone, the profits were worth the investment. One writer noted, "On the road the danger from pirates was particularly acute, hence each truck was followed by at least one car containing armed guards."

Flying down back roads at upwards of eighty miles per hour, bootleggers were loaded to their eyes with whiskey. They had guns at the ready in case they ran into trouble. At $90 per case or more, the 325 they carried in their automobile would bring more than $29,000.

The criminals who made these harrowing trips were quick to draw weapons and faster on the gas pedal. Some were in it for the speed or the thrill of violence, in addition to the cash. One reporter, speaking to Conners, called it the "clamor of flight and battle as a powerful automobile thundered through the night with one man at the wheel and another firing his repeating rifle over the back of the seat at pursuing pirates."

Transporting loads between Cincinnati and Chicago was one thing, but what about truly long distances? Although he did not trust railroads completely, Remus knew that the railways were necessary to ship away from Cincinnati to his other growing markets. Remus set up liquor depots in Chicago, Indianapolis, Toledo, Dayton, Columbus, Pittsburgh, Buffalo, and New York. There were also new operations set up in absolute secrecy and never revealed because the bootleg king transported the bourbon by railcars, necessitating a wide web of bribery and deception that dictated strict confidentiality.

When later asked about where all the booze went after it left his transportation centers, Remus only provided clues to the scope of his criminal operations.

"I don't know," he mused and rambled off a list: "Oklahoma, Missouri, Iowa, Nebraska, Indiana, New York, Pennsylvania, Illinois, Cleveland."

Given that rumrunners and mafia bosses frequently cut and resold the product over and over again, Remus may not have been purposely duplicitous. He actually might not have known just how far his empire reached.

Closer to home, four main distribution complexes were established to centralize and then distribute alcohol: a place nicknamed "Death Valley" in Western Cincinnati, and outfits in Reading, Hamilton, and Glendale. Remus called these his "depots." Each facility operated from a small city or country outpost that ringed Cincinnati. In some locations, Remus owned the site, providing him another means of distribution—selling directly to customers. Hamilton, for example, sat about thirty miles northwest of the Queen City and had gained a reputation across the Midwest as a gambling mecca, far enough away to elude enforcement authorities and other prying eyes. Big-time gamblers could always find a high stakes poker table in Hamilton, so when they tasted the superior bourbon Remus sold, they were eager to procure more. The depot there supplied directly to several prosperous gambling rings. In Glendale, a well-heeled village on a major Baltimore and Ohio Railroad railway line, local suppliers owned the facility. Remus paid them a commission per sale, rather than selling them liquor in bulk.

Remus also created relationships with the rumrunners who came to these locales to get booze, explaining, "At every depot the best customers were the runners, many of whom came from other cities, including St. Louis."

"The demand was greater than the supply," George recalled. "People would come from all over the country to consult and advise with me and try to obtain the liquor."

One rumrunner from Omaha would show up at Death Valley every Monday morning between nine and ten o'clock, Conners remembered. He drove a Dodge and brought his wife with him to throw both potential hijackers and federal agents off his trail. They looked like a typical couple on vacation. They could squeeze twenty cases in the trunk, with Conners charging him $80 to $110 per case, based on the brand and quality.

"That Omaha must be a dry town," Conners joked. "He told me he got $300 a case for it."

The 1,400-mile round trip must have been worthwhile based on the profit from that three hundred percent markup. Like all the experienced rumrunners, the Nebraskan had license plates for every state he passed through, Conners said. At the state line, he would pull over and put on new plates.

Despite the profits flowing in, Remus and his chief aides had to manage the locations and the young organization experienced growing pains consistent with most business entities. When one of his lieutenants complained about Glendale undercutting the other locations, Conners reported the information back to Remus. He held a meeting at his Remus Building headquarters, explaining that it was dangerous for them to resort to unfair practices in dealing with one another. Another violation, Remus explained, would end in that dealer being expelled from the organization.

Remus had to trust his underlings and placed more and more responsibility on Conners. As a bootlegger, George had to travel far more frequently than he ever had as a Chicago attorney. Sometimes this called for extended absences from headquarters, like a several-month stint on the East Coast:

I was spending much time on the road. Today I would be in New York, opening a new drug company; tomorrow in Washington, conferring with certain gentlemen—if I may call them so—on matters pertaining to the conduct of our business without interference from the government. On the train between cities I was busy studying the new prohibition regulations, and devising means to circumvent them as fast as they were issued…it was a very strenuous life.

Conners also hit the road, but in the role of a roving salesman. He traveled to Chicago, spending money lavishly to demonstrate the size of the Cincinnati operation. Next, he cozied up to the top operators of the most exclusive speakeasies and juke joints. The quality of liquor he delivered opened the eyes—and pockets—of the bosses.

From Chicago, he set off across the Midwest, visiting Detroit, Indianapolis, Toledo, and Dayton. At each stop, Conners established ties with local leaders who would send men to pick up bourbon in Cincinnati, Reading, Hamilton, or Glendale. Remus and Conners were often working remotely, so George gave his lieutenants broad autonomy and power, as long as they remained honest and kept the coffers full at his downtown office. They ran their own divisions with near impunity, as long as they did not "cut" or dilute the whiskey Remus stocked.

"I never permitted my agencies to dilute the liquor, it would have to be sold as it was from the distillery," Remus explained. "If they would attempt to dilute it or manipulate it as to the quality of the liquor, I would eliminate them as a distributor. I would never permit that."

*   *   *

It seemed everyone wanted Remus's bourbon—as much of the liquid gold as he could furnish. While he consolidated operations, introducing a distribution and security system, he and Conners reached out to other large players who had thirsty customers to serve. They did not have to look far. Through Remus's associations with Albrecht, Kessler, and others behind the scenes, he had routes into large cities where illegal "speaks" were cropping up as fast as owners could get them up and running.

In Chicago, South Side gambling and prostitution boss Johnny Torrio realized the vast fortune he could amass quenching the city's thirst. Like George, he created an extensive trucking line with steady routes between Detroit, where he could buy smuggled Canadian alcohol, and Cincinnati, where Remus facilitated access to the distilleries in Kentucky. Torrio built saloons and speakeasies in the Windy City and its suburbs to cater to the growing market. Torrio's top lieutenant was Al Capone, who he brought in from New York and trained to run the seedier aspects of his operations.

Capone took charge of getting booze into the organization's speaks and gambling dens. The relatively short trip between Chicago and Cincinnati gave Remus a line into the city, which the mob there exploited. A writer in Chicago noted, "Most of the liquor Remus handled was withdrawn through bribery and other methods from government warehouses. Some of it was sold in Chicago, where it was said the Capone gang was the chief distributor."

George took great pride in selling high-quality products and almost obsessively watched over his men to ensure that value. Some of the New York bootleg titans felt the same way—at least in the early years—like Arnold Rothstein. He wanted to sell primarily to wealthy patrons, just as he wanted the economic elite in his gambling joints. With Remus and Rothstein there seemed to be an honor about their product that was not always replicated. As Prohibition went on, a primary criticism developed regarding the countless deaths and illnesses caused by people drinking tainted or toxic liquor.

John Torrio had no interest in such minor concerns as quality. While some of Remus's finest might make its way to his group of high rollers or local government officials, the Chicago gang cut the whiskey, watering it down to a third or fourth of its original recipe. Capone directed his men to rebottle the cut product and churn it out for their speakeasies, with customers none the wiser.

●　　●　　●

Remus was on his way to cornering the American bourbon supply and cementing his place as an underworld mastermind. But, believe it or not, he had dreams of creating a publicly traded corporation and becoming a Wall Street kingpin. He would accomplish this by dominating the medicinal market—wholly legal—and then sell bourbon from his distilleries to Europe and elsewhere, also completely legitimate.

A primary tenet of the Remus empire was an idea that he called "the circle." Basically, like Rockefeller in oil or J. P. Morgan in steel, George wanted to create a network that controlled all aspects of the bourbon industry, from manufacturing the product in Kentucky distilleries to shipping and distribution, and then through the sales process. If he controlled all these points—thus creating the circle—he would dominate the market.

Under the dutiful eyes of his top men Conners and Gardewig, for example, American Transportation Company trucks—a firm Remus owned—lined up outside the Edgewood Distillery, where Conners was installed as president. Using certificates from the Kentucky Drug Company, they eventually took nearly 17,000 gallons from the plant over a six-day period. Then, the vehicles made their way to the nearby Covington warehouse to store the liquor until it could be taken to other depots.

"From there it found its way to the thirsty public," Remus said with glee. The pull from the Edgewood Distillery alone grossed Remus more than $450,000.

With large customers having alcohol piped in as fast as he could ship it and smaller operators arriving at his distribution centers, George's circle expanded quickly. By some estimates, Remus bought and sold about three million gallons of bourbon in the early years of Prohibition, a figure that equates to roughly 15 percent of all the bonded liquor then held in warehouses nationwide. Despite the magnitude of these quantities, the sums are merely estimates of a sprawling empire.

"We rigged up sets of books for our companies, showing a large volume of sales, and, in order to show large shipments to the customers we pretended to have, we consigned large quantities of drugs to fictitious retail druggists all over the country," George explained.

The circle idea was working, but it hinged on an illegal framework at every turn. The fake drugstores they created had to be filled with all the supplies and stock that an authentic store needed, an illusion that resulted in freight companies sending products crisscrossing around the nation and never being claimed. Remus had made up the addresses, pharmacy names, and everything else that would have seemed legit. But, the deception made these fake operations look genuine and real pharmacies could get whiskey certificates.

The fuel at the heart of the operations—the illegal liquor—was either legally taken from his distilleries via real licenses or illegally through fake whiskey certificates. Drug companies that were also either authentic or phony issued these documents. Then, Remus's American Transportation Company trucks shipped the product or transported it on railways he controlled through extensive bribery.

A significant amount of the bourbon was hijacked by George's own men, who then took it to one of the many depots to be sold at exorbitant prices on the black market or in one of his speakeasies. Much of the heist wound up in the countless roadhouses or brothels that littered the American Midwest.

Other liquor was blatantly stolen from warehouses with well-greased government overseers looking the other way. And, at every turn, George made sure that any potential problems from local, state, regional, or national officials or investigators were papered over through an extensive, blatant bribery network. No beat cop or detective that helped Remus patrol a depot ever walked away without a fistful of dollars or a couple pints of the good stuff.

"From a business point of view," a journalist noted, "their organizing and executive abilities would have been a credit to a Rockefeller."

Rumors abounded that George was close to signing a much larger deal to purchase an additional twenty-three distilleries or warehouses that held about one-third of all the bonded bourbon in America at a cost of nearly $5.5 million.

One writer asserted, "In the sheer imagination of his plan, in the insolent sweep of his ambition, and in the dynamic ruthlessness and power with which he swept upward toward his goal, Remus can bear comparison with the outstanding captains of industry."

As he moved toward this ultimate goal, however, Remus found it impossible to fully lay the groundwork for a legitimate liquor business given the foundation of illegality in America. He could never rectify the competing interests involved in making these kinds of untold riches versus his desired goal of establishing a legal enterprise. He could not slow down.

Remus did not anticipate that the Justice Department would pursue him with vigor or be able to track his operation. There were more stories in the papers about dirty feds than legitimate arrests or indicators that the Prohibition Bureau had any real power. The agency would never be staffed or funded at a level needed to wipe out illegal booze, but it had been gradually upping its investigatory and oversight capabilities. These efforts resulted in several large bootlegging rings being targeted, including Remus's outfit.

When they weren't worrying about Prohis, George's men struggled with maintaining order. The mountains of money they accrued seemed to mesmerize Remus and his underlings. Even though they did not have enough time in the day to count it all, they started taking risks to accumulate more.

No matter how quickly his empire grew or how far it extended, George Remus never found satisfaction in his successes.

He wanted more.

5

Underworld Boss of Death Valley

It was the spring of 1920 when, at midnight, two or three cars lumbered past the gatehouse, slowly climbed the hill, and then disappeared behind a thicket of trees. The vehicles were packed with men, each one with a weapon.

Queen City Avenue was about to come to life.

In the hollow below sat several houses and buildings, Remus's distribution stronghold. Rumrunners dubbed the place "Death Valley," a secluded farm on the outskirts of Cincinnati.

Shielded behind the tree line and having reached high ground, the cars slowed. The men inside reacted quickly, opening fire, filling the air with loud pops and sounds of bullets breaking branches and thudding into wood.

The attack happened so fast that the Death Valley guards could not get one return shot fired before the vehicles sped off.

George Conners left the outbuilding that served as the main office and looked toward the hillside. He guessed that they would be back, the first attack a warning, while the second would be more lethal.

John Gehrum hustled his wife and children into the farmhouse cellar to keep them out of harm's way. He joined Conners out front and they waved the Death Valley defenders into position. Two men would stay at the front gate, while the main group would climb the hill. Others positioned themselves in the trees at the top of the overlook. One man crept over to the farm henhouse, using it as a shield, propping up his shotgun, and readying for the next assault.

Ten minutes after the first attack, the automobiles approached the perimeter of Death Valley, again stopping at the overlook, just as Conners had predicted. He could have laid a bet on it.

Just as before, the men in the cars let loose with a barrage of gunfire, aiming at everything and nothing simultaneously, hoping to scare away anyone who might be at the location. The thugs knew what the farm held and they knew who owned it. By that time, everyone knew about Death Valley. If the bandits could ward off everyone guarding the site, they figured they could steal whatever liquor was there and probably a sizeable amount of cash.

As soon as the volley began, Conners, Gehrum, and their men unleashed hellfire on the hijackers. One reporter called the effort "instant and terrific."

"From the barns, the house, the trees, the sentry box near the gate, and even from the henhouse, a devastating fire raked the top of the hill," Conners told the journalist.

Violence and Prohibition went hand-in-hand. In skirmishes with bandits, criminals, and the ever-present hijackers, the rules were simple—come out shooting. Just like the frontier West, displays of force dictated how events would unfold.

No police were called and no reports filed. Conners did learn that several of the hijackers had been seriously wounded, possibly even dying in the fray. They would never know for sure. If there were fatalities, the bodies might end up dumped in the Great Miami River that ran through rural southwestern Ohio near Cincinnati or left to rot deep in the woods on some forested tract of land.

Later, Conners calmly recounted the firefight and countless others that took place at Death Valley, explaining, "It was a struggle between two bands, both outside the law, and the rule of the jungle uniformly prevailed. The only appeal was to force...the sharpest wits and the heaviest artillery won. No policemen wanted."

The men improvised as necessary to turn Death Valley into a fortress. They used an old voting booth on wheels for a guardhouse at the main entrance. A reporter who visited the farm explained, "The weapons chosen for the defense consisted of automatic shotguns loaded with buckshot, and deer rifles, a style of heavy firearm of large caliber which shoots fifteen times without reloading."

More important to Remus and his lieutenants, though, was that news of the counterattack spread around town and across the region. The name "Death Valley" itself was a powerful tool in representing how deadly powerful Remus had become in such a short time.

Death Valley was a place to be feared. No matter what percentage of truth rested in stories of gunfights and mayhem, the depot solidified Remus's image in criminal circles where reputation mattered. There would surely be more hijacking attempts—the lure of money drew thieves like moths to firelight— but it would take an army to rob Death Valley.

Lucky for him, Remus had the only army in town.

George had listened to his bourbon-industry mentors and followed their advice. He also watched closely as other criminal operatives set up shop in the regions they controlled. He met these overlords in speakeasies littering New York, Washington, DC, and Chicago. In turn, they sent their trucks to load up with Remus's bourbon, the best Kentucky Dew on earth.

His silent partners, according to one reporter, were "practical whiskey men" who brought "working experience" and "an unstated amount of capital" to the growing concern. Remus also had means that they did not, including $100,000 cash and a nearly unlimited line of credit at a Cincinnati bank, deep legal knowledge, and willingness to be the face of the operation.

George also brought new innovation to bootlegging. The creation of the circle enabled the bourbon kingdom to thrive. Remus, Conners, Marcus, Gehrum, and the others saw the cash flowing in and knew it gave them power beyond what they could have imagined. The circle, however, necessitated cash—the bribery grease for its engine. Thinking back to the dozens of small-time crooks and bootleggers he had defended in front of Judge Kenesaw Mountain Landis in Chicago, George realized they had been dealing in chump change compared to what he required now. Remus and his men began disbursing bribes up and down the local and regional ranks of politicians, legislators, detectives, and police officers in both Cincinnati and Newport.

They took graft to a new level, handing out thick stacks to countless judges, Prohi agents, and enforcement leaders—even railway men who could be counted on to look the other way when a large shipment went in or out of the northern Kentucky depots.

But such transactions attracted attention. Without realizing that a federal agent had wiretapped his phone in Room 707 at the Sinton and placed listening devices around the room, Remus had several days of meetings in October 1920 where forty-four men were paid off. They had all arrived downtown to pick up their money. Some were Cincinnati's most distinguished names from its elite families.

The Sinton Hotel itself was connected to the famous Taft family. Annie Sinton Taft—wife of Charles P. Taft, brother of the former president—was the only child of David Sinton, a Civil War profiteer who built the iconic Sinton, one of the largest and most luxurious hotels in the Midwest. Charles and Anna had spent an estimated $300,000 to $750,000 to help get William Howard Taft elected in 1908. The sums hardly mattered to Anna Sinton, who sat on $20 to $30 million inherited from her father—once among the largest landowners in the Queen City.

The vast bribery network in development, the next piece of infrastructure the gang needed was a stronghold. Remus and his men could grease the system—a major component of the circle ideology—but, and this is how the aforementioned Death Valley got its name, they also needed a distribution center. George had already lost a great deal of product from hijackers. He and John Marcus had created a storage depot in Covington, directly across the Ohio River from Cincinnati. A rival gang attacked the location, coldcocked the patrolmen, and stole 250 cases of liquor, worth about $25,000.

This heist and the brutal assault had shaken Remus to the core. He needed a better depot, one near the city, with its convenient water and rail lines, but more importantly, easy to defend. Since Conners knew the city based on his real estate background, Remus sent him off to find a site.

Conners used his connections to find an ideal location—a place where, he explained, "trucks could get in and out easily, but the place could only be reached by that one little road, and consequently would be easy to defend against pirates."

George Dater, a local farmer and small-scale winemaker, owned the 100-acre property. John Gehrum worked there with his wife Ada and their four small children. She served as caretaker of the extended family.

The main compound consisted of a two-story farmhouse, three old barns, and several small outbuildings. Journalist Paul Anderson, writing about Remus's early bootlegging exploits, described the farm and its occupants in a rather unflattering fashion:

> Dater is a fat, unshaven man in the fifties. Gehrum is a little, rat-faced, shifty-eyed individual, described originally by Conners as "a doormat thief," and living in perpetual fear of his wife, a young woman of vigorous propensities and a taste for strong drink.

Originally Gehrum, who had been doing some limited bootlegging on the side, refused Conners's suggestion that he let Remus try to buy it. He wouldn't even take the idea to his landlord.

In response, Conners decided to rent a barn on another farm nearby. Bad idea. The road in the rural area proved too difficult to navigate. After one of Remus's heavy trucks got stuck in the mud and could not make it to the barn, Conners went to see Dater himself. The two men shook hands and agreed to a $100 a week rental of the barns, as long as Conners promised to remove the liquor if Dater wanted it out.

"We drove our truck in and unloaded," Conners recalled. "We hid the cases under the hay in the barn loft."

The next day, against Dater's wishes, Conners and his men unloaded one of Remus's payloads, some 250 cases. Dater worried about getting "pinched," but Conners knew that the local police officers—including the mounted police, who would actually patrol the farm *for Remus*—were already on the bootlegger's payroll. The rental price increased to $200 a week in the hope of diminishing some of Dater's concerns.

Without much concern for Dater's potential objections, Conners launched a full-scale liquor operation almost immediately. Booze came into Death Valley so quickly that Conners had to have his men dig a secret storage cellar underneath one of the barns. Accessed through a trapdoor, the hidden vault provided storage for 10,000 cases in excess of the aboveground storage.

Meanwhile, though Conners didn't really like Gehrum, he hired him. The man could be useful. Gehrum knew the grounds and could run the place during Conners's frequent absences when he traveled to open new markets to Remus's liquor. Johnny's primary task was to oversee the guards and manage security. Conners also hired Ada to cook for the men and provide beds in the farmhouse. He paid her $100 a week to keep the household covered.

Using Death Valley as a shipping depot, the Remus gang obtained bourbon both legally and illegally. George estimated that the stock included "45 different brands of liquor," most of it obtained from distilleries that Remus did not own. Additionally, they had roughly fifteen different brands from the distilleries they operated across three states, including the Fleischmann firm in Cincinnati, the Freiberg & Workum plant in Ohio, and the Rugby Distilling Company in Louisville.

After processing, the gang dispatched the liquor to fake drug companies set up in New York City that would be difficult to trace back to them. George even brought a New York phone directory back from one trip and began mixing real doctors in with fakes when filling out falsified prescriptions. Then, Remus created exaggerated names for entire firms, such as Excelsior Drug Company, Imperial Wholesale, and Alpine. These false fronts secured that Remus could then get the booze to other liquor operatives, including kingpin Arnold Rothstein. Having a foothold in New York City was essential for Remus's success, especially given the city's disdain for the dry laws and slipshod enforcement efforts.

Word spread quickly within criminal circles about what Remus had created out at Death Valley. The place earned its name, according to one writer, because attacks "resulted in casualties, and possibly in deaths. Not a man of the defenders ever got a scratch. It was as a result of these bloody and futile assaults that the place got the name of Death Valley Farm."

Bootleggers within a 500-mile radius descended on the farmstead, eager to buy Remus's booze. Cavalcades of souped-up hotrods and touring sedans forced Conners to hire a legion of men to keep up with demand. They needed privacy and safety, especially when a potential pirate attack could occur at any moment.

As rumrunners from other cities grew more sophisticated—as many as 150 visited Death Valley from cities across the Midwest—they used expensive vehicles to transport the booze. The Packard roadster was most popular. The sedan had room to carry about thirty cases of liquor packed in paper and stacked in the rear.

Bootleggers had to be prepared for anything, including curious stares from local police, so they put heavy-duty suspension springs in the cars so they would not droop or drag. As officers grew more sophisticated about catching the hot-rodders, they used portable scales to weigh the cars and compare them to the poundage of a standard model. Rumrunners also carried extra supplies, like gas and oil—the fewer stops the less risk from cops, hijackers, or Prohi agents.

Conners and Remus won the loyalty of their employees by paying them well. The stern Conners even pitched in when he had the time, showing that he was ready to go to battle with his men. In addition to their regular weekly salaries, usually around $75, he let them carry on sidelight bootlegging as long as they were smart about it. In these instances, the men were paid $10 a case on top of their regular wages and could sell about ten to fifteen cases a week.

Around-the-clock security enabled Remus and his lieutenants to transform the sleepy Dater Farm into an efficient distribution headquarters, bottling facility, warehouse, and transportation hub. Under the watchful eyes of guards toting semiautomatic weapons and hidden forces ready for potential trouble, rumrunners and bootleggers filed into the desolate homestead, filling their trunks and hidden compartments as quickly as possible, perhaps having a drink or two, and then hitting the road out of town. The farm became a kind of make-shift rest stop, which made it more enticing to out-of-town rumrunners.

The money accumulating at Death Valley gave Remus and his delegates power and authority to bribe police and officials at will. According to Conners, they handed out money mainly to the "higher ups" and detectives in the police force, as well as the beat cops who basically knew everybody and everything that went on in their territories. Since Death Valley sat outside the city limits, Conners also worked with the mounted police, giving them a little bourbon and a little cash to patrol the farm and keep hijackers at bay.

Remus's lieutenant explained that the liquor he handed out as bribes allowed the officers to do "a little bootlegging on the side."

Some of the mounted police would even order cases of bourbon directly for their clients, usually wealthy patrons who did not want to mix with the rabble. Remus's underlings would drop the product off at a designated address. The police charged the buyers $90 a case, then took $10 off the top to keep the business running smoothly.

Conners had absolute authority at Death Valley, even over the police who were essentially on the payroll. He was not shy about demonstrating his control. When two mounted officers pulled over some of Remus's Chicago delivery drivers and then robbed them, Conners banned them from Death Valley.

"If I ever see you here again, or hear of you annoying any of our people, you'll get your blocks knocked off," he exclaimed.

After a couple weeks, the mounted officers returned, sullen, and practically begging to get back in Conners's good graces. He relented, and the cops were back on the take.

The lights never went out at Death Valley—it operated around the clock. A flood of smells filled the air. The thick odor of truck fuel mixed with the musky dampness of the hundreds of workers bottling bourbon as fast as their hands could fly. They had to invent contraptions to get the booze from white oak barrels into case after case of smaller bottles. A soft breeze might push the scent elsewhere, providing Remus's men a brief letup from the heat generated in the plant, but the bustle continued nonstop.

Despite the constant activity on the farm, the rickety lane leading up to the hideout was easy to miss from the main road. Since many rumrunners were coming from all over the country and did not know the local nooks, Conners had his men draw a tar line from the main road to the entrance so they could more easily find it.

No one even attempted to count the parade of touring cars and heavily armored sedans that came in and out of Death Valley's gates, always under the watchful eyes of armed guards. Even more sinister, though, a phalanx of gunmen hid away from general view. They bided their time, watching and waiting for the invasion they thought could occur at any moment. The farm seemed an easy score for gangs backed by rival bootleggers or bands of hardened criminals who might attempt a hijack.

Three additional men stayed on alert all night from the central barn, which had an electric buzzer that connected to the second floor of the farmhouse, where another man waited.

"Automobiles entering at night had first to satisfy the guard at the entrance," explained the reporter. "Upon reaching the yard, headlights were dimmed three times in succession. The men in the barn sounded the buzzer, and from a window on the second floor of the house a large floodlight was turned on, brilliantly illuminating everything below."

Watching, waiting.

According to one observer, Death Valley "was an arsenal worthy of any army camp. Every conceivable means of protection was furnished to the guards…shotguns, sawed-off guns, pistols, and rifles."

Conners directed the men in Remus's army to guard the product with their lives. One observer reported, "Whiskey pirates made desperate attempts to take the place, each ending in a bloody repulse." The chief lieutenant paid the guards well and ordered them to shoot first.

A journalist noted, "In the loft of each barn nestled a group of gangsters equipped with machine guns; they needed them, for the place more than once was assailed by hijackers, and men met death in Death Valley."

Threats made security a critical element in establishing Death Valley. The trucks slowly traversed the farm's dirt roads, the drivers careful to not topple the hundreds of cases of illegal booze under their care. Other Remus operatives left the farm in two-car teams, one filled with liquor headed to posh estates in well-to-do neighborhoods around Cincinnati, like Indian Hills and Clifton, while the other carried the men with guns to protect the precious cargo. These rumrunners made personal deliveries to the local politicians, party bosses, police, and wealthy socialites that kept the booze flowing despite the national dry laws. Hardly hiding from local officials—most on the take anyway—workers wrapped the bottles in newspaper and filled the cars to the roof.

While an attorney, Remus was known for his brashness and outlandish speaking style, even in the post-World War I era when people were routinely anti-German and may have been suspicious of him. When he worked on several bankruptcy cases in Hammond, Indiana, a reporter noted his distinct way of glad-handing, walking up to people and announcing, "I'm Remus. Everybody knows Remus."

Despite his thick German accent and deep, guttural voice, Remus fancied himself a distinguished gentleman. He tailored his voice and mannerisms into an overly dramatic style that he believed reflected an aura of refinement. One of the more curious aspects of his idiosyncratic mannerism was the way he frequently referred to himself in the third person as "Remus."

George frequently used this pretense when declaring an important point. It was as if stating his name made an opinion more rational or factual. The verbal tic was actually a kind of "tell," like a giveaway in poker, which provided insight into the bootlegger's frame of mind.

"Remus was in the whiskey business, and Remus was the biggest man in the business," the bourbon king boasted to writer Paul Anderson.

"Cincinnati was the American mecca for good liquor, and America had to come to Remus to get it," he explained further to Anderson.

The third-person affect was one facet of George's personality. Another was baser and more sinister—a cruel temper and quick launch into violence.

Few men doubted George Remus's courage or authority as a criminal leader. Any challenge might land one on the receiving end of his weighted walking stick, which had been purposely designed to crack skulls. Even more convenient were the brass knuckles George carried at all times.

In Remus's mind, the most blatant insult one man could deliver another was to spit in his face or slap him upside the head. If a person questioned his morals or principles, then Remus responded fast and hard.

"He has had a hundred fights and was armed in all of them," his stepdaughter Ruth would remember.

Yet, George's wild temper and emotional response to insult contradicted the smooth veneer and courtly speech he had mastered as an attorney. The duality—coldblooded criminal mastermind and respected, sage attorney—warred inside him. He probably would have described it as his responsibility as a man versus his lawyerly thinking. Emotion versus logic. As a result of the clash, Remus created a worldview that felt black and white, but actually filtered through many gray areas.

George's life as a criminal made little sense. The waves of anti-German hysteria unleashed by World War I, symbolized by the carnage American troops faced on European battlefronts, caused great fear among German-Americans and German immigrants. In Cincinnati, backlash against Germany ranged from Americanizing Germanic street names to open attacks on German establishments. George's ethnicity made him an outcast among the underworld kingpins in the 1920s, primarily Italians and Jews who preferred to work with men from similar backgrounds.

His dissimilarity from men like Al Capone and Joe "The Boss" Masseria, however, had positive consequences. Remus mimicked characteristics of the other leaders that he found useful for survival, but still retained his core sense of refinement, which was central to his self-perception. He built a kingpin's well-armed, well-equipped army to fortify Death Valley, and he hired bodyguards and heavies to exert pressure on adversaries or interlopers. But Remus wrestled with the complexities of being an organized crime boss with a legal degree. Could a person act tyrannical without being a tyrant? Is it fair to kill a thief who attempts to steal your goods, if you initially stole them yourself? Can an unjust law be enforced? Is it okay to defend a murderer, but also commit murder?

Death Valley became almost a physical representation of George's mental map—a fortress to protect the stolen goods of his illegal network that directly countered the Constitution, but an amended Constitution that countered what he believed the Founders had in mind when they created the nation.

Remus later declared, "If our forefathers that drafted the Constitution had ever thought that there would be an amendment to the Constitution setting forth that the only way you may have the spiritus fermenti is along medicinal lines, why they would turn in their graves."

Death Valley also stood as the fulcrum of George's command.

Once Death Valley had been established, George took the next logical step—one that the Italian mafia would have admired—he cut his silent partners loose, though without the bloodshed that marked gang warfare in New York under the control of the Unione Siciliana. By late 1920, Remus wanted full control of his bourbon empire. He bristled at the partnership he had created.

His primary fear was that his two partners might actually oust him from the organization if they realized how quickly it had grown and how much money could be made from the southern Ohio location.

Remus could not trust them, he recalled, because they always wanted to "put the double-cross on somebody." The relationship hinged on the age-old quandary: can a thief ever trust another thief?

His silent partners weren't always quiet. They advocated routine cheating as a method for making more money, whether watering down the liquor or undercutting Remus's main distributors.

The worry was always the double-cross.

"I knew that if these gentlemen were willing to double-cross everybody else they eventually would double-cross me," Remus explained.

Like his counterpart Rothstein in New York, George wanted to build an efficient organization to corner the high-end market for wealthy customers. First, he had to centralize his power.

To gain control, Remus claimed, he paid each of the two primary operators $900,000 in cash, which brought each man's total gains from the year they had worked together to $1.5 million. Remus simply wanted them out of town.

After delivering the cash, he recalled, "I took them to the station and saw that they got on a train for New York."

The move to eliminate his early partners was costly and not without trepidation. They gave him inroads into the alcohol market, so he searched for new suppliers. He found one in Charles Wiedemann, who operated across the river in Newport at the Wiedemann Brewery his father had founded in 1870.

In the early years of Prohibition, the brewery stayed in operation, allegedly manufacturing alcohol for "industrial purposes." Of its one million gallons produced, roughly half made its way to Remus, who had the toxic liquid denatured so that it could be consumed.

Partnerships with men like Wiedemann kept the bourbon empire growing and triggered Remus and Conners to hire even more gunmen to protect their property. No one could be trusted when everyone thirsted for liquor.

Even the Prohi agents who were presumably given the power to administer justice worked the system. Making side deals on dark roadsides and under the cover of night, federal agents frequently teamed with hijackers to stage fake seizures. The men handling the booze tipped off the feds then acted as if the government captured the loot. Instead, the two groups—often with guns aimed at each other—nervously divided up their plunder. Remus knew all about these "knock off" arrangements and fought back with muscle and firepower.

Conners explained, "We didn't propose to have our regular customers harassed and stuck up by a lot of petty grafting, tinhorn coppers. When the big fellows demanded a cut, we had to pay it, but when two-bit grafters tried to horn in we told them to get out of the way or they'd get their skulls caved in."

He had the cops and the feds under control, for the most part, which was important—dealing with criminal leaders in distant locales made it critical that Remus gain respect. Word even circulated that he frequently put his life on line to guard his empire.

Paul Anderson, the investigative journalist who spent months retracing Remus's moves and interviewing the bourbon kingpin and those close to him, claimed that Remus spent "evenings riding whiskey trucks and fighting occasional hand-to-hand battles with armed and murderous whiskey pirates."

Once, Anderson wrote, Remus left his Price Hill mansion at midnight, jumped into a Marmon coupe, and sped off at ninety miles per hour to "take part in a rifle battle between runners and pirates."

Despite the underworld reputation that Remus battled with his fists, weapons, or guns, he did not view himself as a criminal mastermind, but rather like a chief executive of a corporate entity. After all, he was laying the groundwork—like many business leaders in that era—to create a monopoly. Not just a player, he wanted to control the entire bourbon game.

And he seemed to be getting there, which made him a Robin Hood kind of legend. Since Prohibition had turned so many law-abiding citizens into lawbreakers, many criminal leaders developed heroic public personas. Remus grew into a popular, "man of the people" figure around Cincinnati and northern Kentucky, despite the illegality of his actions.

George not only happily accepted the accolades, he needed them. According to one writer, "He thirsted for and obtained newspaper publicity, often posing as a public benefactor and distributing his money where he thought it would do him most good."

Remus had bribed his way through the local police force, detective squad, and mounted officers with cash and liquor. He glad-handed with countless politicians, filling their pockets with incalculable sums. These steps were more or less expected. Remus's star grew brighter, however, as stories of his generosity swirled through the city's gossip mills. He would give newsboys large tips that could feed a family for a month or he would look the other way when neighborhood kids gathered at the baseball field he had built at the far end of his Price Hill estate.

His celebrity status, like that of other noted underworld figures, ranging from the infamous Al Capone to his mentor Johnny Torrio and New York crime boss Bugsy Siegel, changed the way people thought about crime and liquor. The newspaper media also played a critical role in transforming criminality into heroism, essentially turning gangsters into gallant figures—just as dime store novelists had done earlier in American history with notable lawmen and lawbreakers.

The cash came in so quickly that Remus didn't have enough time in the day to make deposits. He couldn't stop to count it. Each of his top men might be carrying up to $100,000 at any given time. George did not really trust the banks, instead viewing them as a kind of necessary evil.

Banks kept records. Remus did not want any documentation that could be tracked by Prohibition law enforcement. George and his men established aliases and fake accounts at regional banks, greasing the employees to keep it all hush-hush. Deposits often ran from $25,000 to $78,000 a day. He and his lieutenants had so much cash stuffed in their pockets that they looked like walking scarecrows.

W.C. Wachs, an executive at the Lincoln National Bank, said that one day Remus closed a major account at the bank and opened another under the assumed name "J.P. Alexander." He deposited $6,000 in the account and told Wachs that he could drop in $2 million more if he wanted.

The legend of "Death Valley" grew alongside Remus's fortune. A journalist at the time called the place, "the great depot through which the river of whiskey from Remus's distilleries and warehouses flowed out upon the country." With Conners and Gehrum overseeing operations, Remus could focus on maintaining the bribery network, particularly with officials on the federal level in Washington, DC.

The combination of the physical stronghold at Death Valley and the constant stream of available cash seemed to fulfill Remus's claim that he went into bootlegging "mostly for thrill and excitement."

There were fissures in the bourbon kingdom, though, that the thrill and excitement plastered over. Remus—despite his best efforts—had imperfect fortifications for his money and imperfect fortifications for his main depot. Both the cash flow and the whiskey flow needed protection from other criminal elements and the prying and snooping federal enforcement efforts. He could hire guns to protect the booze, but he had to rely on people's greed as well, a much trickier challenge. After all, he was violating a Constitutional amendment. The federal government was mandated to stop him.

Even hidden away in rural southwestern Ohio, Remus and his gang could not remain a mystery. The federal government had begun creating an enforcement infrastructure, overseen by Attorney General Harry M. Daugherty, to tear down illegal booze networks . More critically, however, in September 1921, President Warren G. Harding curried favor with female voters by appointing a young former prosecutor named Mabel Walker Willebrandt to serve as Daugherty's Assistant Attorney General. In this capacity, she ran the Prohibition Bureau tasked with bringing men like Remus to justice.

Within a handful of years Willebrandt would be considered the most powerful woman in America.

6
Every Man Has His Price

The train ground to a halt, and as George stepped onto the platform he gripped the handle of a worn leather satchel, squeezing it to feel its heft. He surveyed the station laid out before him. These places all looked the same now.

Travelers scurried around him. The sounds of feet shuffling blended with the sights of the faceless forms of people hustling to get somewhere. Porters and conductors shouted above the commotion. The trains huffed. Steel wheels grinded on rail.

George fidgeted. He moved the bag from one hand to the other, adjusting his grip, and flexing his fingers, ever conscious of his cargo of neatly wrapped tight stacks issued a day earlier by the Federal Reserve Bank in Cincinnati: $50, $100, and $1,000 bills. The bundles formed little lightweight bricks. They'd have to kill him to pry it free.

George had withdrawn the money with checks written out to cash. On each check he jotted down the initials "J. S." The nature of his illegal empire necessitated the utmost secrecy and little formal bookkeeping. A few indiscriminate notes here and there, however, helped the bourbon king remember where his profits were going.

In Washington, DC, like most big cities where he conducted business, Remus had men. They did what the boss wanted and were paid handsomely to remain quiet. His driver today, for example, would pick him up at the station and ensure that no one recognized the famous bootlegger or tried to snatch his bundle.

He was headed to another meeting at a distant hotel far away from Cincinnati and his familiar, scintillating lobby, lights and mirrors, and ornate, oversized furniture. Crisscrossing a region that stretched from the Queen City to the East Coast, George was spending more and more time on the road away from his beloved Imogene, who relished her time in the mansion's luxury and shopping in the high-end boutiques downtown. There were not enough fabulous baubles and trinkets in the world to make her happy, but he would try. Even from a distance. He gleefully stocked the marble palace with all that his riches could acquire.

When his man pulled up at the train station, Remus gave him the name of the hotel where he'd be staying and they sped off. The location meant little, virtually nothing to him. He could afford to stay anywhere in the world. What had value was the exchange.

The simple act of money changing hands was what Remus wanted, all sealed with a handshake. He called it the "gentleman's agreement." A man's word was his honor, and even more critical if it were cemented by money. To his logical, legal mind, meaning took place in the swap. Lots and lots of cash from one man traded for valuable whiskey certificates and protection from the other—simple. He and his men could bully, pound, or shoot their way in or out of any situation, but George knew the truth. Money gave him real power.

The gleaming sedan arrived at the Washington Hotel in the heart of the nation's capital, just across the street from the Treasury Department, and a stone's throw from the White House. Coming to a stop, the driver looked around cautiously, watching for anything out of the ordinary. He hustled around to the back of the car, opening the door for his passenger. Remus popped out, pulling the satchel closer to him, and then adjusted his hat.

George saw Jess Smith enter making long, loopy strides as he scanned the dazzling expanse. Smith did not look like the other men filling the Hotel Washington lobby. His most noticeable feature was the large, round pair of glasses that seemed to give his face a cartoonish look, as if Jess were a character in one of Frank King's *Gasoline Alley* comic strips. His neat little mustache made him appear older.

Among their commonalities, Jess and George shared an affinity for sharp clothes and an elegant personal style. Gaston Means, a one-time Justice Department investigator turned conman and fabulist who knew both men intimately, judged Jess to be "the best dressed man in Washington." Watching Smith walk through the corridors of the Justice Department was a study in carefully calculated taste. He matched from head to toe, from his gray silk socks to the hand-woven gray handkerchief with lavender threads that stuck out of his pocket like a beacon. Jess's gray gloves veiled his favorite ring, set with diamonds and two large rubies. When he entered a room, he would gently pull off his hat and smooth down his hair until it was perfect.

Smith—the mysterious "J. S." that Remus had noted on his checks—was much more than a DC bon vivant. The former small-town Ohio women's clothing store manager was whispered to be the unofficial attorney general of the United States. Jess's best friend and confidant just so happened to be the real attorney general, Harry M. Daugherty. Their relationship put the gossip mill on constant alert. Tongues wagged about Smith's obsessive devotion to his friend. Rumor had it that Harry could not sleep at night unless Jess were nearby.

Depending on Harry's needs, Jess would dutifully serve as Daugherty's confidant, nursemaid for his invalid wife, Prohibition Bureau insider, White House fixer, bartender, or bagman. Smith enjoyed these various roles, no matter how trivial they might seem.

Daugherty, in turn, had recently satisfied his own obsession—getting relatively little-known Ohio Senator Warren G. Harding elected president—which he had miraculously pulled off with the backing of a handful of powerful Republican Party insiders. Daugherty had believed that his man could be the consensus number-two contender for everyone, which would elevate him to frontrunner as others dropped to the wayside. The scheme worked and the popular, amiable, handsome Harding now slept at 1600 Pennsylvania Avenue.

Daugherty's reward for his commitment was a plum position in the Harding White House. A man with Daugherty's appetites—fine food and drink and a parade of much younger showgirls and loose women—demanded a large influx of cash. According to Washington insiders, as soon as Daugherty got his appointment, he was open for business. Tagged as the nation's top law enforcer, Daugherty promptly utilized the power of his office to become an accomplished lawbreaker. His fixation with Harding never wavered, but money filled his heart's greatest desire.

Rushing around Washington, Smith moved from meeting to meeting, searching out a network of investigators, spies, gossipmongers, and clerks that kept him informed about rumors coming in and out of the White House. An informer who asked too many questions often found himself being queried in return. One question too many and Jess would answer, "I dunno—do you?" It was his favorite way to turn the tables on an inquisitor.

When it came to Daugherty and President Harding, though, Smith clammed up. He knew how to skirt a secret and lock one down. Jess would forever be a "willing slave" to Daugherty, Means claimed. Whenever topics got too thick or heated, Smith turned to his first love—fashion—telling anyone who would listen, "The first quality of a gentleman is neatness." He demanded information and gossip but kept his own views hush-hush.

Smart suits and matching socks didn't mean much to the other men who regularly gathered at 1625 K Street in DC. There, in the infamous "Little Green House," Attorney General Daugherty capped off his days of wading through Justice Department paperwork with President Warren G. Harding and his boys. They came to party. Cigar smoke turned the air foul. The sharp sound of glass striking glass echoed off the walls. Playing cards, the men boasted about the hands they'd been dealt and elbowed one another, laughter rolling through the place. And Jess Smith would be there, too, serving as Daugherty's glad-hander at the ultra-private card games. He watched the scene, always ready to serve these powerful men, whatever their needs.

Smith's starring role was to be Daugherty's moneyman. So much flew into their coffers that the group of Harding insiders known as the "Ohio Gang" actually buried much of the profits in a concrete bunker in the backyard. Just like the nation's bootleggers, Daugherty and the Ohio Gang operated in cash. Some of the money fueled their debauchery, and much of it found its way into their personal accounts or those of their close associates.

All the while, few people saw Jess's role in its totality. What they knew, according to one of the era's top newspapermen, was that Smith served as the enigmatic "friend of the General." The power this unofficial title bestowed on Jess—the influential disciple of America's top lawman—provided him almost unlimited clout. Before long, if someone desired a favor from the attorney general, they had to see Jess. He held the cards and took the cash.

Remus and Smith left George's driver in the lobby of the Washington Hotel, and the two adjourned to an upstairs suite. Smith glanced back over his shoulder. He might have been followed. Tugging on his glasses and fidgeting with his cufflinks and vest, Jess looked around for men who looked like federal agents or anyone he might have seen at the attorney general's office. The coast seemed clear. They could plot strategy upstairs.

"There might be a conviction before a jury," Jess assured the bootlegger. The case, however, when it got to the Court of Appeals, he said, "would be reversed."

Smith hoped his explanation would keep the bootlegger from growing agitated. Remus's anger made Smith uneasy, the squat man's physical contortions off-putting. Jess did not like confrontation, but Remus seemed to revel in terrifying people. Smith wasn't sure if George was the snake charmer or the snake.

Remus weighed his options for a moment. He felt the blood begin to well up around his collar. He rested the briefcase on the table and clipped open the snaps with his left hand. This was not the sturdy guarantee he hoped for. However, the exchange had to take place. He could not trust anyone else to deliver it. Placing his faith in Jess's ability to fix the court system by utilizing Daugherty's influence, Remus tugged at the bag, holding it ajar to show Smith the contents—$30,000 in neat little blocks.

All that money, Remus thought. He demanded assurance from his man on the inside. According to George, Smith told him, "The Department of Justice would put up a vigorous battle, but ultimately I would never see the penitentiary."

Smith nodded, "There is no likelihood of your going at any time—you or any of your men." He glanced into the bag, then closed it.

Smith told Remus that Daugherty himself, whom he always called "the General," had assured him that the bootleg leader would never go to jail. Even if his case went to the United States Supreme Court, Jess would make sure that Harding pardoned him.

When their discussion ended, Remus left Smith in the suite and returned to the lobby. "When you have Washington 'fixed' you don't need to worry about 'fixing' anybody else," George later stated. "I had my man in the Department of Justice, right next door to the attorney general's private office. That was enough for me."

Remus liked to joke that Daugherty was "the big permit man" who made bootlegging possible and lucrative.

Exiting the Washington Hotel, Remus rolled the fix over and over again in his mind. The value was in the exchange with Jess. So much money switched hands, but that endless supply of cash resulted in a nearly unlimited supply of whiskey permits. More importantly, it guaranteed George's safety.

They had a deal.

"Regardless of any attempts that might be made to prosecute me," Remus remembered thinking at the time, "I would never go to prison."

George's decision to become a lawbreaker had been unequivocal. When he took that step, he did everything possible to solidify his power and influence. Nearly ending up in prison in his early bungling foray into bootlegging in Chicago had hit him like a bombshell. Yet, the incident and his eventual escape taught Remus an important lesson: perceptions change when a pile of cash is dropped on the table.

"Every man has his price," became George's mantra. He genuinely believed in the sanctity of the bribe, the fair swap, money for influence.

As the tentacles of his bootlegging empire spread, Remus recognized that he needed help. The Volstead Act granted federal Prohibition Bureau enforcement agents nearly unlimited power to snoop and pry. Newspapers around the country led with stories of Prohi raids and arrests. From the Prohibition Bureau the mantra seemed to be: arrest first and ask questions second. Some federal agents clearly circumvented the law in their zealotry for the Eighteenth Amendment.

At the same time, however, Prohi agents were human, with all the frailties and challenges that presented. Like Remus when he saw firsthand the rolls of cash that rumrunners used to pay Judge Kenesaw Mountain Landis's fines in Chicago, the men charged with enforcing Prohibition gathered that they could use their power to line their pockets.

American law enforcement had a deep history with graft. The payoff had been pervasive in police forces around the country for seemingly forever, so there was precedent for bribery. Countless enforcement agents rationalized that since they were the ones putting their lives on the line, they had the right to make some money on the side, especially when so much cash was available. Bootleggers and other lawbreakers were quick with monetary offers.

George had no illusions about what he was doing from a moral standpoint. He saw thugs and other small-time rumrunners purchase the loyalties of everyone from the local beat cop to politicians at the state and national levels, even leaders in the enforcement bureau itself. Remus resolved to buy the patronage of powerful officials who could essentially watch his back.

The Eighteenth Amendment made innovative ways to skirt the law commonplace. The more groundbreaking, the better. Some bootleg operatives had allegedly been brought in for questioning by federal Prohis and then shaken down by the agents who ostensibly represented the law. Whether they paid or not, the criminal would be accused of bribery.

Money purchased information: intel on when raids might occur, who was investigating him, when Prohis were in town, and more. One reporter noted that Remus "possessed his own secret intelligence system for spying upon the movements of government agents."

As a result of Smith's guarantees and Daugherty's closeness to President Harding, Remus would not only expand operations and territories, but he would do so, as he explained, "more openly than ever."

"The moment they would want to tie up some of Remus's institutions, I would have knowledge of it," George confessed. "I was fortified because Washington were our friends."

Remus and his men grew increasingly brazen in disregarding the law, particularly in Ohio and Kentucky. They believed that they had locked down the region through a string of extensive bribes and secret agreements with local and regional officials.

On top of those assurances, they had Jess's word. Smith's guarantee paid enormous dividends. And Remus took pride in letting slip his so-called secret relationship with Daugherty's man.

But, of course, the increased attention came at a price.

"He publicly blustered that he was beyond the reach of the law, claiming he had everything 'fixed' all along the federal, state, and local line," one journalist said. "In effect, he defied the authorities to prosecute him."

As soon as Remus handed over the protection money to Smith, he alerted Conners to commence with the plan to buy the Edgewood Distillery in Cincinnati. Remus used his top lieutenant to front the distillery, naming Conners president. As soon as he had the reins, he knew exactly how to proceed. Agreeing to pay $220,000 for the operation, Conners and his men began plundering.

"We took over everything," Conners divulged. "Office furniture, records, and even kept the office force. When Remus had got the permits, and everything was in readiness, we put our force of bottlers in and started doing business."

In a five-day period, Conners and his men methodically extracted 6,500 cases of Old Keller, 500 cases of Johnny Walker, and 250 cases of Gordon gin. Leading a band of highly paid henchmen eager to make big money for working hard and fast, even Conners himself was stunned by the efficiency of the operation. Once they got the booze to the Kentucky Drug Company warehouse in Covington, they simply deserted the distillery.

"We finished in the morning, put on our coats and walked out, and never went near the place again," Conners boasted. "I don't know what ever became of the office furniture and other stuff. It was excess baggage to us."

The Edgewood haul alone would have commanded more than $650,000 on the black market after being piped off around the country for distribution by a consortium of independent rumrunners as well as larger organizations that bought their supplies in bulk. Remus prided himself on selling the best liquor in the marketplace, but certainly most of the bootleggers were more than happy to pay his prices and then cut the alcohol several times over. And Remus's prices had all of his costs factored in. Take Smith's outrageous costs for protection, for example. When Remus determined what rate he would charge for booze, he just calculated his total costs, including how much graft went into the acquisition.

A journalist explained, "The price of the graft was figured in every case and was charged to the consumer." George's network did not set the prices of bootleg liquor nationwide, but they put so much into the system that his prices became almost standard.

The prices were high, and the secrecy was a sham. Between Remus and the prohibition agents stood a long line of middlemen who collected and exchanged the money in an inane mockery of discretion. Often the "go-between" was a "politician who had got the official his job" and stood ready and able to take a cut of the cash as payment. So many people had their hands out that Remus felt that many of the prohibition enforcement officials had been personally selected by various political leaders as a way to collect such fees. He believed that leaders in Washington used federal agents to line their pockets via extorting the bootleggers.

George had no illusions about the extent of the corruption or the dreaded "double-cross" that could come at any time, but he believed that he could outspend others and secure a modicum of safety. He heard the stories about other bootleg leaders paying off officials. Some of his closest associates, like Mannie Kessler, had already faced federal charges. Although people might disagree on just about every issue, most would take another dollar if given the opportunity. Some enforcement agents and officials developed multiple sources of revenue far exceeding anything they could have hoped to acquire in their lifetimes if national Prohibition had never been implemented.

The corruption in the enforcement bureaus at the national and state levels actually thwarted any efforts George made to sell whiskey legally through pharmacies. He couldn't get his hands on whiskey certificates at a fair price.

Prohibition allowed the sale of alcohol for medicinal purposes, even if most people did not think this was much of a medical cure. The whiskey certificates—distributed by Prohibition directors in each state—allowed booze to be taken out of bonded warehouses. When these transactions took place with corrupt officials, they simply manipulated the system. The director signed blank certificates and disbursed them to underlings who would then sell them to the highest bidder. The power transferred from Remus to the middleman in the arrangement. He had to pay a fee per case withdrawn at whatever price the underling determined.

Remus would testify at one point that he paid $42,000 for a series of permits that enabled his men to take 2,000 cases out of government warehouses, a hefty $21 per case in illicit payments. If the directors were ever questioned about these certificates, they simply declared that they were forgeries or stolen, which placed the burden of proof on the alleged criminal to prove otherwise. If no questions were asked, then the enforcement agents pocketed the money.

Much of the corruption Remus took advantage of came directly from the Prohibition Bureau, particularly as enforcement began. Various state leaders issued whiskey certificates for a hefty fee. "They received considerations," Remus explained. "Otherwise those withdrawals would never have come to the respective distilleries that I was owner of."

As a result of all the various permutations, trust evaporated and criminality ruled, particularly as officials in the Harding administration learned that they could be so dishonest. Much of the underhanded maneuvers originated in Attorney General Daugherty's office and ran through Smith. Jess always ran interference for Daugherty and his Ohio cronies linked to Harding's White House. The money changed hands, which fit with Remus's worldview of how men acted when they had a deal, but he had no guarantee that Smith could do what he said.

Amidst this setting, and with his own loose lips, could Remus possibly keep his central bribe secret? A journalist reported that he heard a rumor around town about George, explaining, "He was once heard to boast that he was immune from prosecution because he had the ear of the private secretary of a cabinet officer."

George continued to pay, explaining, "Always with the assurance that I would not go to prison. If it came to a showdown, I was to get a pardon."

Perhaps not a surprise given the wholesale corruption, there was loads of hypocrisy in Washington, DC. Remus and other bootleggers exploited the thirst of those in power by shipping high-quality bourbon to the nation's epicenter in epic quantities. The duplicity of selling to those who had outlawed drinking was not lost on the bootleg king.

"No, I never had any customers in Washington. But there was plenty of Remus whiskey consumed in that town, with the compliments of George Remus," he explained sarcastically.

"I tried to corner the graft market, but I learned that there isn't enough money in the world to buy up all the public officials who demand a share in the graft."

Fueling corruption at the highest levels certainly kept Remus occupied. It had the potential to pull his focus from another major concern of his national bourbon network. In the beginning, Remus did not take the threat of pirates and hijackers seriously. The oversight cost him hundreds of thousands of dollars in lost revenue. The constant threat forced him to assemble a de facto army of armed guards and a trucking and caravan operation to defend his product. Introducing security measures, however, was a fairly straightforward task. He delegated the work to Conners, Gehrum, and the infamous Buck Brady, the violent Kentucky thug and strongman.

The most important lesson Remus learned, however, might have been the hardest to swallow, because it flew in the face of his natural inclinations. The dictate that was at the heart of his thinking—"Every man has his price"—was simply untrue.

Despite having nearly unlimited funds to bribe anyone who stood in his way, Remus encountered a handful of notable officials that he could not reach, even though he took great risks in attempting to entice them. He and his henchmen made offers repeatedly, and when they were turned down, continued to increase the monetary figures until they reached ten or twenty times what the person could ever hope to make in a lifetime. In several prominent cases, these officials would come back to haunt him.

On one trip to Washington, Remus had asked around about Bert Morgan, the Prohibition Director for Indiana, who happened to be in the city at the same time. George had several of his local thugs follow Morgan around town to see if he did anything that might give Remus leverage in negotiations with him. The flunkies reported back to Remus on the agent's every move, but he did nothing out of the ordinary. Morgan seemed clean.

George questioned some of the insiders that he already had on his payroll, wondering aloud if Morgan could be tempted. He did not like the responses.

Everyone spoke in glowing terms about Morgan, commenting on his upright nature.

When Remus returned to Cincinnati, he ordered his personal secretary, Clem Herbes, and John Gehrum to go to Indianapolis on the double. He wanted them to discuss what he called a "very delicate matter" with Morgan. The two henchmen hustled to the Prohibition Director's office and were able to score a meeting. They wasted little time outlining why they were there.

"Now listen," Herbes urged Morgan, "Everybody else is getting their share, so you might as well get yours."

Clem and Johnnie offered Morgan upwards of $500,000 in exchange for liquor permits. They wanted to remove whiskey from several distilleries in or near the Hoosier State, including the treasured Squibb facility in Lawrenceburg. Morgan would simply have to look the other way for a short time.

"Herbes wanted me to sign all permits that came to me, that is, to okay them," Morgan later explained. "I was the stumbling block in the middle west here. They did not want me to investigate where this liquor was shipped. All they wanted me to do was to sign the permits that were presented to my office."

"Money is the least of our worries," the men explained. "We don't have to worry about that. We can get all we want."

Morgan balked at the offer, but Remus's henchmen persisted. Attempting to convince the eminent Prohibition enforcement leader, Johnnie then pulled out a small notebook that contained a long list of powerful government leaders, including senators and congressmen.

"These are the men we already got," Johnnie explained, all these powerful men "played with the Remus organization."

Since so many high-level Harding administration officials and legislators had already been paid off, Gehrum suggested, Morgan should take part while he had the opportunity.

Despite being presented sums of money that could have changed his life forever, Morgan declined the offers. Sitting there in his Indianapolis office, his annual salary stood at $4,600. Personal honor apparently meant more to Morgan than any cash reward Remus could offer.

"I told them that there was not enough money in the world to buy me, and to give that answer to their head as the final answer."

Morgan added that he not only wouldn't accept the bribe, but that as soon as the two Remus gang members left his office, he would promptly report on their efforts, telling higher-ups that they had attempted to bribe him.

Seemingly unfazed by Morgan's stern warning and threatening words, Johnnie and Clem shook hands with the director and left.

While Morgan watched Remus and his henchmen from the west, further south in Kentucky, Federal Prohibition Director Sam Collins started his own surveillance of the Cincinnati gangsters. Having gained extensive experience with Kentucky moonshine runners in his earlier career as a tax agent, Collins knew that vast quantities of whiskey would be shipped out via back roads if something were not done to prevent it. He instituted a rule that legal bourbon could only be transported out of Kentucky by railroad, which would curb rumrunners and hijackers. It was much more difficult for criminals to stop a train versus a slow moving truck weighted down with cases of alcohol.

When Remus realized that his milking schemes would suffer under Collins's new rules, he sent an attorney to chat with the director.

The lawyer, according to one source, "told him he could have $100,000 if he would resign."

When Collins said, "No," Remus's man doubled the offer to $200,000 just to walk away from his $4,600 a year job. Again, the director turned it down, as he did again when he was offered $500,000.

Later, a newspaperman asked Collins about the bribe and whether he was tempted. "Why, not at all," the lawman countered. "It doesn't cost me any particular effort to be honest. We folks down in this country—the Black Pine Mountain country, near the Virginia border—are not used to much, and what we ain't got we get along very comfortably without."

Despite the occasional upright law enforcement agent, George's power grew. There were other tools besides cash at his team's disposal. According to Conners, they were just as apt to use the iron fist instead of the velvet glove, if someone needed to be persuaded. For a local beat cop or one of the Cincinnati mounted police officers that patrolled Death Valley, a little cash and a couple quarts of "the good stuff" would probably suffice. Other bootleggers and distributors, though, might need some forceful persuasion. The empire required discipline and enforcers to carry out Remus's orders.

What some people assumed about Remus's empire, Cecil H. Kerns brought to light. Kerns was the president of the Victor Drug & Chemical Company in Toledo, one of the many front companies set up to circumvent Volstead regulations. He eventually got caught on liquor trafficking charges in three states. Kerns served a two-year stint in the Atlanta Federal Pen before being paroled by Attorney General Daugherty in 1924 after hiring Daugherty's former law partner John Todd to represent him. Called before a Senate investigatory committee to discuss bootlegging, he told the members that Remus's bribery network—including Jess Smith and Ohio Prohibition director Joshua Russell—was common knowledge in the criminal world.

However, the bootleg king also used his growing power to watch over anyone who wanted to sell outside his network. He used his organization's size and authority to force smaller operators to buy from him, according to Kerns. Only then, could an outfit hope to remain "free from molestation."

Many criminal leaders used bribery and payoffs, but Remus took this to a new level, giving money and booze to thousands of officials, from local police to members of President Warren G. Harding's cabinet. The majority of his bribes went to Attorney General Daugherty.

"Remus and Conners say they never had any serious trouble with the police. They 'fixed' the right men in the right place, and told all the others where to head in," explained reporter Paul Anderson. Bribes included money and a customary two quarts of bourbon a week.

Conners saw the bribery network as part of the overhead in creating a bourbon empire:

> We were in business. I grant that it was an illegal business, but it was a big business…We were paying a reasonable amount for protection, and we didn't propose to have our regular customers harassed and stuck up by a lot of petty grafting, tinhorn coppers. When the big fellows demanded a cut, we had to pay it, but when two-bit grafters tried to horn in we told them to get out of the way or they'd get their skulls caved in.

Remus had distributed enough cash, threats, and violence to ascend to the top of the bourbon game. It was a brutal business that required ruthless tactics. Every bribe, late night protecting a shipment, and moment in danger, however, pushed him closer to the dream world he imagined when he first entered the bootlegging game. His payoff was clear—the grand life that he and Imogene had imagined.

The splendor they had yearned for now unfolded right before their eyes.

7

Epic Grandeur

December 31, 1921. Almost midnight. The countdown is on.

Five hundred bodies in synch. People are radiating heat. The warmth from the water is intoxicating. Everything she's ever fantasized. This isn't a night that anyone has ever lived before—the first instant of a new world.

Perhaps the most spectacular place on earth, the grandest thing she's ever seen. Right here, in this moment.

Surging from the crowd, a noise slices through the music, the buzz of so many voices, and so much laughter. People stumble on wobbly legs. Has there ever been a river of bourbon so wide and deep? The champagne current has swept them here.

The glass shattered and legs shuffled, others dashed away laughing. The most fun that could be had, awash in liquor, as illegal as the day is long.

The smell of vapors and perfume rolls across the room, contained by ten-foot high windows, masking the chemicals in the air. Potted palms scattered. They reflect off the water, immaculate. Dotted across the spread, vats of ice, some bottles float upside down and empty. Dead.

Cloaked, if that's what you'd call it, she feels silk brush against her legs. A pile of cotton towels are stacked nearby, folded perfectly, a great deal of care for something that will be carelessly scattered amid the debris.

These are moments that should be remembered. She pauses to amplify the power. All the seconds and minutes and hours lead to this single instant, just like that champagne flute on the smooth tiled floor. A flash and then that glimmer disappears, not returning even if she begs. The shimmer of memory and the blurry line between real and imagined.

She looks, waits.

Are they watching? Will they capture this moment? Can they see her through fuzzy eyes, through that bourbon river washing over them like darkness? The room narrows as she looks for their eyes on her.

Five hundred people—tables arranged perfectly. They sit, gather, stand, drinks in their hands.

The robe drops, a silky puddle at her feet. Every head in the room turns.

Standing perched on the edge of the diving board, Imogene Remus raises her arms skyward.

Below, two hundred servants cater to the 300 guests at the most fabulous New Year's Eve party the Queen City has ever seen.

George Remus, the master of festivities and host of this spectacle, has spent so much money on flowers alone that tongues wag. The perfume is intoxicating. Even this elite crowd, so used to such opulence, is overwhelmed. The prodigious bottles stacked up on tables are brought around on silver trays by beautiful servers. Each holds dark brown liquor, clear liquid, an unfathomable quantity of lawlessness.

The room is filled with judges, politicians, police, patriarchs, business leaders, sycophants, and stylish shorthaired women garbed in skimpy, form-fitting dresses. They all shimmy around the pool. The younger set cries out for attention, sashaying to the edge, but no closer. The music lilts, then lifts. The ultimate party. Fit for a queen.

Imogene.

The Imogene Baths.

Her party, for her, always about her.

She wiggles at the end of the board. Her white bathing suit is revealing—tight at the bottom and loosely covering her top. She exposes herself in the moment. Gussie wants to be famous. She demands her place. Remus has money, he can buy her anything she desires.

Her mansion, her immaculate pool. The Rookwood tile, the best in the world and found in museums, sparkles below her. The judges and politicians and lawyers laugh and pretend to jump. They won't jump. She will.

George has given them all gold-rimmed liqueur glasses. Then cups made from solid silver and jewelry. And one hundred dollar bills under the place settings. But the big surprise still awaits them, the ones who came to this special celebration. The Imogene Baths.

A gala—the $150,000-dollar pool—immaculate.

Imogene stands there, gathering her breath. A Roman orgy, the newspapers will say. One last pause and then she leaps from the platform, gaining speed as she finishes a picture-perfect dive. She strikes the water, thereby formally christening the Imogene Baths, as her husband so graciously named the pool area.

"Champagnes and other rare wines flowed like the Rhine," a reporter will remember. "One hundred young girls, garbed in Grecian robes of flowing whites served the banquet, which began at midnight."

Four young water nymphs entertain the assembled crowd. Professional swimmers from Chicago, they delight onlookers with exhibitions of diving and swimming. Someday, George hopes to give it all away, turn over the lovely pool to poor neighborhood children who have no place to swim like he did as a young man in the frigid waters of Lake Michigan and the mighty Mississippi River.

Tonight, however, they would celebrate.

Imogene's one-piece bathing suit is held together by intricate, crisscrossed lacing that hints that it might just come undone. The v-shaped back plunges deep, exposing her to the night air and the rapt eyeballs of the men gathered at the edge of the abyss.

The white suit is not translucent, but implies see-through. The high-cut back barely covers her bare bottom.

Imogene knows how to grab their attention. Men long for her.

She has pinned her long, raven-black hair back and up, the nape of her dewy neck exposed in the thick, humid air. Back on the board again, she looks over at the hired water nymphs, smirks, and then dives deep into the crystal drink.

The newspapermen, always transfixed, will proclaim, "The sensation of the occasion was Mrs. Remus herself, who…put the professionals to shame by her exhibition of diving and swimming."

The bathing suit barely contains its parcel, men strain to see more.

"The swimming pool was, as I consider it, very beautiful," George later tells everyone who will listen.

A party to end all parties. Imogene's moment.

Hers.

George Remus enjoyed being surrounded by nice things. As he acquired riches, nothing checked the buying spree. Ownership was what he craved—the new life stood in stark contrast to his childhood in tiny, cluttered apartments with his brother and sisters. Dark, dank, his father's stinking breath, his poor mistreated mother. So far away now.

Without any formal training, he bought art, claimed he was "fond" of it—owned it, like he owned the mansion, which people called the "Dream Palace."

Remus relished collecting, particularly statuary. George had it shipped back to Hermosa Avenue. It was all his.

"Fond of good food, the good things of life," said one observer who studied George.

In conversation with the leaders of banks, lawyers, and politicians, he dropped names of his favorite writers: Goethe, Schiller, Dante, and others. Class and sophistication.

He woke up each morning beneath silk sheets.

· · · · ·

On New Year's Day, 1922, the local newspaper proclaimed: "Cincinnati's lid slithered and bounced as though above a boiling pot as the midnight hour ushered in the infant year to the…throaty walls of hundreds of whistles."

Across town, at George and Imogene's favorite haunt—the Sinton Hotel—three orchestras had blared deep into the night. Yet, the dry laws and the sinister enforcement agents toned down the revelry.

Prohis had been on the march.

"Numerous suspicious-looking individuals emerged from various points of hiding to throw the fear of Prohibition into Cincinnati celebrators, and temporarily halt communication with favorite bootleggers," wrote a newspaper reporter.

Even the luxury hotels had to protect themselves. The grand palaces of hedonism and vice prior to Prohibition had its managers handing out discreet cards with the rather depressing news in overtly large type:

IT IS UNLAWFUL TO BRING LIQUOR INTO A HOTEL OR RESTAURANT.

In the streets, however, reporters sang stories hinting that John Barleycorn had been among the teeming masses. The party hardly stopped in Cincinnati's German district. "Most of the large halls over the Rhine were filled with merrymakers gathered together by fraternal and labor organizations in entertainments, dances, and dinners."

For the Remuses, the New Year's Eve party signaled entry into Cincinnati's elite, like the families in the toney mansions in Indian Hill, where his men hand-delivered case after case of the good stuff. These were the wealthy in Clifton Park and Price Hill, families with names that other men knew.

Simple transactions: a phone call, loading up sedans – cases of bourbon in exchange for handfuls of cash.

Remus was such a man. He would bend them all to his will.

"We had 123 guests from all over the country," George declared.

The registry actually grew to three or four times that number. They lost count as the night wore on. The visitors mixed and mingled with the hired help: servants, dancers, musicians, and harem girls in nearly see-through frocks. Fueled by rivers of George's illegal booze.

"Harry Daugherty's here," George bragged to a reporter, "but he's drinking in a side room and doesn't want to be seen."

Remus treated journalists like visiting royalty when they came to the dream palace. He led them up the hand-carved mahogany steps to the third-floor billiards room. He watched as they touched the railing, saw the statues of Greek nymphs, and wondered what it was like to live like this. The bootleg king, they called him. George acted as if these reporters were his old pals. They would sit around in fat, leather chairs. Remus would reveal things, like they were his confidantes, as the men huffed on the thick, black cigars that he loved. George lit them one after the other, punctuating sentences with a jab of the dark stub.

Remus divulged secrets. Not all of them true, but stories that they would print. Remus, he said with a wink, does not drink, does not smoke—has never touched a drop in his life. Then, clinking glasses, they would sip on some of the finest Kentucky Dew ever made. This was the same bourbon he shared with the local aristocrats that visited the mansion. Those names were hush-hush. They drank his booze, Remus kept their secrets. Took their money and built an illicit empire, then handed them their returns, and another glass.

Never cut, the best liquor in the world.

•   •   •

"Her every glance seemed a caress."

Men loved Imogene. She arrived in her Rolls-Royce, a chauffeur attending to her needs, shimmering from head to toe in jewels that sparkled in the sunshine. She had rubies woven into her hair. Dozens of carats laced her fingers—diamonds as big as the Ritz.

"There was something feline in her every movement."

Wealth wasn't enough, though, Imogene wanted status. The Lackman family was one of Cincinnati's most prestigious. General William Tecumseh Sherman had supposedly stayed with them at the house after the Civil War, enjoying the famous beer baron's hospitality and nights of frivolity. Imogene asked for the Lackman mansion and George gave it to her.

The society women in the Queen City were less willing to allow Imogene or daughter Ruth into their circles. Ruth was sent to the city's finest private schools, but the wealthy children shunned her. Their mothers did the same to Imogene. But, they still came to the parties. They accepted the trinkets she threw at them as favors.

"Imogene Remus always was the kind of a woman that made you think of Turkish harems, oriental dances, and Cleopatra."

"Money meant nothing. Money was coming in so rapidly that I didn't even take time to count it," George said.

The mountains of cash gave his wife power and status, "Permitted her to do anything she saw fit to do."

Remus claimed that he paid $45,000 for the old Lackman house. His wife didn't think it was fit for them in its current condition, so he had it remodeled and enlarged. Construction crews numbering in the hundreds built outbuildings, stables, and elaborate gardens that filled the ten-acre grounds. They spent whatever they wanted to have it elaborately and luxuriously furnished. George said that the grand total, including the pool, upped his total to $750,000 to $800,000.

George and Imogene didn't know when to stop. They filled every spare inch of the mansion with all the expensive trinkets they could. They had so much that they began moving some of the items directly to the attic or they stashed it away above the stables.

Walking inside, the curious onlooker's senses were assaulted with a quantity of indulgence rarely seen in modern America. One observer attempted to describe it, claiming the mansion was a "cluttering of rich things in upholstering, wainscoting, bric-bracrey, tapestries, batik, wood carving, divans, rubrics—everything."

Remus loved the things he collected and relished talking about them. He went on spending sprees, gobbling up art from galleries in Washington, Columbus, New York, Chicago, and St. Louis. He had oriental rugs that cost $150,000. He had another seventy to eighty works of art from galleries in Los Angeles and San Francisco.

"Works of art I got there from the Duke of Abruzzio of Italy…marble statuary," he said. "I enjoy works of art, not that I know much about them, but I like it."

Other items he prized, including "some of Abraham Lincoln's signatures… George Washington's signature, as president of the Cincinnati Society…that I considered a gem."

"We had a lock of hair from Benedict Arnold," George claimed, another of his prized historical treasures.

* * *

Remus's greatest thrill was the bathhouse and pool. The immaculate structure played a starring role in his life. He didn't bother with invoices, but thought he paid between $100,000 and $175,000 for the pleasure, connecting it to the mansion via a long tunnel. He had always felt safe and contented in the water, dating back to long swims with his boyhood chums in local rivers around Chicago. Then there had been the rough-and-tumble days of competitive water polo and the long-distance swimming marathons. He tested his manhood in these events.

Endurance.

George saw the grand pool as a tool in helping his family gain entry into Cincinnati's aristocracy, because it would serve as the centerpiece of the old mansion, which he would essentially rebuild from the ground up.

They stuffed the space around the pool with expensive marble statues. The pool itself was ensconced in light shades of red and similar hues of Rookwood tile, the Cincinnati studio that had launched the art pottery movement in America in the late 1880s. The Queen City had the best tile and pottery artists in the world.

The "Imogene Baths" in honor of his wife. The perfect name.

The splashy soirees and free-flowing liquor could not gain the Remuses real entry into the local aristocracy. Old-money families shut them out. George, however, did bribe his way to the top of the bootlegging empire with an intoxicating mix of booze and cash. Imogene continued to charm the papers with enchanted tales of glorious gatherings in the decade that never seemed to sleep. Their party gifts alone were already the stuff of legend.

Yet, prying eyes had begun plotting their downfall. The couple's brazen disregard for Prohibition offended polite society, particularly as rumors of Remus's bribery network spread.

George was loose with his money. Men with something to lose claimed he was turning Cincinnati into a national laughingstock. By some accounts, he tangled with the Taft family, a major no-no in the Queen City. A reporter explained:

> When George Remus, once more yielding to his wife's social ambitions, insisted on giving the Community Chest as much as Charles P. Taft, multimillionaire brother of the former president, contributed—that was too much.

Polite society had its fill of Remus and his garish wife. They moved to stamp him out, assured that they could find another way to get the booze that powered their own private parties and occasions. They resented the way Remus flaunted his money and had contempt for a cheap immigrant and his low-class wife. There would always be another rumrunner.

· · ·

Federal agents not in his pocket had been hearing the odd name "Remus" for months. The size of his alleged operations virtually dared them to act. Informants and spies in Cincinnati told Remus's stories to the authorities. Wealthy patrons who purchased his best bourbon would later report him to their friends in high places, letting a word slip to a "straight" dry agent who wasn't on George's secret payroll.

Mabel Walker Willebrandt—in desperate need for a big publicity win against the bootleggers—heard the wild tales of George and Imogene's parties and the pandemonium his growing bourbon empire unleashed across the

Midwest. The assistant attorney general turned to the one man she knew she could entrust with bringing Remus to his knees—her star agent Franklin L. Dodge, Jr.

Unlike many of the initial worthless men who made up the ranks of Prohibition Bureau agents, an odd mix of political sycophants and slaves to the Anti-Saloon League, Dodge had a stellar reputation, derived from his upper-class upbringing and tireless work on behalf of Michigan industry as a state investigator.

Dodge was suave, handsome, and knew how to fit in among men from every part of society. He was as comfortable around assembly line workers as he was hobnobbing with aristocrats.

"One of the 'star' members of the Department of Justice's Secret Service," said one newspaper report. "He has had a leading part in virtually every liquor investigation of importance in the United States during the last few years."

Franklin grew up in Lansing, the eldest son of Frank Dodge and his wife Abbie, daughter of James Turner, one of the city's founding fathers. Turner had been a giant in his era, both intellectually and physically, standing six feet, four inches tall and a muscular 245 pounds. Arriving in Lansing about the time it became Michigan's state capital, Turner jumped into building railways and other infrastructure projects. Later, he was an important state legislator and education advocate, founding the Michigan Female College and serving on the board of education for decades.

Frank and Abbie merged two of Lansing's most prominent families. Frank became one of the state's most powerful Democratic operatives and an attorney famous for supporting workers' rights. He kept a prosperous law practice in the Prudden Building, which also housed the American State Savings Bank, the personal financier of Michigan's elite.

As their fortunes grew, they enlarged the Turner family mansion on the banks of the Grand River. Abbie, educated in music in Boston and Berlin, hosted many esteemed politicians and legislators, including members of the Supreme Court and three-time presidential candidate William Jennings Bryan. The home filled with talk of local and national politics and civic events. This was the currency of the Dodge and Turner families.

The mansion also filled with lilting music from Abbie's renowned piano. She was masterful. During the holidays, the Dodge family hosted parties in the third floor ballroom. Large and wood-paneled, the ballroom filled with laughter and raucous dancing.

Franklin grew in physical stature like his Turner grandfather at over six feet tall and 210 pounds. He specialized in undercover work, frequently representing himself to rumrunners as a bootleg operative from New York City. Although many of these men were heavily armed, he made them comfortable. Dodge gathered evidence and fed it to agents in the field to make arrests.

Franklin traveled from city to city, commonly working alone, and armed with two pistols. He made connections in the underworld and started tracking a national whiskey ring that the feds had heard whispers about from informants and assorted gangsters. To maintain his cover, Franklin moved from one luxury hotel to another, ingratiating himself to night managers, security guards, and other staffers who could give him information.

When New York City Prohis nabbed Baltimore whiskey wholesaler Samuel Albrecht, they unearthed documents that linked him to an operative in Cincinnati. Simultaneously, enforcement agents secretly investigated the operation based on a couple recent rumrunner arrests. The men squealed to save themselves, divulging the location of a liquor warehouse outside Cincinnati.

Franklin Dodge left for the Queen City.

* * *

The *Cincinnati Enquirer* noted the Remus party, declaring:

One of the Most Unusual New Year's Eve Celebrations in the History of the City.

After Imogene's diving and swimming exploits, she emerged from the massive pool in her nearly see-through bathing suit, the material clinging to her thick curves. Her deep dark eyes scanned the men looking at her and a broad smile washed across her face.

At the end of the evening, George had one last surprise. He ventured out onto the diving board and called the crowd to order while his wife toweled off, servants attending to her every need.

Raising his voice to rise above the commotion, George made an announcement: the men at the party would receive a diamond stickpin as a gift from Imogene and George Remus. And, he noted, each female guest would find a set of keys next to her dinner plate. They could use those keys to start the brand new luxury sedans he purchased for them. The cars were parked outside.

"I enjoy swimming. That has been my relaxation for years and years," George bellowed above the rapturous applause of his guests.

As bells rang and all eyes remained on him, George was overcome with joy. "Jump," someone yelled.

"On a dare," he said, "I jumped into the swimming pool in a full dress suit."

PART THREE

· · · · ·

Plundering
an Empire

8

Ace Bags the King

The shocking headline in bold type blaring from the April 16, 1922, front page of the *Cincinnati Enquirer*…

NINETEEN MEN ARE ACCUSED OF WHISKY RING OPERATIONS; REMUS NAMED IN FOUR COUNTS

The unthinkable happened—the Federal Grand Jury in United States District Court indicted Remus and eighteen of his men for conspiring to violate the Volstead Act. The bootleg kingpin had been bragging about his safety via Smith and Attorney General Daugherty. Now a chink in his empire appeared.

Six months earlier, in October 1921, Prohibition enforcement officers from Indiana, Kentucky, and Ohio had swarmed Death Valley. The compound had been under surveillance for weeks. Agents knew that illegal activity occurred there, and they had arrested a couple men caught with booze bought at the farm. With just a little pressure, the men cracked like eggs, indicating how to get to Death Valley and who to look for. The fear of jail made some small-time bootleggers weak in the knees.

While the Prohi investigators had gained detailed information about the location and activities, what they really sought were clues that might tie the distribution center to prominent whiskey ring conspirators around the nation. The federal agents had good reason to look in Cincinnati. Just a month before the Death Valley raid, New York enforcement officials had arrested Samuel Albrecht for attempted bribery. Documents seized at his office in the Commodore Hotel in New York and at his headquarters in Baltimore indicated that the operative was at the center of a large national bootlegging network.

"Federal officials believe they are about to uncover the operations of one of the craftiest and richest of the rum rings," the *New York Herald* reported after the arrest and investigation.

Albrecht, who had been instrumental in helping Remus establish his operations, unintentionally provided clues that led to the raid. At that time, the out-of-town enforcement officers—not on Remus's payroll—did not know that the bootleg king and his men ran an operation from Cincinnati. However, the raid turned up bourbon casks, bottles being prepped for distribution, weaponry, account books, and other information that pointed to a massive operation at the farm.

The evidence led authorities to Remus, but they may have received some help from an unexpected source. Underworld rumors suggested that Albrecht turned on several former partners in an attempt to save himself from prison. The Prohibition Bureau gradually started better coordinating efforts to find and share information, including its own spy and informant networks (both legal and illegal), so agency leadership had begun uncovering bootlegging hot spots across the country. Whatever the specific path Prohi officials took to Death Valley, the information they gathered pointed to George and his men.

In addition to what they uncovered through Albrecht, whispers about Death Valley had turned into shouts. Too many people were talking about the depot and the incredible quantities of liquor stored there. Like other monopolies, Remus's operations grew so large, so quickly that the gang naturally attracted attention. Too many people were getting rich by running Remus's booze, and seemingly unlimited supplies of liquor flooded into America's glasses.

Local enforcement officers were kept out of the planning for the raid because there were rumors that they were on George's secret payroll. Insiders, however, soon understood that the raid had the blessing of Mabel Walker Willebrandt, assistant attorney general at the Justice Department and head of the Prohibition Bureau tasked with enforcing the Volstead Act.

While many Justice Department officials had been sufficiently bribed either directly by Remus or via one of his henchmen, Willebrandt stood above the crime occurring in the nation's most powerful law enforcement agency. In the five to six months between the raid and the grand jury indictment, Mabel sent undercover officers to Cincinnati to investigate Remus, focusing on the Death Valley distribution center.

Leading that team of investigators was Franklin L. Dodge, Willebrandt's top detective specializing in undercover operations and investigative efforts. His invaluable work would ultimately bring the king of the bootleggers to his knees.

"He surrounded our house during the investigation of the Remus case," George said about Dodge. "He was at our house, on the outside."

Unwavering in her commitment to put Remus behind bars, Willebrandt traveled to Cincinnati to oversee the case as it was presented to the grand jury. She was one of the sharpest legal minds in the nation, so her work played an important role in getting the indictment. She also brought along her top prosecutor, Oliver E. Pagan, to assist local and regional authorities. There could be no mistake that the federal government wanted Remus locked up. Mabel staked her personal reputation on that outcome.

The Death Valley raid made Remus uneasy, but based on assurances he received due to his continued payoffs to Jess Smith and others in the Harding administration, Remus felt secure that the case would turn in his favor or be dropped altogether.

After Prohi officials uncovered that Remus was the mastermind behind the bourbon ring, Imogene played a vital role in coming to his defense. A local news report called her the "personal aid of her husband in his business."

Initially, Imogene appeared in federal court to testify that she could cover the bonds of her husband and co-defendants. As the wife of America's bourbon baron, she valued her part of the Remus fortune at more than $200,000. She signed bonds covering about $90,000 to get the gang members out of jail. Next, she acted as attorney for her brother Harry Brown, persuading the US commissioner on the case to reduce his bond from $20,000 to $15,000.

Out on bail, and assured by Jess Smith that he and his henchmen would never see the inside of a jailhouse, Remus put the bootlegging operation into overdrive. He still had a team of several of the top attorneys in the nation filing motions and countersuits to assure his freedom, but he directed Conners to pick up production. Chicago boss John Torrio and his top man Al Capone, for example, had a standing order for Remus's whiskey. Remus's men worked around the clock to get the bourbon out of government-bonded warehouses and distillery rackhouses.

What had irked Remus the most about the Death Valley raid was that his subordinates had ignored his command to clean the place out and destroy any written records they had in their possession. George knew that Bert Morgan had come to Cincinnati from his Indiana headquarters. Remus's network of informants kept him abreast of news related to Prohis sniffing around town. One mole had even told Remus that Morgan was plotting to invade the farm.

With Conners away for the day, the men tasked with safeguarding Death Valley directly disobeyed Remus. Johnnie Gehrum, George Dater, and several others were supposed to be on guard. Some of the liquor had been hidden, but they got sloppy.

Gehrum had some customers coming in early Monday morning and wanted to have those bottles on hand when his contact arrived. When Remus called to check on their progress, they lied about what they had done, telling him the farm was in order.

"They sent me word back that nothing was there, so I rested easy," Remus said. "We all paid the penalty for that mistake."

Instead of heeding the boss, the men sat around playing cards, comfortable that the bribery network guaranteed their safety. By the time George got definitive word from a local police officer that Morgan and his small squad of Prohi agents were headed to Death Valley, it was too late.

"I was so mad when I heard about the raid I could not believe my ears," George fumed. "I knew that Morgan was coming over, and I instructed the men to clean up and be ready."

Paul Anderson of the *St. Louis Post-Dispatch*, writing years after the raid, blamed it on Johnnie, who was in charge that day. He contended that "Gehrum's greed and duplicity" led to Morgan and his men uncovering liquor, paraphernalia, and weapons. However, Gehrum wasn't alone—another of Remus's boys failed to convey "a message entrusted to him."

Fielding calls at the mansion in Price Hill, Remus exploded with anger when he found out, minutes after they arrived, that the Prohis were at Death Valley. Morgan and his team hadn't even found anything incriminating yet. George immediately began rounding up his men, calling them in from all over the region. He had an audacious plan.

Rather than wait for the federal agents to find evidence, George plotted a counterattack. His wife expected Prohis to attack them at the mansion, coming over the gates and through the trees lining the estate. Imogene sent some of the henchmen out on patrol, fully loaded with semiautomatic weapons.

"This is an outrage—they'll all get bounced for this," Imogene yelled. Holding her favorite pearl-handled pistol, she said, "They better not come around here."

Armed for a gunfight, the gang members would sneak onto the farm from the adjacent area, gaining an element of surprise. They hoped to trap the lawmen without having to kill any officers, then restrain them until his men could get the 500 cases of illegal liquor off the premises.

Given that one government lawyer called Remus's forces "a near army," there is little doubt that the counterattack would have worked or turned into a bloodbath. "It had orders from the big boss to shoot whenever necessary," the official claimed. "One of the shotguns seized…was nicked with three notches—traditional a symbol that it had struck its mark on at least a trio of occasions."

At the last moment, as Remus got ready to jump into his Marmon for the eight-mile ride to Death Valley, Imogene had a change of heart. Grabbing him, Imogene cried out that he would be murdered. She begged him to stop. At the sight of his wife's tears, George relented and called off the assault.

In 1921, when Attorney General Harry Daugherty had picked a little-known female lawyer from California to become assistant attorney general of the United States, overseeing the Prohibition Bureau, reporters speculated that bootleg kingpins most likely reacted with glee. Certainly, they would not have thought that Mabel Walker Willebrandt had the intestinal fortitude necessary to prosecute them. Could she manage an agency of men created to enforce the Volstead Act? To the criminals, her appointment meant that the Justice Department didn't actually care about enforcement.

They were all wrong.

Soon, bootleggers not only learned that they could not underestimate Willebrandt, but that they should fear her. She became Remus's primary rival, the most important enforcement official that he could not get on his payroll.

No one would have foreseen that such a career would unfold, except perhaps for Mabel herself. Born on May 23, 1889, she would grow to stand just five feet, four inches tall and not much more than 110 pounds, but her influence on the Jazz Age would be monumental.

Under different circumstances, maybe meeting across a Chicago courtroom, Remus and Willebrandt may have developed into friendly adversaries. George and Mabel had many common personality traits, particularly bottomless resolve and deep desire to win. Two legal eagles jostling for victory.

Bringing Remus to justice wasn't a game. Their battles would serve as a microcosm of America's tumultuous relationship with Prohibition. They both transformed to become symbols of the era—Remus a stand-in for wet crime and Mabel the bastion of enforcement efforts.

Mabel's penetrating gray eyes matched her demeanor, reserved and stern. She had a difficult early life. Media profiles repeatedly sketched out her youth in a "sod house" on a Kansas prairie. Her mother demanded that her daughters be educated and Mabel later became a teacher, walking five miles a day to and from the one-room school.

After moving to Arizona with her husband Arthur F. Willebrandt, a former school principal she married at nineteen, the couple eventually settled in Los Angeles. Arthur enrolled in the University of Southern California law school, graduating in 1915. Next, Mabel followed his path to USC. Mabel worked hard to juggle a grueling schedule, enduring eighteen-hour days of full-time teaching, law work, and night school. She also overcame a major physical setback—a problem with her hearing that required her to use a hearing aid. Mabel combed and set her hair each morning in an attempt to conceal what she saw as a defect. After graduating in 1916, she landed a job in the public defender's office, specializing in representing female offenders, an underserved area in the criminal justice system. As a result, Willebrandt created a women's bureau in the office.

Mabel's efforts got her noticed by California Senator Hiram Johnson, a progressive Democrat, who had a great deal of power in Washington. This connection won her a spot on Daugherty's team at the Justice Department. From her first moment on the job, Willebrandt had to overcome doubts that a young female—just thirty-two years old—could lead such an important government agency.

Mabel plunged into enforcing the nation's dry laws with her customary vigor and forthrightness. In her mind, her gender was irrelevant—there was a Constitutional Amendment to uphold. Yet, news story after news story would bring her sex into the conversation.

A profile in the venerable *Saturday Evening Post* proclaimed that in contrast to most women, "there is about as much uncertainty and coyness to the said Mrs. Willebrandt as there is to a rifle bullet en route to its destination."

Mabel disliked when men—it always seemed to be men—compared her to frivolous women or denigrated her for being female. She wanted to be judged on the merits of her character and actions, but wasn't a prude about her femininity. For example, unlike many older women, Willebrandt did not think that flappers degraded society, but should be looked at as exerting freedom.

In early 1925, Willebrandt told a religious organization in St. Louis that the flapper "is a happy-go-lucky definite little miss, who sets up her own restraints." Flappers, she believed, were not "carrying the world to the bow-wow."

In endless press accounts, however, writers could not help but comment on Mabel's physical appearance, frequently "angular" or "sour." In a March 1922 letter to her parents, she complained about the reaction she received so frequently from men after giving a speech to a law association, saying, "these doggone Easterners seem to think that women can't get over the 'girlie girlie' stuff," then criticized the newspaper write-up that ran the next morning, sarcastically wondering, "why the devil they have to put on that 'girlie girlie' tea party description every time they tell anything professional that a woman does, is more than I can see."

If the scribes watched Willebrandt in the courtroom, they may have judged her in ways they did men. In legal circles, Mabel was used to serving as a trailblazer. In many federal courtrooms, she was the first female to argue cases in the nearly all-male bastion of early twentieth-century law.

Mabel excelled at litigation before the Supreme Court. One writer indicated that she had "won nearly all the cases she has argued." The story continued:

> To see her pleading a case before the Supreme Court is to get a good idea
> of her personality. Slim and straight…her thick brown hair brushed simply back from a wide forehead, she seems too quiet and womanly to be a
> formidable opponent. But when she speaks her soft voice and gentle
> manner betray a decision so firm that it needs no emphasis, a directness
> that goes straight to the heart of the question.

"Mrs. Willebrandt," as the press eternally referred to her, took great pains to carve her own personality and path quite different from her male adversaries. While many of them pranced around before the judge like oversized peacocks, wildly gesticulating and ranting in confrontational tones, Mabel spoke calmly and in short sentences. She often impressed onlookers with her "ability to summarize the meaning of great masses of testimony," said one journalist.

In a letter to her parents about getting bootlegger Willie Haar and his brothers locked up in the Atlanta Federal Penitentiary, she bragged, "I raised my own particular kind of H--- around the Department," to get the case moving. The bootlegger, she heard, had told associates that his case sunk because he had everyone bribed, except that "damned woman," which Mabel told her parents, "I consider. . .some of the highest praise I have received."

Mabel also dressed conservatively and presented herself in stark contrast to the fashionable flappers in the latest form-hugging dresses and accessories: dark brown, unbobbed hair; simple clothing. Although she was often a head shorter than her male rivals, she did not overcompensate, frequently speaking in a soft voice that forced jury members to strain to hear her. Tenacity is where Willebrandt equaled and surpassed her male counterparts.

Despite his depravity and blatant corruption as attorney general, once Harry Daugherty appointed Willebrandt, he left her to pursue enforcement without much interference.

Mabel went about her business as efficiently as possible, given the general vice of scores of prohibition officers on the take or agents who looked the other way when illegal booze was on the scene. Her resolve enabled her to become the pillar of national efforts to enforce Prohibition, even in offices reeking with corruption, like Daugherty's.

Remus spread his bribe money thick and the number of flies to the ointment seemed endless. Yet, there were a few key officials who would not accept his payoffs, most notably Willebrandt. She stood almost alone in the overtly corrupt environment Daugherty had fostered. Mabel was a good soldier, though. She always defended Daugherty in public. The successes she had, however, could be considered *in spite of*, rather than *because of*, his leadership.

Given the newness of Volstead enforcement efforts and the rampant stories of bootleggers running wild, Mabel seriously needed a public relations win. She faced relentless pressure to enforce the dry laws. By mid-1920, reporters were chasing down leads that they had heard about "bootleg kings" in various locales around the nation. People feared that organized crime had taken over bootlegging almost as soon as Volstead became law.

When it became clear that Remus was the mysterious leader of a whiskey ring centered in the Midwest, Willebrandt utilized every resource at her disposal to bring him to justice.

Dubbing George "the Cincinnati bootlegger magnificent," reporter Frederic William Wile explained how critical his conviction was to Willebrandt's efforts: "The government is acting on the theory that the suppression and punishment of arch-conspirators of the Remus type are more valuable for law-enforcement purposes than the jailing or fining of ten times as many smaller fry."

Mabel's efforts in Cincinnati were showy and public. According to Jack O'Donnell, she visited the Queen City and "In a few weeks she had Remus on the run." He credited her with personally developing the "salient points of the case" that led to the agency's ironclad position.

Willebrandt tracked the Remus case when back in DC, conferring with state and local officials at every step. She was eager to shut down the whiskey operations, which had brought unwanted scrutiny on her personally and the bureau at large. Mabel and her agency stood in as straw men for the most important morality issue the nation faced since slavery. For most outside observers and many in the nation's capital, Willebrandt was Prohibition.

* * *

Remus had created such an extensive bribery network that much of the Justice Department's evidence-gathering had to be kept confidential. As a result, few knew that Willebrandt had a secret weapon in Cincinnati—Franklin Dodge, her ace detective and undercover specialist. Mabel tasked Franklin with finding the evidence that would convict the bootleg kingpin.

The name "Franklin Dodge" certainly meant nothing to Remus prior to the October 1921 raid at Death Valley. However, it would later seem like Dodge was an evil talisman for the bootlegger. As soon as Dodge charged into Remus's life, George's entire world started to unravel.

While local officials rounded up possible suspects and interviewed people connected to Death Valley, US District Attorney Thomas H. Morrow discovered an informant willing to testify about what had been happening there, a middle-aged woman named Mary Hubbard, who the press would later dub "Mother Hubbard."

Mary and her husband Eli owned a farm adjacent to the Death Valley property. Mr. Hubbard earned $50 a week as a night watchman for George Conners and John Gehrum, but he also did odd jobs around the facility, like burning distillery boxes that were smashed up or broken on the trip to the depot, and most likely bottling liquor that came to the center in charred oak barrels. When Cincinnati officials would tip Remus off, it was the Hubbard farmstead where Conners, Gehrum, and the others would offload whatever booze they had on hand until it was clear.

The federal agents' latest raid pushed Mary Hubbard over the edge. The relentless pressure of breaking the law drove her to a decision. She convinced Eli to turn on the bootleggers and save themselves.

"Tell everything," she urged.

What Mary did not know was that George had spies regionally and all over Cincinnati. These men gladly traded information for cash and booze. Word leaked that Mr. Hubbard had agreed to talk to Prohi officials.

The mysterious Eli Hubbard, just a farmer who took an opportunity to make a little extra money by working for Remus and Conners, turned up dead.

Rumors spread that Remus's thugs might have poisoned him to thwart his testimony. There seemed to be no other explanation for Eli's sudden death. Mary thought she was next, so in fear for her life, she agreed to speak to the authorities. Mary believed that the Death Valley boss ordered her husband's murder, because he "knew too much of the Remus gang."

Government officials watched closely as well, realizing that the woman's testimony could be the key to nailing the liquor ring. Franklin Dodge reported that Mary's "husband had died suddenly and mysteriously."

Not willing to take the chance that the same fate might befall Mary, Willebrandt sent Dodge to Cincinnati to talk to the widow and continue investigating Remus. If her story panned out and could be used to pin the operation on Remus, Franklin was ordered to bring her with him to Washington to keep her safe. He was Willebrandt's star detective and ace in the hole when she needed deep investigative work. He had a special knack for interviewing female informants, a combination of devilish charisma and wit that got the Prohibition Bureau the details it needed to prosecute.

"Dodge was put on the trail, and Dodge got his man," one reporter later noted.

* * *

As much as Mabel wanted to lock Remus away, actually pinning him to the bootleg network proved challenging. Dodge ran the Hubbard angle. The raiding party had gathered mountains of evidence, from bourbon casks to high-powered weaponry found onsite. Yet, none of these pieces alone were enough to guarantee victory, especially if the bootlegger could either intimidate or bribe potential jury members. If tainted juries weren't enough of a challenge for the prosecution, attorneys also had to contend with jury members expressing their disgust for the dry laws by declaring bootleggers not guilty. The case against Remus and his gang had to be airtight and irrefutable.

Willebrandt did not trust the legal system outside Washington. The bootleggers had a knack for convincing hometown juries to side with them. She wanted more evidence of Remus's wrongdoing. Her big break came from a source that George might have never envisioned.

The Remus gang's notoriety in the Cincinnati and northern Kentucky regions continued to escalate as the bourbon network grew. Stoolpigeons and spies littered the criminal underworld and gossip spread about the raid at Death Valley, but it did not seem that any single person could conclusively link Remus with the arrests.

A top-secret informant emerged when Sam Friedman—Remus's silent partner—decided to save himself from potential prosecution by giving Willebrandt and local federal officials the information they needed to nail Remus. Mabel had to firmly lock down the confession, though, because of George's deep fingers in local and regional enforcement circles.

"He had seen I was growing so large that I could ignore him," Remus remembered when asked about his break with Friedman. "He got jealous in a way and tried to oust me as an organization."

Friedman's decision was straightforward. He had never anticipated that George would overtake him as primary liquor distributor so quickly. Rather than risk his own arrest, he gave Willebrandt a great trade: his freedom in return for serving up George as the sacrificial lamb she needed to score public opinion points for the feds.

Friedman had been nabbed in Kentucky, but Sawyer Smith, US Attorney for the Eastern District of Kentucky, deliberately dragged his feet (at Willebrandt's suggestion), which enabled the distillery owner to sell his Covington property and move to Los Angeles. Word leaked that Friedman's health deteriorated—Smith claiming that he "offered medical evidence" to show that he was "broken in health and mind." As a result, and as a kind of compensation for Friedman's information on Remus, Kentucky officials decided to let the case quietly dissolve, taking Friedman's $5,000 fine in lieu of prosecution or extradition.

Ironically, Remus was the one who hatched the scheme for Friedman to claim that he was deathly ill and move to California. When later asked why Friedman was resting easy on the West Coast, a rich man, George could only hint at why, cryptically alluding to "the benefits of my judgment about those things." When pressed on the issue, he claimed, "He was more fortunate than I." Obviously, Remus had no idea that Friedman was cooperating with enforcement agents.

Willebrandt not only stood as the chief architect of the plan to get Remus and his henchmen arrested, convicted, and thrown into the federal penitentiary, but she served as a constant thorn in the bootleg baron's side, repeatedly parrying his legal maneuverings and slamming the jail door on his attempts to gain freedom.

World War I had provided the backdrop for some men to become heroes. One such hero was Thomas H. Morrow, who would go on to lead the local efforts to bring down Remus and his henchmen as the prosecuting attorney. On September 28, 1918, at La Grange aux Bois farm, an American soldier was wounded and unable to escape due to heavy German fire. The enemy held the entire area, the northern edge of the Bois de Cierges region, which one writer called "like the Argonne, although much smaller." And well-fortified: "Snipers and machine guns covered every path, and wire hung from tree to tree. Determined infantry manned camouflaged pillboxes, dugouts, and foxholes."

The American infantry of the First Battalion, 361st Regiment under the command of Major Oscar F. Miller advanced into the valley, which the Germans then "swept with artillery and machine-gun fire." They fought on, despite heavy casualties, and Miller took a bullet in his right leg and right arm, still urging the men on.

Thomas H. Morrow, an infantry captain, led a small party of soldiers into the battle through heavy artillery fire to rescue the wounded man. A reporter later wrote, "He would have perished," if not for Morrow, "who dashed to his rescue and bore him to safety." The major would later die of another bullet wound to the stomach on the front lines.

After the war, Captain Thomas Morrow returned to Cincinnati, and was appointed United States Attorney for the Southern district. From this position, the war hero—roundly respected and admired for his gallantry—would take on Remus. He received personal assistance from Willebrandt, who personally traveled to Cincinnati to lead the federal government's effort to bring George to justice.

Mary Hubbard, the government's lead witness, had to be kept safe. Remus's men—if rumors were true—killed her husband when he threatened to testify and now they were after her. According to government sources, at least one attempt had been made to kidnap the woman. Her life was in Franklin Dodge's hands.

Mother Hubbard's testimony cooked Remus and his gang in the public's eyes. With her guidance, Dodge had unearthed the full picture of George's operations. Morrow and Willebrandt then plotted a detailed strategy to attack the leader of the whiskey ring. However, Remus likely assumed that the trial took place under the guise of Smith and Daugherty's ultimate safeguard. As a result, he only made a passing effort at defending himself. Still, he hired renowned attorneys, including his friend Elijah Zoline, the New York lawyer that introduced him to Jess, and Michael Igoe, a Chicago colleague, who worked previously as Assistant US Attorney in Illinois.

On the witness stand, Hubbard turned out to be a star. She revealed the vastness of Remus's empire, describing the "touring cars and roadsters" that visited the camp "as many as twelve times a day." The parade of vehicles "came from everywhere—Cleveland, Chicago, Milwaukee, Pittsburgh, Minnesota, Omaha, California, and Kentucky," she explained, remembering the scene.

"These men were always heavily armed," Hubbard told the jury. Her husband had been one of the guards toting the semiautomatic rifles, which made her revelation more astounding.

What most impressed the judge and put the nail in Remus's defense was Hubbard's composure as defense attorney Michael Igoe tried to rattle her. She remembered the men who hung out at Death Valley and knew how much time they spent there. She saw bundles of money being exchanged. Most importantly, she knew the brand names of the booze that the workers would bring up to her place when there might be a raid: "Dearborn, Granddad, Taylor, Keller, Johnnie Walker, Scotch, Fleischmann, Clifton Springs, Susquehanna, and Highland Rye." The litany of familiar names gave her added credibility.

In addition to Mary's compelling testimony, the government had evidence of what took place at the farm, not only in confiscated liquor and guns, but in the account books that Gehrum and Conners stored onsite. The lieutenants had broken one of Remus's prime directives by creating a paper trail—it would've been nearly impossible otherwise to keep up with orders when they often had more than $500,000 of booze stored at Death Valley.

"That's crucifixion, destroy them," Remus screamed when he found out that the two underlings had been keeping documentation.

Neither man listened. Conners and Gehrum figured that Remus had such a thorough bribe system in place that they were basically invincible.

During the trial, the prosecution, led by Morrow, scored important points with the jury by carting in the evidence so they could clearly see what had been confiscated, including assault rifles, fifty bottles of rare scotch, barrels of bourbon, and other paraphernalia. Judge John Weld Peck would later rule the evidence inadmissible due to a faulty search warrant, but the damage of seeing the physical evidence had already been done.

The final hole in Remus's plans centered on the basic fact that his mantra—"every man has his price"—backfired after he and his associates were arrested. Captain Morrow had been a partner at the Matthews & Matthews law firm, which had helped lay the groundwork for Remus's purchase of the Parks & Co. pharmaceutical operation. Morrow knew about the transfer, but was not bribed.

George could not take the risk of testifying, because Morrow could then have used his insider information to get the bootlegger to confess the details of the Parks deal. If enforcement agents unraveled that purchase, it might potentially cost Remus millions of dollars in lost revenue and might get Samuel Friedman and others tossed in jail. Remus had to keep his mouth shut or face that huge loss.

In other words, Remus took one hit—thinking that Jess Smith would rescue him—so that another more lucrative deal wouldn't fall apart. In weighing his options, plus the Smith/Daugherty safety net, George put up a half-hearted defense. From his viewpoint, the quicker his lawyers began the appeal process, the faster he could be out in the field, spreading money and expanding the bourbon empire.

Morrow pleaded with the jury to convict Remus, arguing that the criminal was so arrogant that he barely had the decency to shield his law-breaking:

> We listened for days to stories of how trucks were taken through the streets of Cincinnati in the company of armed guards such as Buck Brady and Captain Bell. We heard the story of 'Death Valley' from Mrs. Hubbard, who had seen it in operation.

Morrow implored the jury to look at the case as a desecration of what America had fought for in the recent world war.

"Did the boys who fought and died there think they were fighting for a Mexico or a Russia…Where bribes could be given to government officials? Where records can be taken from federal buildings?"

The jury deliberated for two short hours.

"George Remus—guilty," the clerk read out to the gathered crowd. No one made a sound.

Remus, calm to observers, displayed uncharacteristic frailty when Judge Peck asked him if he had anything he would like to say before the sentence was passed.

"'I have nothing,'" he said, his voice, according to an eyewitness, "so choked that it could hardly be heard."

. . .

WHISKY RING MEMBERS GUILTY; PENITENTIARY TERMS IMPOSED

The *Cincinnati Enquirer* ran the headline in thick black type on Wednesday morning, May 17, 1922.

Judge Peck gave George the maximum penalty: two years in the Atlanta Federal Penitentiary and a $10,000 fine. His men were all given slightly lesser sentences and fines. Conners and Gehrum were both sentenced to eighteen months and $5,000 fines. Following their boss's lead, neither man said a word prior to sentencing. Loyal soldiers to the end.

Captain Morrow, who the jurors did not want to disappoint, issued a statement thanking the people who had helped win the case, including Willebrandt, who he declared, "has most efficiently aided in this matter," as well as several of her colleagues. Franklin Dodge, whose work depended on secrecy and stealth, remained in the background, hidden away.

Remus, who had been called the "master mind" and "big gentleman" during the trial, learned an important lesson in the way the proceedings unfolded. Based on his relationship with Jess Smith, he did not take the stand to defend himself. He lost the opportunity to spin the jurors to his side, the magic he seemed to conjure which had been the highpoint of his past legal work. His silence was a detriment. Remus would not make that mistake again.

With George and the men out on bond and launching the appeal, he had to return to trial again to face a "public nuisance" charge for operating Death Valley. Basically, the first trial was replayed, both sides reiterating everything. George wasn't as calm or collected during the second trial.

"Remus paced the courtroom floor and corridor, chewed gum continually, and talked with various persons," a reporter noted.

The legal team repeatedly shouted "double jeopardy" at Judge Peck, hoping that he would dismiss the charges, but he ignored their pleas.

Michael Igoe labeled the proceedings "persecution instead of prosecution." He continued, "Remus is the man they want," but countered, "And I say this man's business transactions were no crime."

"The hand of the Anti-Saloon League is plainly seen in this pro-
ceeding. Not one gallon of whiskey has been disposed of or sold
by me for bootlegging purposes. Whatever acts the other defendants have committed were done solely and entirely pursuant to my
suggestions and directions and if any violations have taken place,
I must take the consequences for them." —GEORGE REMUS

George remained resolute after the conviction, maintaining his innocence and emphasizing that his bourbon dealings were legal under the mandates of the Volstead Act.

He had launched a nationwide network that reached from the shores of the Pacific Ocean to the tip of the Atlantic Coast on ever-drunken Long Island. Remus didn't anticipate a limit to his growing empire, just a sea of thirsty citizens eager to circumvent the despised Prohibition legislation. His operation outgrew the local Cincinnati, Covington, and Indiana pharmacies that seemed the most logical way to get booze into the hands of eager patrons.

George sent the majority of the alcohol to the large population centers in New York and Chicago. This is where demand surged, insatiable. His underworld contacts in those cities were behind the endless speakeasies and gin joints that seemed to pop up on every street corner. Remus also had to serve the local market. He ensured that a vast web of influential public officials, politicians, and cops had enough whiskey to grease his path.

Morning, noon, and night, men from the Remus gang hopped into fancy touring cars and armor-reinforced trucks filled to the brim with illicit alcohol. The demand for liquor never ceased.

He had his own ace in the hole—Jess Smith and the hundreds of thousands of dollars he had personally given him to ensure such convictions disappeared. The power was in the exchange. George just needed to wait for the agreement to unfold.

While his crackerjack team of attorneys filed appeal after appeal to get him the valuable time he needed, Remus went back to work.

9

Business as Usual

"I am not worried about the raid at Death Valley because I bought my way from the suburban cop to Washington."

George's boast, delivered to yet another Prohi, was meant to demonstrate his swagger, even after being convicted in the showy Cincinnati trial. He believed that he and his men would never see the inside of a jail cell, despite the guilty verdict.

George Winkler, an assistant to Bert Morgan, looked back at Remus. Morgan was a legendary figure in Indiana, known widely for his moral rectitude and forthright nature. The bootlegger had tried—and failed—to get dirt on Morgan to blackmail him. He then tried—and failed—to bribe him outright.

Although Winkler's boss had turned him down, Remus thought he could make headway with the underling. George wanted Winkler's assurance—offering him a $40,000 bribe—that he and his henchmen would be able to drain about 1,500 barrels of bourbon from the Rugby Distillery in Louisville, then transport it from Kentucky to New Albany for storage at Remus's Indiana farm.

Unlike Louisville, situated directly across the river, New Albany, Indiana, was a sleepy village with greater opportunity for George to create a new version of Death Valley.

All Winkler had to do was get Theo Williams, a federal agent stationed in New Albany, out of the area for six weeks. In return, the Prohi would make in one illicit transaction double what he would earn in the next twenty years combined.

"I have everything fixed on both sides of the river to remove my whiskey without interference if you will accept my terms," Remus explained.

Despite the chance to become rich, the agent turned him down flat. Instead, he roared for Remus to "keep his whiskey out of Indiana if he did not wish more trouble." Winkler immediately reported the conversation to the District Attorney, promising to testify against the bootlegger if he went to trial.

The raid on Death Valley halted Remus for a moment. In his mind, the bribe was offered and turned down. Unfortunate, but the agent's prerogative.

Men shook hands and walked away.

Of course, he never anticipated he would encounter Morgan and his men's zealotry and dedication to such a hollow piece of legislation.

On the positive side, Remus still had significant rural Ohio distribution centers in Reading, Hamilton, and Glendale. His New York operations in Buffalo and New York City were supplying large networks across the Empire State. Rumors confirmed what most people already knew—if a person were drinking "the real thing" in the East or Midwest, it most likely came from George or his bourbon kingdom. Many more distilleries still awaited his plunder, as did towns and cities filled with thirsty patrons.

"At the Remus Building, I always had from twenty to forty thousand dollars in cash, because many of the distillers would not deal directly or indirectly with Remus, on the theory that I had gotten a lot of publicity and notoriety," George explained.

Regardless of the feelings of individual distillery owners, however, the circle framework enabled him to make money on every part of the illegal booze industry. And, he had teams of lawyers and lieutenants who would stand in as purchasers if the heat on Remus increased.

Distillery owners might feign the high road, but many were desperate. Their holdings seemed like relics from an ancient past that looked blurry in the new world. When he peered into the future, though, George saw a different portrait—one with him at the center of a consolidated bourbon empire sending out the American product to ports worldwide.

Yet, he had local challenges in Ohio and Indiana, two states renowned for dry zealotry. These issues forced him to regroup to some extent. He looked south to the Kentucky distilleries, the traditional home of the bourbon industry. He could replicate Death Valley near Louisville, hiring better men who understood the need for secrecy, and service the growing metropolitan area there.

Later, he thought, Louisville would serve as a path deeper into the Midwest, setting up operations in St. Louis with its transportation hub on the Mississippi River. St. Louis would open the West to Remus's network. Far away from Washington, DC, he felt that the future was on the West Coast.

Shifting locations was part of the cat-and-mouse game George and his boys had to play with the feds. When operations were halted in one region, they quickly increased production in others. Remus had outrun his own problems in Chicago by relocating to Cincinnati.

Newport remained a stronghold. People there hailed Remus like he was the king of Sin City. He put men to work and his illegal operations put money in their pockets. George's Kentucky team continued to move denatured alcohol out of the Wiedemann Brewery. He hired dozens of Newport thugs to protect his shipments, men with reputations for itchy trigger fingers. The intricate delivery system they devised utilized "highways by the truckload" and "rails by the boxcar load," and the increased traffic necessitated a sophisticated bribery web that enabled George's hitmen to get the liquor out of Newport.

"Remus," according to one report, "elevated the level of organization in local corruption to a point at which it became routinized. The regular, scheduled, weekly payoff became a way of life in Newport." The skill he applied earned George the nickname the "Gentleman Grafter."

Despite the increased notoriety the trouble in Cincinnati brought, George still had his pact with Jess Smith. That was the handshake that mattered most.

Remus looked to the West and saw his future, like so many immigrants who viewed it as the fulfillment of the American Dream.

His recent criminal conviction conviction be damned. His bribery network would keep him free.

Business as usual.

* * *

The cash that flowed into George's coffers and the tremendous demand for good booze masked several chinks in the bourbon king's armor. These small fissures had taken hold before his conviction. The raid on Death Valley proved that he needed men who would not screw up, who listened to his orders, and understood the consequences. Such men were difficult to find, reminding Remus of the simpleminded thugs he had defended back in Chicago.

After the trial, the glare of the media spotlight made it more difficult for him to operate. Before the Death Valley raid, his quickly growing operation could stay hidden, a rumor of an outpost here or there, but nothing concrete. The ruse rested on a silent handshake between the Cincinnati establishment and the bootlegging newcomer. These were not teetotalers—they wanted untainted liquor and would continue to imagine that Remus was a legitimate business-man, as long as they maintained a semblance of decorum.

The guilty verdict lifted that veil. The documents uncovered at the farm had exposed his network to authorities. For the wealthy elite and powerbrokers, it was one thing to be rumored to consort with a bootlegger, but being physically tied to a convict was quite another. A handshake, not a photo of the handshake.

Money, demand, respectability, exposure—how would Remus and his or-ganization respond?

George ordered his men south. They would scout Louisville for new headquar-ters. Perhaps they could outrun the attention on them in Ohio by turning to the Bluegrass State.

"You can get away with anything in that town if you stand in with one or two of the big boys," Jew John told George.

Louisville offered everything that George and the boys needed, including Marcus's experience rumrunning in the area. Remus began with his play-book—searching for operatives to bribe.

Remus had actually made connections long before he would be raided in Ohio, initially sending his brother in-law W. C. Campbell to Louisville to es-tablish a friendship with city Republican Party leader Chelsey H. Searcy. The Remus gang even took up offices in the Realty Building because it also housed the Republican headquarters. Campbell and Searcy spent a great deal of time visiting one another in those rooms, exchanging vast amounts of money and drinking Rugby bourbon.

In spring 1921, Remus made an early foray into Louisville, purchasing the Rugby operations at 34th and Rudd Avenue for about $250,000 to $275,000. His men moved in with forged permits to remove the bourbon there before Prohis could react.

Using the fake whiskey certificates, they orchestrated the delivery of 1,000 cases each to the Akron Drug Company, the Armand Drug Company of Cleveland, and the A. R. Park Company, all part of the sham wholesale pharmacy ring Remus established. While trucks were shipping the liquor out of the plant, several competing truck lines—each supported by different bigwigs in the city—fought over which would get shipping rights.

The initial dispute turned into a total fiasco. Soon, rival politicians were involved and many of the local men Remus hired double-crossed him. Without muscle to arm the plant with men he could trust, others started robbing the bootlegger, a flagrant kind of internal hijacking that Remus could do almost nothing to stop.

Simultaneously, Prohi agent L. A. Burnam conducted an investigation into alleged siphoning at Rugby. Sam Collins, Kentucky's top enforcement leader, issued a citation and ordered that federal officials seize the distillery. Eventually, the federal government took over the plant, but not before another 417 cases were stolen.

All indications pointed at one of Remus's own men: Fred Stewart, who had been named president of the Rugby Distillery when it was purchased. He supposedly conspired with two federal agents.

"Inside job," Remus said about the heist. "A crowd of armed bandits arrived with trucks, bound and gagged the guards and drove away with the whiskey."

Stewart hightailed it to Chicago after being briefly detained and questioned by police. After some perfunctory investigation, they let Stewart go. Getting approximately 3,500 cases of bourbon out of Rugby would have netted Remus a street value of about half a million dollars, more than justifying the purchase price for the factory and grounds. However, the feds seized the factory and, once again, George's name surfaced.

Too much heat.

"Nightmare," George called Louisville.

Instead of becoming a home base for future operations, the city turned into a mess. Remus did not have men he could trust and the old boys network there shunned him after accepting his bribe money.

As Remus put it, "I received such a rotten deal down there at the hands of my own men and some people they had on their string. I do not like to think of it."

When Louisville turned sour, Remus looked deeper into the Midwest, thinking St. Louis might be a better option. When he considered his options, he thought that perhaps he could replicate his earlier move from Illinois to Ohio, which had stalled officials from chasing him, and gave him enough time for the bribes to win his freedom. If Remus relocated to Missouri, he could wait there while Smith and Daugherty overturned the Cincinnati conviction. If he kept running, maybe he could stay one pace ahead of the law.

There were other benefits on his mind, as well. St. Louis could be an entry point to the entire American West if he were able to create the legitimate bourbon corporation that he planned. Jew John had connections in St. Louis, both with local bootleggers and the city's powerful gangs. He had run large loads of whiskey out of St. Louis. That experience gave him a path into the local power structure, including Republican politician Jack Kratz and liquor wholesaler Morris Multin.

Marcus suggested that Remus enter a deal to purchase whiskey from the Jack Daniel's Distillery, which had closed down its historic Tennessee facility in Lynchburg, and deposited its stock in a local warehouse at 3960 Duncan Avenue. Jew John assured Remus that he could get the booze out "without any trouble," especially with powerful local associates watching over the transaction.

Kratz went with Marcus to visit Remus in Cincinnati, where they discussed logistics and safety precautions for slowly draining the whiskey, which the bootleggers called "milking," without tipping off the government agent assigned to watch over the supply. After the Louisville debacle, George was hesitant to move if he didn't have men on the ground to run the operations.

The intermediaries convinced Remus that he should go to St. Louis to meet with the other high-profile investors involved in the scheme, including political boss Nat Goldstein, an adviser to President Harding. Safely getting the whiskey out was George's primary concern. He asked Goldstein about Arnold J. Hellmich, the St. Louis Internal Revenue collector who was responsible for overseeing the supply in the city. Goldstein assured him that he had Hellmich controlled, glibly explaining, "I made the Dutch boob for a purpose and now is the time to use him. He'll be right and he'll see that the gauger is right."

Although he thought the co-conspirators were too intermingled, Remus agreed to buy a minor interest in the operation. Remus negotiated the deal with Lem Motlow, the favorite nephew of Jack Daniel himself who had inherited the property when his famous uncle died in 1911. Tennessee had voted itself dry in 1910 and Motlow moved operations to St. Louis as a last ditch effort at saving the distillery.

Initially, Motlow wanted $300,000 for the buildings and liquor, but Remus kept whittling away at that figure. George eventually offered $125,000 in a "take it or leave it" ultimatum, he claimed.

Motlow did not like the deal, but he agreed to prevent the St. Louis politicians who conspired against him from commandeering ownership of the facility. George put $50,000 into the purchase and was supposed to direct the milking efforts in exchange for 60 percent of the profits. Imogene made a separate investment of $28,000. There were 896 barrels of Jack Daniel's whiskey in the warehouse, each holding a little less than forty gallons, with three gallons making up a case of liquor.

Remus planned a year-long heist to subtract six gallons of whiskey from each barrel and replace it with water and alcohol to keep the proof up. The government's gauger would then be bribed to looking the other way. The first batch would deliver the conspirators about 5,000 gallons of whiskey, which Remus thought would make $30 a gallon. That revenue installment would earn them back their investment. The second milking, according to Remus, would be "all velvet and the danger of discovery would be negligible."

George had a bad feeling about the siphoning business, which he did not totally control, but he needed to keep supplying his contacts with quality booze.

Harry Boyd, Remus's driver, took George and Imogene to St. Louis for meetings. Although slight, the 30-year-old was armed, serving as both chauffeur and muscle, if needed. Boyd would manage George's interest in siphoning the warehouse.

During one trip, Boyd drove a Reo truck to the warehouse where he met with Edward Meininger, who directed his efforts in the city. Remus's man then drove cases of booze to area drugstores. In July, John Marcus brought an electric pump from the Fleischmann operation in Cincinnati to begin siphoning.

"The warehouse was on the second floor," Boyd explained. "The only way to reach it was from an elevator on the Duncan Avenue side."

They had to find a creative way to get the whiskey into trucks. "We ran a hose through a hole in the concrete floor, and through a hole in the first floor, into the boiler room. The hose passed out through the basement window and across an areaway into a garage," Remus's man said.

"The trucks with the empty barrels in them drove into the garage, and the whiskey was pumped into them through the hose."

Using the pump that Jew John brought with him from Cincinnati, the men devised a system of filling the trucks, which lined up outside.

"Meininger and I had put a buzzer system between the garage and the warehouse. When the trucks drove into the garage they would give one ring, which notified us up in the warehouse to start pumping. Two rings meant the barrels were full and to stop the pump."

The men ran this intricate hose and bell system for fifteen days. They were able to siphon 893 barrels in that span. As long as the government gauger didn't investigate, the plan would work. The single barrel with actual whiskey in it remained inside the warehouse, nearest the gauger. The other barrels were refilled with water. Whenever he sampled the whiskey, which he had to do in intervals, it would test positive. The rest could be gradually filled with alcohol to mask that they had been stolen.

Meininger and Boyd visited George and Imogene, who stayed in the posh Hotel Chase, while the milking procedure took place. Remus cautioned that the men had to keep the operation secret.

"It only means ten years if we get caught," he warned.

George then sent Boyd to the Arcade Building to meet with Morris, Sidney Multin, and Harry Levin. The St. Louis operatives led him to a secret location where they stored stolen liquor. At the new spot, Boyd loaded 110 gallons into the car in five-gallon tin cans. Driving a Ford, Sidney Multin then led him through East St. Louis with the illegal stash.

That summer, Boyd and an armed guard named Miller made four trips loaded down with Jack Daniel's whiskey. Boyd also delivered a load directly to Chicago, traveling solo. Sometimes George and others would join the trips, which created a caravan of illegal smuggling that might thwart hijackers.

Remus ran into trouble after he outlined his strategy to his St. Louis partners. He cautioned them against greed, instead counseling patience. He "protested most vigorously," but they thought about the profits and wanted to institute a "get rich" plan to steal it all at once and sell it quickly.

The St. Louis gang dismissed George's objections, and instead went behind the boss's back to start milking with speed and recklessness. A few days after the decision and back safely in Cincinnati, Remus wrote to one of the partners, exclaiming, "these amateurs were going to ruin us all with their greed."

He likened the robbery to the St. Louis men "simply trying to break into the penitentiary." Remus left for another round of business meetings in DC, not realizing that the Missouri crowd immediately started milking the warehouse. With Jew John Marcus's blessing, they emptied the barrels with an electric pump and filled the casks only with water.

They did not even try to cover their tracks.

Boyd saw what had happened while George was away. He reported to Imogene and George later at the Chase Hotel, explaining how Marcus directed distribution and other Remus men operated the hoses.

"Tell them to be careful and keep quiet about this," Imogene warned. "We could all get ten years for this job."

As Remus fretted over the ill-advised plan, more bad news came in a dire message from William P. Colbeck, the leader of Egan's Rats, the gang that controlled the region. The gang boss, who friends called "Dinty," threatened Remus that if Egan's Rats were not "cut in" on the action, that he and his men would raid the storage facility at a nearby farm and steal all the liquor for themselves.

"All Colbeck did was to stick us up for a slice after we got started," Remus claimed.

George had confidence that his gunmen could stare down the Egan sluggers. However, they were in unfamiliar territory and a long way from their Cincinnati home, which afforded safety in numbers, if nothing else.

When the St. Louis leaders heard about Dinty's warning, they panicked. The insiders had a more immediate sense of the gang's ferocious reputation. They had no doubt that Dinty would keep his word. No one wanted to stare down Egan's Rats in a hijacking battle, especially with so much profit available, so they paid Colbeck off.

The gang was not the last challenge George would face. Once the whiskey went into the black market, Remus realized that his partners were double-crossing him. They claimed that sales were slow at $30 a gallon or $90 a case, but Remus's own spies had seen how briskly the booze flew out from the local distributor. George's informants, who had been running liquor between St. Louis and Cincinnati, reported selling for $135 a case.

At either price, the Jack Daniel's warehouse accounted for between $1 million and $1.5 million in profits. The greed and double-crossing were one side of the coin for Remus. Even more egregious, he found that his partners were cutting the whiskey that had already been cut under Motlow's supervision, which meant about one decent gallon was being diluted into three mediocre ones.

"There I sat in the office, twiddling my thumbs, and compelled to accept whatever they gave me," George complained. "I was helpless. I realized how unwise I had been to get in such a position."

Remus called in reinforcements from Cincinnati. His boys arrived in droves in oversized touring sedans ready to haul liquor. They began their own double-cross, filling the cars with booze under the guise of being washed near the warehouse. Then, as soon as they were full, George's men put their guns in their laps and hightailed it north.

The heist was discovered on September 20, 1923. When Prohibition authorities finally realized the extent of the Jack Daniel's thievery, which they valued at $1.8 million, they shut down operations immediately.

Remus demanded his share of the liquor from his partners, but they claimed it was too "hot" to move. What Remus did not know was that he was being watched by Treasury Department agents while in St. Louis. His phones at the Rex Realty Company offices were tapped. Another group of officers set up across the street and watched George come and go via opera glasses. They heard whiskey orders on the wiretap and used the transcripts to get arrest warrants.

Remus's men later told a reporter that they knew the phones were tapped and "loudly announced receipt of an order for a case of whiskey from President Coolidge, another case for Wayne B. Wheeler." The same lieutenant, however, also watched the St. Louis group rob Remus of an estimated $500,000.

Despite his skill in building the bourbon empire, Remus proved naïve in assessing how his enemies would conspire against him. He did not realize that the more distilleries and whiskey warehouses he purchased, the more he threatened other illegal operators with grand desires. The sheer size and magnitude of Remus's bourbon kingdom made its continued existence a menace.

The pressure frayed his already unsteady nerves. Suddenly, the great bootleg king who had prided himself on bribing everyone who could possibly bring harm found himself incredibly alone. His circle of trust was reduced to a few select lieutenants and Imogene. Relying more on his wife for mental stability and solace in the midst of his legal wrangling, George attempted to exert more control in his own home.

More independent with the influx of money and George's absence, Imogene pushed back.

In early October 1922 she traveled with a group of friends, including her personal chauffeur and his family, to the luxurious Claypool Hotel in Indianapolis, one of her main haunts where she could unwind from the constant pressures in Cincinnati. She also enjoyed being treated like the aristocrat she fancied herself to be. Showing off Remus's money was one of her primary joys. Nicholas B. Shammas, a local lace salesman, came along to negotiate a deal for Imogene to trade one of her cars with a seller there.

When Imogene left Cincinnati, George had been in Loretto, Kentucky, at the Burks Spring Distillery he owned. His driver brought him back to the Hermosa Street mansion at about 2 a.m.

Finding out that Imogene had gone with friends at 10 p.m. while he was hundreds of miles away, he got angry. His rage boiled over when he learned that she took a friend named Schmueling, who he had forbidden her to associate with. He exploded when he heard about Shammas.

"That Syrian had been selling her little table doilies for as much as $1,000 apiece," George fumed. "This fellow Shammas had a record as a 'woman killer,' he was strong with the women."

"I was very much exercised to think she would go and leave the city at that hour of the night for Indianapolis," Remus said.

He asked his driver to "shoot on" toward the city to "see why in the heck she leaves with a man and [group of] women at that hour of the night."

Arriving at 6 a.m. and speaking with the desk clerk, Remus found out which room Shammas occupied. He went directly to the seventh floor, two floors above where his wife stayed, and thumped on the door.

When the man answered, he immediately recognized George, and saw that he was angry and suspicious. Shammas launched into an explanation about the auto swap. He realized that George assumed he had caught him in a compromising position with Imogene.

"That is a nice thing, for you to go out with a woman at night, although she has got a chauffeur and his wife and another woman as alibi," Remus bellowed.

Heated words escalated into a screaming match.

"What do you mean, Shammas, taking my wife this way?"

Fists were thrown.

Then, George swung the heavy cane.

A short while later, a police officer near the Indianapolis statehouse found Shammas wandering the streets disoriented. The injured man told detectives that he was "struck several times behind the ear on the right side of his head with a cane wielded by Remus."

A reporter investigating the assault and the "supposed automobile trade" after the fact, checked with the Nordyke and Marmon Company sales manager. The man explained that he had never heard of anyone named Shammas. The car dealer did, however, corroborate the potential sale, admitting that he "had dealings with Mrs. Remus."

Shammas never reported that he had punched George during the argument, but Remus explained that they came to blows when they became "hopelessly divided" over a business deal when Cincinnati police officers informed him of the charges. Remus claimed that the two got into a fistfight but that he never hit the salesman with his cane.

Although Imogene did not see the assault, she later told detectives that Shammas "insisted" that he go with her, because "he could obtain a larger amount" for the vehicle because of his connections in the city. Imogene and her entourage checked out of the Claypool at 8 o'clock that morning.

Two days later, on October 13, 1922, the Indianapolis police asked their brethren in Cincinnati to arrest Remus for assault and battery with the intent to kill. He was released on a $1,000 bond arranged by Imogene. Indiana officials immediately filed a lawsuit to extradite the bootlegger, which his legal team fought. Remus eventually returned to Indianapolis and surrendered to local police.

Nine months later, Judge James A. Collins threw out the charges against Remus, because Shammas, who the court reported was actually "Naseem N. Shammas," could not be located. Without the witness on hand, the courts could not pursue the charge.

Shammas disappeared into the wind.

• • •

George thought that all his recent woes in Louisville, St. Louis, and elsewhere would be wiped away when the Death Valley raid conviction was overturned by Jess Smith's machinations. Moving in secret, he had been paying Jess off wherever they could arrange a meeting.

"The Department at Washington could handle the situation," Jess had explained after the raid.

Smith's bravado in the face of Remus's anger was a ruse.

Actually, the Daugherty aide feared for his life. Everywhere Jess went, he thought he saw eyes on him. He sensed federal agents or government spies at every turn.

Like the fall guy in a hard-boiled crime fiction page-turner, Smith believed that influencers close to President Harding were setting him up as the ultimate scapegoat. If he were pinned as the criminal mastermind behind the scandals plaguing the administration, then no one in the Harding White House would be implicated.

Too many times—including some cases that he knew intimately—a person on the wrong side of such an equation would be "taken for a ride" by hired thugs or gangsters, "sluggers" as they were often called. The newspapers filled with stories of these disappearances. Never to be seen again…

Jess's trust began and ended with Daugherty. But Smith realized that he knew too much to be incarcerated. Jail would not be his bitter end. Smith believed that his knowledge of the corruption in Daugherty's office and the Harding administration in general would put him on the wrong end of an assassin's bullet.

In early 1923, feeling the weight of the indictment grind down on his life and his bootlegging operation, Remus met with Smith and Elijah Zoline, the attorney that brought about this long, illicit relationship at the Washington Hotel in DC. The bourbon king did not comprehend Smith's fragile state or that Jess couldn't clear up the mess in Cincinnati.

"What assistance will you give me now," George demanded.

Smith's earlier guarantees were the lynchpin of Remus's empire. Without safeguard from prosecution, his beautiful creation would crumble at the feet of crusading Prohis. The big win orchestrated by Franklin Dodge and Willebrandt allayed public fears about the increasing power of the criminal class. The small-time bootleggers didn't matter. Willebrandt railed against the large operators and thought convicting them might turn the public in favor of the dry laws. Remus was a kind of mounted trophy from her successful hunt.

"There is no likelihood of you ever going at anytime or any of your men," Jess assured him, attempting to sooth Remus's growing temper.

Smith implied that he and Daugherty had spoken directly about the case and that the attorney general had promised to back Remus. He never used the name "Daugherty," but alluded to "the General" to indicate the clandestine nature of the conversation.

Although suspicious, George had no choice but to deliver another payment. He dropped $30,000 off in a deluxe suite and sulked off.

Jess, however, could not wrest the demons from his head—no matter what amount of money he took in for himself and Daugherty. Desperate, Smith reached a point of no return. He turned to his soul-mate Daugherty, who realized the man's delicate constitution and allowed him to move into his personal apartment to clear his mind. If they were under the same roof, as they had been when they first moved to DC, Daugherty believed he could help his friend. Perhaps a respite would do him well.

On May 30, 1923, Jess startled awake in the middle of the night. He drew a pistol from a bedside drawer, stumbled to the bathroom, and lay down on the floor. Positing his head on the side of a wastebasket, Jess put the revolver to his temple and pulled the trigger.

Smith killed himself a little more than two months before the shocking death of Warren G. Harding, who declined quickly on a trip out West and ultimately passed away on August 2, 1923, only 57 years old. The Ohioan was wildly popular at the time and mourners lined the train route that brought the dead president back to the nation's capital. Only after his death would the full weight of his scandal-ridden administration become unraveled by a series of congressional investigatory committees and reporters hot on the trail of his Cabinet members and their cronies, many who seemed to specialize in corruption. For George, the deaths of Smith and Harding left him with little hope. Worse, the tragedies severed his ties to Daugherty.

"Misfortune came fast, suddenly," Remus said.

"Jess Smith was found dead in his bathroom. President Harding died. The Senate called for the impeachment of Harry Daugherty. The game was over. I had no place to turn."

According to a reporter covering the bootlegger, "Remus's 'ace in the hole,' the friend on whom he had counted to save him when all else failed, was gone."

With Smith dead, George put all his hopes in the series of appeals that his lawyers had filed to keep him out of jail. He doubled-down on his bootlegging operations, convinced that his extensive bribery network would eventually lead to the conviction being overturned. Every moment counted as his attorneys argued motion after motion.

Yet, the legal wrangling ended rather quickly. On January 7, 1924, the US Supreme Court ruled that it would not consider Remus's appeal. A little more than seven months after Smith's suicide, the bottom fell out of the protection he thought he had purchased.

Just a few weeks after the Supreme Court refused to hear Remus's case, which Mabel Willebrandt urged in a plea to the highest court in the land, she wrote a memo that circulated across her agency and throughout the upper reaches of the federal government, explaining:

> George Remus and his group of co-conspirators are defiant, dangerous lawbreakers. I am reliably informed that Remus is now engaged in the distribution of illicit liquor in St. Louis…He has never settled in full his income tax liabilities with the Bureau of Internal Revenue. In all of his conspiracies he has exhibited a rare ability to surround himself with seemingly respectable and important citizens while he hides behind their operations.

Officials reading the memo had no doubt about the prosecutor's feelings for Remus. What was less inherent in the piece, however, was that she needed to make an example of him and his men for political and publicity purposes.

Mabel knew that the American people were complicit in defying the Volstead Act. She also understood that George's bribes had put many significant leaders in a corner opposite hers. Her choice—upholding her office and the pledge she had made to enforce the law—was to make a stand. Remus's demise would be her defining moment, the one she would stake against her own political and professional reputation.

Willebrandt also had other motivations. She dreamed of someday being nominated for the Supreme Court. As a result, any negative chatter about her work in the Justice Department had to be challenged.

The Supreme Court response denying Remus's appeal echoed Willebrandt's argument against setting him free. She explained the stakes involved, calling it an:

> Extraordinary case of conspiracy involving many individuals who adopted ingenious methods of law evasion, interstate in scope. It was one of the first important cases and up to that time the largest case prosecuted for conspiracy to violate the National Prohibition Act.

· · ·

The unthinkable happened. It was the scenario George had planned against and unleashed a tidal wave of bribes to keep from happening. The Supreme Court ruling sealed his fate.

George had months to prepare for life behind bars, but when Mabel Wille-brandt intervened in the Supreme Court appeal, chaos ensued. He had to tighten up what remained of the empire, while ensuring that Imogene would be okay and that he would have enough liquidity to rebuild while inside, even though his chief lieutenants were also facing their own sentences.

George claimed that he quit the bootlegging business prior to entering Atlanta in January 1924, saying that at that time he had "no business."

However, he understood the value of the whiskey certificates, which were nearly priceless. Like a blue chip stock, they would only appreciate over time. He called this "conserving," storing away the documents that gave him access to 3,900 barrels.

In his calculations, the bourbon stash represented by the certificates could resurrect Remus's empire after a short stint in the federal pen, perhaps two to three months. On the open market at the time, those barrels translated to revenue of about $5 million.

Remus was going to prison. But Remus had a stash.

10

Life in Hell

• • • • • •

The six by nine cell seemed to be shrinking.

Men in the other cages gasped for air.

George felt the hard metal scrape across his brow. Tremendous heat seemed to billow down the hallways, choking everyone inside. Sweat beads rolled down his cheek and the back of his neck. Perspiration soaked his thick wool collar.

Anything for a moment of relief. He splashed water on his face and felt his skin tingle. A few more flicks of the razor and done.

Looking up into the mirror, Remus saw a different man staring back at him—gaunt. He was thinner than he had been since childhood.

Over the tender, red skin burnt by the razor, his eyebrows were gone. No more hair on his head. Only his eyelashes remained. Raw scalp—small rivulets of blood dripped down his neck where he had cut himself.

What did it matter?

There were no prying eyes in "Big A," what the inmate population called Atlanta's massive federal penitentiary. No more reporters asking for a quick word. No one hovered at his elbow waiting for decisions. The gunfights were over for now. The world that he had worked so hard to create seemed like a distant dream.

The prison was his new circle—an enormous concrete box housing some 3,140 men in hellacious conditions—dark, blistering, and always reeking of unclean bodies and filth. The diseased criminals in the penitentiary were the most wretched and truly feared. The risk of catching some horrific sickness from a cellmate drove some men nearly mad. Some prisoners hinted that getting caught stepping out of line might lead to being bunked with one of the sickly men at the warden's order.

"There was some vermin in the prison, naturally, I suppose," George said, explaining later why he cut off his hair. However, he claimed, "It was not on that account. Rather, because of the heat."

Although many convicts in Atlanta took the razor to their scalps, Remus mystified guards and prison staff when he shaved off his eyebrows. The peculiar behavior exemplified his physical and mental deterioration.

Nothing seemed to matter. Staying alive in these conditions was his primary concern.

They had separated Remus from his fellow Queen City henchmen, probably for his own good. They had worked together to build the bourbon empire. He paid them well, but they had trusted him. Yet, now those same men found themselves locked up. They knew the risks but were imprisoned because George assumed—incorrectly—that his extensive bribery network would protect them.

Some of these hoods—like Buck Brady, a murderer who kept Remus's bourbon safe from armed hijackers—wanted revenge. Remus might die in this stinking hole.

He stared ahead, glancing again at his new face.

Prison life pushed him to the edge. He could not digest the boiled rations they served—basically slop masquerading as food. Boiled potatoes, boiled beans, boiled meat.

The bootleg millionaire, used to a private chef and fine dining on the outside, was reduced to begging for scraps of bread from other inmates. He offered prisoners money in exchange for the basic means of survival. Once, prison officials caught Remus with a sandwich smuggled in from the outside—what officers deemed "contraband." He was locked in solitary confinement as punishment.

George had always exercised to stay centered. He attempted to stay fit while imprisoned now, but did not have enough to eat to stay healthy. He dropped from his natural 225 pounds down to just 172. The drab wool clothes that had been fitted for him when he arrived at the Big A hung from his frame like window drapery.

Remus kept up a frenetic pace over the last several decades, from pharmacist and business owner to attorney and later baron of the bourbon empire. He had difficulty acclimating intellectually to prison time, let alone the relentless heat and humidity. Naturally, he worked in the jail's law library, filing endless briefs for reconsideration of prisoners' rights. He helped his fellow criminals prepare appeals, but mostly performed simple legal tasks that he could do with ease.

When speaking with other inmates, George felt their angst. He digested the vileness of being jailed. "You see the misery that is being showered upon the families…starvation, no money."

What he realized night after desolate night behind bars was that his many bribes and so-called "friends" on the outside washed their hands of him once he was incarcerated. His life would never be the same.

The dark, stinking nights were the most difficult for the lifelong insomniac. On the outside, Remus only needed a couple hours of sleep each night. On his small cot, however, the darkness seemed to last forever. Nighttime also gave him time to think. Almost everything on the outside seemed a pack of lies.

Who could he trust?

Maybe no one…

"In the incarceration of the human makeup, a man loses every bit of identity that he has ever had," George said, attempting to make sense of how the pen had broken him.

So much time to reflect and ponder. Remus began to piece the story together. What he realized infuriated him, but he was caged, nearly shattered.

"Where you think you can smash it away from your thoughts—never. Incarceration is with you every minute of the day, every minute of the night, even in a subconscious condition. You can't help but have tantrums in an institution of that kind. You look out at those steel walls, it is tremendous."

"If I had known the tortures that I have undergone in stepping into the Atlanta penitentiary, I would have taken a dose of cyanide," Remus said, remembering later the horrific conditions and the utter despair that took over his life while incarcerated.

Lying there in the cell, the hot Georgia sun beating down on the concrete fortress, Remus felt hopeless. He tried to imagine his future. He knew only one thing: there would be retribution.

He'd set it all up before they took him in.

Remus woke suddenly, tossing a bit in his soft bed. He felt the silk sheets slide smoothly on his skin. Around 3:30 a.m., most people were sleeping and would be for hours, but this was Remus's regular routine. The extra hours that he squeezed from each day gave him time to think. Then he put himself through the physical exertions that meant so much to his spirit.

January 24, 1924—George had been dreading this day. A mere twelve hours of freedom left.

The cold night air broadcast a dreary day, both physically and existentially. Remus had just woken on his last free morning in his Dream Palace mansion. The last moment he would wake with Imogene by his side, a free man. Tomorrow, he would wake up on a train, and then go to bed a prisoner in the Atlanta Federal Penitentiary.

George flipped through his clothing. He stopped at his favorite—pearl gray with matching spats. He stuck his best diamond stickpin through the silk tie. A touch of class for the cameras and reporters at the depot.

The chauffeur waited outside to deliver him to the Federal Building downtown where he and his men would be checked in before being bussed to the Grand Central Station railway depot. The final thing Remus did was to sign power of attorney over to Imogene. She wept as he scrawled his name on the paperwork.

"I gave her full power of attorney to act for me while I was in prison," Remus explained.

Imogene instantly became one of the richest women in Cincinnati, if not the entire Midwest. She now controlled the vast spoils from the bourbon empire.

"To her, I assigned the Price Hill home, almost $1 million in whiskey certificates, the stock of Fleischmann's Distillery which I valued at $300,000, my jewelry, three automobiles, and all my private records."

Then, as a final nod, he wrote out a check for $115,000 to cover Imogene's living expenses, almost $5,000 per month if her husband had to serve the entire two-year sentence.

At the moment, the power of attorney designation seemed of little consequence. George struggled to comfort Imogene. He pulled her close to him, urging her to see that it would all be okay.

Remus always had a plan. Gangland rumors circulated that the warden down in Atlanta would "play ball." If money were all he needed, then George would bribe his way through. Despite Willebrandt's interference and watchful eye over the prison system, as well as enforcing the Volstead Act, he heard that other big-time bootleggers were bribing their way into easy jobs, not hard labor. And, they even had gourmet food delivered to the jailhouse to make life as easy as possible.

Imogene knew where the hidden vaults of cash were located, as well as the dummy bank accounts, which George set up using a series of fake names. His wife could then smuggle the money to him on visits.

It would all work out.

Remus had even figured out how to regain what he stood to lose while behind bars. He told Imogene that they would go somewhere far away—maybe Africa—then when enough time had passed, they could return to the fabulous life that the illegal booze trade had afforded them. Sitting atop a mountain of hidden money that he had stocked away, Remus believed that his reentry into mainstream society would materialize in a matter of time.

George had money from the bourbon empire in banks scattered across the Midwest and East Coast, including New York City, Chicago, St. Louis, Louisville, and several others. Someone had to watch over those accounts, because the cash there would be necessary to jumpstart operations once George was freed.

Imogene was the only one he could trust.

Federal Marshal Stanley Borthwick scanned the crowds gathering at the train depot. He grew increasingly uneasy as throngs of onlookers massed around the platform. Were there gunmen in that crowd willing to put their lives on the line to free Remus by force?

Government informants and a network of spies paid to funnel information to the authorities had alerted the lawman that the train might be hijacked. In response, Borthwick gathered a team of seven special deputy sheriffs to accompany the Remus gang to Atlanta. He would prevent a possible attack by taking them all on one passenger car as quickly as possible from Cincinnati to the jailhouse. They would use the cover of darkness as an ally, leaving at 8 p.m. and traveling all through the night.

Hijackers risked a bloody showdown if they hoped to stop a moving train filled with armed guards.

The scene at the Union Central Railroad station depot grew progressively more frenetic. Newspapermen peppered George and the dozen of his men who were sentenced to Atlanta with questions. Cameras popped as photographers took pictures of the train and the Remus gang. George's men laughed and joked among themselves. They acted tough for the curious onlookers who hoped to catch a glimpse of the infamous bootleg king and his accomplices.

The men said farewell to their family members who had gathered together and clutched at their loved ones. Several of the men had children who were bundled up against the January chill. George Conners's wife Alma carried their two-year-old daughter Rose.

Imogene, who the press reported had "specially cooked" the men "a chicken dinner" for their trip to Atlanta, shied away from the scene at the station. She earlier announced to the newspapermen, however, that she would be relocating to the Southern city during George's stay. Imogene slipped into the train at the last moment.

Buck Brady, whom wags considered the toughest, most violent villain in Newport, had been the first to show up at the Federal Building, with his wife by his side. Buck came directly from Covington, where he had just turned himself in to federal authorities after being found guilty for violating Volstead in a different case. He was the biggest wildcard on that train and the one who might have had the audacity to plan a hijacking.

George still believed that his litany of bribes would pay off. The day before, after filing a motion to have his freedom extended a week while he dealt with back taxes issues with the IRS, he announced that he "regretted sincerely that no action yet had been taken by the President." Remus fully anticipated that Calvin Coolidge would step in, believing that "executive clemency for his associates…may be taken within the next week or two."

As George prepared to board the special passenger coach attached to the Cincinnati Southern train, however, Coolidge, Daugherty, and even poor dead Jess Smith were far from his mind. He wanted to soothe Imogene.

George told a reporter that Imogene's presence in Atlanta would be "a great solace to him." Her love and nearness, he said, "will enable him to maintain his cheerfulness during his confinement."

The train pulled away from Cincinnati's Grand Central Station at precisely eight o'clock. Imogene tried to console her husband.

"Never mind," she said bravely. "When it is all over, we will go away somewhere together and forget the disgrace."

On the way to prison, George and his men ate gourmet meals. They played cards, joking and backslapping as a way to pass the time and avoid thinking about the long prison terms they faced. Sometime in the middle of the long, overnight trip, he and Imogene retreated to his private quarters.

Remus read a copy of Dante's *Inferno* that he brought along from his vast personal library.

O gente umana, per volar sù nata,
perché a poco vento così cadi?

[O human race, born to fly upward,
wherefore at a little wind dost thou so fall?]

—Canto XII, lines 95–96

About six weeks before her husband left for Atlanta, Imogene pulled George aside. She had an important matter to discuss.

"She showed me $275,000 in cash at the First Trust and Savings Bank in Chicago," he recalled. This was not an account that George had opened or authorized.

Without providing detail, Imogene announced that this was her personal account. In revealing the stash to her husband, she was trying to demonstrate that he could trust her. Imogene put her cards on the table. The bourbon empire would be in safe hands while he awaited release.

George was dumbfounded.

The idea of a secret account that he hadn't funded haunted Remus. Imogene claimed that the hidden reserve would help them reestablish themselves when he got out of prison, but George viewed the stash from a different perspective.

The money, he figured, enabled her to "get this power of attorney so she could go ahead and act as she would see fit while I was incarcerated." He had given her an opulent lifestyle, and now Imogene could continue living that way while he was in prison.

Jailed. Like an animal.

Cincinnati Southern officials and federal authorities ensured that the railroad car would be routed to the prison, arriving around noon. The first stop was a terminal in Atlanta, where Imogene would disembark. There, George and his wife had a long talk, her final instructions before he went inside. He slowly stripped off his treasured diamonds, handing them to Imogene. She had to keep those safe.

Finally, Remus realized that he would not need the fancy silk shirt that he had worn on the train ride. In an act of generosity, according to a nearby reporter, George "made the car porter a present of his last silk shirt." He then waited as the railroad car was switched to a track that led directly to the prison.

George was supposed to be the star in the papers that day, but Imogene stole the show. As usual, her appearance mesmerized reporters who greeted the train. They *had* to talk about her.

"Mrs. Remus," reporters noted, "was lavishly dressed, wearing a magnificent gray sealskin coat." She promised that the water in their $100,000 Rookwood-lined pool "would sparkle the same as ever," while she tended it during her husband's incarceration.

The new, infamous prisoners arrived at the facility while the current inmates ate lunch and hung out of windows to see. "Millionaire bootleg king of the Middle West," was what the press called him, and those inside the walls wanted a look at the kingpin and his gang. George waved at the inmates without saying a word, though a reporter noted that he walked in "flashing an infectious smile," and "jauntily swung a light cane." Remus waved to newspaper reporters who had gathered at the jail as he filed into the assignment room where he would wait for his cell to be ready. As prison guards began measuring Remus for his drab prison attire, something snapped in his mind. The totality of what he faced finally overtook him.

"With the click of that big door down, there came a feeling of humiliation that was almost intolerable," George explained.

Remus assessed the enormous facility on McDonough Boulevard, dubbed "Big A." The prison held some 3,140 men. The overwhelming majority were detained in row after row of tiny cages stacked on top of one another several stories high. Big A looked like an efficient factory from the street, but on the inside, the dark prison ran dank and hot.

Fighting through the gripping anxiety, George resorted to what he knew— making deals and spreading around cash to get what he wanted. Bootleg millionaires, or so the underworld network chattered, could buy special treatment at Big A. The boys who ran the facility would make prison life easier…for the right price.

Separated from his men, who were thrown in among the common prisoners, George bought his way to a comfortable life in Atlanta. Like the other wealthy bootleggers in the prison, Remus found that with enough cash, he could buy privileges.

Willie Haar, head of the infamous Savannah Four rum smuggling network, was the de facto leader of the small band of wealthy prisoners. His partners Graham Baughn, C. C. Tuten, and Richard Bailey had also been pinched. Haar, dubbed "The Admiral" for his role in the bootlegging scheme, had a fleet of ships that worked off the coast of Georgia. Like Remus, Haar and his crew grew too big, too fast, attracting the attention of Willebrandt and her ace, Franklin Dodge.

Haar, Remus, and the others found that the rumors they had heard were true—Warden Albert E. Sartain and other members of the prison leadership would play ball for the right price. These were terms that the bootleggers understood. They greased prison officials with enough money to make many people rich, many times over.

Imogene played a critical role. She was George's cash mule, secretly delivering thick stacks of bills. Not everyone was on the take and silence was at a premium. Even those taking the bribes had to pretend to follow the system's basic rules, which outlawed monetary exchange.

"She distributed the funds or paid the bills pursuant to my instructions," Remus explained.

George's slice of the overall pie cost him $17,000, which Imogene siphoned from his many outside accounts, not much more than pocket change when the empire was operating at full tilt.

One reporter later claimed that while at Big A, George had a servant, lived in luxury in the prison's isolation unit, and ate fine foods. He called the sentence "a prisoner's paradise." Rumors of late-night card games with Willie and others cited rounds of drinks and cigars, allegedly served by a black butler whom the men all called "Cincinnati."

For George, one significant privilege was using the phone to call Imogene. He had entrusted Blanche Watson, his longtime personal secretary, to oversee his businesses, and his wife would deliver instructions. A native Kentuckian, Blanche played a critical role in the bootlegging infrastructure because she understood the bourbon industry and the false-front pharmacies in the distribution network. Remus had made her president of the Kenton Drug Company which—like his other operations—mixed legal medicinal alcohol business with illegal acquisition and distribution, constantly maintaining the illusion of propriety. If there were going to be anything left of the Remus empire, it would be Blanche's duty to preserve it until some of George's chief lieutenants were released from the prison.

The key to maintaining the bourbon empire was Imogene's serving as a conduit of information and instructions. When George paid off prison officials, one of his primary motives was to get daily access to a telephone. Willie Haar later asserted that George and Imogene spoke on the phone for ten to fifteen minutes most nights. Remus used affectionate expressions like "sweetie" and "little bundle of sweetness."

The cash also enabled Imogene to have unlimited visitation rights. When she arrived, George doted on his wife, and she returned that affection.

Willie claimed that Imogene got down on her hands and knees to wash the floors on several visits, cooked for George, and brought fruits and other delicacies that her husband could not obtain inside.

Cracks did begin to appear, however, with the stifling strain of incarceration. George and Imogene argued, sometimes launching into shouting matches. The mental turmoil boiled over, according to Haar. He saw Imogene crying after one screaming match because George "had accused her of different things and abused her."

The intensity inside the jailhouse, growing greater by the day despite the luxuries the bootleggers could afford, was matched by Willebrandt's office who had heard rumors of misappropriation in Atlanta. When word leaked that Sartain was on the take, Mabel had to act fast.

Willebrandt was in the unique position of directing enforcement of the Volstead Act *and* controlling the nation's prisons. These two worlds collided at Big A. When Mabel heard rumors regarding the luxurious incarceration of Remus, Haar, and other prosperous bootleggers, she sent Franklin Dodge to investigate.

Willebrandt could not afford any undue negative publicity directed at the Prohibition Bureau. She gave her favorite agent a blank check. His orders were to root out the corruption in the prison and bring to justice anyone who had been involved in wrongdoing.

With that security, Dodge used every tactic available—legal or illegal—to carry out his boss's order. When necessary, he would threaten local officials who he thought withheld information from him. Dodge intercepted personal and business mail sent to prison leadership. When these tactics failed to turn up information, he resorted to turning prisoners on one another, in turn ratting out the warden and his underlings. Dodge and Willebrandt knew that the corruption in Atlanta was widespread and pervasive. Mabel, however, turned a blind eye to Franklin's strong-arm tactics. She needed proof and evidence for a conviction, not the hassle of worrying how it was gathered. Willebrandt demanded Sartain's resignation.

On January 16, 1925, the assistant attorney general hired John W. Snook, an Idaho lawman, to serve as warden of Big A. Standing six feet, four inches tall and barrel-chested, Snook had served as a marshal in the West, winning fame for rooting out "bad men of the old days," as one reporter declared. The new warden, under Willebrandt's watchful eye, promised to reform the prison, emphasizing efforts "to clean out all 'dope'" that had been smuggled into the facility under the previous warden.

Snook quickly launched initiatives to clean up the prison, but he balked at Mabel's oversight and Franklin's meddling. He worried about Dodge's methods and the consequences. From what he could gather, the federal agent "had been sent among the prisoners and was freely offering pardons, paroles, and commutations of sentences in exchange for testimony that would land others in jail."

Franklin lured Remus into his web by dangling parole if he would squeal on Sartain and the others. However, George might not have had a choice. According to Snook, the federal agent could also strong-arm prisoners, suggesting, "no parole could be hoped for if they refused." It was at Willebrandt's urging, the warden claimed, that Franklin began "conferences" with Imogene.

Franklin's diligence and commitment to fulfilling Mabel's every wish nearly led to riots inside the federal pen, Snook later grumbled. The only thing that saved the prison, the new warden ventured, was that most of the men housed there were not hardened criminals and did not wish to risk longer sentences if they tried to escape. Time meant everything to the inmates. They won possible early release for good behavior and few of them were willing to risk breaking rules if it meant increasing their prison time.

Turning on his boss as he realized the state of the jail and its population, Snook laid the blame for deteriorating conditions at Willebrandt's feet, calling her "Meddlesome Mabel" and accusing her of "misrule." She had given Dodge and Federal District Attorney Clint W. Hager virtually unlimited power over individual prisoners, allowing them to order harder work details and take away privileges.

While Snook attempted to maintain order at Big A, the former warden and his administrators went on trial, a showy courtroom drama that seemed another sure nail in the coffin of the Harding Justice Department under the crooked rule of Harry Daugherty. Sartain, who had worked in the prison system since 1902, had been appointed by Daugherty, which tied the prison operations directly to him and Willebrandt.

Sartain, Deputy Warden Looney J. Fletcher, and Lawrence "Heinie" Riehl were charged with conspiracy to accept $10,500 from members of the Savannah Gang in exchange for "soft" assignments and upgraded accommodations. Authorities did not even bother to include the money Remus had paid to the warden and his staff. They felt that the charges would stick regardless.

Prison Chaplain Thomas P. Hayden admitted that he received $2,100 in return for special privileges. As Hayden made clear, in February 1924 (just a month after Remus had entered Big A), the chaplain and his bosses met with a man representing the Savannah Four. The bagman offered three prison officials a total of $15,000 to look after the wealthy criminals.

The allegations and subsequent accusations made by Hayden, Sartain, and the others as they turned on one another captured media attention. The juiciest details were ones that included Daugherty, since he was a Harding Cabinet member. However, the attorney general and his underlings were so corrupt that it was difficult to track where one scheme began and another ended.

Daugherty's lawyer in Columbus, James N. Linton, served as a roving courier for his boss and sometimes as a shakedown artist. Linton wrote a threatening letter to Willebrandt and signed Daugherty's name on it. The note demanded that the investigation surrounding the corrupt Atlanta prison administration be halted or that Daugherty would "go to the president." Given Daugherty's close relationship with Willebrandt, it is doubtful that he knew about the forgery, though the heat of the prison investigation and trial and subsequent negative publicity may have pushed him to make the threat.

Desperate to prove his innocence, Sartain had also used his power to force the multimillionaire bootleggers to sign affidavits "as to his own good character and record" and that of his staff members. The list included Willie Haar, Sam Goldberg, Morris Sweetwood, Mannie Kessler, and Remus.

The changes at Atlanta Federal Penitentiary after Warden Albert E. Sartain's downfall were brutal for the prison's celebrity inmates. For Remus, it meant Imogene's visits were restricted, which made it difficult for him to conduct his bootlegging affairs. Often their correspondence was reduced to letters and notes, rather than face-to-face meetings. Once Willebrandt toppled Sartain, Remus had to do hard time, just like the common thieves and murderers who were housed in the prison.

Remus realized that he had made many powerful enemies in Washington, DC, despite his assumption that the payments to Daugherty and Smith would bring him protection. Mabel Willebrandt was his most important foe and she viewed the bootlegger as one of the nation's biggest threats. Staking her own reputation, as well as the Prohibition Bureau itself, she did everything she could to keep him in prison. Willebrandt repeatedly thwarted his attempts to gain an early release. The assistant attorney general, one historian noted, "had so far resisted all of his bids for freedom." Willebrandt's efforts were wide-ranging and decisive, including personally arguing against his appeal when it came before the Supreme Court.

Despite the new physical hardships, the prisoners at Atlanta were still fueled by the wholesale rumor mill that fed the institution gossip, real and fake news, and kept the inmates somewhat connected to their lives outside the penitentiary walls.

While in prison, Remus finally pieced together how the government orchestrated its plan to shut down his operations, regardless of the mountains of bribes he had disbursed. He also grasped that Willebrandt had given her star detective Dodge almost unlimited power to bring him down, including highly suspect search parameters to invade Death Valley and leeway in interpreting what they learned from witnesses who had been at the illegal liquor depot.

Remus wasn't the only one with powerful enemies, though. Daugherty's reign of unfettered corruption had peaked. The irony was that the more successes Willebrandt had, the more it made her boss look like a criminal. Harry was in too deep, wallowing in the loss of his best friend Jess, the persistent health challenges of his wife, and a new distraction, the alcoholism of his son Harry Jr., who made headlines for his antics.

•　•　•

If Remus's star was starting to fade, Senator Burton K. Wheeler, a progressive Democrat from Montana, and Senator Smith W. Brookhart of Iowa, made it shine. The bootleg king would become a national celebrity again. In January 1924, less than a year after Jess Smith killed himself in Harry Daugherty's apartment, Wheeler had introduced legislation to open an investigation of the alleged corruption in the attorney general's office.

Two months later, the committee launched its high-profile work with George testifying on May 10, 1924. Although George had not been in prison long, he craved freedom. Remarkably, he still anticipated that his stay would only be a few months, believing that his deal with Smith would grant he and his men early parole. The testimony before the Wheeler Senate committee, he believed, might be another way to get early release.

George confessed to the payoffs to Daugherty that he made through Jess Smith, admitting that the total ran between $250,000 and $300,000. Remus's revelations of the extensive wrongdoing further tainted Harding's legacy and the reputation of the current Republican Party.

The headline yelled at readers of the *New York Daily News* as they perused the paper over morning coffee on May 17, 1924:

RUM'S GOLD FOR DAUGHERTY PAL

Remus had amplified the coverage of the Senate investigation. The news of the bribes and the amount he had forked over gave the public a shocking look into the heart of the corrupt Harding administration. The reporter noted, "the story came from the lips of the prisoner with an intense and trembling earnestness."

All around the nation's capital, officials ducked for cover as the news broke. Yet, despite the widespread and pervasive fraud in the Justice Department under his rule, Attorney General Daugherty dug in for a fight. Simultaneously, President Calvin Coolidge put on his best "Silent Cal" routine. He made no public comment about the Senate hearings. Privately, however, he waited to gauge how the public would construe the battle between the Democratic legislators and his Republican administration.

The president worried that the hearings would jeopardize his 1924 election hopes. Coolidge was a feisty politician. He realized the stakes at hand, particularly due to his own shaky standing. He was not widely popular among Republican insiders: too conservative for progressives and too liberal for the conservative core. Wheeler's investigation could only do further harm to Harding's legacy, regardless of how much the people loved and admired the man. The residual flack also dinged Coolidge, since he had been vice president during the many scandals. People doubtlessly wondered if he had been involved.

In national headlines, newspaper reporters took full opportunity to examine the entire range of indignities, from Secretary of the Interior Albert B. Fall and his role in the Teapot Dome transgressions to the wholesale fraud in the Veterans' Bureau under the direction of Charles R. Forbes.

The senators investigating Daugherty wanted irrefutable proof of the boot-legger's payoff claims. George attempted to wrangle them into letting him out of jail long enough to procure the necessary documentation, which he had hidden away. He proposed several stops to pick up the materials.

Once again, however, Willebrandt jumped into the fray. She denied George's possible release, writing to the committee, "We do not feel justified in allowing a man who, during the past two and a half years we have been prosecuting him, has brought pressure to bear on every public official he could approach in an effort to secure favors, to be absent from prison walls for a trip around the country in the informal manner requested."

During the Wheeler-Brookhart hearings, Willebrandt was so convinced that Remus had to be a scapegoat for all bootleggers that she publicly took on Sena-tor James A. Reed, a Democrat from Missouri, who had written to President Coolidge asking that he personally intervene to keep Remus and his codefend-ants out of prison. Without naming Remus specifically, Reed wrote that certain inmates should be given clemency. The senator then noted that the irregularities of the case demonstrated "the complete innocence of certain of these parties."

When the White House referred Reed's request back to the Justice Depart-ment, Willebrandt showed an uncharacteristic public display of anger, testily informing Wheeler that Remus "tried to influence even the White House it-self" in his attempts at clemency. She produced no evidence that confirmed Senator Reed was on George's payroll, but the insinuation was telling. The an-imosity between Remus and Mabel escalated during the Senate hearings.

Then, Mabel shifted the blame to "senators and congressmen themselves" for making Volstead enforcement "difficult" via "unreasonable requests" for whiskey permits and appointment of federal agents that she deemed "crooks or useless."

Mabel's stern constitution and experience as a prosecuting attorney helped her through several hours of grilling, what one reporter called "accusations" by Wheeler and the committee members, which she "threw…back in the faces of the senators."

For George, his national testimony had one goal—early release. What he learned, however, was that Willebrandt would not let him go free under any circumstances. After the shocking public revelations, a Daugherty and Repub-lican Party insider named Blair Coan visited George in prison.

He presented an enticing offer, telling Remus, "If you will repudiate this statement [about the payoffs to Smith] made before the Senate Committee, we will see that you are liberated on parole, that your men will be liberated on parole." Coan also promised that the Jack Daniel's-related charges against George and Imogene would be dropped. Despite his own troubles and public shaming at the hands of Wheeler and the Senate investigation, Daugherty feared that Remus's testimony would hurt the Republicans in the upcoming presidential campaign.

The attorney general also sent word to Remus via Sartain that he "never forgets his friends." George, he said, would win favor by renouncing his testimony and might be freed early.

Remus countered. Mabel Willebrandt would have to guarantee his early release before he would say that he had lied in front of the committee. Sartain later lied to George, asserting that he found out from Willebrandt "that matters had been satisfactorily arranged."

Under increasing pressure to refute his accusations against Smith and Daugherty, George protested, explaining that all he had left was his honor and that signing a false affidavit would brand him a perjurer.

Sartain and Daugherty increased the pressure, threatening, "you know the power of Harry M. Daugherty," while also promising that Remus would be freed. On August 28, 1924, attorney James N. Linton (another Daugherty insider) and Coan watched over Remus as he signed an affidavit that rescinded his previous testimony before the Wheeler committee. They immediately sent the document to the media.

Daugherty, defending his own honor and that of his party, released a September 19 letter he wrote to Democratic Party presidential nominee John W. Davis, who had been criticizing the attorney general in stump speeches. Daugherty declared that Remus "published a full retraction and repudiated his testimony."

The attorney general chalked up the Senate committee as a witch-hunt, asserting that its investigation amounted to little more than a "contemptible conspiracy of fraud and deceit…to destroy my character and injure the Department of Justice." Later in the letter, Daugherty invoked red-baiting language equating the criticism of him as part of a larger Russian and Communist ploy to destroy the nation.

Although he did as Daugherty requested, George did not get liberation. He stayed in the Atlanta prison while Wheeler and others unleashed a renewed barrage of criticism against Sartain and Daugherty. Wheeler urged Coolidge to immediately fire Sartain, claiming that the warden was part of the corrupt "Daugherty gang."

The senator also revealed that Imogene had personally given Senator Smith W. Brookhart copies of checks that were "cashed and the proceeds paid to Jess Smith and to other go-betweens for Republican officials in Ohio, Washington, and New York."

George recalled feeling "persecuted, hounded, unfortunately treated" while in Atlanta, because he would not tell Willebrandt or others how he had built the bourbon empire.

"Mrs. Willebrandt came down to Atlanta for a few days and talked to me," George said. She wanted details, but "I wouldn't give them to her...of course, those matters...irritated them." He realized that many of the people he worked with and sold illegal liquor to would have been subject to arrest and imprisonment if he ratted them out to Willebrandt.

According to Remus, Willebrandt would visit him in Atlanta, making many promises that she would conveniently forget once she got back to Washington.

"The attitude of Mrs. Mabel Walker Willebrandt was inconsistent with the attitude that she took in my presence," he explained.

* * *

The Sartain probe and the fallout it generated had even more direct consequences for George, throwing him back into the general prison population and severely restricting his rights within the jailhouse. As his life behind bars quickly crumbled, his rock on the outside started collapsing as well.

Imogene grew more distant as George's special treatment ended. The new restrictions severely curtailed their ability to interact. When his wife did visit, George found that the consultations ended up causing him additional headaches. After the high-profile Senate hearings and his prominent role in the Sartain investigation, he stood on the verge of collapse.

At one point, George heard rumors about Imogene driving around Atlanta with a known ladies' man named Higgins, who happened to be a civilian employee of the deputy warden. According to other prisoners, Higgins had successfully seduced the wives of other inmates by taking them for car rides. When George confronted Imogene, he grew livid.

"I told her I didn't think it was the proper, decent thing for a person to do under those circumstances," he remembered, particularly since he had given her a life filled with "everything that money will buy."

"I told her that if she would do those things, I didn't want her to come back to the institution no more."

Behind George's back, she had taken additional steps to generate cash flow. On July 2, 1924, she surprised Cincinnati observers by holding an auction at the Hermosa Avenue mansion. She had sent notices to several regional newspapers that listed the countless valuables that would be sold off or carted away.

George later claimed the auction was all a ruse "for the purpose of making the authorities believe that there were no funds to pay the income tax," which totaled about $188,000 in 1921. However, for the onlookers who attended the event, it seemed like a giant publicity stunt to show off the mansion and its owner. And, whatever money the auction took in went into Imogene's coffers, despite what George intoned.

Imogene's behavior rocked George. He needed her strength and support to get through prison. Just as important, though, George needed Imogene to bring him information from the outside and then deliver his instructions to what remained of his gang. Remus needed a partner. Imogene began to pull away.

. . . .

Although George had been famous most of his adult life for possessing nearly unmatched physical stamina, including swimming in frigid Lake Michigan for hours on end, nothing he had experienced on the outside prepared him for the mayhem of the Atlanta prison. At first, by bribing Warden Sartain and his cronies, George ate well and had free time with members of the infamous Savannah Four gang. Once Mabel Willebrandt and Franklin Dodge turned up the heat on the warden, however, Remus and other notorious criminals were pushed back into the general population.

George's body withered with each passing meal—little more than vats of boiled meat and vegetables—wrecking his stomach and leaving him shrinking in pain. Remus traded with his fellow inmates, his slop for slips of bread. Although used to hot summers in Chicago and Cincinnati, George guzzled down water to fight the relentless heat and humidity. The physical toll would soon be eclipsed by mental anguish. No matter how determined he was to win freedom, Willebrandt stopped him cold. He grew more famous by testifying in the Wheeler-Brookhart hearings, but the notoriety only made him a sturdier target for Mabel. His collapse was her publicity windfall.

In addition to gossip about Imogene and Higgins, Remus had begun hearing rumors about Imogene and Franklin Dodge, of all people. As he neared nineteen months behind bars, he must've wondered if the allegations were true and how long they may have been going on. In that span, no hardship, not starvation nor solitary confinement, could have prepared George for the ultimate treachery of Imogene's betrayal.

"There was nobody in the world who I trusted so fully," Remus explained. "We agreed that when my term was out we would take a long trip around the world, and then settle down where the disgrace would not follow us."

His optimism was misplaced. Imogene and Franklin meant to destroy his life.

"I've been three years in hell," Remus later explained, looking back on his time in the pen. "I, behind the prison bars, helpless; they on the other side plotting my destruction."

11

Freedom

Late in August 1925, Remus anticipated his sentence in Atlanta coming to an end. He had a laundry list of important tasks that required his attention, decisions that had to be made as he regained his freedom. He didn't know the exact date of the release, but knew it would happen soon.

George needed Imogene to be at the ready during this crucial time to relay messages and information. He had attempted to telegraph his wife at the Price Hill mansion in Cincinnati. Imogene hadn't responded. Her disappearance had left his business in disarray.

Now, as the hours wound down, Imogene sat next to him in Warden Snook's office in the vile penitentiary.

"Don't get angry, Daddy, you know I love you," Imogene cooed.

George pressed her for information. Every day mattered as he prepared to reenter society. He needed money to pay his team of lawyers attempting to nullify the public nuisance charge that bedeviled him. The last thing in the world he wanted was another year behind bars.

Imogene, coy as always and flirting with her husband to distract him, admitted that she had gone to Lansing, Michigan, with friends.

Shocked that his wife could be so flippant, George implored that she tend to his "important business," explaining that his "liberty was at stake." Rather than travel the countryside, he demanded she "stay in Cincinnati where he could reach her, so that she could handle his business."

His tone scared Imogene. She jumped from her seat and turned to face the warden. Cozying up to Snook, who stood nearly a foot taller than her husband, she cried out, "I am afraid of him! He threatened to strike me."

Snook, experienced in the trauma that couples faced in such moments, shrugged off her peculiar behavior, answering calmly, "He is not threatening to strike you." The warden asked her to sit down.

Then, George jumped in—bewildered—exclaiming, "I won't strike you, I have no reason to."

Imogene took Snook's advice. After that first outburst, she and George spoke about business matters. Snook noted that "she kissed him goodbye and they parted."

As Imogene prepared to go, George called out, saying goodbye to his "little honey bunch."

Two days later, Snook again brought George to his office. As warden, he had official business—serving Remus with the divorce papers that had just arrived by messenger.

"He was a very much surprised man," Snook remembered.

Franklin Dodge became Mabel Willebrandt's top undercover agent, remaining in the shadows as he interviewed—and later protected—Mary Hubbard during the months leading to Remus's first trial in Cincinnati. That testimony was decisive in putting the bootleg king in jail. Dodge also had success in another case, this time posing as a New York City rum baron looking for liquor in the South. The undercover agent then conned Willie Haar, the head of the Savannah ring, into divulging his secrets, ultimately putting the gang behind bars. Next, when he was ordered to Atlanta to investigate and clean up Warden Sartain's mess, he used Mabel's trust in him as a weapon. Dodge browbeat and threatened prisoners until he had exposed just about every secret at the facility.

During the latter investigation, Remus had heard about Dodge's power in the Prohibition Bureau. But, he also learned from Haar that the agent might take a bribe for the right amount of money. This was Remus's specialty. In response, he hatched a scheme for Imogene to cozy up to the star fed in a last-ditch attempt to have his sentence reduced.

"It was necessary for this very efficient agent to call on Mrs. Remus at Cincinnati in order to get some information," Remus explained later. "The main information he seems to have obtained was the amount of money I turned over to her."

At the launch of Dodge's investigation, before the totality of Warden Sartain's corruption was known, Remus asked him to broker a meeting between Franklin and Imogene, so that she could plead her husband's case for a shorter sentence. What George did not know at the time, though, is that Dodge knew everything about George Remus. Secretly, the undercover man had been at the heart of the investigation in Cincinnati that led to his conviction. Dodge read the ledger books that had been found at Death Valley. He knew what kind of money Remus made.

The results of the meeting could not have been more disastrous. Instead of setting a trap for Dodge, George had set a trap for Imogene. She instantly fell under Dodge's spell, falling desperately in love. And Dodge knew that he stood before the Remus empire with the owner of its golden key. He became Imogene's full-time companion.

A genuine lothario, Dodge used Imogene's affections to press her into divulging all the secrets of the bourbon empire, including where Remus hid his money and the priceless whiskey certificates that granted access to the booze socked away in the Kentucky distilleries. If they could just keep Remus in the dark depths of the Atlanta pen or keep him locked up via the public nuisance charge he had hanging over his head, Dodge and Imogene had access to a nearly unlimited fortune.

After meeting Franklin, Imogene became increasingly distracted and resentful toward her husband. In the beginning, as she fell deeper in love with Dodge, she feigned faithfulness, but the pressure mounted, and Imogene had to work hard to continue the deception. Franklin did not make it easy. Still an undercover agent, he had to keep his cover, which often placed him in compromising positions, both as a federal agent pretending to be a bootlegger and as Imogene's secret lover. These worlds collided as the deceit compounded.

George and Imogene both caught a glimpse of Franklin in his dual role when the investigation into Warden Sartain began. It began with wealthy prisoners in Atlanta using bribe money to buy their way into weekend furloughs at downtown hotels. During one of these trips with Imogene, George found out that Franklin Dodge "had two naked women in the room" down the hall from theirs. Remus did not know that the affair between his wife and the Prohi had already begun.

George thought this was preposterous behavior for a federal agent, so he told Imogene what he had heard. Her reaction startled him.

Imogene, Remus later explained, "was crying out [about] why a government official should have that kind of woman in his room."

At the time, the bootlegger thought that it was the impropriety of the other prisoners that caused Imogene's consternation. Dumbstruck, he later came to a harsh realization: "Lord sakes, here I thought she was ashamed to think that that kind of a happening would take place, when it was her love for Dodge."

He mocked her tone, adding, "Oh, gush, oh gush! Can you beat that?"

"The one you loved and trusted most had betrayed you with the man who helped to send you there."

George fully realized that Imogene loved Franklin much later, not really believing it, even when he heard rumor after rumor about the pair.

"This scum, Dodge!"

George could barely stand to think about the Prohi agent and Imogene, his beloved wife, together. As a matter of fact, he really didn't believe it. Sitting in Warden Snook's office, holding the divorce papers late in the summer of 1925, the totality of the message didn't sink in.

Long before, Snook had also heard about Imogene's dalliances, but decided against informing her imprisoned husband. Jailhouse gossipers divulged to Snook that Imogene "was traveling around with Dodge." The warden feared that telling George would just disrupt his "peace of mind...When a man is in the penitentiary, he is very susceptible to listening to any rumors."

George had heard things, though, small particulars that started adding up. Night after night, he lay motionless on his tiny cot sorting them out—the missed telegrams, the mysterious travel, the talk of her running around. The anger swallowed him up.

Caged in the Atlanta pen, he had no way to make Dodge pay, if the rumors were true. Remus was going to be released soon, five months early for good behavior. He could not risk his freedom.

"His wife and Dodge together, spending his money and enjoying themselves," he kept repeating.

"In all the pain and humiliation of the thing, my one consolation was my wife," George explained. "She had been my partner in everything. She knew the inside of all my deals. She kept books on transactions, which could not be entrusted to the office force. She often invested her personal funds in my enterprises."

"While I was locked up she was poisoned against me," George cried out in agony.

The deception infuriated Remus because his wife had so fully and convincingly tricked him at a time when he could not have even guessed the truth.

"I was in prison, helpless. A man behind steel bars," he told a reporter.

Even other inmates and the guard staff worked against him, on the take from Dodge, who gave them money from George's plundered coffers.

"She had her paid satellites," George said. When they got information, the guards were "to report back to Dodge as to what was going on."

Initially, Imogene had played the role of dutiful wife and caretaker of his bourbon empire.

"She came to me with smiles!" George bellowed, the anguish engulfing him. "When she was not at Atlanta I received letters from her every day. Letters filled with loving words." He remembered thinking, "How faithful my wife? Every day she writes to me. I am always in her thoughts."

Later, George pieced together the truth.

"These letters were only a part in the scheme of betrayal. She wrote ten or a dozen letters at a time and had them mailed daily from Cincinnati while she went about the country."

On August 11, 1925, Franklin resigned from the Prohibition Bureau to tour the country with Imogene and manage her business affairs. Rumors insinuated that Franklin and Imogene were establishing their own bootlegging venture, but it turned out that they were simply attempting to offload George's invaluable whiskey certificates to different syndicates. Dodge claimed that he left government service to take a position in the investigation department of the National Credit Men's Association in Cleveland.

Franklin had years of insider knowledge about liquor sales and circumventing the Volstead Act. He had led operations against many of the most devious minds in the industry. Dodge also had a letter from Mabel Willebrandt that served as a kind of calling card.

"She had given Franklin Dodge a letter setting forth that he was a good, efficient officer," Remus claimed.

The former agent used that authority to open doors to the criminal underworld. It is unknown whether or not Mabel realized Franklin's duplicity, but there were many investigations into his actions as the whiskey certificate operation became more widespread.

.   .   .

On August 31, 1925, while George spent his final agonizing days in the Big A lockdown, Imogene took a decisive step—filing for divorce in Cincinnati. The rationale couldn't have been clearer. Coldcocking George on the eve of his release, she would be able to tell her story to the media first. George would be forced to play defense.

The divorce between the bootleg king and his status-hungry queen promised to be played out on a public stage.

Imogene launched her publicity campaign by telling the world that Remus had been "guilty of extreme cruelty." In making her case, Imogene outlined a recent incident in Atlanta when her husband, following a torrent of verbal abuse, also threatened to strike her in front of prison officials ("I am afraid of him! He threatened to strike me."). Imogene asserted that she fled the warden's office in tears. She did not reveal, however, that the confrontation she had described had just taken place a couple of days earlier and her divorce paperwork had already been in the works. Whether her husband was abusive or not, Imogene never let the truth stand in the way of a great story.

George, she argued, could not control his vicious outbursts and acted in fits of rage. In the past, such episodes had resulted in destroyed property at the Price Hill mansion and endangered her and Ruth.

The petition she filed in Cincinnati explained that "she has conducted herself as a dutiful wife," but that he had "been guilty of extreme cruelty...displayed a terrible temper, shouted and yelled...threatened and attempted to strike this plaintiff."

The divorce document further declared that Imogene believed "She is in great fear of being done bodily harm by this defendant, and that she has reason to believe and does sincerely and earnestly believe that he will, if not restrained, do her severe bodily harm."

Judge Robert LeBlond responded by issuing a temporary restraining order against George, barring him from the mansion. He would leave the Atlanta Federal Pen, but he could not return to his beloved Dream Palace.

With the divorce suit filed and the judge's order in place, Imogene left to visit friends in Chicago. Couriers would take a couple of days to deliver the papers to Remus while he was still behind bars. Her legal team waited for her husband's response. Given the wrecked state of their marriage and George's fragile mental state, Imogene knew his next move would be malicious.

George's March 1924 testimony at the Wheeler Senate hearings had restored him to national celebrity. The lurid details about the pervasive corruption in Daugherty's Justice Department had sparked deep interest. As a result, Remus's release from prison on September 2, 1925, made headlines across the country.

Many newspapers published George's photo as he exited Big A. Flanked by two much larger deputy sheriffs who were ordered to return him to Ohio, the now-thin bootlegger enjoyed fleeting freedom. The moment he left the federal pen, he was rearrested on the nuisance charge stemming from the Death Valley operation.

"I would not be in the penitentiary for thirty days again for all the money in the world," George told reporters on the morning of his release. "I don't mean thirty months or thirty years. I mean thirty days. Not for every cent there is in the world."

Reporters wanted to know more about the Wheeler committee and what the criminal mastermind planned to do next. Did the bourbon king intend to dive back into the bootleg network? The details that had come out about the size of his operation and the amount he had paid in bribes were great fodder for newsprint, particularly since bootlegging had been professionalized to a great extent while Remus served his prison sentence.

"Crime does not pay," George said dutifully, as if a reformed man. "There are no dividends declared on a life of criminality. The only result is that you have to pay—pay with mental, moral, and spiritual anguish."

George issued a statement clearing up the Wheeler-Brookhart controversy. When he rescinded his early accusations against Sartain, he claimed, he had done so because Sartain, Daugherty, and their henchmen had forced him. They made threats, telling him that denying their wishes would mean longer prison time.

"Many promises" had been made, George admitted. Linton, Daugherty's attorney, "knew that when I made such a statement it was not true."

Remus simply signed the affidavit in an attempt to win parole. But Daugherty and Sartain double-crossed him after the heat grew too intense. Too many eyes were on the bootlegger, specifically those of Mabel Walker Willebrandt and her team of attorneys. And Harding's death had pulled the lid off the Teapot Dome scandal and other misdoings in the highest levels of the federal government.

Remus's freedom had come at last, then lasted only minutes as he briefly spoke with reporters before the deputy sheriffs from Cincinnati returned him to Ohio. From Cincinnati, he was then whisked off to St. Louis to discuss his role in a whiskey heist at the Jack Daniel's warehouse. Remus knew this step was coming based on protracted discussions with Willebrandt and his willingness to turn state's witness. The Atlanta to Cincinnati to St. Louis whirlwind epitomized George's life after getting out of prison. He would endure a series of trials, constant interviews with reporters, and intense legal battles in an attempt to have the public nuisance sentence rescinded.

Mabel Willebrandt had continued to play mental games. She repeatedly dangled freedom, alluding to her ability to have the nuisance charge dropped, if Remus gave federal investigators information to convict his partners in the Jack Daniel's heist. His testimony—basically turning into a "rat," the underworld's greatest shame—was Willebrandt's demand. George really had no choice, and the assistant attorney general knew it. He went to St. Louis to prep the attorneys for the impending trial.

Willebrandt had no intention of cutting Remus a deal. In her mind, every day that the bootlegger served behind bars was a good one. Given his fears about losing his mind in prison and yearning for freedom, George paid her price, despite realizing that his chances were slim. Even if Remus felt that he might make some inroads with Mabel by trading insider bootlegging secrets for goodwill, she instead listened to her closest associates regarding how to proceed.

Franklin Dodge and other federal agents were constantly disparaging Remus. Before he resigned from the Prohibition Bureau, Dodge repeatedly spoke out against the bootlegger, while maintaining his secret relationship with Imogene. Dodge even had one of his colleagues, Agent Henchin, urge Mabel to increase George's bail in the St. Louis warrant from $5,000 to $50,000.

George did not have a full understanding of how his world was falling to pieces, but the picture began taking shape with the combination of the divorce papers, underworld gossip, and the information he was given by federal attorneys. First, however, he had to find a way to get out of the St. Louis lockup. He thought the $50,000 bond, ten times more than the other defendants had to post, was vile. He perceived it as dirty business and saw Dodge's large shadow behind the increase.

"It was the rankest injustice in the world to place a man in the position of sending him to jail when he can give a reasonable bond."

Imogene and Franklin "were succeeding in depleting my property, squandering it throughout the country," all the while using Franklin's "past relation" with the government to keep authorities on George's back.

During the preparations for the Jack Daniel's trial, George spoke to Imogene on the phone, but the conversation quickly devolved into name-calling and accusations. Finally, unable to control herself, she blurted out a threat.

"I had talked to the Mrs. in St. Louis," Remus confessed. And as the discussion fell apart, according to George, Imogene exclaimed: "If Dodge had come to St. Louis, he would make mincemeat of me, and a lot of that kind of nonsense."

George now knew his marriage was over.

"She said she had more love and affection for Dodge in her little finger than myself a thousand fold," he acknowledged. The conversation sent him into a rage, particularly since they were spending "the illicit gains that I had made."

Reports circulated in St. Louis that George would testify against the sixteen other defendants in the Jack Daniel's case, including Imogene. But he denied that notion in the press, contending that he never spoke to the district attorney or had been subpoenaed to appear in front of the grand jury. Certainly, the catcalls of "rat" and "smelling like cheese" that the bootleg baron had endured in Atlanta still rang in his ears. Snitches were the lowest form of scum in the underworld hierarchy.

What tipped the scale toward testifying was Willebrandt's forcing George's hand and the chance at getting revenge against Imogene. If his testimony put her behind bars, then she would not be able to keep spending his dough.

Remus told reporters that he would defend himself in St. Louis, clearly still smarting from the double-cross he felt he received in his first trial. He wasted hundreds of thousands of dollars in bribe money to Jess Smith who could not keep him or the Remus gang out of jail.

With his mastery of media relations still intact, even after his long stint in the federal penitentiary, George flatly declared, "It is my judgment that I can handle the case better than another lawyer."

Reporters in St. Louis wrote about his "easy, dignified manner" and "deference," noting, "even his most emphatic utterances are politely qualified by such expressions as 'Don't you know?' or 'Doesn't it strike you that way?'"

•   •   •

Remus hired legal ace Benton S. Oppenheimer to represent him in the looming divorce case against Imogene. Oppenheimer had earned widespread respect as a county judge, which the bootlegger thought would help him in the divorce courtroom. When Remus finally returned home to the Price Hill mansion about two weeks after getting out of prison, the judge went with him. Oppenheimer wanted to be on hand in case authorities showed up to enforce the restraining order Imogene had served on her husband. If she knew Remus were on the property, Imogene might alert the police. Neither Remus nor Oppenheimer could be sure if his neighbors or others were spying on the house for Imogene.

"I entered the place and found it stripped, the doors locked," George said about the day he returned. "I had to break a window to get in."

For an emaciated ex-prisoner, the agony over the state of the Dream Palace was too much to handle.

"I became unconscious when I saw that happening," Remus recalled.

The two men encountered a shocking scene: George's tailored clothing was piled in a heap on the back porch, rotting in the early fall heat. All the expensive paintings and statuary had been removed. Imogene had left behind sixty-three pairs of shoes and slippers.

"She took everything out of there," George exclaimed. "She even took some of the valuable doors off the hinges and took them away."

There was nothing left.

The sight of the ravaged mansion, after nearly two years in prison, cast Remus into despair. Imogene had been so spiteful that she'd had the doors locked, the keys thrown away, and spikes driven into the doors so they'd have to be destroyed to be opened.

George had made several attempts to contact her after receiving the divorce papers on his last day in prison. He was able to get her on the phone, but the conversation turned sour and he verbally threatened her.

George screamed that he would "get even with her or get her if he had to follow her to China."

When he saw what Imogene had done to his house, George later recalled, he began to "entertain the idea" of killing her.

With George out of prison, fighting to find his fortune and battling to stay out of jail, Imogene knew her husband was unstable. She had experienced the rage when the pressure on him mounted. With no money and desperate, Remus was a threat to her life.

"Mr. Remus is bitterly angry at me," Imogene confided to federal agents and attorneys investigating her role in the Jack Daniel's whiskey heist.

"He is seeking revenge," she admitted, telling anyone who would listen that she utterly "feared" George. She had no idea how he might exact retribution.

Although at this point they could barely speak to one another, the husband and wife were also greedy and vengeful. Imogene had the upper hand because she had hidden away the money that George wanted back. But she knew he was dangerous and might kill her if she pushed him too far. Their meetings frequently devolved into shouting matches, so they both had bodyguards and lawyers with them. Imogene thought she could outmaneuver George by making promises about returning some of his valuables.

One evening she visited the mansion around 8:30 p.m. with Johnnie Gehrum, as her driver and bodyguard. He drove her to Price Hill in a Packard sedan that she had bought as a gift for Franklin, certainly something she knew Remus would notice. Although they had been trading incriminating barbs and lawsuits, George and Imogene had important financial details on the line. Imogene was going to hammer it out with George, whether he liked it or not. When she and Gehrum arrived—unannounced and uninvited—George was in his bathing trunks and a robe, just having finished a swim in his beloved pool. The ever-faithful George Conners was with Remus.

Regardless of what Imogene hoped, she was on Remus's turf and he knew exactly what he wanted—to know where she and Franklin had hidden the money, whiskey certificates, and stock information. He launched his line of questioning immediately, but had to stay calm, in the hope of getting answers. Remus knew his financial future might depend on finding the cash, valuables, and extensive collection of jewels that Imogene stole.

"I wanted to know what she had done with the securities, with the Liberty Bonds, with the whiskey certificates, with the jewelry," George said.

Standing there face-to-face with her husband, Imogene wavered. John Gehrum was there as her personal bodyguard, but he couldn't stop Remus if he attacked her. Imogene told George that she and Franklin had hidden much of the jewelry. But Imogene promised to "gather it up," so they could account for its value.

Imogene, like Franklin, was a deceiver and wasn't going to give her husband anything. She had been liquidating George's assets from the moment she met Franklin, and had in fact sold the holdings of the Fleischmann Distillery operations for $81,000 earlier that summer while her husband sat in prison. She sent Remus a mere $100 of the profits. The accompanying postcard exclaimed: "You will soon be out and we will be together again."

What Remus didn't know was that his wife wrote out that card while she sat in Leonard Garver's law office. Franklin hovered over her shoulder, watching. Then the two lovers took off for Cleveland together in the car she had purchased for him.

"By this time I was almost crazy," Remus explained. "I was broken-hearted and disgusted."

When none of the politicians or his cronies would pay back any of the money he had made them in St. Louis for his portion of the Jack Daniel's warehouse, George knew he had nowhere to turn.

With her husband desperate and enraged, Imogene recognized that Franklin could not protect her, regardless of his broad shoulders, thick arms, and overt masculinity. Not even his training as a federal agent could keep Imogene safe. Franklin was heavily armed, a handgun tucked into his shoulder holster or secured in the back of his pants, but he had to remain hidden. The lovers had everything to lose.

If Remus saw them together and alerted the police, they could be arrested under the tenets of the Mann Act, which made it illegal to transport a female across state lines for illicit reasons. Congress passed the law to thwart prostitution in America's big cities, but the Mann Act could also be utilized by husbands who demanded that their wayward wives return to them. Such an arrest would certainly give Remus a way to save face, while simultaneously making Imogene and Franklin pay for their transgressions. They traveled to Indianapolis determined to get out of public view.

Tangled up in George's bourbon empire and her own greed, Imogene also faced incarceration for the way George's partners had bungled the whiskey robbery in St. Louis. The constant scrutiny she faced as the estranged wife of one of the nation's most notorious criminal masterminds forced Imogene and Franklin to use aliases anytime they were in public.

Imogene's picture had also been in newspapers across the country. There were always people watching her. It seemed as if federal authorities or newspapermen constantly trailed her. For so many years, she yearned for the spotlight—now reporters begged for her story, and she just wanted anonymity. Early in their lives together, George's fame was an intoxicant. In what felt like a lifetime later, she did not want to answer questions about Remus or their marriage.

To protect herself, Imogene tucked her favorite pearl-handled revolver into her purse, hoping that she would not have to actually use it. In the past, just flashing the steel had gotten her out of danger. No one expected a sophisticated lady in tailored clothes, lace collars, and expensive furs to be packing. Most, even hardened criminals, saw the gun and beat a hasty retreat. Imogene hadn't yet had to pull the trigger.

While Imogene agonized over the Jack Daniel's trial and Franklin remained out of sight, George had little time to adjust to freedom.

Through appeals and countersuits, Remus avoided jail for the time being, but he had been subpoenaed to appear in St. Louis for the Jack Daniel's theft. Short on cash and unable to recover funds from Imogene, George could not raise enough to initially post bail. Once he arrived in St. Louis, they put Remus in jail because he lacked bail money. State prosecutors agreed to free him after he acquiesced to turn on his co-conspirators.

When George made it back to Cincinnati, he heard rumors that his life was in danger. Assassins had been hired to murder him.

"I was advised not to go to the house, because I would be killed," Remus said. The situation grew so precarious, he claimed, "My lawyers wouldn't walk the streets in Cincinnati with me, expecting me to be killed at any moment."

Anonymous underworld sources reported to Remus that someone had placed a $15,000 hit on him. George soon learned that Imogene and Franklin were behind the assassination order.

George Conners took his boss in, hiding him away in his house with his wife and young daughter. Before long, however, they received confirmation that their cover was blown.

"Our lives are in danger," Conners told his boss.

During the day they set up shop at the Sinton Hotel, figuring they were safe in such a public space. But even the Sinton became too dangerous. Hitmen had been casing the place, asking about Remus's whereabouts. So George went back to the mansion.

Most of his fortune spent or hidden by Imogene and Franklin, George couldn't hire the squad of bodyguards he might have at the height of his power.

So, as the trial in Indianapolis approached, Remus went into exile, hiding even from Conners and Blanche Watson, his two closest companions. He left for New York City, purposely avoiding the Waldorf Astoria, where the staff knew him.

"I was registered anonymously," he said. "Under an alias, at either the Astor Hotel, [or] the Commodore Hotel." George still had connections in the city and an extended line of credit, plus several thousand dollars that Conners had given him. He set up business meetings, but kept away from his old haunts. Remus couldn't trust anyone and if his location were revealed, he might be killed.

When the high-profile Jack Daniel's trial arrived less than three months later in December 1925, Remus railed against Imogene, Franklin Dodge, and the poached millions. The bourbon empire he so carefully constructed had fallen apart while he rotted away in Atlanta. Imogene had spent the time careening around the country with a rotating group of toadies, including many sycophantic family members, eager and happy to spend Remus's money while he wasn't there to protest. She and Franklin had spent wildly on fancy accommodations and exquisite restaurants. Every tip Remus had collected from informants painted a portrait of Imogene robbing him blind.

Husband and wife—both defendants in the Jack Daniel's whiskey theft trial—were reunited in Indianapolis, but there was no guarantee that George would see her privately. And it wasn't just the threat of George's violence against her that kept Imogene away from him—she didn't want to be collateral damage. As word leaked that he might turn against the other Jack Daniel's robbery conspirators, George's own safety was in doubt. Several federal agents protected him, and with what money he could scrape together with loans from George Conners and Blanche Watson, he added to the security detail with some of his own men.

Despite these obstacles, nothing would stop George from confronting Imogene. She had tried to stay out of Cincinnati and Ohio to avoid county deputies who would serve her papers in the many countersuits and legal maneuverings Remus and his lawyers concocted. Yet now, in Indianapolis, something had to be done. So, he waited.

George knew how to find Imogene, knew his wife would put on airs for her travel companions. She and her entourage would most certainly stay at the Claypool Hotel, the grandest spot in Indianapolis and one of the finer hotels in the Midwest. Remus simply waited outside for her to show up.

Despite his celebrity profile, at this point, he enjoyed almost complete anonymity. The feds had George holed up in a room at the Claypool, not on the books in any way, and outside of those officials, only George's lawyers, and Russell Moritz—the Prohi agent assigned to guard him—actually knew where

Remus was in Indianapolis. There had been too many rumored and real threats against his life.

George did not have to wait long for his wife to arrive at the Claypool, and when she did, he could not believe his eyes. Franklin stood there at Imogene's elbow, just about to enter the hotel's expansive lobby.

Franklin did not notice the powerful, compact man stalking him from behind. When the larger man got inside, the bootlegger slipped in behind him. In an instant, George attacked. He pummeled Franklin with his heavy, gold-handled walking cane, the high-society prop he used to put on an air of sophistication. "The animosity of Remus flared forth once when Remus followed the man into a hotel and attacked him," a reporter noted.

The brief flash of brutality could not have satiated George's hunger for revenge. In what seemed only a moment, police rushed in and promptly arrested Remus.

There were many newspapermen in town covering the trial, but none of them pieced together Franklin's name or even realized that he was the victim. In published accounts, they simply referred to him as "the man." Indianapolis police, in league with the Prohibition officials prosecuting the case, hushed up the felony. They needed Remus to be perceived as a credible witness in front of the jury, so they could not afford a row. Besides, no one pressed charges—Dodge could not stick around. His mere presence would have given George all the ammunition he needed to back up his claims about Imogene's infidelity. As a result, the onslaught and its consequences slipped into the ether, just another rumor encasing Remus and his ever-evolving myth.

Surprisingly, given the harsh words and accusations that had volleyed back and forth for nearly a year, George and Franklin did not turn the cane assault into a gunfight. Moritz, the Prohi in charge of guarding Remus during the months leading up to the trial, grew so spooked about the possibility of hired assassins, that he had given George a .45 caliber pistol to protect himself. Franklin and George had been sparring in the press regarding accusations that each had hired hitmen to take the other out. Franklin spoke openly about being armed. He claimed that he had two guns ready and waiting for Remus, just in case.

With the exception of stalking Imogene and Franklin near the hotel lobby, most of George's time in Indianapolis was spent hunkered down with Prohibition agents, who nervously guarded him at the secret fourth-floor hideout. George received a telephone call from an anonymous tipster in St. Louis. Moritz recalled, "They said gunmen were to be brought to Indianapolis to 'bump him off.'" Later, when the federal agent and the bootleg baron were in the hotel restaurant for breakfast, George spotted two large, muscular men he knew from Chicago. "Two other fellows were with them," Moritz said. "Remus said these other two were gunmen."

Moritz conferred with Claypool Hotel officials and learned that the two hired thugs had rented a room across the hall from Remus, which meant that they had informants. According to the Moritz, the Chicago hitmen had "no baggage" with them.

Realizing that their star witness might get mowed down, Moritz and his boss, Special Assistant Attorney General John R. Marshall, kept George from buying a noontime train ticket back to Cincinnati and stayed by his side.

"Remus feared these men," said Moritz. "We didn't want to lose him as a witness. Only Marshall and I knew he was in Indianapolis, so we put him in an apartment house." Officials heard that there were men sent by Dodge and would be paid $20,000 to carry out the gruesome task.

"I'm better than Remus and he knows it," Imogene told reporters once the Jack Daniel's trial began.

She walked cautiously to the second floor of the Federal Building. The grand hall featured granite and marble pillars that lifted to a stained-glass skylight, as well as a judge's bench of intricately carved walnut.

Though fearful of what Remus would do to her if given the chance, Imogene couldn't resist boasting to journalists. They flocked to her, the most intriguing of the Jack Daniel's conspirators. Yet, when pressed, she knew that she was playing a dangerous game with the bootleg baron. Turning state's witness would be another volley lobbed at her and Franklin in an attempt to rattle the couple.

George wanted them both behind bars, but would settle for Imogene first. His wife told federal agents that she feared him, but Imogene and Franklin had also unleashed terror by placing the target in the middle of his chest.

In the early moments of the trial, Imogene "burst into hysterical weeping and left the courtroom." A reporter wrote that a man had approached her and claimed he was a federal officer. He said that he would interrogate her after she entered her plea.

"This is another threat from George Remus," she cried. "He is persecuting me." She left the room with her attorney, Joseph Breitenstein, a lawyer from Cleveland, demanding that Remus be searched for weapons before she return.

The mystery "fed" told a reporter that he wanted to question Imogene in a "white slave" case, but provided no additional information. In response, Breitenstein claimed that Remus was "annoying" and "threatening" his client.

George and Franklin launched verbal warfare, taking shots at one another through newspaper stories and reports. Whenever the assassination plot against Remus made it into the papers, Franklin countered that "George Remus offered a man $8,000 to kill me."

Not willing to back down, Remus responded: "No, Mr. Dodge; only one hand would have had the satisfaction of doing that."

Despite news of a mysterious attack at the beginning of the trial and the subsequent rumors among criminal sources, no one had pieced together that George and Franklin had tangled, although the younger, larger man could not risk fighting back. The two nearly came to blows several other times during the trial, but in each case, men interceded to keep the two apart. Later, people who saw the near-fights claimed that Remus went after Franklin like a bull. Observers professed that George plunged into "hysteria" when he saw the former federal agent who had stolen his wife.

"Here was Dodge sitting with the defense, where he had worked to corral the evidence against those unfortunate defendants…acting in a dual capacity," George explained.

Imogene sat with Franklin in the dining room of the Claypool Hotel, Remus asserting that "they had come on from St. Louis together in the same compartment. I knew these things. It is a serious proposition."

John T. Rogers, an eminent journalist from the *St. Louis Post-Dispatch*, recalled, "Remus was shrieking and out of his mind. I struggled with him for an hour and a half to subdue him and keep him in the room."

Rogers and George Conners became de facto handlers, trying to keep Remus from assailing Dodge. They knew that if George fought Franklin the federal government would erase any chance he had of a commuted sentence. Their task wasn't simple.

Late one night, when Remus, Rogers, and Conners walked through the lobby, they saw Franklin in the room, only about fifty or sixty feet away.

"Remus broke away and made a dive in the direction of Dodge," the journalist explained.

He and Conners were able to stop the bootlegger, enabling Franklin to get into the dining room unscathed.

"Remus acted like a madman in the elevator for us not letting him get Dodge."

Rogers also served as an informant for Remus. He had spies who watched the St. Louis underground. He relayed information about the hit that Franklin and Imogene had orchestrated. He claimed that a Cincinnati gangster and ex-convict admitted to him that "Mrs. Remus, on two occasions, in St. Louis and Cincinnati had sought to employ gangsters to assassinate Remus."

Remus also had to contend with supposed old allies who now either wanted him out of the picture or were aligned with Imogene. No one was completely safe in this charged environment. George was on a mission to get even with his wife and her lover. Imogene and Franklin were just as determined not to be pulled down.

12

Heavy Lover

• • • • •

Feeling the chilly night air on his neck, Franklin Dodge grabbed the gold-plated railing and quickly climbed the six short steps from Superior Avenue into the Hollenden Hotel. The massive building did little to divert the brisk breeze whipping off Lake Erie, an icy wind that constantly swirled through the streets and alleys of downtown Cleveland.

Just past the end of a late-February workday, dusk had fallen on the city. The nearly deserted streets betrayed the Hollenden's opulence. The massive building rose into the night like a sumptuous red brick mountain. Everyone staying in Cleveland wanted to be at the Hollenden. The hotel's postcards had turned into keepsakes, with guests sending them to family and friends far and wide. Most observers felt it was the most luxurious hotel in the Midwest.

Franklin pushed through the heavy door and into a space lit by rows of chandeliers. The deep mahogany walls held large windows topped with beautiful gilded arches. The marble floor shone.

Dodge scanned the reception area for a familiar face. Behind the desk stood night manager Samuel Carlos Clapper. He greeted Franklin with a smile. They had grown friendly over the last two years that the federal agent had been staying at the Hollenden.

Everyone at the hotel recognized Franklin. The staff gave him a wide berth—they knew that he was a Prohi. Seeing him up close did little to alleviate their sense of awe or nervousness at having a federal agent in their midst. Others, certainly, had no love lost for a man whose job it was to enforce the Volstead

Act. Hotels were the country's party headquarters. The lack of legal alcohol threw a bit of dirt on that luster. Franklin moved in and out of Cleveland frequently, staying at the hotel several times a month.

Clapper had arranged Franklin's room, placing him in fine accommodations on the sixth floor. The night manager had one of his bellboys settle the enforcement agent in his chamber. Clapper did not see Dodge for the rest of the evening.

Many hours later, at 2 a.m., night watchman Fred Yocke reported that he had heard loud noises coming from Room 902 as he conducted his customary corridor patrol. The disturbance was out of character at the Hollenden. After checking with the front desk clerk on duty, Yocke learned that the ninth-floor room was registered to a woman from Detroit named Miss Charlotte Conan. Not sure exactly how to handle the situation, Yocke went to his boss and asked Clapper if he should investigate the incident further.

"I told him to let it go for another hour, and when you make your rounds again, if you still hear anything let me know, and we will see about it," the night manager remembered.

When the patrolman returned an hour later at 3 a.m., he approached the room quietly. Again, he heard loud talking and commotion. He returned to the ground level and alerted Clapper. The two men dashed up to the suite. They pounded on the door, urgently attempting to get the occupant's attention. No one answered, so they continued to knock.

Yocke was sure he had heard voices and that the room was definitely registered to a woman, so the two men stood there for 15 minutes. They were not going to leave until someone responded.

"I knocked at the door and Dodge came to the door, sticking his head out of the door," Clapper explained. "We looked into the room and there was a woman in bed there."

Franklin peeked out, his big frame blocking off the entrance. Clapper, now nervous about having to confront a man that he knew was a federal agent, demanded that he be allowed to enter.

"He wasn't going to let me in, and I was very much surprised to see him in that room, as there was a woman registered in the room," Clapper said. Determined to enter, "I stuck my foot in the door, and finally pushed my way in."

Dodge relented, standing awkwardly with his extra large shirt unbuttoned and draped over his shoulders like an old pajama top. He had not even attempted to wrap his collar around his thick neck.

Assessing the potential calamity on his hands, Clapper then noticed that Dodge's "trousers were unbuttoned in front." He looked across the room, and then turned to Yocke. Worse: "The woman was laying in bed with just a night-gown on."

"I asked him what he was doing in the room at that hour in the morning," Clapper said.

Grasping what the night manager insinuated after catching an unmarried couple together, Franklin launched into a story about the woman. Franklin told him that she was "his sweetheart and that they were going to be married in a short time." She suffered from a "sick headache," Franklin explained. He had to be in the room to nurse her.

Not accepting such a flimsy excuse, Clapper turned toward the bed, asking the woman how she felt. She replied that she was sick and Dodge was "keeping her company." When Clapper countered by offering to call a physician to treat her, the suggestion led to an argument between the two men about her ailment. Dodge wanted the Clapper and Yocke to leave immediately, but they would not budge.

Clapper had reached the end of his rope. This was a desperate situation. The Hollenden could not risk gaining a reputation for this kind of behavior. In a deep growl, the night manager demanded that Dodge return to his own room. Franklin looked at him, but did not move.

Then Clapper put his foot down, explaining, "If he was going to be in this room he should notify the desk downstairs." The woman would have to go, Clapper noted, demanding, "the lady would have to check out...I didn't want to throw her out at this time in the morning, it was so late, but that she could stay until seven o'clock in the morning, and she would have to be out at seven."

Dodge, he insisted, "would have to take it up with the manager himself in the morning." Clapper and the guard demanded that Franklin go to his room and then waited there until he left.

The next morning, promptly at 7 a.m., Franklin appeared at the front desk. He paid the woman's bill. She slipped out a side door.

Clapper never forgot the strange incident with one of his favorite guests. A few days later, he saw Dodge and the woman again. This time, Franklin was driving a long, shiny limousine.

Authorities later quizzed Clapper about the mystery woman's identity. They showed him a photograph of the female that he and Fred Yocke had discovered in Franklin Dodge's bed, half-naked.

Clapper recognized her instantly—it was Imogene Remus.

In the early rhapsodic moments of her affair with Franklin—a few years before the incident at the Hollenden—Imogene took elaborate precautions to hide their forbidden bond. Polite society would not accept loutish behavior, so she went out of her way to cast an aura of decorum wherever they traveled. More urgent, however, were the troubles that would result if they were caught, including the possibility of being arrested or detained. For one of the first times since she met George, Imogene shunned the news media.

"Mrs. Remus," according to her husband, "always had as an alibi, her mother, her sister Grace Campbell, and her daughter Ruth, so as to cover up any possible illegality as far as she was concerned."

Imogene's friends and associates were more than happy to travel with her and spend George's illicit liquor gains. They moved across the Midwest and East Coast staying in luxurious hotels and resorts. Imogene understood the legal ramifications if she were caught with Franklin.

"They all fostered, connived, schemed, after they got whatever monies they had from me…they could obtain from me. They condoned all the adulterous practices that she had done," Remus would recall.

Imogene used a series of aliases to register in the different luxury hotels she frequented with her entourage. She had no choice. Married women were not allowed to sign the guestbook alone or even walk the halls of these grand establishments unescorted. George had gained so much notoriety that she could not risk using "Remus" when she checked in.

Using an alias also helped conceal that Franklin was her lover. Different names on the registry gave them an alibi. Dodge habitually signed the guestbook as "John Gray," his customary pseudonym. Imogene listed her hometown as Chicago, hoping to throw off anyone who might recognize her.

Imogene did not know that George had a team of private detectives and operatives secretly chasing her and passing information back to him. While George served time, his chief aide George Conners would sometimes track Imogene, hearing about her escapades and checking up on the rumors himself. Remus trusted Conners, so the lieutenant needed to corroborate the stories with his own eyes.

"They were hobnobbing together in Canada, in Michigan, in Wisconsin, in Illinois, in Georgia, and New York, together," Remus eventually heard from his undercover agents. Ruth or another family member, he learned, provided "an alibi to cover up her adulterous practices throughout the country with Dodge."

Imogene had to be even more careful at home in Cincinnati, since George's men patrolled the Dream Palace and its grounds. Death Valley strong-arm John Gehrum served as a frequent driver for Imogene while George served out his prison term. He chauffeured her and Dodge on many occasions. It is clear that he kept this arrangement from his imprisoned boss. In subsequent years, Remus never mentioned knowing about Gehrum's assistance to Imogene.

William Mueller, a member of Remus's bourbon gang and caretaker of the Hermosa Avenue mansion, testified that he saw Imogene and Franklin together three times while George wasted away in prison.

Imogene ran the home and had absolute authority over the staff. Realizing that Mueller was a threat and might notify George about seeing Franklin at the Price Hill mansion, the lovers tried to keep the Prohi hidden. Mueller claimed that he had seen Franklin actually crouch down behind a car in an attempt to avoid being seen. Another instance, Imogene closed all the window shades to keep Mueller from peering inside.

She sent the house staff away at times so that they could begin emptying the mansion. Using the same kind of covert tactics she had watched Remus employ in building his secret liquor network, Imogene covertly scooped up things she wanted from the house. She unloaded some of the exquisite furnishings at a Canadian roadhouse she purchased in Ford City, Ontario, a sprawling community town founded by Henry Ford in the early 1900s. The town housed a large Ford Motor Company manufacturing plant. Her brother Harry, who had done time in Big A with George, set up shop in Ford City and provided Imogene and Franklin with a safe haven there.

Imogene and Franklin hired a trucking company to cart the valuables and furnishings they wanted from the mansion. But they were unable to avoid Mueller, who confronted them and said that his boss would want to know all about this when he got out of prison.

"Mr. Remus is not coming back," Imogene snapped.

"We're going to have him deported. It's all arranged. He's going back as he came, with his little bundle."

* * *

"Mrs. Remus told me she was madly in love with Dodge," said John S. Berger, one of George's boyhood friends who attempted to serve as an intermediary between them.

John had become one of the country's foremost managers of large-scale fairs and expositions. He was regarded for his negotiation skills, but Imogene did not want to contemplate a settlement. She and Franklin had hidden or spent vast portions of the fortune, but she didn't want to leave her husband with a single penny.

Berger went to one of their parties at the Statler Hotel in St. Louis, a city where he had staged a wildly successful grand exposition.

"I went to see her to ask if she would take a few hundred thousand dollars and return the rest of the property to Mr. Remus," he recalled. "She said no, that she wanted her divorce and would keep everything, because she loved Mr. Dodge."

Imogene couldn't help but brag to Berger, knowing that all she said would make it back to George.

"Mrs. Remus told me, and I told George, that she and her heavy lover, Franklin Dodge, were going to kill Remus," Berger confessed.

He delivered this information in late 1925 during the Jack Daniel's siphoning trial in Indianapolis, at a suite at the Claypool Hotel. George knew that Imogene and Franklin were in the same building. He went berserk. He snatched up two revolvers from his things and declared that he was going out searching for Dodge and Imogene.

"I had to persuade him not to kill Dodge," Berger remembered.

Franklin and Imogene had gained reputations at several luxury hotels around the country for having racy parties and dressing suggestively. They kept the festivities rolling with bootlegged liquor, champagne, and wine.

Berger was blunt in his assessment: "Later, I told Remus how Mrs. Remus and Dodge were in almost nude attire."

Imogene became more brazen as her affair with Franklin intensified. Perhaps the vast amounts of wealth she had purloined increased her blatant disregard for the illusion of decorum. Even in the wild days of the roaring 1920s, such immodesty placed her and Dodge in harm's way. George still had the upper hand from a legal viewpoint. Trying to reason with the bootleg king, John S. Berger suggested that he attempt to catch Imogene and Dodge in the act, which would lead to favorable divorce terms.

"I told him how they had connecting rooms" as they traveled around the country, he said. However, Berger pushed too far, saying, "When I told him how his wife and Dodge were hugging and fondling each other, he wanted to break through the door and get them."

If George could track her down and get detectives on the scene, he could have Imogene and Franklin arrested. He came close on several occasions. Once after his release from Atlanta, he did track her down at the Mayflower Hotel in Washington, DC. However, a night clerk tipped Imogene and Franklin off. They were able to slip out of the hotel at 1:00 or 2:00 in the morning, before George could alert the police.

Imogene and Franklin were safer when they stayed far away from Remus.

The couple found a hiding spot in Lansing, Michigan, which was Dodge's hometown, and one of the few places they felt they could avoid potential spies. During Remus's final days in Atlanta and then during his frantic search for them, the city provided a respite.

Franklin's family had a long history in Lansing and central Michigan, helping found the city. Dodge paraded Imogene around the area like a queen, rarely taking the same kind of precautions that were necessary in other cities.

Shoppers and office workers jammed the bustling streets in front of the Prudden Building at the southeast corner of Michigan and Washington Avenues. One of Lansing's architectural highlights, the twelve-story structure lit up in the midday sun. The red brick middle floors were a majestic scarlet, which contrasted with the light stone of the gallery and top levels. From across the street, a person looking up at the Prudden would see a kind of gleaming white top hat.

The companies and firms housed in the Prudden were some of the most noted in the Michigan state capital. The American State Savings Bank occupied the ground floor, a sweeping office lined with high, bright windows, allowing in ample natural light. The bank had a long history of serving Lansing's civic leaders.

People scurried back and forth over the city's manicured streets, built with wide thoroughfares to allow the trolley to crisscross the downtown area. Workers hustled between automobiles and their offices, nervously glancing at watches, as if marching in step as they hurried about their days.

In spite of the frantic pace outside, heads turned to watch a shimmering touring sedan pull up in front of the bank. The dashing Franklin Dodge emerged from behind the wheel, his suit cut perfectly to fit his tall, muscular frame.

Franklin beat a path around to the passenger side of the car and opened it. All eyes trained on her, Imogene stepped into view. She tugged at the fur wrapped around her shoulders, attempting to ward off the late September chill. Imogene pulled a black leather satchel from the car and struggled to hand it to her beau. Then, Franklin slipped to the back of the vehicle, opening the passenger door so that Imogene's young teen daughter Ruth could step out.

Imogene took Franklin's arm, looking up at him, as the trio moved toward the door. Ruthie tagged behind a step or two after the couple. J. Edward Roe, president of American State Savings, pushed the door open, smiling wide, and welcomed the striking couple and beautiful youngster. Roe, like Franklin's family members, the Dodges and Turners, was one of the city's most prominent citizens. He had been part of the generation that had built Lansing through savvy planning, determination, and fortitude, rising to lead the town's most important savings trust. Later, he would play a key role in bringing Oldsmobile to the city. The manufacturing plant provided countless jobs for generations of Lansing workers.

As the three disappeared inside, people in the street whispered questions and asked pointedly about the well-heeled woman with the dashing 36-year-old Franklin Dodge, who had grown famous as a federal Prohibition agent. Some wags even postulated that Franklin had been a spy in Germany during the First World War, using his German language skills to cozy up to the Kaiser himself. Now, the hero materialized in the flesh. Should they take note? Was this "the one" for Franklin or just another in the long line of well-bred, wealthy women that appeared with him in Lansing? Regardless, any anonymity they hoped for had disappeared. Lansing was Dodge country.

Once inside, Franklin and his brother Wyllis, one of the city's top real estate executives, chatted with several bank employees. They knew these people and their families, some dating back generations. Franklin introduced Imogene to everyone as "Mrs. Holmes." After more handshakes and chitchat, they walked to the back of the building.

Freda Schneider, the assistant manager in charge of security boxes, met them there, situating the couple in front of the large camera. Photographs were required of each security box owner. Even in Lansing, where the Dodges were so well known, the bank had to have verification on file. Mrs. Holmes then filled out the requisite paperwork, listing her address as "Milwaukee." Ruth co-signed the papers, her tiny handwriting barely legible on the legal forms. In securing the containers, they used Franklin's name and "Mrs. A. H. Holmes," one of the many pseudonyms Imogene used to hide from her husband's noto-riety and unique moniker. "Remus" would have drawn scrutiny, particularly in Lansing, where nothing Franklin did could avert prying eyes.

The trip to the bank was clearly a formal occasion, and usually when they were in public Imogene liked to show off, allowing people to overhear her as she spoke to Franklin in syrupy language, calling him "sugar lump" and "Daddy Dodge." But on this errand she maintained a reserved aura.

Imogene and Franklin stayed at the Turner-Dodge homestead in Lansing when they visited the city. However, most of their time together they criss-crossed the nation in search of good times. Staying out of Cincinnati was easy when they could enjoy the luxury of fine food and hotels in Detroit, Indianap-olis, Cleveland, Chicago, and New York. Imogene controlled the illicit Remus bourbon fortune and had finally "rolled him for his roll," just as she had pre-dicted almost a decade earlier to her friend at the State Street appliance store in Chicago's Loop.

Moving around the country in large touring sedans and aboard fast trains in first-class compartments, Franklin and Imogene were rumored to have trav-eled to South Florida, far away from suspicious minds in Ohio. While in the Sunshine State, they stayed at a rotating series of fashionable resorts and spas. Among the elite patrons, the couple kept far away from any of George's busi-ness associates or potential scrutiny from private detectives he could have hired to tail them.

A main destination for Franklin and Imogene was Hialeah, a 1920s boom-town chiefly built for its wealthy clientele to enjoy the Florida sunlight. It was also the home of the Hialeah Park Race Track, which had just opened in 1925, catering to the rich with its sixteenth-century French Mediterranean architecture and thoroughbred horse racing on a one-mile dirt track. The park also featured a dance hall and a rollercoaster. Since the track sat near the Florida Everglades, it had a designated snake catcher who brokered the peace between horses, spectators, and reptiles by fishing the latter out of the infield lake each day.

Imogene and Franklin invested an untold amount of George's liquor money in the hotel on the property. Allegedly, they also had many of Remus's art pieces and statuary shipped to Miami to decorate the resort.

At Hialeah, Franklin and Imogene could sunbathe in privacy. The establish-ment was renowned for its discretion—at the right price. Imogene never lacked in that department.

Prior to his release from prison and the lead-up to the Jack Daniel's whiskey siphoning trial, George did everything in his power—as diminished as he had become in Atlanta—to convince himself that the mountains and mountains of rumors he heard about his wife and Dodge just couldn't be true. According to George Conners, he continued to deny it to himself right up to his final days in the federal pen.

Remus "had a statement prepared to give to the press, stating how happy he was to be released and to be with his loving wife and daughter," the chief lieutenant offered.

When Remus and his top man returned to the Price Hill mansion, however, "the house was stripped."

When he began connecting events with what he thought might have transpired, Remus established that Franklin and Imogene had begun their affair within two months of his sentence, which had begun on January 24, 1924. His legal team uncovered documentation that revealed Franklin and Imogene had an ongoing business partnership as early as January 9, 1925, while Dodge was still employed in the Prohibition Bureau. At that time, Dodge had helped negotiate the sale of whiskey certificates to Cleveland boxing promoter Matt J. Hinkel at the Hollenden Hotel.

In October 1925, George had countered Imogene's divorce suit with one of his own. The spectacular charges against his wife—that Imogene engaged in "misconduct" with Dodge—resulted in a series of shocking headlines in newspapers across the country. George took his report public, claiming that the improper relationship took place in Chicago, Cleveland, Atlanta, and other cities while he served out his jail sentence. For several weeks prior to the public announcement, Remus had an investigator in Atlanta digging into the background of the case and establishing Dodge's role.

George claimed that Dodge used his influence with officials in the federal government to keep him "held in prison under exorbitant bond." That way, the bootlegger said, Franklin and Imogene could "obtain and keep possession of monies, securities, and other valuable property belonging to him."

One report noted that George accused Franklin "of having conspired with Mrs. Remus to railroad him to prison in order that they might live off his fortune."

What launched George into bouts of rage was hearing about Imogene's escapades from his network of spies and informants. During the Jack Daniel's trial in Indianapolis, he found out that his wife and Franklin "were having drinking parties two floors above" almost nightly in the hotel where he was sequestered.

Recalling how the news sent him into madness, George explained, "they were feelings of anger and remorse, humiliation, pride," trailing off as he remembered the anger welling up inside.

George's testimony in the Jack Daniel's trial was supposed to be a highlight of the proceedings, even though many in the courtroom wanted to hear from Imogene. On December 17, 1925, at 11:30 in the morning, Remus took the stand. He looked at Imogene and prepared to launch into an invective certain to pin her to the crime. However, just before he began, Imogene's lawyer Joseph Breitenstein objected. The attorney claimed that based on the fact that the two were still married, George was precluded from testifying against Imogene.

Not willing to risk losing the entire case on a technicality, District Attorney Albert Ward dismissed the charges against Imogene, essentially trading her freedom for a shot at jailing the other coconspirators. With this chance of putting his wife behind bars squandered, Remus continued, but deflated. His testimony raised eyebrows, particularly when he revealed that he had deposited almost three million dollars in the Lincoln National Bank in less than a year. However, he displayed few of the theatrics that observers hoped they would see.

Once again, Imogene slipped through his fingers.

Still trying to find ways to get his wife and reclaim his wealth, in March 1926, Remus hired Cleveland attorney Charles S. Reed in an attempt to counter Imogene with a new lawsuit that focused on the documents he claimed she hid, as well as all of his valuables, from stock and whiskey certificates to cash and deeds. George told the press that he would battle Imogene in a "fight to the finish" over the divorce and hundreds of thousands of dollars of whiskey certificates she still held, worth about $600,000.

The move came one week after Fiorello La Guardia called Dodge out on the floor of the House of Representatives for attempting to sell more than $200,000 worth of Remus's certificates to George W. Wallenstein in New York.

George could not shake his legal training. He relied on facts. His conscience demanded that he uncover concrete proof of Imogene's duplicity, that he take elaborate steps to catch them together. The criminal underworld had its own informal communications network filled with a mix of rumor, fact, gossip, and innuendo.

Unfortunately, his darkest days still lay ahead.

On July 1, 1926, George ran out of appeals and luck. After barely surviving the hellhole in Atlanta, he was headed back to jail to serve a 12-month stint in the Montgomery County Prison in Dayton, Ohio.

Caged.

Once again, Assistant Attorney General Mabel Willebrandt had thwarted him. Her promises of freedom in exchange for information and testimony meant nothing. Knowing that George had the public nuisance charge hanging over him gave Willebrandt power, which she used to manipulate him. Her innuendos were all Remus had to bank on, but in the end, she turned on him.

Several months earlier, he had his legal team argue before the Court of Appeals in Cincinnati that he had served the two sentences concurrently. Judge Smith Hickenlooper would not accept George's plea. The failure meant that he would serve out the one-year sentence, although none of his lieutenants were required to serve it.

Remus had one last shot. He took the argument to the United States Supreme Court. However, his application to present the case was denied by the justices, in no small part due to Mabel's relentless intervention.

"I have had quite a number of interviews with Mrs. Willebrandt," George explained. "When I make the statement that she is directly responsible for I doing that additional year, I know it."

Remus also pointed the finger at Franklin, claiming, "It was through his activities that I was not released with the others." According to the bootlegger, as Willebrandt's "trusted agent," Dodge exerted his influence to ensure that George would stay locked up.

"She gave Franklin Dodge a letter saying he was a good government representative," Remus explained.

Dodge perceived the Willebrandt seal of approval as a kind of immunity card. He used it to work angles with lower-ranking officials in the prison system and to later negotiate to sell Remus's liquor certificates.

Mabel, however, had an even more direct route to keep Remus behind bars. According to the bootlegger, Willebrandt took his "case to the president." The results, in his mind, were obvious: "She was responsible for my additional years in prison." President Coolidge could not afford the additional negative publicity he might receive if a criminal mastermind of Remus's stature were allowed to go free.

Remus did not need much prodding to see a conspiracy to keep him locked up. No matter the number of appeals or the information he gave the Prohibition Bureau, the public nuisance sentence remained.

Why had Mabel kept him dangling? The media attention his case attracted may have played a role. Willebrandt's name repeatedly showed up in newspaper stories about sending Remus back to prison, certainly boosting her public image, as well as the image of federal efforts to curb bootlegging. President Coolidge also had a reputation to manage. Remus was the "bootleg king" and the assistant attorney general wanted him to pay the full price for his transgressions.

13

Plundering the Bourbon Empire

The move from federal penitentiary to county lockup made incarceration no easier. The closed-off, tiny cell that Remus would call home starting in July 1926 caused mental anguish that harkened back to the darkest days at Big A.

"I was at the Troy jail for nine months and I never saw the street or anything," Remus said. "No windows in the walls, the place is an old army thing, and I didn't see anyone but the prisoners for months and months and months."

A new volley of legal challenges exacerbated the trauma caused by the physical conditions. In August, officials in the Department of Labor announced that they had issued a warrant for George's arrest on grounds of "moral turpitude." The charge was the first step in an attempt to deport him.

Realizing that Imogene had destroyed or hidden all his valuable documents while he served in Atlanta, Remus figured that she and Franklin had to be at the root of the charge. Without proof of naturalization, which Imogene threw out, George would have little chance to prove he was an American citizen.

"The only time I saw the street was when the deportation proceedings were on," Remus said. "That was to deport me to Germany after she and Dodge had gone down to Atlanta to urge that stuff on."

Based on the rough treatment in the tiny Miami County Jail, George's legal team lobbied to get him transferred to a different location. He claimed that jail officials had discriminated against him, a charge that Judge Hickenlooper in Cincinnati and federal officials took seriously.

"I was transferred to Portsmouth on account of the way they treated me there."

In Portsmouth, an even smaller facility, Remus found more humane treatment. He shared a desk with the local sheriff to work on legal proceedings. And, when he was with the other inmates, George did his share of typical prison duties, such as peeling potatoes and washing dishes.

The new environment was better for Remus, but he later admitted that the conditions were still often as vile as he had faced at other institutions. The small space was overfilled with sweaty, rotten men.

Although he had a little less than a month left in prison, Remus continued to face threats from the outside. Franklin and Imogene used every dirty trick they could to make his stay more difficult.

The couple wrote anonymous letters to the sheriff at Portsmouth warning him that Remus "is trying to cause you trouble, same as he does wherever he goes." In case the official needed further proof, they pinned ex-Atlanta warden Albert Sartain's ultimate demise on George based on his "lying testimony."

Remus, the letter claimed, was a "lying, squealing rat…He has sent more people to the penitentiary than most judges."

Even more revealing, the letter brought to light George's mysterious role in the August 20, 1923, murder of Brookville, Indiana, sheriff William Van Camp, who died in a gunfight with rumrunners. The writer claimed that Remus had seen the homicide and had even ordered his thugs to dump the body in the nearby woods. Some people even believed that George pulled the trigger himself.

Remus, the letter said, "has committed everything from murder down, bribery, arson, highjack liquor; nothing he has missed; don't let him catch you asleep."

As George's countdown to freedom grew closer, only four days until his release, Conners arrived with terrible news. His Chicago spies reported that Imogene and Dodge had accosted Romola, George's 27-year-old daughter from his first marriage, at her apartment in the Windy City. Probably tipped off by Imogene, the media then followed up on the story, clarifying that Imogene had a court order allowing her to take $10,000 worth of furnishings and artwork that she claimed had been stolen from her during George's months of freedom.

"Dodge met them out there with Mrs. Remus's automobile," Conners told his boss. "Dodge got into the car and had two or three gunmen with him."

"My God," Remus exclaimed. "If I just had a chance, but everything they are doing, they are doing when I am behind the bars."

Remus worried about how his daughter coped with the stress, and the intensified anxiety rapidly deteriorated his health. Conners remembered that after talking about the rough business in Chicago, George fell ill for two or three hours, nearly comatose, barely able to move or speak.

Later, George claimed that Franklin and Imogene accosting Romola was the clincher for him. He considered the news the "first actual knowledge of the adulterous practices."

"Up to that time I wouldn't believe it. I couldn't believe it," he confessed. "That was the first absolute, definite, real knowledge—lawyerlike knowledge—that I had."

Finally understanding that Dodge had stolen Imogene's heart hurt George's pride, but what had happened with Romola also added to his dire financial straits. Although he would later boast that he had more than enough money to last him the rest of his life, the $10,000 in goods they took from his daughter would have provided Remus with a bit of breathing space. Attorney fees and rental charges from his stored bourbon had been piling up.

Unlike the end of his stint in Atlanta, authorities in Portsmouth granted him some small favors. Remus paid for three gourmet meals for the fifty-six prisoners held there. The final feast took place just hours before George's release. Treating it as a grand affair, the defrocked bootleg baron donned a white uniform and served the inmates by hand. He wanted to give them one last gift before leaving the institution.

The continuing Remus saga remained a newspaper staple, so his impending release instigated a series of new interviews. Most reports were run-of-the-mill, the same "what's next" questioning that Remus had been answering for years. Some reporters noticed, however, that the great bootleg king had changed as a result of his three-year stint behind bars. They had heard wild rumors about how he acted while incarcerated. Remus's sanity seemed in direct correlation to the disturbing stories he heard about Imogene and Franklin dismantling his bourbon empire. Each new revelation seemed to make him more unhinged.

A story circulated that he once banged his head off the cell wall over and over again, barely pausing at the self-inflicted pain.

"The only mark prison has left is the destruction of his continuity of thought," contended journalist Charles Swafford. "His conversation rambles."

Then Swafford revealed George's worst nightmare, the bootleg king's being "haunted by a secret fear that his punishment and troubles have affected his intellect."

Speaking to a reporter the night of his release, George claimed that he had offers to write a book about his experience in prison. He had also been approached by contacts in Hollywood to turn his story into a film. Yet, he lamented the years spent behind bars.

"It isn't worth the price," he exclaimed, when the topic turned to what he thought about the wasted years. "There is nothing better in life than freedom."

He also asserted that bootlegging was in his past. When pressed on whether he would reenter, he shrugged the answer off with a sarcastic, "What for?"

Incarceration ended for Remus at one minute past midnight on April 26, 1927. George Conners met his boss outside the Portsmouth facility. They sped off toward the shimmering lights of the Queen City and the Dream Palace in Price Hill, some 100 miles west. First, however, they would have breakfast with members of the Remus gang at Conners's house at 3801 Llewellyn Avenue—to hash out plans for reviving what was left of the empire and plot a way to get back at Imogene and Franklin.

* * *

"Well, I'll take care of him," Imogene said as she slammed down the phone.

The noise startled the two companions sitting near her in the cramped Rogers Park apartment, sisters Edna Heicher and Olive Long.

Edna and Olive had reconnected with Imogene when she returned to Chicago. While they were used to her frequent outbursts and loud talk, this time they looked away. Neither woman wanted to take on the brunt of her anger.

"While the big boob was in Atlanta, he gave me power of attorney," Imogene told her friends. "Absolute power over all of his property. I have all of it. He'll never get one cent."

In the years since she had married George, Imogene often visited the sisters at Edna's tiny place only a handful of blocks away from Lake Michigan in the northern Chicago suburbs. The Windy City remained Imogene's home away from home. When she fled to her old friends in the early days, she did so to escape the pressures of Cincinnati. George's illegal bourbon empire caused tremendous strain on the couple, even before Franklin Dodge had entered the picture.

Now that she and Franklin had dismantled the marriage and the empire, and now that George was about to be released from the lockup in Portsmouth, Imogene had to act quickly.

She pulled out a square black bag that she always had handy. Olive peered inside and gasped. The satchel was filled with jewelry, unset stones, money, and bank securities.

Olive and her sister overheard Imogene on the telephone with her mother, who had dialed in from Cincinnati. Her mother reported that George had just been released from the county jail in Portsmouth, Ohio, and had subsequently broken into the mansion.

"I'll get him, he can't put anything like that over on me. He's crazy," Imogene announced.

She plotted her next move, telling Edna and Olive, "His father died in an asylum. His brother is in an asylum. I'll send him to jail or have him deported."

Looking directly at her friends, Imogene then professed her true intent: "Or else I'll kill him and plead self-defense. I got him right where I want him."

Then, as if forgetting all about the murder plot she just hatched, Imogene quickly picked up the receiver and asked the operator to place a long distance call. "I want to talk to Franklin Dodge of Lansing," she exclaimed. She hung up and waited for the connection.

Imogene revealed how she had taken control of the bootlegging empire, explaining to Olive and Edna how George's transfer of power of attorney allowed her to gain control of the whiskey certificates.

"He's wise now," she said, trembling with the thought of what her estranged husband might do in retaliation now that he was free. Imogene, though, had Franklin to protect her, so she would not cower before Remus, saying, "Before he knows it he'll either find himself back in jail for the rest of his life or we'll deport him!"

When the phone rang, Imogene snatched it up, telling the person on the other end of the line that she wanted to talk to "Franklin Dodge Junior." She turned to Olive and said that it had been his father, Frank Senior, that had called her back.

When the son came to the phone, Imogene went into pleading mode. "Franklin, dear, he's out and in Cincinnati and has broken into the place. I think you ought to do something about it immediately." Then she thought, "I think he's going to Washington, and I wish you would go right down there and see Mabel Willebrandt." Then a glimpse of fear crept in. Imogene explained, "You ought to get down there before he does, dear, and offset anything he might do."

Franklin agreed to book passage on the midnight train from Lansing to Washington. Imogene smiled then, and asked her lover: "Do you love me, dear? Well, how much? Tell me again."

Then, without hesitation, Imogene put the phone up to Olive's ear. "You know I love you, dear," Franklin said.

Imogene then pulled the receiver away, happy that Dodge had followed her instructions. She hung up, beaming.

"I love Dodge and when Remus finds it out he'll be wild, but it won't do him any good, because he'll either be in jail or out of the country, or penniless," Imogene confessed to her friends.

Since that fateful meeting at the penitentiary in Atlanta where Imogene first laid eyes on Franklin, the Prohi had become the center of her universe. She even admitted to her Evanston friends that she had gone as far as to change all the monogrammed silver that George had purchased for her from the "R" in "Remus" to the "D" for "Dodge."

Imogene even gave Franklin one of Remus's treasured diamond stickpins, which he now wore as a sign of his feelings toward her. George had given these valued diamonds to the men who attended their roaring New Year's Eve parties and other special occasions.

Then there were the cars. Expensive cars. Imogene bought her lover a Packard roadster, detailed with his "F. D." initials, and a Pierce Arrow. The second vehicle cost $6,300, remembered Pierce Arrow Motor Company sales manager Fred C. Wendell. Avoiding public scrutiny that could lead to possible charges of violating the white slavery act, the woman who purchased it told Wendell that her name was "Mrs. Julia M. Brown." Years later, scanning a photo of Imogene, the sales manager identified her as the mysterious "Mrs. Brown." He also knew Franklin Dodge, who accompanied her on the shopping spree one day in April 1927.

Imogene kept George from returning to the Dream Palace in Price Hill by filing a restraining order against him. Although he loved the mansion, he found staying away only a minor frustration. He returned to his old haunt, a large suite at the Sinton Hotel downtown. There he could conduct business meetings with George Conners, Blanche Watson, and others as they attempted to pull together what was left of the bourbon kingdom. A nuisance, little more.

What angered Remus was finding that Franklin Dodge and Imogene had lived in his home while he had rotted away in jail.

"I had been made aware of the fact that Dodge had been a tenant at my home, slept in my bedroom, for days and weeks, spent my money," George sputtered.

He vented his frustrations to Conners, who dutifully listened, and then attempted to calm his boss down. He had seen too many fits of rage and incoherence since Remus returned to Cincinnati. Each incident had been unleashed when they spoke about Franklin and Imogene's transgressions. Remus had a litany of ills that had been done to him by his wife and her "heavy lover." He repeated them over and over.

"They were the direct cause of seeing that I was placed in solitary confinement," George continued.

"They were hobnobbing at the Ainslee Hotel and the Biltmore, loosely, with my money. They took every bit of jewelry I had, and I had about $20,000 worth of jewelry, and my watch, cuff buttons, etcetera."

When the rant fixed on what Remus had found at the mansion, he choked out his words, as if the air had left the room, even falling to his knees and sobbing uncontrollably.

"My God, aren't they going to leave anything for me? They are taking everything and leaving me nothing," he had moaned, seeing the utter destruction.

Every stick of furniture and all his art and antiquities were gone, including his prized George Washington collection.

"Ravaged and robbed," he exclaimed.

In addition to the fine art, statuary, and books for the mansion, Remus had purchased several historical artifacts, including a document signed by the nation's first president and Founding Father for $3,800. He treasured that piece and hoped to donate it someday to the Cincinnati Art Museum or a local historical society. He also had an autograph of Abraham Lincoln and an authenticated lock of Benedict Arnold's hair.

More importantly for George's immediate future, Imogene and Franklin had also cleaned out or destroyed all of his personal and financial records. Without the necessary documents, including stock certificates and records of money owed to him, the bourbon king had no means of authenticating ownership of the remaining pieces of his crumbling empire.

George focused his ire on Franklin Dodge, who he believed had duped his wife. Imogene, in his mind, was clearly a woman who could be easily deceived.

"The thing that shakes him and stings him and sends him into berserker rages is the mention of his wife's defection. It has become an obsession with him," an investigative reporter wrote.

Seeing the state of his home and realizing the totality of the treachery, Remus determined that he "already hated [Dodge] with all the vigor of his forthright nature."

George's hatred and disgust seemed to observers to be getting the best of him. *Cincinnati Post* sketch artist Manuel Rosenberg visited Remus after he returned from the Ohio jail in Portsmouth. He noted the bootleg baron's odd behavior as they nervously surveyed what was left of the home and its furnishings.

"Every time he came to an empty room Remus sang in a peculiar manner," the journalist related. "He was peculiar in his actions whenever his wife or Dodge were mentioned."

As the two walked around the mansion, Remus complained endlessly. He lost his cool when William Mueller, the mansion caretaker, joined them. He screamed at the man whose sole purpose was to guard the house.

Later, when they walked to the immaculate, Rookwood tile-lined swimming pool, George shrugged and exclaimed, "Well, at least she left me that." He continued singing in an exaggerated tone.

When asked about Remus's mental condition at the time they toured the grounds, Rosenberg admitted that he thought the man "was a little off on that one subject."

George could not comprehend the level of deception. Although he had made countless millions breaking the law, he felt some topics, like a person's word or the sanctity of their home, were above reproach.

"She took everything out of there," George exclaimed. "She even took some of the valuable doors off the hinges and took them away."

There was simply nothing left.

•   •   •

After two years chasing down Remus's lost fortune, paying Imogene's delinquent bills, and searching for ways to delay the divorce proceedings, any meeting between George and Imogene required loaded weapons, bodyguards, and witnesses.

According to Conners, Imogene came to the Price Hill mansion in the summer of 1927 to determine a cash settlement that would allow the couple to split as amicably as possible. Despite having been the one who'd stripped the lavish home bare with Franklin Dodge, Imogene came in fuming and lashed out at Conners, Remus, and George's secretary Blanche Watson.

"What are you people doing here? This is my house," she barked.

"Of course it is," Remus spoke up. "You can stay here if you want to. I'll go to a hotel if you don't want me here."

"I'll settle this!" Imogene screamed.

She looked down, opened her purse, and fished around for a moment. Conners saw a flash of steel in the satchel. He knew that she kept a pearl-handled pistol tucked into the lining.

Before she could take hold of the weapon, Conners grabbed her arm and kept her fingers from the smooth grip. Enraged, she continued screaming.

She stormed out of the house without a settlement. No one was injured.

How long had it been going on, George wondered? He looked down at the stack of invoices piled up on his desk. Carpenters and furniture makers, service providers, and bills from practically every high-end retailer in the Cincinnati. All these unmet obligations, he thought.

She'd had access to at least $715,000 in cash when George had left for Atlanta.

Only one answer made sense—Imogene had been stealing from him. She hid the money away in secret bank accounts. It must have commenced as soon as they arrived in the Queen City from Chicago.

Once, while Remus sat in prison, Imogene demanded that Orin Weber, one of the mansion caretakers, drive her to Charlotte, Michigan, with a pillowcase she had stuffed full of valuables. When he later told Remus, Weber recalled, his boss "got red in the face and his eyes bulged out."

"I told him she had four guns and wanted to get him," Weber continued, upping the ante from robbery to a more life-threatening situation. "Remus walked around the room, shaking his head. He was kind of wild. He was mad."

Astonished at what Weber told him, Remus looked down at the bill for his magnificent pool. That wonderful safe haven, the hours that he had spent soaking there in pure joy—Ben Shaffer and his men had built it exactly as Remus instructed and then his wife had dodged the bill. He had instructed Imogene to take care of it. How could that still be due? Hadn't she paid the man?

"When I found out that she had not taken care of those notes, after I had given her the money, I was peeved," George recalled.

Rather than admit that his wife had pocketed the money, Remus staged an argument with Shaffer. "I didn't tell him that I had given [Imogene] the money to pay them because I didn't want that additional humiliation and embarrassment," George admitted.

His wife had pulled similar cons all over town. She evaded bills and bill collectors, while stashing away money. Shaffer sued, claiming that Remus still owed him $20,000 for the famous pool.

So much now came to light. The magnitude of the betrayal was tremendous.

Conners showed Remus copies of contracts revealing that Imogene was paying Dodge and some outside liquor brokers to sell off whiskey certificates that covered 4,085 cases of bourbon in storage at the H. E. Pogue distillery in Maysville, Kentucky. Other documents Conners had were forged in Remus's name, which may have been a crime to him, but didn't matter to the various buyers.

Remus claimed that Dodge had brainwashed Imogene and forced her to turn against him. He was after the money and swooped off her feet to get at the fortune. The two, the bootleg king argued, had conspired to "frame me behind my back."

Given Franklin's deep knowledge of the bootlegging business, he knew that the whiskey certificates alone could have jumpstarted Remus's vast network. Coming out of jail, George needed cash to resuscitate his illicit operations, but stripping the house and razing the proof left the ex-con in a state of collapse.

When rumors that Dodge was attempting to sell whiskey certificates to various known bootleggers and operatives got back to Willebrandt in DC, she let it be known that he risked too much to continue. Each day it seemed as if papers reported on how some lowdown Prohi had betrayed the public's trust. She could not have her ace fall from grace.

Ultimately, Cleveland fight promoter Matt J. Hinkel ended up with the Pogue certificates, which Remus claimed would bring in about $300,000. Dodge negotiated the deal with Joseph Breitenstein, Imogene's attorney, and Hinkel's lawyers. Dodge received a broker's fee as part of the arrangement. When Breitenstein heard about George's plans to thwart the sale, he came out firing in the press: "Let him file all the suits he will. I've whipped [him] in every one so far."

Instead, Remus took to the road. He stormed down to Maysville, Kentucky, the home of the Pogue Distillery, one of the oldest in America, and one that had always been central to his operations. He claimed ownership of the 3,000 barrels of bourbon in the distillery's large riverfront warehouses.

As George and his men pulled up to the gates, they were met by federal officials who had a restraining order. The document prevented the bootleggers from taking the bourbon. Someone at the distillery or one of the Prohibition enforcement officials had probably tipped off Franklin, Imogene, or Hinkel, who was able to get a judge to issue the injunction.

While the legal fight continued to play out in courtrooms and judge's chambers across the Midwest, Breitenstein battled to keep public perception about Imogene and Franklin positive.

"I want to keep the record straight about Franklin Dodge," the lawyer told newspapers. "He was one of the best agents the Department of Justice ever had."

For his part, Dodge remained steadfast in denying George's accusations. He said that his relationship with Imogene was platonic—a business partnership. Remus, he countered, was simply out for revenge because the former star undercover Prohi detective had been the one responsible for putting him behind bars.

In response to George's charges against them, Franklin and Imogene went to Atlanta to interview witnesses and take testimony that would refute his claims. They were attempting to make the divorce case ironclad, not only through depositions with corroborators, but by hiring undercover detectives in hopes of catching George with another woman.

The years of wealth and living like an aristocrat made Imogene think she was above reproach, but she was still bound to George and the failed marriage in an era that demanded a wife remain subservient. On May 11, 1927, detectives in Cincinnati arrested Imogene on a warrant from Portsmouth, Ohio. Officers detained her for obtaining money under false pretenses, related to the certificate sales.

Franklin also faced charges, but was not arrested because he was not with her in Cincinnati at the time. Wholesale dealer Frank Brahm charged them with obtaining $1,750 from him for the sale of 100 barrels of bonded liquor. Documentation, however, revealed that George still owned the certificates.

According to a reporter on the scene, "She also telephoned Dodge's father and advised him to notify Dodge to surrender."

At the proceedings, Imogene told Judge Chester R. Shook that the false charges were "her husband's ways of annoying her."

Detective Chief Emmet D. Kirgan suggested that Imogene go to the sheriff's office to finish the proceedings.

"Mrs. Remus, who appeared to be somewhat perturbed throughout the proceedings, started to protest and then suddenly broke into tears," said one writer. "For several minutes she sat in the courtroom, dabbling at her eyes with a handkerchief."

"This is terrible—the disgrace of being arrested for something you did not do," she exclaimed.

Within two weeks, Cincinnati police detectives released Imogene from the warrant because Sheriff Elzey Canter of Scioto County failed to appear in court with the original warrant or subsequent dismissal order. The sales were real, but the charges against Franklin and Imogene were fabricated.

"Somebody is going to get hurt," reporter John Rogers told Imogene. Rogers had become friends with Remus and had heard too many stories of competing hit contracts.

"I'm sure Daddy won't hurt me," Imogene shrugged. "He's very kind to me." But, she then added, "Don't let him hurt Mr. Dodge."

"He is a craven coward. But he will not live long," Remus announced to the press, when they asked him about Dodge.

A Chicago news story provided details about Remus stalking Franklin and Imogene. On September 22, 1927, Remus missed a chance to kill the couple in the Windy City at the Dempsey-Tunney fight.

Remus later told the paper that he missed them by 35 seconds. Hearing this account, Dodge's father claimed that his family had been on a vacation in Pelham, New York, a Long Island suburb, where his nephew William H. Dodge lived. Frank Dodge even produced itineraries and trip details, along with postmarked postcards the family had sent to Franklin's brother Wyllis as they traveled.

Dodge started his own publicity campaign, maintaining his innocence. Franklin outlined a different narrative.

As a federal agent, he had worked with Mary Hubbard, who lived on a farm neighboring Death Valley. She came to Franklin offering aid in incriminating Remus. Her husband, who worked for the bootleg baron, had died mysteriously. Hubbard suspected that Remus had him poisoned to prevent him from turning state's evidence.

Franklin claimed that he first met Imogene on January 15, 1925, when Remus had been in the Atlanta pen for about a year. Dodge went there in an undercover role on the order from his boss Mabel Walker Willebrandt. The extent of the corruption at the jail had recently been exposed, resulting in Remus and some of the other high-profile criminals being moved to a county facility.

When he met her, Franklin said, Imogene scrubbed George's jail cell and prepared his food, "all that she could for the comfort of her husband."

"To my knowledge, [she] has always acted as a perfect lady," he said.

Franklin admitted that Imogene wrote to him after their initial meeting. She hoped that Dodge would help her free Remus. Later, however, Dodge claimed that he met with Imogene's lawyers in St. Louis and New York "in behalf of Mrs. Remus," but that the attorneys paid his expenses, not Imogene.

He reiterated that the few times he had seen her were "all in connection with official business."

Franklin also said that contrary to common belief, Remus was "broke" when he went to prison. His investigation in Cincinnati uncovered that George had made about $3 million in revenue, but had little to show for it.

"Mrs. Remus had a little money, I realize, but I do not know where she got it," he said. "Remus was a poor man when he went to prison."

*　*　*

George's manic and hysterical behavior startled his close associates, including Conners. It seemed as if any mention of Imogene or money led to a rant so furious that people began to question Remus's sanity. Judge Oppenheimer, a formidable legal scholar who had taken up private practice, concluded that he could not represent Remus in his impending divorce case. He simply could not control Remus and feared that his outlandish outbursts would turn the sitting judge against them.

Once word about Remus's behavior traveled through the Queen City legal community, he could not find another attorney. Some were scared off when they heard rumors that multiple hits had been placed on the bootleg king. No one wanted to risk their own life by getting caught in a gangland crossfire.

Given these challenges, George decided to represent himself as legal counsel in the divorce case. Before Oppenheimer stepped down, his legal team, according to George's estimate, had accumulated fifty-one depositions that proved the adultery between Imogene and Franklin. They had a slew of witnesses willing to appear in person as well.

A reporter who interviewed Remus as he prepared to leave Portsmouth claimed that the bootlegger "glares vindictively" and "curses bitterly" when mentioning Imogene. The years in prison, he secretly worried, had deteriorated his intellect.

Soon after he was released from Atlanta, the reports of sluggers on his trail forced him to hire bodyguards, request assistance from federal officials, and begin carrying a pistol.

"I was notified that Jew John out of Toledo had a crowd in there to go ahead and knock me off and had the outside watched at the Sinton Hotel," George said of just one assassination plot he knew about.

Everywhere he went around in Cincinnati, Newport, Hamilton, or other local areas that he formerly controlled became sites for hitmen to lay in wait.

"Wherever I would go, someone would be placed there to knock me off."

The underworld that conspired against him actually also saved his life. A boss in one city would have to clear a murder with the boss in another. Leaks occurred in those discussions.

"Mob leaders," George explained later, "interchange courtesies."

Since Remus had been helpful to many mob bosses while in the Atlanta pen, "they would let me know through someone" if they heard his name in these conversations.

When Dodge heard that Remus countered by placing a bounty on his head, he showed an onlooker his matching set of revolvers and said that he had two barrels waiting for Remus.

The battle was far from over. Everything was on the line, including the mansion, money, luxury cars, and whiskey certificates. For George—seemingly being driven closer and closer to the edge—the fight was also for his freedom, his name, and his dignity.

PART FOUR

· · · · ·

A Very Dangerous Man

14

A Shot Rings Out

Early morning sunshine and the promise of a dazzling Indian summer day. . . . Glinting off the glass, the light gave the taxi's windshield a sharp edge. On this spectacular October dawn, a cab pulled up to the Queen City's brand new Alms Hotel.

Erected just two years earlier, the ornate building had row upon row of deep red bricks lining its upper levels, while natural stonework dominated nearer the ground level. It was imposing yet welcoming, like an overgrown Swiss chalet come to life in Cincinnati's well-heeled Walnut Hills neighborhood.

Two passengers slid into the backseat of the vehicle. Imogene Remus and her daughter Ruth, who would celebrate her twentieth birthday the next day. The women—dressed head to toe in black—nodded in approval as the driver doffed his cap and held open the door. Closing it behind them, cabbie Charles Stevens navigated out of the hotel's wraparound drive. He pulled onto Victory Parkway, heading toward downtown Cincinnati where the two women would meet with Imogene's attorney.

The mood within the cab mirrored the morning glow, happy and energetic. Mother and daughter felt a sense of relief. Ruth took a letter from her purse and started reading it to Imogene. They giggled as Ruth read aloud.

Stevens stepped on the gas and the car pitched forward into traffic. His passengers had an appointment with Edward T. Dixon, former judge and currently Imogene's attorney. At his office, they would prepare for the divorce hearing scheduled later that day. Imogene was desperate to win her freedom from the "King of the Bootleggers."

George had just returned to Cincinnati as a free man five months earlier, following his year-and-a-half stint in the Atlanta Federal Penitentiary and another year in rural Ohio. Husband and wife had spent the time hurling lawsuit after lawsuit at one another.

Remus accused Imogene of adultery. His legal team attempted to have Imogene's divorce case nullified or overturned, yet his unruliness caused his lawyers to drop him as a client. He had exploded in bouts of yelling and erratic behavior when they discussed the details of the lawsuit.

Dixon had fought off each successive charge on behalf of Imogene, who stayed on the move, often well clear of Cincinnati or Ohio. She neither trusted her estranged husband nor the many Ohio police officers and law enforcement officials on his payroll.

As Imogene and Ruth rolled away from the Alms Hotel, George sat a stone's throw away, riding in the front seat of his large blue touring sedan next to George Klug, one of his henchmen. The car belonged to Remus's longtime aide and confidant George Conners. Klug had no special skills as a chauffeur; this was just the job Conners needed him to do that day. Drive the boss around town.

George had sent a messenger into the hotel in an attempt to contact his wife. He wanted to set up a meeting with her to hash out their property disputes before a judge would need to settle the matter. Both husband and wife thought the other was hiding assets.

The courier had emerged from the hotel with bad news. The front desk clerk wouldn't let him deliver the message to Imogene or even leave one for her. "No one was to be admitted, no telephone messages to be received, no messenger to be sent into the room," George recalled the man telling him. With the news, Remus moved from the front seat next to Klug to the back, where he could think for a moment.

For the next fifteen minutes, Remus and Klug sat less than a block away, anxiously waiting for signs of Imogene. Despite what the clerk said, he knew she was in there. George had spies stationed at the Alms Hotel. They had been paid for information, reporting directly to Remus that Imogene had been spotted several days in a row having breakfast with Franklin Dodge, right in public view.

"I waited for them," George would recall, expecting the couple to appear at any moment.

And then George saw his estranged wife walk out of the building with his adopted daughter, not Dodge. His anger grew, he recalled later, particularly after he "saw her laughing and joking as she left."

Mother and daughter ducked into a waiting cab.

The bootleg baron lurched forward in his seat, eyeing his wife, and grew consumed with anger. He screamed at Klug to follow them. "Run them down if you have to," Remus roared at the driver. George had to speak to Imogene before the divorce hearing.

But before they could close the half-block gap between the vehicles, the taxi pulled away.

Klug gunned the big engine, shooting southward on Victory in hot pursuit. He kept up the wild pace, weaving through the morning commuters as the parkway narrowed to become Eden Park Drive. The roadway severed Eden Park, Cincinnati's ornate urban green space on the northeast border between downtown and the growing suburbs.

"There's Remus," Imogene shouted when she recognized the commotion. Ruth, nearly frozen with fear, blurted out to Stevens, "Go ahead!"

Both cars rushed through more traffic. Klug accelerated, surging out in front of the other vehicle several hundred yards later. Remus leaned forward, grabbing the wheel and wrenching it from his driver's hands. Turning fast, he forced the smaller vehicle up onto the berm, both coming to a screeching halt.

Remus leapt from the car and moved toward the cab. Imogene yelled at Stevens to do anything to get them away from her estranged husband. The cabbie hammered through the grass in a desperate attempt to escape. George jumped back in with Klug and continued the chase, cutting the taxi off a short distance away at the foot of Mirror Lake in Eden Park. A dozen yards away, on the near shore, stood the Spring House Gazebo, a popular picnic spot for families and young lovers hoping to enjoy the green oasis and the reservoir pond. Children played in the shallow basin while mothers stood together and gossiped.

Shrieks of panic cut through the air when the sounds of roaring engines, squealing brakes, and twisted metal shattered the scene. A line of cars ground to a standstill, some blasting into the ones that stopped short just ahead of them. For morning commuters, the day had just turned into a nightmare.

Both women moved toward the car door. Ruth tried to get out and run, but her mother grabbed her and pushed her back in. Imogene escaped from the taxi on foot. Remus, already out and moving toward her, chased her a short distance, eventually seizing her right wrist. Imogene could not break free from the powerful grip. She twisted her arm and kicked at her husband. George held tight, screaming obscenities at Imogene and then smashing his fist into her face. Onlookers froze in fear.

Remus wrenched Imogene close to his body, as if they were caught in a timeless photograph of a loving couple on the ballroom dance floor. In the rush of madness, George had drawn a pistol from his coat pocket.

Imogene pleaded, "Oh, don't hurt me, Daddy, you know I love you! Don't do it, don't do it!"

She begged for her life.

"You degenerate mass of clay, take this…" he yelled, blind with rage.

George pressed the small pistol against his wife's belly and fired. A single shot blew a hole in Imogene's abdomen. He gripped her waist tightly and continued shouting.

Bystanders watching the horrific scene could not hear what he said, but he raged on. Feeling Imogene go limp, George then dropped her to the ground.

"It made me sick, but I looked her straight in the eye," George confessed. "I was as cool as I will ever be. Then, I pulled her against me and let her have the gun."

Klug, Remus's driver and bodyguard, had heard the gunshot. Looking left and right, he panicked. There were always thugs and hijackers around. Were they after the car? He did not wait to find out. Klug sped off in the sedan.

Meanwhile, Imogene struggled to her feet. In a daze, she crawled back into the taxi and tried to edge through the vehicle, hoping that somehow it would provide her a means of escape through the far door.

By now, Ruth had emerged from the taxi. She hadn't seen the gun, but she had heard the shot. From only a couple feet away, she'd watched George drop her mother to the ground and heard him cursing her.

As Imogene struggled to get back into the taxi, Ruth stepped in front of George, blocking his pursuit of her mother. Then for a wild moment, the girl started beating his broad chest with her fists. Grabbing him by the lapels, Ruth yelled, "Do you realize what you are doing?"

"She can't get away with that," Remus answered flatly.

Ruth then turned back to Imogene when she heard the woman cry out. Imogene had fled into the street and screamed for someone, anyone, to help her. Her daughter chased her, following the bloody trail left in her wake.

Time must have stood still for George then. He turned away from the women, tuned out the screaming, scanned the horizon for his vehicle.

"I walked away," he said. "I continued on in a somewhat dazed condition."

Klug was gone, so George kept walking, then he began jogging away from the scene. Scores of onlookers shrunk back in horror. Drivers dashed from their cars to see what had halted their commute. Some of them saw the squat man before he disappeared into the lush trees lining Eden Park.

Imogene struggled to remain on her feet. Ruth had caught up to her and provided support. The older woman threw her hands up in the air as she stumbled into traffic, and then dropped to her knees.

"Help, I've been shot," Imogene cried out.

Evander Raulston, a bookkeeper who lived about a mile away from the crime scene, had been in his Ford well behind Remus's sedan when the bootlegger's car had raced under the stone archway that marked the entrance to Eden Park. The chaos on the street caused a backup and when the car in front of his stopped suddenly, Raulston had bumped into it.

"I started out of my machine to see what damage had been done, when I heard a shot," he explained. "Then I saw a woman lying on the ground and a man, with a pistol, over her."

Ruth helped Imogene back toward the taxi, then changed direction to a different car. The driver shook his head in fear, so they hobbled to Raulston's vehicle.

"I noticed blood on her clothes near the belt, with a smear of black," Raulston said later.

The kindhearted bystander hit the gas, weaving through the jammed cars and groups of people gathering in the park. William C. Knight, a police sergeant attempting to direct traffic, saw the speeding car coming straight toward him. Throwing up his hands, he ordered Raulston to stop, but then heard Imogene scream. The policeman jumped into the car next to Raulston. They sped the wounded woman and her teenage daughter to nearby Bethesda Hospital.

"George Remus shot me," Imogene cried out. "Take me to a hospital quickly. I'm hurt terribly."

"Why'd he do it?" Knight asked.

"Oh, I don't know, I don't know," Imogene moaned.

Imogene remained conscious as Raulston drove, sitting in the backseat before kneeling on the floor with her elbows on the seat. She told her daughter, "I know I'm dying. Isn't George terrible for doing this?"

Ruth tried to direct her attention away from the wound while comforting her. "She talked a great deal," Raulston remembered, "but in a hysterical manner. I heard her groaning and talking."

"Her clothes were all full of blood," Ruth said later. "I got blood all over me."

When they arrived at the hospital, the victim had lost consciousness. Doctors quickly prepped her for surgery. On the operating table, just before the ether took hold, Imogene blurted out: "My God, do you think I'm going to die? Oh, God, I don't want to die!"

Two hours later, Augusta Imogene Rumus died without ever regaining consciousness.

* · *

Several miles away, Remus marched into Cincinnati's District One police headquarters. He had walked away from the murder scene, been mistakenly driven to the downtown train station, and then taken a cab to the police building. He blurted out that he had killed his wife. He paced back and forth in front of the long table between him and the officers.

While there with Cincinnati detectives—and having been told that Imogene would likely die from the gunshot wound—Remus recounted the murder repeatedly. Remus had already crafted his plan. He remembered William Cheney Ellis—the poor, broken man he had saved from a death sentence more than a decade ago. He beat the executioner. He—George Remus—had devised the ultimate con.

Chief Detective Emmett D. Kirgan brought Remus back to the present, telling him, "You accomplished what you set out to do."

Calmly, with a slight hint of satisfaction, Remus shrugged and said, "She who dances down the primrose path must die on the primrose path. I'm happy. This is the first peace of mind I've had in two years."

* · *

George roared to the reporters who gathered in front of his cell: "I am sane as any man now, but at the time I fired the revolver I was insane. There is no doubt that any man is insane during the commission of a deed of that sort."

As he bellowed out to the newspapermen, Remus paced. For emphasis, George smacked his left palm with his meaty right fist. He hated the bars, feeling the dread of again being caged. But this was his courtroom now. These men would help him sell the ruse.

Reporters lined every available inch in front of Remus, catcalling the infamous bourbon baron with question after question.

"What have you to say now?" they yelled.

"What more can I say?" George barked back.

Then, regaining his composure, he looked up at the men, revealing the softness in his eyes that had won over so many juries during his days as a criminal defense attorney in Chicago.

Then, referring to the murder he had just committed, Remus said almost casually, "It is the penalty one pays for being contrary to what he owes society."

George Remus had confessed. A few days after he fired that shot, which the reporters called a "gut-wound," he proclaimed: "If it should cost me my life, I would pay the penalty rather than go on the way I have felt the last two and a half years."

Imogene and Franklin had turned him into a chump.

"This immense sum tucked away in the trust company," George sputtered, drumming his fingers loudly against the table, "filched from the Remus business."

His businesses had suffered and the legal proceedings that might have regained some of his fortune slipped away as he grew more preoccupied with the duplicity. George railed against Franklin Dodge.

"This man," he spat, "how I have had to follow them, here and there, driven by this compulsion, this sense of outrage."

Law enforcement agents might have expected Remus to be some kind of crazed maniac. However, Robert L. Dunning, the head of the Department of Criminal Identification for the Cincinnati police, saw him as "courteous, intelligent, coherent, and without regret for what he had done." In Dunning's mind, Remus was perfectly sane—dangerous, but sane.

According to Dunning, George's only remorse was not catching Imogene and Franklin together so that he could murder them both at the same time. Remus even admitted to the officers investigating the shooting that he had been following Imogene and Dodge around for about a year and a half "trying to catch them and kill them," even though he had only been out of the county lockup for about five months.

There were other factual details that Remus did not remember. George claimed that he shot Imogene three times under the gaze of that crystal blue sky. The coroner would release the death certificate in short order and the newspapers carried the truth—just one shot had ricocheted around Imogene's stomach and chest cavity, ripping everything to shreds.

Hamilton County Coroner F. C. Swing and Dr. D. C. Handley released the details of the autopsy report the next day. Imogene had no chance of surviving the bullet wound, the coroners agreed. The projectile had entered her abdomen, but then tore through her liver, spleen, and stomach. Each wound on its own "would have been fatal," according to Swing.

Despite what Remus had said earlier to Dunning and Cincinnati detectives, he changed his tune once he stood in front of the judge. In a brief arraignment hearing on October 7, 1927, which lasted only a handful of minutes, Remus pleaded "not guilty" and asked that his case be adjudicated before the grand jury as soon as possible.

George also declared: "Remus will defend himself!"

For the outside world looking in, the theatrics had already begun. George, the master legal tactician, simply had to launch the attack. These fireworks would be followed with repeated volleys directed through the media, just like the old days in Chicago.

"I'm going to put the whole case to a jury on its merits and let my peers decide my fate," Remus declared.

Remus's friends and allies played a significant role in setting the tone. They hung from the rafters, packing Judge William D. Alexander's courtroom to capacity. Instead of being shunned, the bootleg baron took on an air of respected benefactor, as if the congregation were gathered around for a church service or Sunday picnic.

All these spectators, George certainly implied, would not give such overwhelming encouragement to a murderer.

Remus played a fine victim.

George looked the part of a patrician, dressed in a sharply cut gray suit and topped with an ever-present smile. There would be no contrition from Remus. It was a peculiar pose for a man undeniably guilty of murdering his wife.

A journalist who watched the short proceedings said that George "appeared as if ready for a day of pleasure." The night in jail "brought no change in the air of confidence, almost of satisfaction, which has marked Remus since he shot and fatally wounded Mrs. Remus."

Now, he turned his efforts to playing the victim to the world. And the world would be reading about it in the days ahead. This story was hot.

As he left the courtroom under armed guard, George paused to greet visitors who swarmed around him. Shaking hands with supporters, he took on the sunny disposition that marked his days as a trial attorney. Without hesitation, he also chatted with reporters from the city's daily newspapers, divulging that he had suffered extreme anxiety in the role as both scorned husband and defender of his home. Batting his lashes and speaking calmly, he looked each reporter in the eyes, wondering aloud if any man could make it through such "extremely trying circumstances."

Planning to draw out all the details of an already sensational event, reporters dug for more information about the murder. George, always ready to comply with the media to manipulate the narrative, gave them what they needed.

When a reporter declared to George that the murder placed him at the center of a "bad mess," Remus had an answer—and an opponent—ready at hand, his nemesis Franklin Dodge, the man he accused of stealing both his wife and his fortune.

"Do you think I am going to let Dodge get away with that sort of thing forever?" Remus asked, letting the weight of the betrayal set in.

"I tell you it was a matter of principle. I am a man of principle, despite what people say about me."

"I cannot stand for the sort of thing this man and Mrs. Remus have been carrying on for a long time." The disgust rang out in his voice.

The newsmen asked the question on everyone's mind: "Where'd ya get the gun George, why'd ya have the gun?"

"I found the revolver in the garage at home."

"Mrs. Remus forgot to take the little pearl-handled revolver when she removed everything from our home except a cot, table, and chair."

With an air of finality, he proclaimed:

Plead insanity? Certainly not! Did I do an insane deed? Nothing of the kind. What would you have done had your wife been unfaithful and wasted your fortune with her lover? She who dances down the primrose path must die on the primrose path. I am happy. The unwritten law will free me. I did a duty I owed society.

Given the limited time between the murder and Remus's turning himself in, there is little chance that he could have contacted his daughter Romola, then living near Lillian in Chicago. However, Conners or Blanche Watson probably requested that she speed to Cincinnati as soon as possible, since they greeted her at the jail when she arrived from the Windy City.

Remus needed props to win this case.

Romola, a stunning, 23-year-old beauty with raven-black hair sporting the latest flapper style and batting her dark eyes, stood by her father's side and spoke with eager reporters.

"I'm here to help my father. I don't know anything about the case. It's such a terrible mess," she explained in her most melodious voice. The years of musical training were now paying off.

The young woman pledged her support, saying, "I'm going to stand by him. I'm all he has. I'm so sorry for him."

The reporters covering the story ate it up. Newspapers ran large photographs of the young beauty. They were immediately sympathetic to the girl. She looked typecast from Hollywood, as if a story about young love in the pages of a magazine came to life.

Sensing their sympathy, George played along.

"It's hard on her," he explained, dragging out each word and appearing repentant. "That's the only thing I hate about the whole mess—the notoriety for her."

When the papers tracked down George's first wife Lillian in Chicago, she was strident in defending her ex-husband. More props in George's fight for his life.

"I hardly can believe he has shot her," she said. "But if he did it was in self-defense. She made his life so miserable he was driven to it."

Lillian then provided the outline of the public plea, explaining, "She made him a pauper. Again and again she threatened his life." Finally, summing up, she told reporters, "George Remus wouldn't hurt a fly."

Despite her own checkered past with George, Lillian revealed that Imogene always carried a pistol, even in her younger years in Chicago when she and George were still married.

"Pursued him night and day, and she carried a gun," George's ex-wife told the papers.

Lillian asserted that when George tried to break off the relationship with Imogene and rekindle his marriage, he was "obliged to warn her to keep away from his home and office."

Remus and his supporters continued to vilify Imogene, making a sport of publicly shaming her. In contrast, no one rose up to speak for the dead woman. Franklin Dodge was nowhere to be seen. Her daughter Ruth, traumatized by what she had seen, was in hiding at the Alms Hotel with Imogene's older sister Grace.

"I will ask the death penalty for George Remus."

The words hardly left the mouth of prosecutor Charles P. Taft, II, before they were splashed in headlines nationwide.

The dashing son of William Howard Taft, former president and current Supreme Court Chief Justice, was chief prosecutor for Hamilton County, Ohio. The call for the death sentence immediately upped the stakes in the public battle for George's soul.

Taft soon found a ready ally in Ruth Holmes Remus. The young woman, who celebrated her twentieth birthday the day after losing her mother, had watched in horror as Imogene got "snuffed out" by her adoptive father.

Ruth characterized Imogene's marriage to George as "terrible years." She was "constantly filled with fear and dread" because of his "brute instincts" and "frequent fits of temper."

She recounted a time early in the marriage when George had punched Imogene in the face during an argument about renovations to the Price Hill mansion. "In a rage Remus struck mother in the nose," she remembered.

In her daughter's eyes, Imogene was a loyal and faithful wife who had endured years of beatings and verbal abuse.

The final straw, according to Ruth, was when George brutally attacked Imogene in front of Atlanta prison officials. Ruth claimed that from then on Imogene resolved to divorce her rampaging husband to escape his thrashings.

Each time Remus exploded, he would later beg for forgiveness.

"I can cite places and dates when he threw a pickle jar, a box of candy, and anything handy at my mother," Ruth explained. "The times he has struck and beaten her were without number."

Then, she said, "We actually were sorry for him and time after time forgave the cruel blows and bitter abuse he heaped on mother as well as myself."

Meanwhile, George went on a cuckolded husband offensive.

On October 17, 1927, his first appearance defending himself, he made several impassioned pleas to Judge Shook maintaining that he should be allowed to orchestrate depositions in ten cities around the country to prove the intimacy of his wife and Franklin Dodge, as well as their conspiracy to steal everything he owned.

George also used his time in the spotlight to talk about the many letters of support that poured in from all over America and Canada.

The letter writers, George asserted, alerted him that Imogene had liquidated all his assets and then set up secret cash deposits in the neighboring country to the north. An anonymous missive from Canada, George claimed, expressed hope that Remus would go free.

Roguish, inspired by the publicity, Remus gave the media its quote of the day: "Remus's cause is just. If not, Remus will go to dust."

• • •

Remus's plight returned him to folk hero status around Cincinnati, much to the chagrin of polite society. Visitors overwhelmed the Hamilton County Jail. Excited by the stories blanketing the papers, crowds were curious, hoping to catch a glimpse of the famous bootlegger who had murdered his wife. As he prepared for the fight of his life, George had to plead with officers guarding his cell to curb the steady stream of guests. Media only, please.

The interviews and subsequent stories gave Remus free reign to pontificate and spin. Relying on his experience as one of the nation's top criminal defense attorneys in Chicago and his increased notoriety as the "Bootleg King of the Middle West," Remus swayed the media's message. One strategy, a kind of faux modesty, transformed into great sound bites when translated to the page.

"I hope the public will reserve judgment of this case, whether I rot in jail or in my grave," George requested, full of mock earnestness.

"I do not forget that I am fighting for man's dearest and most sacred possession—his liberty."

At the core of George's plan was a smear campaign designed to persuade any potential jury that he was the victim of a carefully conceived plot—Imogene and Franklin robbed him of his dignity and fortune. Could he convince readers—and future jurors—that murder could be justified? The cornerstone of Remus's efforts concentrated on giving newspaper reporters the juicy details they needed to keep him in the headlines.

"She took the things that I loved more than money. She took my works of art. There was a signature of Washington that I treasured, and a signature of Lincoln," George told the *Cincinnati Post*'s Alfred Segal.

He pleaded with the reporter: "Can you understand my state of mind? Can you put yourself in my place?"

These were the precise questions George wanted people across the nation to ask.

As a criminal defense attorney, Remus had deep experience teaching juries about difficult legal concepts. He returned to his strategy in the Cheney murder case, deciding to use temporary insanity as justification for pulling the trigger. He had to make the concept something that people could grasp.

George created a legal term—essentially a slogan for his campaign—that rationalized the murder: "transitory maniacal insanity." Remus later defined it for observers, but he felt that jurors didn't require precision.

"As a result of the emotions that have been reflected in the mind," he said later, "as a result of the activities, that, impulsively, something takes hold of you and you do an act for which you are sorry after it has been performed."

To make it clearer, he applied the concept, explaining, "He was irresponsible at the time of the shooting of that pistol, a temporary insanity only at the time of firing of that gun."

During the initial days and weeks of planning for the trial that would determine his fate, George's favorite word became "unbalanced." The notion perfectly captured the idea he wanted to convey, while also depicting the mood he wanted readers and future jurors to absorb.

To win over a jury, his case had to be less about pulling the trigger and more about whether he was a man they felt like they knew and would like to spend time with. How could you blame the likeable Mr. George Remus for this death when his mental and emotional scale had been so horribly tipped by his cheating wife and her conniving lover?

"Unbalanced."

George also understood that creating villains for the jury would help him frame the battle. If he were successful, then reporters would pick up on the clash and aid him in winning over public opinion. Remus had done much the same in the William Cheney Ellis case, turning the jury's attention from the heinous crime to the affair that Eleanor Ellis supposedly had with William Cauldwell.

While Remus planned the defense in the courtroom, his friends and associates worked on the outside, throwing a nonstop party with the finest booze in town to entertain reporters and get them to cover George positively. Ed Sweeney, one of George's close allies, played a pivotal role in the overall defense scheme—he entertained out-of-town reporters. Many of the national correspondents were visitors to the Queen City, so they had to be shown around the area, including "Sin City" across the river in Newport.

"Chairmanship of the Remus reception committee," one reporter called Sweeney's role, noting that he was "charming."

George read as many newspapers as he could while in jail preparing his case. He kept a keen eye on how reporters depicted him. Then the bootlegger rewarded the journalists for their support by granting interviews and bartering information.

"The press of the country certainly has been fair to me," he told a local reporter. "I am grateful."

Taft attempted to turn the public in his favor with compelling statements focused on the bootlegger's guilt, explaining, "Remus committed a cold-blooded murder and I have no doubt that he will be electrocuted for it. He will get nowhere with the defense which he seems to be planning."

An Ivy League gentleman from a prestigious family, Taft could not imagine the public's capacity for supporting a person like Remus, even though his father warned him that the public would root for the bootlegger. On the other side, Remus realized that if he turned the trial into a circus, he could keep the jury both amused and dazed by the spectacle.

Part of Remus's act centered on remaining optimistic and friendly, which gave the jurors a positive impression of him. One reporter for the *New York Times* remarked that Remus's "optimistic attitude" basically "amazed" people attached to the court.

"Daily he has smiled, laughed and chatted with friends as though he never had seen the court where his life is at stake," the newsman said.

The media even bought into George's kindness to other jailed inmates in the Hamilton County Courthouse. One reported on the impending Thanksgiving feast, disclosing that "due to consorting with King Remus," the "jail birds" would enjoy "celery, cranberry sauce, spaghetti, young roast turkey, giblet gravy, ice cream, nuts, assorted candies, and coffee."

On the other hand, the press remained indifferent—or worse—regarding Taft and his prosecutorial team. As the two sides argued over legal details before the trial began, reporters must have sensed that public sympathy shifted to Remus. The tone of countless stories swung to the bootleg king.

The Cincinnati Post presented the legal efforts like a ballgame, proclaiming, "The defense has won three victories over Charles P. Taft II, county prosecutor, and his assistants."

15

"Ready for the Battle—It's a Fight!"

"I'm sorry to meet you under such circumstances," George said to each stranger as they passed. The first day of the trial…all eyes were on Remus.

The onlookers smiled. They finally caught a glimpse of the king of the bootleggers up close. Considering the crowds, it was amazing to just be admitted to the courtroom. Many felt weary after standing in the long line that snaked through the courthouse hallways. Four deputy sheriffs examined them as they entered.

Sheriff William Anderson did not take security lightly. He couldn't. The underworld rattled with rumors that assassins might come looking for Remus. Murdering the king of the bootleggers in the courtroom would make someone famous.

Anderson's men toted shotguns in addition to their service pistols. They stopped each person who wanted to enter. Spectator after spectator shuffled to their cramped seats, and the air buzzed with anticipation.

After speaking to spectators, Remus continued to stand in front of the defendant's table, surveying the crowd. The newspapermen were at a large table over his shoulder and observers filled every single seat, eager to see the man whose life hung in the balance.

He'd had twenty suits delivered to the jailhouse. Today was special, so he selected one in deep blue, offset by a black four-in-hand tie. George did not look like a man who had killed his estranged wife in broad daylight. He cut the figure of the distinguished defense attorney that he had been in Chicago. Only the tailored, cream-colored silk shirt would have given him away. Yet, Remus wasn't filling out expense reports or balancing ledger books—he was about to defend himself from a date with the electric chair.

George also realized that he couldn't defend himself alone, as he had planned to do in the divorce proceedings. Despite having trumpeted his confidence to the newspapers, his life was on the line and he needed assistance. Remus hired former county prosecutor Charles Elston to help represent him. Elston had what George favored in an attorney—a history of successes in cases that no one thought he could win.

Elston's reputation had recently skyrocketed in Cincinnati legal circles when he won the acquittal of George "Fat" Wrassman, a bootlegger from nearby Hamilton, one of Remus's main haunts. Fat owned a speakeasy on Court Street in the city and got into an altercation with local thug Dutch Concannon, who ended up shot dead. Elston's client cried self-defense and the lawyer argued masterfully, ultimately winning acquittal. Remus kept his eye out for winners.

When his young colleague Elston sat down, George did too. He adjusted his weight on the dark wooden chair and looked upon the several law books, from his own private library, heaped on the table in front of the attorneys. Next to the books sat a steel filing box that held the strategy he and Elston had contrived.

Sunlight filled the courtroom through the tall windows, framing George as he sat there. At the front were paintings of American heroes, including Washington and Lincoln, two of the forefathers he admired most. George was now deep in thought, tapping a stubby pencil on the tabletop, running it through his thick fingers. His most important case was about to begin. He would later tell reporters that it was his fiftieth birthday that day, but it was actually his fifty-first—anything to divert attention from the murder. For several heartbeats he stared out at the light blue sky.

Judge Chester Shook entered the courtroom. The crowd murmured for a moment before silence filled the space. People snapped to attention, including George and his co-counsel Elston.

"And now," Remus said, turning to Elston, "we are ready for the battle. It's a fight!"

Judge Shook realized that the Remus murder trial would unleash a media feeding frenzy. Everything about the event would be outsized and intensely scrutinized, so he arranged to accommodate the escalation, creating additional room for spectators and setting guidelines regarding photography. Eight large tables were lined up in the courtroom to seat twenty reporters, while another area would be for photographers, as long as no tripods or flashbulbs were used.

The courtroom next door became a holding area for witnesses. It just so happened to be the courtroom of Judge Thomas H. Morrow, the former district attorney who had prosecuted Remus in the case that landed him in Atlanta. According to one news report, he also "loaned" his jury room to Western Union and AT&T, who installed eight telegraph transmitters to keep the rest of the nation informed. They also installed an additional four wires for general reports.

The nation's attention centered on Cincinnati, a battle between Remus and Taft that would uncover the kind of gruesome details the public devoured. People wanted accounts of how the German immigrant had become the "bootleg king," wanted to wrap themselves in details regarding the criminal underworld that Remus represented.

Most significant of all, George would defend himself from the proverbial hangman's noose. Remus had been an opponent of the death penalty dating back to his attorney days in Chicago. Certainly his close relationship with Clarence Darrow played a role in his thinking. Supporters of the death penalty, however, had surged in the 1920s, in part because of the fear instilled by the Russian Revolution and rise of socialism, America's entry into World War I, and a change in thinking by criminologists who argued that putting offenders to death was the only just way to deal with heinous crimes against humanity.

Darrow remained a key figure nationally, particularly after defending Nathan Leopold Jr. and Richard Loeb, the teenage sons of two wealthy Chicago families who had been arrested for the murder of Bobby Franks, a 14-year-old neighborhood boy. The boys confessed, claiming that they committed the crime for the excitement of it, which outraged the public. Cries went up for the death penalty for Leopold and Loeb. Darrow, in a cunning effort to save their lives, had the boys admit their guilt, and then closed the case with a twelve-hour argument that convinced Judge John Caverly to give them life sentences instead of death because they were mentally ill and had no emotional gauge to comprehend what they had done. With the final plea, the great legal thinker even managed to sway public opinion to agree with Caverly's sentence.

Now, three years later, the Remus case—with its question about temporary insanity—kept people on the edge of their seats. Across the country, they eagerly waited for every scrap of information that surfaced. It was almost as if Prohibition *and* the death penalty were on trial with Remus.

"I face my future with the greatest pessimism, for I am charged with first degree murder. Yet I am told the sentiment on the outside is for me," George told reporters covering the trial. His plan to win the publicity campaign seemed to be gaining traction.

Because Remus had initially announced that he would be his own counsel, Judge Shook granted him privileges that he otherwise would not have been given. He had private quarters on the top floor of the Hamilton County jailhouse, which one reporter described as "a five-room suite."

George had also convinced Shook to allow him to bring Vernon Chumbley to Cincinnati to serve as his legal assistant. Chumbley, a fellow bootlegger, had being doing time at Leavenworth, including a stint in the insane ward there.

No attorney could operate efficiently without books, either. So, prison officials had shipped in much of George's law library and given him access to local libraries. And along with the twenty of his finest suits he had on hand, some reporters who visited George in his cell claimed that the bootlegger even had a liquor stash for visitors.

"I had my working library there and I would work until eleven or twelve o'clock at night," George explained later. "Then I would be up at 2:30 in the morning."

Shook had even allowed Remus to retain the books and suite after the bootlegger decided that he needed help to beat Taft. He remained co-counsel with Elston.

Although he enjoyed all these privileges, the most critical might have been the freedom to go out onto the roof for fresh air. In the morning, he was even permitted to exercise. He had a photographer take pictures of him in various workout gear, some images in boxing regalia and others looking tough in his exercise clothes and winter cap perched atop his bald crown. The photographs found their way into the newspapers.

More props to make him seem human, approachable, but also a fighter.

* * *

Remus's number-two man, George Conners, continued to serve his boss during the trial—in the role of witness coach.

"George used to be crazy, see, you can swear to that, can't you?" Conners said to one man as he led him toward the courtroom doors.

"Crazy as a bedbug," said the witness.

"But don't you get up there and say George is crazy now," the tutor warned. "The first sap who pulls that will get his ears knocked off. He used to be crazy, but not any more."

"How long was he supposed to be crazy?" the witness inquired.

"Until he killed Imogene."

"I got you," the witness confirmed before taking the chair waiting him beside Judge Shook.

Even under the glare of the law and press, the man did his duty.

⁕ ⁕ ⁕

Remus's faux plea—temporary maniacal insanity—created challenges for Judge Shook, let alone the prosecution. Struggling with how to proceed, the judge brought in three alienists (the era's name for psychiatrists or psychologists)—E. A. Baber, head of Longview Hospital for the Insane, David I. Wolfstein, and Charles E. Kiely—to evaluate Remus.

Judge Shook charged them with creating a report that assessed George's sanity. The three doctors sat in on the proceedings during the pre-trial meetings and during the trial itself, watching Remus's every move. They also had the opportunity to interview him at length after each day's proceedings ended.

Remus's strategy centered on introducing the perfect dilemma for judge and jury: if he were deemed insane, then how could he possibly defend himself adequately at trial? If he were deemed sane, then he would proceed with the attack on Imogene and Franklin, thereby turning the spotlight to their misdeeds, rather than his actions. He calculated his odds of winning and figured that he only needed one or two jurors to buy his reasoning. That would bring them to a standstill.

George had plenty of ammunition in proving his temporary insanity. Elston called witness after witness who had seen odd behavior from Remus after he was released from Atlanta in September 1925.

Under oath, *St. Louis Post-Dispatch* journalist John Rogers testified that when George found out about a "cocktail party" Imogene and Franklin were having one night during the Jack Daniel's distillery trial, he "at once flew into a rage."

Rogers and Connors struggled for fifteen minutes to stop him from going to confront the two lovers. Rogers took the brunt of the collision, getting knocked to the ground by the stout Remus.

Remus cried out that he needed "to avenge his honor."

From his years in the courtroom, George had gained deep experience with legal experts. He knew how they thought and how they persuaded juries. So, he had to put on a show for the alienists.

"Sometimes I would see electrical stars or something, you know, up in the mind," George told them, "as though someone hit you in the nose and you are knocked out and see stars."

Despite Remus's best efforts, the alienists knocked him and Elston for a loop when they issued the report to Judge Shook on Saturday, November 26:

REMUS SANE

The headline blared from coast to coast.

"George Remus is now sane and was on Oct. 6, 1927, sane," Wolfstein, Baber, and Kiely concluded.

Taft and his prosecutorial team turned relentless in portraying George as a petty thief, consummate liar, and serial adulterer. Suddenly, what seemed like a steady path toward victory for Remus was turned into a knockdown fight.

While the sentiments of the jurors remained a mystery, the opinions of observers watching the trial were still mixed. Attorneys and reporters watched as spectators and others were respectful—deferential, even—as they approached Remus in the wide courtroom corridors. While an attorney in Chicago, George had mastered the defense attorney's balance of compliance and aggression, utilizing whichever he found necessary. He could switch masks in a moment. Men doffed their hats in deference, which he matched with a slight bow of his own. At the same time, George kept the pressure on the prosecutors by relentlessly hammering home Imogene's infidelity.

"She's dead, thank God," he exclaimed in an interview with Paul W. White, a United Press national correspondent.

Remus equated the murder with a man preserving sanctity in his home, essentially saying that the killing was an "obligation." Reporter Alfred Segal, who covered the trial extensively, described the bootlegger's populist appeal, explaining, "Remus, the legendary hero of big money, now has become in many minds a hero with a flaming sword striking down the wicked and making wrong right."

Another reporter on hand for the entire trial explained how the defense's position unfolded: "She took his wealth while he was in prison, ran away with

Dodge, plotted to have Remus deported, and then schemed to have him murdered."

While Taft attempted to vilify Remus, he and Elston hammered them back with a parade of people who would counter that notion. George stacked the trial with associates and business partners who backed him, like former Assistant United States Attorney General John R. Marshall, who testified that he attempted to get Remus's sentence reduced after the bootlegger turned state's witness in the Jack Daniel's distillery proceedings. Marshall wrote a letter to Remus's archenemy, top Prohibition enforcement officer Mabel Willebrandt, then later spoke to her about Remus.

"Rarely has one of our more prominent murderers been equipped so lavishly with witnesses," wrote Frederick H. Brennan, a newsman covering the trial.

"If I had you in the corridor I would wreck you physically," Remus bellowed at Charlie Taft in the packed courtroom.

He slammed his shell-rimmed glasses on the table in front of him and shook his fist in the prosecutor's direction. George then stepped toward him, stomping his feet.

Although his face turned red, Taft smirked when the smaller man stopped short.

"Pitiful offshoot," Remus said, hatred directed at the young prosecutor. A moment later, he glanced over at the spectators.

"How much of this stuff is the court going to stand, this personal vilification?" asked Carl E. Basler, the feisty assistant prosecutor, a World War I veteran who had been praised for training Army troops for the war.

Judge Shook allowed these exchanges to a point, but eventually shut Remus down.

Taft grinned when later questioned about Remus's threats. The president's son had played football and basketball in his undergraduate days at Yale. Plus, he had twenty years on his foe. Although few doubted Remus's toughness or well-conditioned, stocky physique, Taft probably would have made short work of him in a fistfight.

Without backing down, the prosecutor said that if Remus continued with these kinds of outbursts, he would have two bailiffs stationed next to him and then "be prepared for an assault."

To counter, the press reported that Remus said he would "relish" the chance to fight Taft.

"Remus daily has been shadowboxing in the jail to keep fit," reporters noted.

George railed against any attempts by Taft or the prosecution to portray him as physically weak or intellectually feeble, particularly if his standing as an attorney were assailed. At the slightest provocation on either of these topics, the bootlegger erupted.

After repeated outbursts, George continued to toy with the attorneys on Taft's team, particularly Basler.

Whenever he had the opportunity, Remus called out Basler publicly for drinking "pints and pints of whiskey" on the deposition trips. The provocation caused Basler to lose his cool, particularly since he had built a fine reputation in the Queen City as a thoughtful, compassionate lawyer and civic-minded leader.

Remus heaped on the threats until Basler reached a boiling point.

"Get back on your own side of the railing or I'll take a crack at you myself," he threatened.

When George hovered too close to Basler, the assistant prosecutor told him that if he came any closer, he would "punch" him.

In a rhetorical counter-attack, Basler attempted to goad Remus, thinking that the murderer's outbursts would give the jury a negative impression of him. But the ploy seemed to backfire. Remus consistently defended himself as a tough guy and man willing to fight. These kinds of taunts and the threats of violence from both sides revealed how deeply the rascally bootleg baron got under the skin of the prosecutors.

During Willie Haar's testimony, Basler tried to demonstrate Remus's disingenuous personality and vicious, quick temper by having the former prisoner explain that the other criminals called Remus "a rat."

As the two sides objected and argued about admissibility, Remus leaped out of his chair.

He shouted, "There wasn't a man down there big enough and strong enough to insinuate such a thing."

Remus then threw accusations back at Basler, again accusing him of drinking and calling him a "hypocrite."

The outburst forced several bailiffs to intercede and form a circle around Remus until he regained his composure. However, when Haar said that inmates did call Remus a rat, George again jumped to his feet and objected. Basler reacted, too, which caused Judge Shook to intervene.

The demonstrations of anger, bluster, and aggression had made George seem like a fiery underdog to jurors, while simultaneously vilifying the prosecutors. He wanted to portray himself as a man who took care of slights with his fists in an age where manly aggression was viewed as a fundamental character trait.

Remus stuck his finger within inches of Taft's face.

"They are doing the bidding of Franklin L. Dodge, that degenerate mass of nothingness, kicked out of the Department of Justice," he bellowed.

From the moment he decided to replicate the temporary maniacal insanity plea that he had used successfully in defending William Cheney Ellis, Remus had to magnify his role as hero and plug in a villain. Prohibition as an entity itself already served as one bad guy. The other was going to be former federal enforcement agent Franklin Dodge, who Remus had been kicking around for months.

Dodge was an easy target. First, the general public hated the dry laws and what they forced them to endure if they wanted a little nip. The Prohis were the personification of this disgust. The news constantly featured stories of feds who overstepped their bounds or had taken money to look the other way. Remus had set Franklin up from the start. Whether any of it was true didn't really matter—the opposition gave George the straw man he required.

A screaming headline the morning after he had murdered his wife left little doubt about who allegedly caused George's passing madness.

Other Man Denies Remus' Charges Against His Wife

In the Remus murder trial, even something as nondescript as depositions made front-page news. The added intrigue kept readers interested, since each day brought some additional mystery.

The most damning evidence came from a trip to Lansing to secure depositions. When Elston found out about the security deposit box shenanigans there, he and George used the information to demonstrate collusion between Franklin and Imogene. They pointed to the sinister nature of her securing the compartment using the name "Mrs. A. H. Holmes" and its taking place in Dodge's hometown, under his guidance.

J. Edward Roe, the president of the bank, had taken Imogene's photograph when she rented the box, which made it easy for Remus's legal team to identify her and negate Dodge's assertion that he never really knew Imogene. Frieda Schneider, who managed the bank vaults, also testified under oath that she saw Franklin and Imogene visit the safety deposit boxes together several times.

Elston entered the identification photos into the record. Then, in a deft cross-examination of Frank Dodge, Sr., he got the elder Dodge—a venerable lawyer and town statesman—to confirm that the man in the photo was Franklin Jr.

What happened next cut the legs out from under Taft and the prosecution who hoped to keep the Imogene and Franklin relationship out of the proceedings. On the record, Elston asked: "Did your son ever introduce to you a woman who resembled the woman in that photograph?"

"Yes, I think I met her with her sister on the streets of this city," Frank Dodge, Sr. answered.

"What name was given?" the attorney countered.

The older man replied: "I have not the slightest recollection. If it was some assumed name like, something different from her name, I have no recollection about it."

"You do not recall the name Remus being used," Elston queried.

"I do not recall it, but I presume that might have been the name, but I do not remember that face at all, to be candid about it," Frank responded.

For most observers, this was more than enough evidence, even though the older Dodge had attempted to be cagey about the facts.

Franklin and Imogene were lovers.

Newspaper headlines shouted the information—the illicit relationship that Remus had been ranting and raving about for more than two years came out in bold lettering, staring readers directly in the face.

Remus had done it. He made the affair real.

On the other side, the esteemed older Dodge had cemented his son's relationship with the bootlegger's wife because he did not have the capacity for deviousness. He simply could not lie, even though he tried to muddy the truth by claiming a faulty memory. It would be incredibly difficult for Taft, Basler, and the prosecution team to keep the affair from having an influence on people's thoughts about the defendant.

Elston was so confident that the depositions proved the illicit affair—and that they proved Remus's bout with insanity—that he issued a press statement in late October announcing their success: "The relationship between Franklin L. Dodge and Mrs. Imogene Remus," the lawyer wrote, "which was known to

Remus and caused transitory insanity so that he killed his wife, has been established definitely."

The investigative team had moved on to St. Louis and more testimony, but Elston explained that the move "is merely cumulative, but of equally startling nature." The startling information about the intimacy and betrayal at the hands of Imogene and Franklin, the attorney contended, would "free Remus."

While Elston dropped media bombs, newspaper stories pictured Taft as a dud. With Olive Long, one of Imogene's best friends from Evanston who had overheard a loving telephone conversation between Imogene and Franklin, for example, the *Cincinnati Post* reported that the golden boy prosecutor "could not shake her story" in cross-examination.

"Dodge," the paper said, "could not be found to answer the charges," even though he was in the Windy City with Taft and his team.

When Taft attempted to counter Remus's media advantage he looked clearly out of his league. The same day that Elston made his proclamation linking Franklin and Imogene, Taft told reporters, "I am working on a story that may be the real reason for Remus killing his wife."

"Mrs. Remus knew of an alleged murder that Remus is said to have committed." The prosecutor revealed that George had supposedly killed Sheriff William Van Camp in Brookville, Indiana, in 1923, a local police officer known to be tough on the gangsters hot-rodding through his town on the route between Indianapolis and Cincinnati.

The logic proceeded that George killed Imogene to prevent her from making the murder allegation in the ensuing divorce proceedings. Although rumors swirled that Remus or his crew might have been involved in the unsolved murder, Taft added, "I have no substantiation that any part of the story is true, but it is being investigated."

What the wild accusation actually did, however, was further draw the public's attention away from the main point Taft had in his favor—Remus admitted to killing Imogene and plenty of people saw it. The tangential argument about Van Camp amounted to Taft shooting himself in the foot.

"Propaganda," was George's retort: "innuendoes, mudslinging, and insinuation."

Franklin also jumped into the fray, criticizing Remus for the "fishing trip" depositions. He labeled Olive Long's testimony "bunk," professing that he had been ill in Cleveland the day he allegedly spoke to Imogene over the phone.

For George and his legal team, the nationwide trip stopped the trial cold so that the defense could get witness depositions. This tactic added eleven days to the proceedings. More importantly, the interruption gave Remus, Elston, and their allies time to plot strategy and win over the media. There would be no way for Remus or what was left of his henchmen to tamper with the jury, but at the same time, no one seemed willing to stop his publicity onslaught.

Readers wanted more, and each new nugget of information led to greater newspaper coverage and further questions. Relentlessly painting Dodge as the rat was all he needed to get them on his side. George repeatedly won the war of the words versus an outgunned Charlie Taft and a beleaguered, overwhelmed Franklin Dodge.

When the deposition phase ended, Taft seemed out of sorts, discussing the overwhelming "interest" in the case nationwide, while simultaneously alluding to the press favoring "Remus developments."

He pointed to the frantic efforts to take Franklin's picture as part of the favoritism, essentially not respecting Dodge's wish for anonymity.

Franklin took up that call, claiming, "I am innocent of all the charges made against me." He explained, "I don't want my picture taken so that evidence can be framed against me."

While privacy may have been Franklin's aspiration, the public's fascination with Imogene's murder and George's role created arguably the most sensational news story of the Jazz Age. The former fed's declaration of secrecy actually made him look suspicious. Neither he nor Taft saw the proceedings as a strategic battle with the bootleg king that would primarily be waged in the media.

16

Cutthroats and Assassins

Witness after witness marched to the stand and unfurled a portrait of life in the criminal underworld that surpassed breathtaking. The tales they told topped any accounts people had read on the newsstands, perused in men's magazines, or glimpsed in the latest crime novels.

"The Egan's Rats had received $15,000 from Dodge and Mrs. Remus to 'knock off' Remus," said Clarence Owens when he took the stand.

Owens ran a bail bonds business in St. Louis. His friends called him "Gully." For better or worse, most of Gully's closest acquaintances were members of the city's notorious Cuckoo gang, led by Herman Tipton. Before Prohibition, the Cuckoos had been a group of guys who played baseball together. Over time, though, the boys who played ball grew up. As they got older, the Cuckoos took a degenerate turn. They devolved into a group of vicious thugs that hung around saloons looking for trouble. Owens had run a joint where Cuckoo members liked to hang out. He had a ringside seat to countless assaults and murders. Since the city police force did not like associating with the Cuckoos, innumerable homicides were never solved. St. Louis was a rough town in the early decades of the twentieth century.

The dawn of the dry years gave the Cuckoos newfound purpose. They eagerly jumped into the lucrative bootlegging business. The gang had little problem with murdering rivals to facilitate business transactions or maintain their turf, particularly when Italian gangsters infringed on their territory. Some of Remus's liquor probably ran through the Cuckoo outfit, but—despite George's desire to distribute the best of the best—they certainly would have diluted it many times over.

Men like Gully traveled in a dark world, full of gossip and innuendo. He had one tentative foot in everyday society as a business owner, but trafficked most frequently in the gang world. Gully had secured George's bond so he could keep Remus out of the city lockup. Owens had spies who funneled him rumors. He felt that if the bootleg king ended up in jail for an extended period the penalty would probably be the equivalent of a death sentence.

"Remus was supposed to go to jail and then the gunmen were to be arrested and placed in jail with him and kill him," Owens testified at George's murder trial.

The Egan's Rats gang was another St. Louis operation, arguably even more brutal and bloodthirsty than the Cuckoos. They specialized in robbing banks, stealing about $4.5 million from 1919 to 1924. The underworld swirled with gossip about George and his partners not allowing the gang a slice of the Jack Daniel's profits. Knocking off the top boss would send a sufficient message to the other conspirators.

Federal agents and prosecutors also heard the stories about a hit on Remus. They locked down protection to keep him safe.

"There were two different gangs there to try to take me unawares," the bootleg king reported. He had thugs searching for him while he was hidden away and a detail team of "three to five secret service men" watched over him.

The government protection and hidden lair worked. When the Egan's Rats assassins were unable to kill the bootlegger, they went to visit Gully. The new plan was to force the bondsman to set Remus up by requesting that the bootleg baron visit the bond office to sign additional paperwork. This plot would lure George to a spot where a slugger from the Egan gang could ice him.

Despite threats on his own life, Owens refused to help, remaining loyal to Remus and his Cuckoo friends. But, he would pay a steep price for that allegiance. For several months, members of Egan's Rats returned to Gully's headquarters with machine guns blazing. His decision to not sell out Remus had basically cost the thugs $15,000. The inability to collect on that money fueled their revenge against Gully.

"After Clarence Owens signed my bond of $50,000," Remus said, "he had to put up iron shutters on his place of business. Machine guns were used and twenty-eight people killed. Owens was wounded so badly he was in a hospital for seven months."

Courtesy Jack Doll Papers, Delhi Historical Society, Cincinnati, Ohio

Remus during his pharmacy years, pictured standing in front of the nine-story Geo. Remus and J.A. Taggart Office Building at 4520 North Clarendon Avenue in Chicago, near Lake Shore Drive and on the edge of Buena Park and Uptown. Lillian is in the driver's seat, while Romola is sitting behind her.

Author's Collection

George, seated at the far right, business associates, and family members posing at a party in the Price Hill mansion, circa 1921. Imogene is standing at George's right, while stepdaughter Ruth is at his left, with her arm around his shoulder.

Courtesy Jack Doll Papers, Delhi Historical Society, Cincinnati, Ohio

George, Imogene, and Ruth pose with their guests for a formal portrait inside the famous "Imogene Baths" prior to its opening on December 31, 1921. Reports estimate that Remus paid up to $150,000 for the Grecian swimming pool, lined with Rookwood tile.

Author's Collection

The exterior of the Gatsby-like "Dream Palace."

Courtesy Jack Doll Papers, Delhi Historical Society, Cincinnati, Ohio

The solarium inside George and Imogene's grand mansion at 825 Hermosa Avenue in Price Hill on the Westside of Cincinnati. In the 1920s, fashionable homes were built with solariums, private spaces filled with therapeutic sunshine and large windows. Solariums were considered chic and provided untold health benefits.

Courtesy Jack Doll Papers, Delhi Historical Society, Cincinnati, Ohio

Imogene Remus poses for a photographer in her elaborate private quarters in the Dream Palace mansion. Designing the room, the mansion, and the swimming pool area in Louis XVI style, Imogene adorned the spaces with flowers and plants.

Harry M. Daugherty (left) helped get Warren G. Harding (right) elected President. In return, Harding made him Attorney General. Remus believed that his payments to Daugherty, via his right-hand man, Jess Smith, would protect him from arrest or imprisonment.

Courtesy Public Library of Cincinnati and Hamilton County, Cincinnati History Slide Collection

At the height of his power, George Remus purchased an office complex at 225 Race Street on the southwest corner of Race and Pearl Streets, renaming it the "Remus Building." The lobby tile display spelled out "Remus," which he thought demonstrated his authority. For his second-floor office space, Remus spent $75,000 on lavish furniture, accessories, and equipment, as well as a personal chef.

Library of Congress

The stylish Sinton Hotel at the corner of Fourth and Vine in downtown Cincinnati served as George's primary headquarters as he built the bourbon kingdom and after, notably while he searched for his lost millions and Imogene's whereabouts. Modeled after a French chateau, the Sinton was dubbed "the finest hotel in the West."

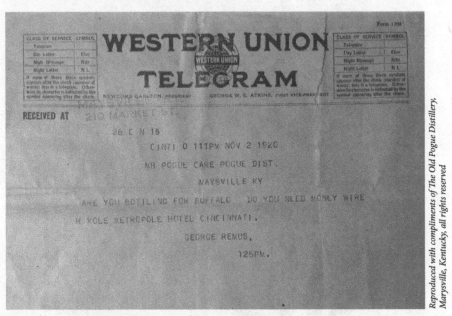

A letter dated November 5, 1920, from George Remus to Henry Pogue, Jr., the owner of Old Pogue Distillery in Maysville, Kentucky. The letter demonstrates how quickly Remus had begun purchasing distilleries and selling off bourbon. This payment is most likely for a shipment of bourbon to one of Remus's false-front drug companies or storefront pharmacies in Buffalo.

The Western Union telegram from George Remus to Henry Pogue, Jr. demonstrates how quickly the bourbon kingdom grew. By early November 1920, Remus has already set up a depot in Buffalo, which is being supplied by the Pogue Distillery in Maysville, Kentucky. The telegram also mentions the mysterious "H. Kole," one of Remus's earliest business partners who helped him establish the whiskey ring.

When Tennessee passed statewide dry laws in 1910, Jack Daniel shifted operations to St. Louis, including a large warehouse at 3960 Duncan Avenue. Remus joined several dozen city politicians and influencers in an effort to purchase, then steal the whiskey from the warehouse. Before officials uncovered the theft, Remus was double-crossed, got in trouble with local gang members, and ultimately he and Imogene were arrested. The trial made national headlines, with George turning on his coconspirators.

Imogene Remus sits for a photograph with her arm around George. Her daughter Ruth sits at her stepfather's feet.

"King Remus" Ruler of a "Bootleg Empire"

Ruled Like a King, Lived In a Palace, Scattered Huge "Overnight" Fortune In Revelry and in Largess To His Retainers---Wife Was His "Prime Minister"

Now Dethroned, His Empire Has Crumbled and His Incalculable Wealth Has Shrunk to a Paltry $1,000,000

Mrs. Imogene REMUS

Geo. R. REMUS

$100,000 Marble Swimming Pool

At the Height of the New Year's Revelry Mrs. Remus Donned a Bathing Suit and Her Fancy Diving Put to Shame the Four Water Nymphs Who Had Been Hired to Entertain the Guests.

The DATER FARM in "Death Valley"

Author's Collection

Joseph Pulitzer's *Evening World* published an embellished, mythmaking story about Remus and his "Bootleg Empire" on June 7, 1922, one of many that established the legend of "King Remus." The Bourbon King personally orchestrated many of these media opportunities, enabling him to craft his public image. The national media seized on the lurid details that emerged during the trial in Cincinnati.

Widely considered the "best dressed man in Washington," Jess Smith (left) was Attorney General Daugherty's confidante, friend, nurse, and bagman for the mountains of cash he was able to extort from America's bootleg barons. When he committed suicide on May 30, 1923, it ended what little hope Remus had of staying out of jail.

Imogene Remus sits for a formal portrait in her finest fur shawl and feathered hat. Her stunning diamond wedding ring is prominently displayed, which may indicate that this photo was taken shortly after she and George were married in Newport, Kentucky, on June 25, 1920.

President Calvin Coolidge, who succeeded Harding after his untimely death, is seated, preparing to sign a document. Assistant Attorney General Mabel Walker Willebrandt (left) and Ohio Congressman I.M. Foster stand behind him. Willebrandt led the Prohibition Bureau in its efforts to shut down Remus's bourbon empire. Her work with top undercover agent Franklin L. Dodge, Jr. eventually brought the bootleg king to justice and unleashed a string of events that resulted in embezzlement, mayhem, and murder.

George Remus is flanked by two Cincinnati detectives moments after being released from the Atlanta federal penitentiary on September 2, 1925. Remus was served with divorce papers and re-arrested, and then escorted back to the Queen City. His lawyers battled to keep him out of jail on the public nuisance one-year sentence, and federal prosecutors questioned him about the Jack Daniels whiskey theft case.

Remus's spectacular rise and fall as "King of the Bootleggers" made headlines nationwide in the 1920s. In April 1927, papers speculated about what he would do next and gleefully recounted the tale for readers increasingly interested in stories about bootleggers and gangsters. The montage features an image of the Price Hill mansion and the Death Valley liquor depot that was the site of the initial raid. Remus, after another year-long jail sentence, is thin. He worried about what the time in jail did to his mental faculties.

The grand Hollenden Hotel on the corner of Bond and Superior Streets in downtown Cleveland served as Franklin Dodge's chief residence while he worked as an undercover agent in the Prohibition Bureau. After he resigned, it became a lair for him and Imogene. It was here where the night watchman caught him—half-dressed—in Imogene's room. When Remus found out about the liaison, he knew the rumors were true—his wife had run off with the Prohi.

A rare snapshot of George Remus leaving a Georgia courthouse in the trial of former Atlanta federal pen Warden Albert Sartain and several prison officials who were accused and convicted of accepting bribes in return for providing wealthy convicts easy privileges while imprisoned there. Remus had paid Sartain and his aides to have telephone access, unlimited visitation for Imogene, and a private chef.

From one of Michigan's prominent families, Franklin L. Dodge, Jr., became a top undercover agent in the Prohibition Bureau, helping bring down Remus and other bootleg barons. In this image from the Dodge family archives, the young Franklin stares confidently into the future, unaware of how entwined he will become in the Jazz Age criminal underground.

Imogene Remus on May 23, 1924, two days after being arrested for violating the Volstead Act in connection with the removal of 30,000 gallons of whiskey from the Jack Daniel's Distillery warehouse in St. Louis. After her murder, this photo would become the one used most frequently in subsequent news stories.

A 186-acre park in the Walnut Hills/Mount Adams neighborhood of Cincinnati, Eden Park features the Spring House Gazebo, which sits next to Mirror Lake reservoir. Just on the other side of the roadway, George forced Imogene's taxi off the road, where he produced a pistol and murdered her in broad daylight.

After fatally shooting his wife Imogene on October 6, 1927, George Remus was taken by a squad of Cincinnati detectives back to Eden Park, the scene of the murder, to re-enact the shooting.

Romola Remus (left) and her mother, Lillian Krause, George's first wife, announced to the press that they would stand by him after he was arrested for killing Imogene. Romola played an important publicity role during the trial as the grieving daughter, sitting with Remus throughout the trial, and defending him to newspaper reporters.

MORGUE, HAMILTON COUNTY, OHIO.

The Hamilton County, Ohio, morgue report for Imogene Remus (misspelled "Imagene"), noting her time of death at Bethesda Hospital and that she died of a "shotwound in abdomen."

George Remus (left), his flapper daughter Romola (middle), and co-counsel Charles H. Elston (right) sit at the defendant's table during the sensational murder trial.

George Remus's chief lieutenant, George Conners, is shown testifying at the bourbon king's 1927 murder trial. Conners's testimony, particularly identifying the occasions where Remus seemed "insane," helped convince the jury that Remus suffered from "temporary maniacal insanity" when he shot Imogene in Eden Park.

A lifelong fitness enthusiast, Remus worked out daily on the rooftop of the Hamilton County Jail in Cincinnati. These photographs were widely published, demonstrating George's fighting spirit and toughness in preparation for his "courtroom fights."

Remus, photographed in a jail cell, after being arrested for the murder of his wife Imogene on October 6, 1927. The photo was widely distributed on newswire services and appeared in hundreds of newspapers eager for information about the "wife-slayer."

Charles Taft and the prosecutorial team hoped that Ruth Remus's eyewitness testimony of her mother's murder would sway the jury and sink George's chance for exoneration. She spoke in such a soft voice that jurors had to lean in so they could hear her.

Acquitted after the jury deliberated for merely 19 minutes, Remus's ensuing celebration lasted all night. Although not free, George (either in makeup or touched up by the photographer to make his facial features more prominent) was mobbed in his jail cell, and posed for publicity photos taken with members of the jury, including the "flapper" member Ruth Cross (middle) and Robert E. Hosford (right).

Snapped in late October 1927 as he prepared for the start of the murder trial that would decide his fate—life or death, George Remus does not look pleased to be photographed. This image would be the one that newspapers used most frequently in presenting the bourbon king to the world. The rectangular crop lines are seen in this image.

George Remus, smiling, is shown with a Christmas tree and stacks of congratulatory telegrams after being acquitted by the "Christmas Jury." He would spend the next six months proving that he was sane, and ultimately he would win his freedom.

A savvy, yet mysterious, financial manager with deep ties in the Kentucky bourbon industry, Blanche Watson served as Remus's personal secretary as he built his illicit liquor empire. Some observers saw her as the brains behind the operation and credited her with starting Remus in the business. Blanche and George married in the 1930s and were together until his death in 1952.

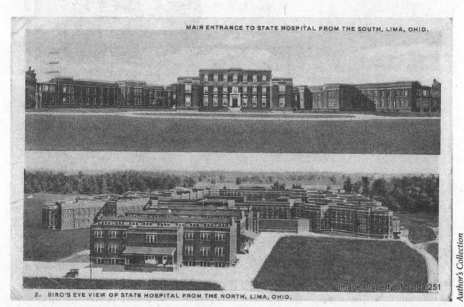

George Remus spent about six months in the State Hospital for the Criminal Insane at Lima in Ohio. He despised the facility, calling it the "dumping ground of humanity," but served his time counseling other inmates and buying them gifts. He earned the nickname the "Johnny Appleseed of Lima State Hospital" for planting an apple orchard on the grounds, dubbed the "Remus Grove."

Critically wounding Gully and murdering many of his henchmen did not fully satisfy the bloodthirsty Egan thugs. The lost bounty made them crazy and pushed them into disarray. The gang's leaders were so irate about allowing Remus to escape that they eventually turned on one another. An internal feud ensued, heightened by a snitch in their midst who had begun cooperating with federal prosecutors when he felt his life was in danger.

As the rat ratted out the Rats, federal agents and state police officers put most of the top leaders behind bars. Authorities then hunted down what was left of the gang. The remaining Egan's Rats dispersed, but they blazed a lethal trail. Many became freelance killers and criminals, continuing to terrorize the Midwest and other regions where they relocated.

The trial testimony and deposition revelations regarding the depravations of the criminal underworld titillated the spectators and jury members of Remus's murder trial. Many observers considered these shocking accusations the highlights of the trial, which like most legal proceedings, would frequently stall out on arcane jargon and tedious minutiae. What the witnesses revealed shook polite Cincinnati society, exposing a dark underworld of hired cut-throats and assassins, murder, machine guns, and shady maneuverings by powerful government officials.

During the trial proceedings, through witness testimony and depositions, jurors were given a recent-history lesson on Prohibition's deadly underworld and the forces at play in Remus's war against Imogene and Franklin. Imagine a juror, an average Cincinnatian, being confronted with it all. And imagine how it may have painted Remus as a man constantly in fear of betrayal and murder since his release from the Atlanta prison in September 1925.

A highly publicized long-distance shouting match with Franklin and Imogene in the press was one thing, but the revelations at the trial shocked the jurors, hundreds of spectators, and the reporters who sent all the salacious details out over the newswires. When accusations turned to allegations involving murder plots and assassinations, the warfare became very real for everyone paying attention to the Remus murder trial....

George, Imogene, and Franklin had each carried guns. Frequently, George and Imogene employed bodyguards, some little more than hired killers willing to shoot quickly and accurately in response to a threat.

Imogene's divorce suit had infuriated George. His greatest rage, however, was sparked by Franklin's role in the affair. From the moment of his release from the Atlanta Federal Pen on September 2, 1925, until he was jailed in Ohio seven months later in April 1926, Remus lived on the edge. On one hand, the bourbon baron launched a spirited campaign to regain his lost riches. He employed a team of lawyers and detectives to hunt down Imogene and the money she and her lover hid. Simultaneously, he fended off the efforts of courts trying to throw him back in jail.

The hell he endured in Atlanta made him fear prison time nearly as much as the assassins always prowling around the periphery. He could not trust anyone. His circle had been reduced to George Conners and his faithful business manager Blanche Watson. Of the thousands that had worked for him, this was basically all that was left. More often than not, he had to turn to Willebrandt and federal officials for protection.

"Remus told me that when he was in the Claypool Hotel in Indianapolis two gunmen followed him continually," Conners told a reporter.

Later, a different pair of killers tracked him to his Cincinnati headquarters at the Sinton Hotel. "Remus was under guard and the gunmen were afraid to go through with the program," the reporter noted.

To make matters more complex, some underworld figures floated the idea that Willebrandt herself was in league with members of the Egan's Rats gang to assassinate Remus. George brushed off these accusations, instead targeting "Dodge" and his "henchmen." For Remus, Franklin was always the target.

"Dodge was using Mrs. Willebrandt's offices to bring about that killing."

Mabel Willebrandt did not get a free pass, though. The assistant attorney general had a deep network of informants—sometimes including Remus—and received a great deal of information about dry enforcement, particularly among the elite bootleggers. She needed to make an example out of Remus, while simultaneously attempting to squeeze him for information.

Her anger regarding George's flagrant testimony before the Wheeler Senate committee, and his constant efforts to use his influence to be paroled or pardoned, pressed her to demand Remus's St. Louis bond to be posted at an unreasonable $50,000—it had initially been set at $5,000.

Although she probably did not believe that her former star undercover agent Franklin Dodge was behind the death threats against Remus, Willebrandt knew that there was an active contract on George's head. In turn, how could he not see a larger conspiracy at work?

Knowing that his life was in danger, Remus attempted to get Willebrandt on the phone long distance, but reportedly she was on vacation in Maine. He then tried John R. Marshall to no avail. George did not believe that Mabel worked directly with hired thugs and assassins, but he did know that he might be knocked off at the jailhouse if he could not raise the bond money. To him, the figure was unjust and the potential downfall could mean his life.

"When you know they put up $15,000 with a crowd of people that have killed fifty-three people within forty-two months, that is, the Egan Rats, you would become a little exercised as well. Yes, I was very much provoked," Remus stormed.

"I was very tense," George explained. "I had been at the St. Louis jail for a day and a half, didn't know how soon my head would be cracked, I didn't dare to say a word, because I didn't know who were the agents of some of those people."

Remus declared that going to St. Louis would be "reasonably certain death."

The rumors had reached the district attorney's office. "They were very dubious as to whether I would return."

"I was laboring under a tremendous suspense," Remus said. "It was not thought of death as much so as the mortification and the humiliation to think that I should be placed in that kind of a position through a scheming, conniving woman."

Imogene still controlled the purse strings and she had put as much distance as possible between herself and George. His estranged wife basically disappeared, letting him twist alone and with little money to his name.

John Berger, the famous exposition director and George's lifelong friend, went to see Imogene at her hotel room, asking her to give her husband $25,000 of his own money back. When Imogene demurred, her mother Julia Brown asserted that Berger warned, "if you don't give George this money, he has men already here in St. Louis to kidnap you, and to carry you away, and to break your legs, arms, and mutilate you."

Federal officials attempted to intercede in the assassination plot against George. John Marshall sent George Conners to see Noonan, the leader of the Egan's Rats gang, according to Remus, "to see whether we could not beg off so that they would not kill me."

Remus said that Conners informed him of another potential attack planned to take place outside the Springdale dog track in the rural Cincinnati region. Springdale was a frequent haunt for Remus, his henchmen, and other local criminals.

Conners had warned him, "I had better not ride home in his car, as there were some killers in from Toledo that was likely to get us."

Since Conners had driven with his wife Ada and small daughter, Remus did not want to endanger them. Instead, he hitched a ride with August Bruck. On their trip back to Cincinnati, George contended that men driving a large Hudson touring sedan tried to push them off the road in Mt. Healthy, a small town outside Hamilton. Bruck gunned the engine of his Paige luxury car, which easily outdistanced the bandits.

"It was a very close call," George said. "I was subsequently told that Jew John had employed some people...they were going to turn the machine guns on us and exterminate me and kill whomsoever was there, but on account of the five women folks being there, they didn't want to do it. They were afraid the smack-back would be too serious...the indignation would be too severe."

Threats against Remus's life, jurors learned, became a consistent theme after he left Atlanta. How could he possibly *not* be a man on edge? Many people had their ears to the ground in the 1920s, especially as the dry laws turned people against one another. Everyone who drank and all those responsible for getting the liquor down people's throats constantly strode back and forth over the law of the land. There were many other plots, which George learned about through his own informants and friends. He credited his friends with saving his life on many occasions.

"Some sluggers from New York had come on and as it is with the underworld characters, they sometimes get in touch with the leaders of the underworld in a large city," Remus explained later. "That communication may have come to me through some of those men out of Cincinnati that I befriended."

· · · · ·

While learning of the constant threat of assassination against the defendant, Remus's jurors also absorbed the melee over Franklin Dodge's affair and illegal business maneuvers with Imogene. For Remus, the testimony and depositions furthered his defense as a wronged husband driven mad. The prosecution, meanwhile, needed to counterattack—"Remus should have killed me, not his wife, if he wanted to do the honorable thing and I had been guilty of so much wrong," Franklin Dodge announced to the press after Remus murdered Imogene.

"Lies," he proclaimed when reporters pressed him about George's claims of the illicit relationship between the former enforcement agent and his now-dead wife.

While Remus had innuendo, Franklin claimed that he held "documentary evidence" to prove his claim, including "railroad tickets, hotel receipts, and affidavits of individuals."

The constant fireworks between the two men persisted, despite Remus being behind bars awaiting trial and Franklin being in limbo—partially in hiding, but also spouting off in the media to refute George's claims. Charles Elston also joined in the fray, keeping up the pre-trial pressure and journeying to ten different cities to interview people who could prove that George's allegations about Imogene and Franklin were true.

In Washington, DC, the lawyer took testimony of J. L. Doran, head of the Federal Prohibition Department, and Judge James J. Britt, the department's chief legal counsel. The two government officials would have had a great deal to lose if they lied under oath.

Elston found out from Doran and Britt that Franklin and Imogene discussed the fate of 1,800 barrels of bourbon with David H. Blair, the internal revenue boss, on June 14, 1926, some three months prior to George's scheduled release from the Atlanta pen. Remus and Elston used the information to negate Dodge's initial claims that he did not engage with Imogene beyond the initial meetings in Atlanta.

Franklin had earlier provided sworn testimony in support of Imogene for her divorce case. He had testified on her behalf, giving "specific denial of undue intimacy with Mrs. Remus."

At the same time, however, Dodge also admitted that he served in "capacity of confidential adviser" to her as she tried to break free from George. Imogene worried that her husband would attempt to frame her for some of his liquor deals in retaliation for filing the lawsuit.

In the immediate days after George killed Imogene, Franklin did not waver in clarifying to the press corps—which hounded him at his parents' family estate in Lansing—that he saw Imogene only "on business."

Appearing with his father, Frank Dodge, Sr., a prominent attorney and political insider who had helped elect Democratic Presidents Grover Cleveland and Woodrow Wilson, the younger Dodge lashed out at his avowed enemy.

"George Remus is a dirty coward who lacked courage to harm anyone other than a woman," he said.

Franklin then recounted that Remus offered a thug $8,000 to kill him. In contrast, Dodge characterized Imogene as "a perfect lady."

The public declaration that Remus had actually tried to have Dodge assassinated was founded on the Prohi's odd friendship with Willie Haar, the Savannah Four leader who was sent away due to Dodge's own undercover work. There were many strange codes in the underworld and it seems that Haar respected Franklin for nabbing him. Mabel Willebrandt had also received these kinds of greetings from rumrunning kingpins who wanted to shake her hand for doing such a bang-up job in chasing after them. Even among thieves, respect for doing one's job trumped hatred or animosity.

Dodge did not name Haar specifically in the interview published by the *Cincinnati Enquirer* on October 8, 1927, which was picked up by newspapers all over the country. He just explained that a would-be assassin had squealed, admitting the alleged plot to the former dry agent. Franklin claimed that he didn't think much of the warning at the time, because enforcement agents received many death threats. The rationale the killer gave was that he turned down the potential payday because Franklin had always been such an honest broker.

"This agent came to me and told me of an $8,000 offer for my life."

When further pressed about the potential killer's name, the former Prohi detective would not reveal it.

"No, I can't mention this man's name," he said. "For the reason that it wouldn't be safe for me."

Franklin did, however, tell a hometown Lansing newsman that the assassin had been a powerful bootlegger in the South and had since become "a well-known gunman."

Dodge explained: "I have no desire to bring unwelcome publicity to the man who, instead of taking my life for $8,000, saved it."

Franklin then reiterated his business-only relationship with Imogene and lambasted George for bringing him into the case. The former Prohi said that he obtained the evidence against Remus in Cincinnati without the assistance of Imogene. This declaration was to snuff rumors that it may actually have been Imogene who squealed to Dodge and Willebrandt, leading to her husband's demise.

In the *Lansing State Journal* article, Franklin claimed that he met Imogene on January 15, 1925, when Remus had been in the Atlanta pen for about a year. He explained that he went to Big A in an undercover role on an order direct from his boss Mabel Walker Willebrandt. The extent of the corruption at the jail had recently been exposed, resulting in Remus, Haar, and some of the other high-profile criminals being moved to a county facility. When he met her, Franklin said, Imogene scrubbed George's jail cell and prepared his food, "all that she could for the comfort of her husband."

Dodge asserted that Imogene, "To my knowledge, has always acted as a perfect lady."

Franklin used more choice words for Remus, calling him "A coward and a shameless liar—one who would never personally offer violence to anyone except to a woman or a child, but who would hire assassins, if necessary, to remove enemies from his path."

Franklin told the reporter that he often received death threats while working for the government, but shrugged them off in his duty as ace detective under Assistant Attorney General Willebrandt. For example, the former Prohi agent claimed that he got forty-two telephone calls or letters that threatened his life for investigating vice at the Atlanta Federal Pen. Newspaper readers could not have missed the contrast between the cowardly Remus, who murdered his wife, and the brave Dodge, who stood up to the nation's fiercest criminals.

Frank Dodge, Sr., the venerable state politician and advisor to several US presidents, called Remus's claims "too absurd to merit denial."

The younger Dodge, scion of the Turner-Dodge family, admitted that Imogene wrote to him after they met, asking for help in freeing her husband. And Franklin also said he met with attorneys in two cities—St. Louis and New York—as an agent for Imogene, expenses covered by the legal teams. When he had seen Imogene, he said again and again, it had never been inappropriate.

Both men went after the other with bombshells meant to garner additional press coverage. Franklin told the interviewer that contrary to common belief, Remus was "broke" when he went to prison.

The millions Remus had made, according to his arch rival, had mostly disappeared.

Was that money now in Imogene's possession?

Dodge claimed not to know.

The rumors and assertions about Franklin and Imogene had been splashed across newspapers nationwide since October 1925, a little more than a month after George had been released from prison. Remus had been able to delay the second sentence for operating a public nuisance at Death Valley for about seven months, until April 1926, when he went to prison again to serve out that term. He spent that entire span trying to catch the two together and blasting them in the press for stealing his money and other valuables.

Dodge fired back, repudiating Remus's story and making him seem cowardly. Each day the former fed and the bootlegger hurled accusations and insults back and forth. The battlegrounds were the newspapers and in front of the jury in the courtroom, where Dodge was conspicuously absent and Remus a forceful personality who seemed to overwhelm Judge Shook and Charlie Taft.

The sensational allegations continued to materialize as Elston and Remus revisited the events surrounding the Jack Daniel's investigation in St. Louis and the subsequent December 1925 trial in Indianapolis. The jurors listened to the lurid details, enraptured by the claims each side made and the specifics of how Dodge and Remus used their extensive connections in the criminal under-world to try to have the other murdered.

George, Franklin, and Imogene had faced real danger at the time, and the added fear that they might be arrested at any moment. George and Imogene were deeply embroiled in the Jack Daniel's theft, while Franklin had engaged in selling Imogene's whiskey certificates while still an enforcement agent.

John Rogers, who had extensive relationships with sources in St. Louis, in-formed George that a Cincinnati gangster and ex-convict told him in the pres-ence of another thug: "Mrs. Remus, on two occasions, in St. Louis and Cincinnati had sought to employ gangsters to assassinate Remus."

When the news of the latest allegations hit the newspapers, the reporters covering the Remus murder trial ran to Dodge for comment.

"Lies," Franklin blurted. The former lawman did not, he claimed, have two guns on him or threaten Remus.

Later, George countered that he had proof of the contract on his life from John Marshall, one of Willebrandt's underlings. The attorney, Remus said, "told him that five gunners and bandits, some of the Egan Rats and two sluggers from Chicago were in Indianapolis to kill me."

Marshall also had information that one of the teams of killers had registered at the Claypool Hotel in a room across the hall from Remus under the name "John Murphy." The next day, Marshall would not let George leave the city. He saw five men staking out the Indianapolis train station waiting for a chance to take a shot at Remus.

John Marcus, who had served as a quasi-mentor and partner for Remus when he first entered the bootlegging business, claimed that Imogene wanted him to kill her husband. She had the money, and the friendship between the two men would enable Marcus to get close enough to do the job.

Marcus took advantage of Remus's many distractions to take over large parts of the bootleg baron's territory. George Conners, Remus's unflappable second-in-command, appeared cool and collected in public, but spent most of his time looking over his shoulder for would-be murderers.

He and Marcus despised each other. According to Walter A. Shead, a reporter looking into Queen City criminal circles, "They had sent word to each other they would shoot on sight." Yet, they agreed to a ceasefire while Remus fought for his life—part of the underworld creed that criminals would put aside their differences if they faced the electric chair: "to never desert one of their own who is in the shadow of the noose or the chair." Marcus, despite his hatred for Remus and desire to kill Conners, even testified for Remus during the murder trial.

And there was further corroboration that Remus was a marked man after his first release from prison. According to August Steinbach, a deputy United States marshal who took George from Dayton to St. Louis in September 1925, Remus had to travel secretly, because he faced multiple death threats.

"Our office had information that a gang known as 'Egan's Rats' were trying to take Mr. Remus's life," the marshal recalled. Remus was so nervous about the trip that he sent a telegram to Willebrandt in her Washington, DC, headquarters requesting protection.

Imogene, George asserted: "Agreed to pay the Egan Rats of St. Louis $15,000, she and Dodge, to knock me over."

With death looming all around, Remus and his legal team fought the public nuisance charge that would put him back in jail, but Willebrandt wouldn't sign off on the charge being dropped. Realizing that his safety was constantly in question, George began carrying a small handgun that he had stumbled across in a box in the garage. He stashed it away in the butler's pantry, just in case his wife came back for it.

The pearl-handled pistol was the one that Imogene had always had on her, but she must have mistakenly left behind in the frenzied rush to empty the mansion before her husband returned from Georgia. The last thing George did each morning, whether at the Price Hill mansion or downtown at the Sinton, was grab the little gun and slip it into his pocket.

Remus always had the weapon at the ready. It might not save him in a shoot-out, but he hoped the gun would fend off anyone who might lack the courage to murder him. It was one thing to kill an unarmed man, but quite another altogether to face down one who was also packing.

"I had been advised by Tom Wilcox, who was working out of the Department of Justice in Detroit," Remus remembered, "that there was no question about the fact, but that this combination of people wanted to take my life."

Wilcox proved a kind of odd ally for Remus. The federal official even disclosed that Franklin and Imogene were under watch for Dodge's role in threatening George while he served as a government witness, including the Egan's Rats $15,000 assassination offer.

Meanwhile, at the Price Hill mansion, George set up armed sentries along the driveway to the house. He also had workers install pillars along the path so that if someone unloaded on the house with tommy guns, many of the bullets would be deflected. Access to this new firepower forced Remus to turn his home into a fortress.

According to Remus, Gully Owens, who had driven him back to Cincinnati from St. Louis with Conners, "told me how dangerous it was for I to be anywhere near the house and I had better leave the city."

Although Dodge continued to deny the assassination accusations, members of the Justice Department thought enough of the threats to give George a large handgun for protection during the Jack Daniel's trial in Indianapolis.

"Go ahead and shoot anyone that would come near me, with the authority of the government," George said the agents told him when they gave him the gun.

In addition, federal authorities, including John Marshall, would sometimes guard Remus at the Claypool Hotel. According to George, Marshall was just as nervous as he was. The fed "would barricade himself with great big trunks and everything—the door in between." Marshall and others urged Conners to stay with his boss as an extra level of protection.

Years of looming death could certainly cloud a man's mental and emotional states. That's undoubtedly what jurors and American newspaper readers gauged from the corresponding testimony and depositions given at the murder trial. But the atmosphere right outside the courtroom heightened the tension even more. Cincinnati had become explosive since George had killed Imogene. Jurors, spectators, and especially the defendant himself could feel it.

There were too many gangsters coming into the region. Many of them felt they had a score to settle. Remus might have been weakened and jailed, but he commanded the respect of some criminals who wanted him to go free. Simultaneously, George was hated by other thugs, mainly for selling out his co-conspirators in the Jack Daniel's case and turning himself into a laughingstock for murdering his wife in such an explicit fashion.

The pressure of the trial forced more dirty laundry into the light. Just before Thanksgiving, Cincinnati police hurried Franklin Dodge out of the city to a secret suburban location. They heard rumors that Edward Sayler, a known hitman from San Francisco, was in the area with orders to kill the ex-federal agent.

Detectives had been spotted searching numerous gang haunts on the west side in search of the assassin. "Rubbing out" Dodge would prevent the former Prohi from testifying in Remus's murder trial.

Ironically, George was the one that launched the manhunt, even though keeping quiet might have led to Dodge's demise. Remus shared with Judge Shook a letter he received from Sayler.

The hitman wrote that he hoped to "reach Cincinnati in time to kill that dirty rat Dodge."

Sayler claimed that Dodge and Imogene had visited him several months earlier, urging him to "go out and bump George Remus off," adding that the former agent would "give you a thousand bucks."

Sayler also wrote that Charles Taft had paid him $200 to "get something on you." Taft quickly countered when the story hit the media. He claimed to have never heard of the man.

Even the charges against Charlie Taft could not have prepared people for what happened next.

* * *

Hearsay, past trial records, second-hand testimony, depositions, news from outside the courtroom.... It all grounded the jury in the storyline that George Remus had lived the past few years knowing that death was right around the corner, either at the hands of the criminal underworld or of his own wife and her paramour.

It felt real now.

George glanced outside. Sleet pelted the windows. The temperature hovered around freezing, turning the sidewalks and streets slick. As he sat and waited for the courtroom action to unfold, the bourbon king was immune to the slight whir of the heating system that kept the space warm on this December morning. He also seemed oblivious to the gentle murmurs and ruffling sounds emanating from the spectators in the packed stands behind him.

The warm smiles and emphatic handshakes that had marked the early days of the proceedings had receded into memory. Despite the frequent outbursts and arguments between the prosecutorial and defense attorneys, the trial looped into a series of endless objections, followed by mountains of arcane legal wrangling. The trial had turned Remus's life into sport, but only he faced the electric chair if the jury sided against him.

Next to the bootlegger sat the faithful Elston. The younger man, wisp thin and stately—a rising star in the competitive Cincinnati legal community—brushed aside the difficulties of defending someone with Remus's deep legal knowledge. No matter how smart, though, Remus had a notoriously short fuse. Part co-counsel and part defendant, he attacked trials like a bulldog. He constantly wanted to interject, to show off for the jurors, to demonstrate that his legal mind remained sharp. He faced life or death pressure, yet he remained aggressive, coy, and pleading—whichever he needed to adopt for any given situation. Everything hinged on the state of George's mind.

Glancing at Judge Shook, Elston stood and called the next witness. Every head in the room turned when the man entered. Tall and rugged, he took long, loping strides toward the stand.

"Harry Truesdale," he said slowly, when the bailiff asked him to state his name. He dropped into the chair next to the judge, easing his large frame into the cramped space. No one in the crowd had heard the name "Truesdale" so far during the proceedings. Each new witness was a hope for some shocking new revelation.

A hush fell across the crowd, although some of the women snickered, covering their mouths with their hands. Harry looked like a silent film star, or one of the many handsome clerks selling the latest clothing styles down at the Alms & Doepke department store. Making himself smaller than he was, Truesdale hunched slightly, glancing over at Taft, and then back at Judge Shook.

Harry peered out behind dark, detached eyes. In little more than a low whisper, the thug, whom the dozens of reporters would later refer to as a "gunman," looked at Remus across the short distance and calmly explained how Imogene and Franklin had offered him $10,000 to kill her husband. As a matter of fact, Truesdale told about following Remus for days in an effort to gun him down.

"I lay in wait for him at the Sinton Hotel. I plotted to kill him in his room, but too many people were going in and out of there. He always had a lot of callers coming in and out," Harry revealed in a deep voice, barely audible to the spectators craning their necks toward him.

As the words sank in, a feeling of stunned disbelief fell over the room. A reporter covering the trial explained that Harry outlined his role "without any outward sign of emotion," explaining "in a matter-of-fact way how he waited near the elevator on the floor where Remus had his rooms in the Hotel Sinton."

While Harry slowly unveiled his plot and repeatedly referred to "Mrs. Remus," George began to sob at the defense table. He pulled a handkerchief to his lips.

Rising partially out of his chair, unsteady, George then squeaked in a high-pitched voice, "Will you adjourn Court for a minute, Your Honor?"

Judge Shook asked that the bailiff clear the jury, but not before George had sunk down into his chair and collapsed forward, his head falling into his arms. "His shoulders were shaking," revealed an observer. "It was evident he was sobbing."

Sheriff William M. Anderson and his deputies on guard rushed to surround Remus. At the same time, Romola, sitting at the table, hugged his neck before launching into a hysterical fit, sobbing against his thick shoulders. As the jury filed out, 58-year-old jury member Anna Ricking and 23-year-old Ruth Cross began crying. Reporters noted that several of the male jurors were also teary.

Two deputies helped George to his feet and moved him toward Shook's chambers. "Excuse me, Your Honor, I couldn't help it," he muttered on his way. Then, as they moved closer to the door, right behind the jury members, "there burst from his throat an eerie yell, a half-strangled wail with a peculiar nasal intonation, that swept through the courtroom and electrified the audience, already in a state of emotional suspense."

Romola, also supporting herself with the aid of an officer, wept loudly with her father as she trailed him out of the courtroom.

Reporters, court employees, police officers, and the three alienists crowded toward the anteroom. Although in the other room, George's wails echoed when the door opened. He wrestled with the men, finally pulling his knees up under his chin and crying out, "Will this never end? Oh, will it never end?"

Remus wailed and struggled for fifteen minutes, eventually being taken back to his jail cell on the advice of the psychiatrists. Hours later, after conferring with Elston and the doctors, Judge Shook announced: "The defendant is unable to appear in Court."

Back in the cell, Remus stripped off his clothes and lay on his cot, covered with a bathrobe. Jailers applied ice packs to his head and hot water bottles to his feet in an attempt to alleviate his misery. Almost as quickly as the doctors determined George was okay, the prosecution and defense lobbed insults back and forth about whether the trained lawyer was faking it or not.

As a state of shock descended over the crowd after Remus's exit, Shook just sat in his seat, high above the proceedings, while Truesdale remained on the witness stand without changing expression. This lack of emotion added to the bizarre scene. "He sat in this calm attitude, for the full half-hour," a reporter recalled.

Harry's statements and George's bizarre reaction became a defining moment in the murder trial. "The outbreak was by far the most spectacular of the entire trial, filled as it has been with the unusual and dramatic," one reporter noted.

For the first time, after volleys of accusations and counterclaims over several weeks, the jury had heard firsthand testimony that Imogene and Franklin hired an assassin to kill Remus. The would-be-assassin himself had confessed.

When they closed their eyes, the jurors surely could still hear Remus's sickly shrieks as he was rushed from the courtroom.

Certainly, reports about the Egan's Rats gang were sinister. But no one from that crew appeared to testify at George's murder trial.

Harry Truesdale, the hired thug who was both physically imposing and handsome, provided the defining moment. Remus believed that Harry was part of a larger gang of Hamilton criminals in the virtually lawless town.

"A man by the name of John Marcus told me he knew how I could make $10,000," Truesdale admitted, "and I asked him how it would be, and he told me that if I would kill a man that I could get that much money."

Jew John Marcus, George's one-time partner and hired gun, had become Imogene's on-again, off-again bodyguard and advisor while George had been behind bars.

Just with that knowledge alone, George parted ways with Marcus on bad terms, basically guaranteeing a violent end. Rumors in gangland asserted that George Conners planned to take care of Marcus. The two were rumored to have a "shoot first" pledge against one another. Marcus went to see Imogene, who asked that Jew John and Truesdale visit her at the Alms Hotel in Cincinnati to work out the details.

When Truesdale and Marcus went to Room 708 at the Alms, Imogene only met with them for a few moments because she had a party to attend to in the other part of her suite.

"I went back there by myself," Harry explained. "I talked to her again, and she told me that I would get $10,000 if I would kill Mr. Remus."

Then, she broke down the payments, half from her and half from an unnamed source. When the hired gun protested, Imogene assured him. She "says it was a man by the name of Franklin Dodge." Imogene would not give Harry a deposit, but did press $250 into his hand to pay for expenses.

When Harry later met with Imogene again in Hamilton, she pointed at a dark figure sitting in a touring sedan across the street. She told Truesdale that it was Dodge, who would pay the remaining balance of the fee.

"Mrs. Remus went across the street to the automobile…and came back with a pistol." She then declared, "If I see him tonight, I'd kill him myself."

Truesdale feared being double-crossed by Imogene, because everyone in the criminal underworld knew that Imogene had left Remus for Dodge. The lovebirds were conspicuous in traveling around together, never adequately concealing their illicit affair. Since they consorted with criminals and thugs, the rumor mill worked in overtime. Neither realized that her blatant disregard for George while he was in prison broke a significant jailhouse rule about being true to one's marriage while the husband did time.

The manager of the Mayfair Hotel reported that Imogene carried a thick satchel filled to the brim with $500 bills, so she could have paid Truesdale's fee. The would-be hit man, however, simply did not trust her or Franklin to hold up their end of the plot. Murders had been splashed across the headlines recently, so killing a person as high-profile as Remus would launch an intense manhunt. Truesdale feared that Imogene or Franklin would rat him out to the police after not paying for the hit.

Harry went to the Sinton Hotel and admitted to Remus that he worried that he would have "committed the act and never have gotten his money and she would double-cross him."

"I had been at the hotel that very same night," George remembered later. "She was down at Hamilton with Dodge and the thugs and the sluggers."

The day before he killed Imogene, Remus claimed that there were three other gunmen waiting for him at his headquarters at the Sinton, Room 327. When Truesdale admitted his role, George and his closest associates were holed up in the hotel, afraid that leaving would spark a gunfight.

After Truesdale's confession, Remus went home. The next morning he saw a car carrying three men pull into his yard at the Price Hill mansion. The vehicle had a Pennsylvania license plate.

"Your honor," George said softly, standing before the judge, "I want to apologize to you and the jury for my unmanly conduct of yesterday."

After the hysterical outburst of the previous afternoon, George's quiet apology restarted the trial. Judge Shook did not respond.

According to an observer, Remus appeared "fit" and sat quietly for the rest of the alleged assassin's testimony.

The jury, however, noted every tiny movement.

17

Let's Give Him a Nice Christmas

"Observe, gentlemen, the quality of my mind," Remus bragged. "How it sparkles. How keen it is. How quickly it thinks."

The bootleg baron sprang from his chair, motioning to the jury. He swept his hand through the air as if chopping alternative ideas to pieces.

"Have you ever seen a mind more sane, gentlemen? Does it behave as an insane mind would?"

Before anyone in the packed courtroom had a chance to consider the query, Remus provided them with the preferred response. "No gentlemen, I am not insane today. I was insane at the moment I killed my wife, but I am sane today."

Then he finished with bravado: "Is this speech I am delivering that of an insane mind?"

With the question still dangling in the air, Taft nearly leapt from the chair. The prosecutor rebuked Remus for yet another grandstanding outburst—playing politician rather than defending himself. The younger lawyer had anticipated that Remus would use any trick he could to deflect the attention away from the unassailable fact that his finger pulled the trigger of the pistol that had murdered Imogene. Irrefutable fact was the crux of Taft's strategy. Although Charlie did not trust nor like Remus, believing that the bootlegger had poisoned his city and sullied its reputation—which his family had worked so diligently to shape—Taft had faith in his fellow citizens. It seemed like an open and shut case. They would find Remus guilty.

Charlie Taft's father, the ex-president and current Supreme Court Chief Justice William Howard Taft, had warned his son that the bootlegger would launch into "a sensational appeal through the newspapers."

Ultimately, the elder Taft explained, Remus would direct his remarks at the female jury members who he believed would be "in favor of the rights of a man to kill his wife for disposing of his property while he is in jail and changing to the home of another man."

The elder Taft knew Cincinnati and its people. This was his city. And just as he predicted, the crowds that packed the Hamilton County Courthouse each day could not get enough of these heated arguments. At any moment, it seemed the antagonism between the infamous defendant and golden boy prosecutor might spill over into violence. Everyone yearned for a fistfight.

When George stood to face the court as his own counsel, he went back to the tricks and manipulations that had served him so well in Chicago. He ranted, raved, and waved his arms wildly, as if punctuating his own thoughts. Then, if he sensed that his theatrics might push the jury too far, he would back off.

When Remus thought the jury was losing focus or interest, he would embrace a tough-guy persona. He acted bored stiff when Taft and his fellow prosecutors questioned witnesses. Frequently, George would dance over to the opposing counsel, getting mere inches from the prosecution's table in an attempt to intimidate them. Observers held their breaths as Remus moved closer to Taft. The crowd wanted more than yelling and legal minutia, they craved fireworks.

Looking on incredulously, a local reporter attempted to explain the attraction between George and the crowds that showed up each day. Clearly, he believed, both the spectators and jury members fancied Remus as a kind of folk hero.

"The multitude of the people stood in long lines in the corridors, seeking the privilege of a glimpse of him in the courtroom. This had never been seen before—a killer arguing with his prosecutors."

Realizing the power he had to sway the proceedings, George began to laugh and snort out loud while Taft and his team spoke or probed witnesses in a way that he did not like. The simple reaction—only occasionally rebuked by Judge Shook or the deputy sheriff—undercut Taft's case.

In other instances, Remus shouted out comments about Taft's questioning of witnesses or legal moves. When the prosecutor tried to prove William Mueller's bias for Remus based on his employment as George's groundskeeper at the mansion, the bootlegger yelled out, "You should familiarize yourself with the facts." Judge Shook merely warned him against making similar outbursts.

Later, Remus kept up the pressure on Walter Sibbald, the able young assistant prosecutor, giggling into a handkerchief while the lawyer spoke. As a result, an onlooker reported, "four members of the jury giggled with him."

Near the end of the witness testimonies, Remus's actions took on an outlandish quality clearly meant to influence the jury and rattle the prosecutorial team. Judge Shook hit him with a contempt charge after George waved what one reporter called the "red flag of ridicule" at Taft and his colleagues. Remus later openly ridiculed them, saying that they were "novicing prosecutors."

"This has gone far enough," Sibbald cried out in response to the bootlegger's insinuations. "Remus's antagonism to the prosecution and his hatred of Taft particularly have brought down his house about his own ears. He has proved to be the bull in his own china shop."

Shook agreed with Sibbald, particularly after countless warnings directed at Remus. "The judge is nearing the limit of endurance," reporter Walter Shead explained. "His nerves are becoming frayed, and although he is courtly dignity personified, he is hurrying the attorneys."

Observers in the courtroom could sense the crowd turning in Remus's favor as the many witnesses spoke about the travails he faced as a result of Imogene and Franklin's scheming.

"Locked out of his own house," one man said to himself quietly. "It would drive me crazy," a woman nearby breathed.

"One need only sit in the audience of the courtroom to learn what the jury is thinking about, for the audience is composed of the same kind of human beings as the jury," explained reporter Alfred Segal, who from his vantage point at the press table had heard every gasp and whisper.

"It certainly would knock me cuckoo to hear a thing like that," said one person watching the proceedings. Those feelings reflected the mindset of a nation enthralled by the spectacle.

Newspapermen wrote insider accounts of the trial as it pushed forward, boldly predicting that Remus would be acquitted. In early December, Frederick H. Brennan of the *St. Louis Post-Dispatch* claimed that "arrangements for the acquittal" were "so complete" that George's friends had "laid plans for a big party to celebrate" and welcome the bootleg king back into the free world.

Outside the courtroom, Remus supporters flocked to the Queen City. They ran the gamut from preeminent Chicago lawyers to shady, violent underworld figures. Many would eventually testify as character witnesses on George's behalf. Others showed up with little to do except keep the story churning, as if the threat of violence pervading Cincinnati would somehow hasten a "not guilty" verdict.

Meanwhile, Remus and Conners attempted to run the shattered bourbon empire during the murder trial, with the lieutenant and Blanche Watson taking the reins. Conners visited Remus in jail daily, staying for two to four hours at a time, and keeping business transactions afloat.

Gangsters and tough guys flaunted their power across the region, filling up the luxury downtown hotels and haunting the speakeasies there and across the Ohio River in Newport, which nightly upheld its rank as America's premier red-light district. Newspaper accounts speculated that the price of illegal liquor had risen throughout the trial as the influx of activity downtown put a dent in local supplies.

As the first week of the trial came to a close, a Remus henchman took up a perch in the ballroom of one of Cincinnati's luxury hotels. Pulling out a revolver, he rapped the pistol on the table and then loudly announced: "A bullet in there goes for anybody who thinks that Remus is going to be tapped for this racket."

The flustered journalist who watched this scene wisely kept the thug's identity anonymous, but the threat of violence did not prevent it from appearing in the local newspaper. No one is quite sure whether hotel patrons dove for cover at this dire threat or leapt to their feet, giving the hooligan a standing ovation. Either way, such a public display of support revealed how deeply Remus had won people over.

As he portrayed himself as a man of the masses and a husband defending the honor of his home, George took on a bizarre kind of Robin Hood role. He particularly enjoyed juxtaposing his impoverished childhood versus the aristocratic, Ivy-infused Taft and his famous father.

Remus also offered up the corrupt world Prohibition had created. Without the immoral law, George argued, there would have been no temptation for him to become a criminal mastermind in the first place. Imogene's murder was more or less placed on the backburner, replaced by the much more compelling portrait that Remus and Elston had crafted for the eager public and jury members about the despicable Dodge and the couple's robbing him of his ill-begotten bourbon gains. Prohibition was responsible for Imogene's death, not the criminal mastermind it created.

Deflect, deflect, deflect.

While many bandits and desperados filled the streets, reporter Allene Sumner took a different approach, but no less important for Remus in winning the public relations battle versus Taft and Prohibition itself. She profiled "Grandma Remus," George's 77-year-old mother, who during the trial allegedly slept on a plain cot in the Hermosa Avenue "Dream Palace." Sumner's story ran with a picture of the elderly woman and the subtitle "Mr. Remus Needs Me Now" as she stood at the stove cooking soup in a large iron pot. The elderly Mrs. Remus could have starred in the perennial grandmother role in any Hollywood flick—wizened and with gray hair swept back into a bun. Betraying her formal German roots, she always called her oldest son "Mr. Remus."

Rendered as a simple immigrant who shunned George's flashy lifestyle and disliked the mansion's priceless furnishings, Grandma Remus cooked her son lentil soup or hasenpfeffer—rabbit stew, a traditional German treat—which she then delivered to him at the county jail. According to Sumner, the criminal mastermind had a soft spot for his elderly mother, "smiling" up at her when she dropped off "mama's soup." When she wasn't cooking for him, the journalist claimed that Grandma "sweeps the cobwebs from the bare tinted walls of Remus's stripped home or on her knees scrubs the corners of the priceless, marble fireplaces." All the while, Sumner explained, the elderly woman muttered in German about the fate of her son and what the dastardly Imogene had done to him. "If only Mr. Remus hadn't wanted too much money," Grandma moaned in heavily accented German, instead wishing that her son's life had taken a different path.

Back inside the Hamilton County Jail, the lights went out at nine o'clock in the evening, forcing Remus to snap shut his law books and drop his favorite fountain pen. He hustled to gather up the notes he'd worked on, stuffing them neatly into the heavy steel box that he carried in lieu of a briefcase.

Although in the late afternoon or early morning hours Remus could venture out to the rooftop for a breath of fresh air, the holding cell where he slept was narrow and small. He had his own room, the bunk above his folded up to give him more space. A lone sink across from his bed allowed him to wash up and shave before appearing in court.

Once the lights were clicked off, the darkness must have amplified the sounds of other prisoners shifting and moving in their cells. Three years of incarceration in Georgia and Ohio had not made it any easier to sleep through the night. Jailer Eugene Sheridan, a middle-aged man dressed in a dapper three-piece suit, sat outside the door, ensuring the prisoner's safety.

George surely spun the same ideas in his mind during those lonely nights. Imogene wasn't grateful, even after he had lifted her and Ruth out of the gutter in Chicago! He had given her everything, and what did he get in return? The woman who had been the love of his life stripped him of everything he had while he was helpless in prison.

TAFT DEMANDS DEATH PENALTY FOR DEFENDANT

Charlie Taft upped the ante as the newspaper headline swept across the nation on December 18, 1927. He implored the jury to see George's crime through a simple lens: he had, in fact, committed it.

Taft explained to the many assembled reporters: "Remus killed his wife that morning when she was on her way to court to divorce him because he knew she was going to reveal things about Remus's business that he did not want disclosed."

He dubbed Remus a "deliberate murderer" and demanded that the jury send him to the electric chair. "The only way the people will be safe is when he is given the death penalty—when he is dead!"

Charlie Taft wanted Remus to fry.

So did Imogene's young daughter Ruth Holmes Remus, the prosecution's star witness. She had been the only person who had witnessed the murder.

Ruth had taken the stand as the final witness Taft and his team would call. The entire nation was yearning to hear her tale. The young girl had watched her stepfather murder her mother in cold blood and then bravely jumped between them so Remus could not shoot Imogene more than once.

The media circus rose to the effort, preparing to zip the story nationwide to eager readers thirsty for every nuance. She had been a hero in that moment and now appeared in the Hamilton County courtroom as a victim.

Slowly walking to the witness stand with tears streaming down her face, Ruth had worn a long, silky black dress, accentuated by a thick fur draped over her shoulders. The dark attire drew attention to her frail, thin frame. She had most of her hair tucked under a tight black felt hat. Yet, even in the guise of a daughter in mourning for her dead mother, Ruth's stylish flapper hairstyle gave away hints of her recent prosperity as the stepdaughter of one of the kingpins of illegal booze in the Midwest. Wisps of bangs curled down her forehead, nearly covering her left eye. More curls were matted down to line the side of her face.

Ruth could have stood in for a heroine in the latest F. Scott Fitzgerald short story published in the *Saturday Evening Post*. Newspapers across the country ran her photo—a large image of the dark-clad young woman with a black veil mysteriously covering her face.

In a low voice, trembling, and frequently descending into bouts of uncontrollable sobbing, Ruth had testified, often stopping to catch her breath. Assistant Prosecutor Sibbald, a young man himself, had gingerly led the young woman through the tragic events that she witnessed.

Unlike all the others to testify in the murder trial, she had seen everything that happened from just feet away, including the fatal gut-wound. Ruth stared at George as she spoke, but then looked away when he caught her eye. These moments of bravery in facing her mother's killer receded and the emotion of the event overwhelmed her. Ruth had frequently dabbed back her tears with a handkerchief, while other times she covered her face completely. At times, Judge Shook had to ask her to speak loud enough for the jury to hear, even though they were barely more than an arm's length from her. The jury strained to comprehend the young woman, just as the crowd leaned closer in an attempt to catch what she said.

In one horrific instant, the prosecution had introduced Imogene's dress into evidence. Sibbald held it up at arm's length. The dark bloodstains and the bullet hole led many in the room to gasp. Jurors paused, realizing what they were seeing, before a volley of heads snapped away. Ruth could not hold herself together. She wept violently. Sibbald halted the questions, hoping to remain in the jury's good graces, despite attempting to prove Remus's actions were those of a vengeful—but sane—man.

While Ruth spoke in halting spasms filled with anguish, George had acted unmoved. He riffled through papers stacked up in front of him on the desk or whispered into Elston's ear about some legal point or another. At other moments, Remus chewed on cough drops or fiddled with his glasses, leaning back in his chair nonchalantly.

According to one observer, "Even the appearance of his slain wife's bullet-marked clothing failed to shatter his stoical attitude."

Few could believe that the garment did not shake Remus, even if Imogene had died at his hand. Courtroom staffers, who had seen an inexhaustible number of murder trials, told reporters that "no greater display of nerve or indifference...ever was witnessed in Criminal Court here, than that of Remus during the time his adopted daughter was testifying." Ruth's description of Imogene dying in the hospital did not stir George, according to one journalist, producing "not a tremor in Remus's face."

For Charlie Taft, the murderer's indifference demonstrated his coldblooded calculation in stalking and killing his wife. He noted the way the bootlegger altered stories as an indication of his scheming.

Taft thought that exposing Remus's contradictory stories would seal his fate. He laid the inconsistencies out for the jury after Ruth's testimony, noting that Remus claimed that he shot Imogene as part of the "unwritten law" that made it acceptable for a husband to defend the sanctity of his home. "Then he said he was driven to kill his wife by an irresistible impulse," Taft argued. "And, lastly, he claims now not momentary insanity, but insanity that existed two years before the murder."

The prosecutor considered the efforts made by Remus and Elston to be little more than "subterfuge" to "justify this murder."

While Taft's effort to explain and expand on Remus's con made sense on paper, few spectators or those following along in the newspapers seemed to care all that much. Logic went out the window as Remus and Elston pushed multiple strategies from multiple angles. George, as pugnacious and aggressive as he had been in the Chicago courtrooms, punctuated his defense with heated words, open threats, and lengthy arguments with Taft, Sibbald, and Basler.

George Remus, a lifelong lover of endurance swimming, had always me-thodically and calculatingly worn down potential adversaries. And he found ways to use his well-honed charm and charisma as a weapon. Despite Taft's statesmanlike reputation, Shook's wagging finger, and Ruth's emotional outcry, Remus discovered ways to burrow inside the jury's hearts and minds.

Observers tracking the trial could see the Remus effect at work.

"The jury is becoming a giggling jury," one reporter cautioned. "At one time yesterday five of the thirteen were laughing or giggling to themselves."*

George latched on to this attention like a shark to chum. "Remus, always the showman, plays to the jury. He casts sly glances at their direction and at least two smile broadly at him." Two members of the jury were all Remus needed. After trying hundreds of cases, he had a sixth sense for understanding how juries thought and felt.

Later, George thought back yet again to the William Cheney Ellis murder trial. The gruesomeness of that attack had soured the public to Ellis, but Remus had still managed to save his life. "Many of the essential elements of that case apply,"

---

* One juror would end up being dismissed, making the number twelve.

George believed. "Ellis killed his wife because she was in love with another man." The fundamental difference, however, stood in the "atrocious killing," he said.

Remus knew that if he just kept up the pressure on Taft, throwing the young prosecutor and his team off balance, that it would undermine the factual evidence they introduced. At the same time, George rode Franklin and Imogene's duplicity to show that it had driven him mad—for one moment—that fateful second it took to pull the trigger. His life hung in the balance. This trial was his last chance. Remus fought like never before…

Endurance.

While Remus danced with the jury, Taft left a glaring hole in the middle of his case, the one element that might have countered George's antics and brought the jury to his side—calling Franklin Dodge to the stand. Taft simply let Franklin sit on the sidelines waiting, jilted, and otherwise disposed for the duration. On Saturday, December 17, just before final arguments were scheduled, Dodge grew so upset that he basically dared Remus to call him to the stand. He could not force the bootlegger to face him physically, so he attempted to undercut the basis of the defense's assertions about him and Imogene.

"At no time in the trial of this case have they sought or elicited the truth," Franklin maintained in a rare interview granted during the proceedings. "The truth would be most disconcerting to them and they dare not produce it."

Dodge hoped he could coerce George into a hasty judgment, which would give him an opportunity to speak before the jury. "Remus knew when he killed his wife that she was about to reveal the truth about him in a court of law," Franklin added, letting the mystery of what she knew hang in the air.

Neither Elston nor Remus took the bait, despite the effort at shaming the defendant into subpoenaing him.

"We dare not put Dodge on the stand because we can not vouch for his truth and veracity," Elston countered. "If he wanted to take the stand why did he wait until too late to insist…Why didn't the state put him on the stand?"

⋆ ⋆ ⋆

The final arguments in the Remus murder trial took place on Saturday, December 17, and Monday, December 19. The fact that Dodge did not testify continued to hang over the proceedings. Conversely, the courtroom buzzed with excitement knowing that Remus would argue for his life on the last day of the trial.

Taking his turn in front of the jury, Elston quickly launched into the same line of reasoning that they had been establishing about Dodge and Imogene, claiming that the infidelity and their pilfering had caused Remus to suffer "the greatest wrong ever done to any man."

Elston implored, argued, and outright begged for the jurors to confer the "not guilty" verdict that would set his man free. Considering that Franklin had not taken the stand to defend himself or the woman he loved, Elston argued that the jury members and all the other people packed into the courtroom "have a right to assume he was guilty."

Letting the word "guilty" hang in the air with its association to Dodge, Elston paused a moment, then took up his argument again, explaining, "There isn't a man or a woman on this jury who would let such a charge go unchallenged." His voice growing louder, Elston asserted, "There isn't a red-blooded man anywhere who would let it go unchallenged."

Getting in one final shot, the barb that he knew Franklin would take personally, Elston concluded that Dodge had not taken the stand because he was "afraid" and a "filthy louse."

Several times during Elston's fervent plea the spectators erupted into applause, drowning out the counselor as he methodically portrayed George as a fine man and caring husband. Judge Shook had to intervene and threaten to halt the proceedings several times.

On Monday, December 19, George stood up to deliver his final argument. What took place over the next two hours left the jurors and spectators dumbfounded. His performance matched the excitement in Cincinnati, a city that yearned to hear him. The crowds were so thick at the courthouse that bailiffs had to use force to keep spectators from gaining entrance. The noise from the hallway grew so loud that it drowned out the proceedings if opened.

"Ladies and gentlemen of the jury, here before you stands George Remus, the lawyer." His voice, usually deep and powerful, cracked with emotion.

George then pointed to the empty spot that he had occupied next to Elston. His extended arm trembling, he exclaimed, "There in that chair sits George Remus, the defendant."

The packed courtroom waited for George to continue. Regaining his footing, Remus the attorney thanked the court and the jurors for their patience. Then he warned them of the impending fireworks he was about to unleash.

"If I become somewhat emotional, somewhat shaken by emotion, I want to beg the indulgence of this jury," George calmly explained. "For more than two years I have lived with this pent up in my breast."

He paced in front of the jury box, almost matching his footsteps to the howling winter wind rattling the courthouse windows. Jurors leaned closer to hear the man, those in the front row merely inches from the mythic figure they had watched for weeks from across the room.

They saw a man in a perfectly tailored, light gray suit, fine silk shirt, and stiff, starched collar. George had made headlines by giving partygoers diamond stickpins for their ties, but on this occasion he wore a simple, yet radiant, white pearl. He looked prestigious, like a bank official or politician, the type of man these jurors from the ranks of the working class were used to treating with deference. On the advice of a newspaperman, he stuck a sprig of Christmas holly in the lapel of his coat.

The strain showed, however, and at times Remus rambled off topic. During these soliloquies, Judge Shook interrupted and scolded him. George kept talking, slapping his thighs, and pacing in front of the jurors.

"It is upon the evidence from this witness stand you folk must find whether the defendant is guilty of the charge in the indictment or not," Remus explained to them, pointing again to the empty chair.

Newsman Walter Shead viewed George's argument and its theatrics as "a never-to-be-forgotten picture—a Jekyll and Hyde—Remus the lawyer, pleading for Remus the defendant, who still sat in the empty chair."

George's voice once more grew agitated and aggressive, almost reaching a falsetto as he returned to attack mode. Remus called Dodge a "deuce with women" and criticized him for traveling with Taft—"this scion of the house of Taft." George made sure he also spoke in the language of the jury members, calling Dodge a "social parasite" and "leper among men."

George gave "a highly athletic performance," noted reporter Kenneth Doris, "crammed full of the many trick gesticulations that are characteristically Remus." The defendant used every means at his disposal, from wild theatrics to a soft whisper forcing jury members to strain to hear him. "He leaped and he paraded," the reporter said. "At times he bowed himself almost double."

When the wild, almost dance-like spectacle came to a close, George stood directly in front of the jury box—these souls that would determine his fate— and then humbly submitted to them. "As you ponder your duty, bear in mind that that which is most sacred is your home and family," Remus said softly.

Then, with renewed vigor, announced: "I thank you. Merry Christmas to you." The bourbon king's final swing.

Charlie Taft had argued against Remus on Saturday, but surprisingly, on Monday afternoon, he turned the reins over to his assistants, Carl Basler and Walter Sibbald. Basler began the attack, questioning why Remus had never taken the stand—a deliberate attempt to counter the same line of questions about Dodge. He then made it more personal, calling George a "coward" and "snitch."

Basler completed his argument by attempting to match Remus's over-the-top antics. He stood directly in front of George and shouted to the jury: "The only verdict you can return is one that says to that man, 'You die.'" As he said this, he waved his hand within inches of Remus's face, as if wiping him off the table.

Basler's exclamation might have been positioned as dramatic, but a handful of spectators burst out laughing, causing Judge Shook to boot two of them from the proceedings.

Walt Sibbald took his turn before the jury and continued an aggressive line. Both Remus and Elston made objections, which led to brief shouting matches and caustic remarks thrown back and forth between the bootlegger and young prosecutor. After being reprimanded by Judge Shook, Sibbald tried a calmer approach.

He made clear that many of the people in Remus's circle—including Imogene—were not good individuals. However, Remus, he said, should not be allowed to get away with such a heinous act:

> The king of the bootleggers killed his queen. We are not trying to paint the deceased as a lily. She could not have been and been the wife of Remus. She was the queen of the bootleggers. But Remus had no right to kill her.

3:55 p.m. December 20, 1927, Hamilton County Court House, Cincinnati, Ohio.

The courtroom was filled with spectators. Judge Shook saw the overflowing room and declared that no one else would be admitted, ordering the deputies to slam the doors shut. Outside the doors, the officers used clubs to push back the crowds.

Harry Byrd, the jury foreman, handed the verdict to clerk of courts Sherman Balmer, who glanced at the paper and read it out loud...

In the wide marble hallways and on the concrete downtown streets, throngs of onlookers screamed and shouted when they heard the news, their breath steaming in the freezing air. Electricity buzzed through the crowd as the last minutes of daylight faded in the clear, cloudless late afternoon sky. Women's "hysterical screams," according to one newspaperman, "reverberated through the building." A steady beat of photographers' flashes pulsed…pop, pop, pop… then muffled bursts as reporters jockeyed for the best position.

Remus would go free!

> "Mrs. Remus got what was coming to her."
>
> —Anonymous Juror,
> December 20, 1927

The twelve members of the jury in this highly publicized trial deliberated for just nineteen minutes before declaring George Remus innocent of killing his wife Imogene on the sole ground of insanity. If Judge Chester R. Shook had not intervened, the jury members later affirmed that they would have allowed the defendant to walk away free.

"If the court had submitted a straight 'not guilty' verdict that would have been the one returned," one jury member told the gathered newsmen.

"That man suffered the agonies of hell and Dodge certainly was guilty of all that was charged against him or he would have insisted on taking the stand to defend himself," another succinctly explained, outlining the rationale for the group's decision.

Clearly, the jurors felt sorry for George, not his murdered wife: "We all felt Remus had been persecuted enough, hauled through all those jails," explained one juror.

Hearing the verdict, Remus's blood rushed to his head. The defrocked bootleg king burst into tears.

"I wanted American justice," he shouted at the jury members, "and I thank you."

Friends and onlookers immediately swarmed Remus. They had been waiting for this moment for six weeks—cheers and applause created a roar. A sea of hands reached out to George. He grabbed them, pumping up and down, full of emotion. Women jumped from the crowd and threw their arms around him. Jubilant!

George led the parade back to his jail cell for more celebration. When he arrived, the crowd let out a round of applause and screamed for ten solid minutes. Romola, his faithful daughter who had been by his side since mere hours after the murder, threw her arms around her father. With tears streaming down her face, she declared, "All my congrats, Daddy. I'm so happy!"

Remus's deep blue suit looked worn and his black tie flew from its position as he skipped from supporter to supporter, giving hugs and slapping the men on the back.

Next, a procession of jurors visited George, shuffling through the herd to greet him. Robert E. Hosford, a young, married juror, shook hands with Remus. According to a reporter on the scene, one of George's men, "a tall, tough looking man hanging about the jail," leaned down to Hosford and said, "I knew we could depend on you Bob."

"Yes, I was steady from the start and I was for Mr. Remus from the start," Hosford beamed.

Another juror explained to reporter Martin Sommers, "He didn't have any Christmas last year, and we wanted to see him have one this year."

The cheers of family members and cronies continued deep into the night. George, however, would not be free. Judge Shook and Charlie Taft had guaranteed he would remain behind bars by negotiating to eliminate the conclusive "not guilty" verdict. Adding the "insanity" piece meant that they would hold Remus until another judge in the Probate Court determined Remus's current mental state—whether he was now sane or insane.

No matter—Piffle!, as Remus might say—he had avoided the gallows.

"THE CHRISTMAS VERDICT"

During the murder trial, George Remus created a new guise for himself—underdog. People embraced this scrappy persona. On the scene in Cincinnati, when he cried, spectators and jurors shed tears, too. When he harassed and threatened Charlie Taft and his junior prosecutors, onlookers cheered him on. In the court of public opinion, it seemed as if Remus had triumphed over Taft, Franklin Dodge, Mabel Willebrandt, and Prohibition itself.

Then everything changed.

When the jury members declared him not guilty by reason of insanity after their nineteen-minute deliberation, the entire world seemed to turn on the bootleg king. Newspapers that had pushed his agenda began wagging their fingers in shame.

The Indianapolis News, which had drawn criticism for its positive coverage of the trial, turned on its golden cow after the verdict came in, calling it "disgraceful" and "amazing." Leaving no doubt where they stood, the paper's editorial team declared: "There is, we repeat, no justification whatever for the Remus verdict. The case was clear, and the proof of guilt conclusive."

A collective roar rang out: How could they do such a thing? Another pundit dubbed the jurors "the Christmas Jury" for letting Remus off—the ultimate present.

"We can not help but wonder if the 'King' was really crazy," questioned an editorial in the *Virginia Law Register*. "If so, he is about the most sensible insane man we have heard of in a long time, if ever."

The venerable publication called his orchestration of the trial "spectacular," noting his "masterly manner." Remus, the writer claimed, "was shrewd to a degree that makes us look beyond its vaudeville aspect and see the masterful mind who played upon the feelings of that jury to the tune of 'save my neck' with such artistry."

Yet the journal ultimately deemed the jury's decision a "miscarriage of justice which will shake the public confidence in jury trials."

"Probably never before in the history of American jurisprudence was there such a strange and spectacular courtroom drama," wrote one reporter.

Martin Sommers, on the scene for the *New York Daily News*, commented, "What's sauce for the goose is sauce for the gangster."

"Time and again he turned on his 'personality' for the benefit of the jury of ten men and two women," explained James L. Killgallen, who had covered the trial from its earliest days.

The main question is a simple "why?" Why would a dozen Cincinnatians let a cold-blooded killer walk free?

An editorial from St. Louis condemned Ohio for its "farce of justice," which let Remus escape the death chamber. The paper pinned the blame on the jury, explaining, "At his trial Remus strutted and acted before a jury that seemed amused at his antics." Then, wearily, it concluded: "He is now free to resume his activities, to indulge his temper as he sees fit."

Perhaps most provocative, though, was Judge Shook's reaction. From his place at the center of the proceedings, he accepted none of the blame for Remus's antics, but wagged his finger nonetheless:

It may be that the verdict in the trial in Cincinnati was a miscarriage of justice. We frankly say that if his mental condition was, at the time he committed the homicide, as it was shown to be during the trial before us, the verdict was a most flagrant and reprehensible outrage of judicial administration which cannot too strongly be condemned.

* * *

Remus would not actually go free. At Charlie Taft's insistence, Judge Shook had instructed the jurors that if they found George not guilty by reason of insanity, then the defendant would have to face a sanity hearing to establish whether he were sane or insane at that time.

Remus would not die for murdering Imogene in cold blood, but the state would not give him his liberty either, especially since the prosecution and judge saw the verdict as a travesty of justice. George would, in fact, spend his Christmas holiday in prison. But this was a small price to pay considering the alternative.

After the grueling murder trial, Remus and Elston faced off against the same prosecutors, this time in the probate court of Judge William H. Lueders. If George were found insane, he would be committed to the State Hospital for the Criminally Insane in Lima, Ohio. Lueders had three alienists help him assess Remus during the hearing, and he granted them the ability to ask questions and interview witnesses. And unlike the jury trial, the power for determining George's sanity rested solely with the judge.

Just days after the initial trial ended, Elston had no doubt that he and Remus could have proven Imogene's deceit in court, if given the chance. "We had evidence and introduced the evidence of two men who caught Dodge and Mrs. Remus at a hotel in Cleveland occupying the same room, Mrs. Remus without clothes on and Dodge half clad, at two or three o'clock in the morning," the attorney told Herman H. Hoppe, one of the alienists assessing Remus's sanity for Lueders.

In what seemed like a deliberate attempt to provoke George's infamous temper, Hoppe asked George if Imogene running away with Franklin served as some kind of karmic justice, given that he had cheated on his first wife Lillian with Imogene. The alienist claimed that the affair made sense, citing oft-used logic in this case, that "sauce for the goose is sauce for the gander."

Straining to keep his cool, George defiantly stuck to his story: "When you sacrifice the beauties of womankind for junk or rubbish, and it turns out to be junk and rubbish, it is tremendous."

He then added, "The mental depression is something tremendous as a result of it."

Dr. Hoppe kept pressuring George about whether or not he would kill Dodge if released from custody. Whether Remus actually wanted to finish him off or not, he would not give in to the insinuations.

"A most depraved person" and "an ulcer on the social fabric," Remus labeled Franklin. But, he did lament that the illicit affair and subsequent murder caused him to lose "a wonderful daughter."

When the alienist asked if he had the "right to remove this ulcer by cutting it out," George responded: "Absolutely not!"

The probate hearing to determine Remus's sanity took many odd turns. People who had argued that George was sane during the murder trial when he wanted to be considered *insane* now reiterated their arguments in his favor. However, there was no jury to sway. Remus also testified at the hearing, enduring constant grilling from Walt Sibbald, who seemed to relish the verbal sparring with his adversary.

*   *   *

The St. Louis Post-Dispatch front-page headline on December 30, 1927, burst from the page at the reader.

REMUS INSANE, JUDGE ORDERS HIM TAKEN TO ASYLUM

Judge Lueders decreed George "insane and a dangerous person to be at large." The judge's decision contradicted the findings of the three new alienists he brought into the case to serve in an advisory role. They believed that Remus was then sane and had been when he murdered his wife. The alienists, however, differentiated between sane and technically sane, the category Remus belonged to. They did not mince words when it came to assessing George, using provocative language meant to elicit reaction.

"We believe that he is a dangerous psychopath because he is unmoral, lacking a sense of ethics, emotionally unstable, being subject to unrestrained outbreaks of temper and rage, and egocentric to a pathological degree," they concluded.

According to the alienists, Remus did not believe it would be wrong for him to kill Dodge, too, which meant a great deal to Lueders, who wanted to keep a dangerous individual off the streets.

"The evidence further discloses that George Remus at this time does not believe it morally wrong to commit further homicide," the alienists' report noted.

The challenge for Lueders was that his ruling contradicted the alienists' report so conclusively. He certainly had to know that his judgment would face a great deal of scrutiny in the courts and the court of public opinion. George relayed his thoughts about the decision immediately. He laughed out loud at the verdict when he heard it from reporters who rushed to his jail cell to tell him.

"Is that so? Well, well." He thought for a moment, and then said, "The decision is so farcical, such a joke that it makes a sane person laugh. It is so humorous."

Despite the initial reaction and certain censure he faced, Lueders coldly decreed: "The law rests with me."

• • •

Remus had been through hell and back during his stint at Atlanta. In his opinion, though, the Lima Hospital was not much better. He called the facility the "dumping ground of humanity."

On February 1, 1928, Elston and Remus filed a writ of habeas corpus in Allen County, which they hoped would be a friendly venue for George's appeal. Remus hired two Lima attorneys—Francis W. Durbin and D. W. Henderson—to help Elston with the fight they expected at the local level. During the proceedings, they shuffled out six Lima doctors who had examined him, each declaring that George was sane and praising his mental acumen.

Taking the stand for his own defense, George endured four days of give and take with Hamilton County Assistant Prosecutor Walter K. Sibbald.

"He flayed Sibbald and the Hamilton County prosecutor's office for their actions in prosecuting him," said one newspaperman.

Throughout the proceedings, though, George expressed little remorse for killing Imogene.

"I feel sorry for the unfortunate woman to think that she would contaminate herself with that kind of a human parasite so as to go ahead and contaminate the moral atmosphere," George explained.

His concern was not that Imogene was dead, but that she sullied her name (and his) by carrying out "adulterous practices throughout the country." Later, he called killing her in cold blood "a very pitiful, sorrowful incident happening to her," as if he hadn't committed the crime himself.

A month later, on March 30, the Allen County Court of Appeals issued a 2-to-1 decision to free Remus. The court determined that George was sane and illegally being detained at Lima. The state, still smarting over Taft's egregious loss in the first trial, immediately appealed the decision to the Ohio Supreme Court.

On May 16, the justices gathered in Columbus to hear arguments for and against the lower court's decision. Charles Elston continued on as George's attorney, after his masterful earlier win. Sibbald argued that Remus should remain at Lima.

On June 19, 1928, after enduring the Lima facility, George was ordered freed by a 4-to-3 decision upholding the earlier determination. Judge Thomas A. Jones authored the majority decision, awarding Remus his liberty at long last. He noted in the report that "22 out of 25 experienced persons" declared the man sane. Another judge, Reynolds R. Kinkade, wrote that while public opinion might determine that freeing Remus is "unpopular," the law established that Lima "is an institution for care of the insane and not a place of punishment."

Remus had spent about six months at Lima, all the while using the legal system in an attempt to prove his sanity and win freedom. He served his time counseling other inmates and buying gifts for them. Later, he earned the nickname "Johnny Appleseed of Lima State Hospital" for planting an apple orchard on the grounds, dubbed the "Remus Grove."

· · ·

George stepped out of Lima a free man on the cloudy afternoon of June 20, 1928. He had been locked away in the insane asylum for nearly six months.

"It's wonderful, it's wonderful," George cried out to reporters after the announcement.

"I'm going back to Cincinnati and make my home there." Attorney Durbin picked him up at the gates in his car and drove him to the train station for the trip south.

Later, supporters and curious onlookers greeted Remus as he stepped off the train at the Central Union Station downtown, the grand depot at the corner of Third Street and Central Avenue that looked like an enormous gothic mansion. Looking healthy after eight months in Lima—one reporter said he was "tanned to a ruddy bronze"—Remus grabbed Elston's hand in jubilation, raising their fists in a sign of victory. Conners and others cheered.

"I'm in good condition," George called out to a friend who said he looked well. "I've been exercising."

The *Cincinnati Post* covered Remus's arrival as if it were a triumph, pasting it in the middle of the front page. However, several inches to the left, the Cincinnatus editorial—named in reference to the Ancient Roman statesman who symbolized civic virtue—offered its advice for the former bootleg king:

"Mr. Remus must get out of his head that he is any sort of a hero. He is a most ordinary sinner and the wages he paid for his sinning was very light."

The paper claimed that the public had grown "quite tired of him as an attraction and would be glad not to hear of him again." They calculated that George's best course of action would be to "obscure himself."

Despite the *Post*'s admonishment, the scene at the depot was markedly different. Throngs of onlookers wanted to touch George or exchange brief words with him.

"Only smiles greeted him," said a reporter. "Many who recognized him ran along at the heels of the party, seeking to shake his hand. Remus again was the center of the public eye. And Remus seemed satisfied."

PART FIVE

· · · · ·

Lost Millions

18

Rise of the Gangster

· · · · ·

Charles E. Kiely, one of the original alienists to examine Remus during the murder trial, never considered him insane: not before, during, or after pulling the trigger that killed Imogene. Testifying later as a witness at the insanity hearing in late 1927, the doctor declared George:

A very dangerous man to be at liberty.

Among other things, Kiely characterized him as a megalomaniac with a vicious temper. He informed the court that Remus had made "definite threats" to track down and kill Franklin Dodge, thus satisfying his desire for revenge.

From the perspective of the alienists, George's mental state emerged over the course of many long discussions. Herman H. Hoppe, one of the doctors who had assisted Judge Lueders, asked pointedly about Remus's emotional condition after having had time to reflect on the murder.

"Got any feeling about your dead wife, having killed her?" Hoppe asked impatiently, attempting to get an answer that felt authentic after long hours watching and studying Remus.

"None in the slightest."

Then, when Hoppe asked about the idea of remorse, Remus revealed his true feelings.

"Oh, I feel sorry to think she was unfortunate—that she would be tied up with that kind of human parasite." Over and over again, George simply returned to the kind of running script he had in his head—Imogene had destroyed their marriage after being seduced by the less-than-human Franklin Dodge, who conned her for Remus's riches.

The alienist then prodded George to speak about his murdered wife from a religious perspective. Although acknowledging the idea of heaven and an afterlife as a reward for what takes place on earth, Remus did not relent:

> A woman—I mustn't use the word 'woman'—a person that is so depraved, so degenerated as to lose all person of womankind the way she did, that whatever is in the future, in the hereafter, so far as she is concerned, cannot be bad enough or good enough.

Later, David I. Wolfstein, one of the original alienists working for Judge Chester Shook, explained during the sanity hearings that the murderer had already outlined his defense by the time they had first met.

"My defense is going to be temporary maniacal insanity," Remus had told Wolfstein. "I got Mr. Ellis off on that plea. I got his sentence reduced."

Remus had pulled off the strategy, exactly as he predicted to Wolfstein.

*   *   *

Remus correlated Imogene's death with his perception of overall justice, even though he had pulled the trigger. That he had played Imogene's judge, jury, and executioner made sense within his larger worldview.

"I am quite strong myself," he explained in probate court. "I have my way of looking at things. If I want to throw something at a man or spit in his face, that is my business."

In Kiely's estimation, Remus was thoroughly "criminal," holding both "criminal tendencies" and "strong criminal sympathies." Even dating back to his career as a practicing lawyer, the alienist said, he had never served as prosecutor.

"His sympathies were always with the criminal," the doctor disclosed. "His criminal sympathies and his states of rage and intense egotism are included under the symptomatology of the psychotic individual."

Remus's history of violence demonstrated that his quick, sadistic temper led him to strike out. He had caned both Dodge and Nick Shammas, attacking each unprovoked while fueled by his uncontrollable anger. Grudges, not actions.

He nearly killed the Evanston plumber Herbert Youngs because he had simply argued with Imogene over ten dollars. In these cases, his sense of right and wrong triggered a focused but dangerous response.

When he surfaced from the Lima facility, George walked into an environment that was categorically different than when he had ruled the bourbon empire as its undisputed king. Similar to other criminal operatives who had emerged during Prohibition's earliest years, Remus did not end disputes with widespread murder. Gang leaders, like Chicago's Johnny Torrio, who had learned the prostitution, gambling, and liquor trades at the feet of his mentor "Diamond Jim" Colosimo, advocated more efficient, business-like operations.

"Violence should be avoided whenever possible," Torrio explained, "because bullets brought headlines and crackdowns."

By the late 1920s, a new breed of gangster had emerged. The next generation wanted power, but also security from progressive politicians and police squads that had fought back against vice in the early half of the decade. The authority of these new underworld kingpins stemmed from violence and undisputed control. Murder became a fairly routine tactic, not a last resort. Strategy centered on wiping out the competition.

When Remus left the Lima State Hospital on June 20, 1928, he could not return to the bootlegging business, no matter how acutely he understood the industry. As Prohibition further gripped the nation and enforcement work expanded, a new brand of gangsters emerged.

These men were hardened and vicious. They used coercion and violence to establish themselves as the new rulers of the underworld. Stretching from the neighborhoods of New York City and gradually to the budding oasis of Las Vegas and out to the shimmering lights of Los Angeles, gangsters like Al Capone gained virtually unlimited power and used that to run the nation's dark underbelly. Capone tightened his grip on Chicago, running the city like his own personal fiefdom in ways that Remus could barely imagine.

The viciousness of gang warfare did not suit Remus. He was a punch-first criminal now adapting to life in a shoot-first world. For George, the bootleg empire was as much an intellectual game—for excitement—as anything else. For the men who followed, criminality was their livelihood. They were playing to win and wanted everything, even if it meant placing their lives on the line and killing to achieve their ends.

Remus had been able to win over the jury and press corps with his sad sack story of being duped by Imogene and Franklin, but this portrayal didn't jibe with the more aggressive, manly aura of the new leaders at the top of the criminal underworld. George had lost face during the trial and sanity hearings. His every move was exposed to the public far and wide in stories, that while quite gripping for the general public, were unacceptable to the more hardened criminal class. Killing Imogene, rather than Franklin, was not a manly way to handle one's affairs.

Most damning for the violent men who divvied up the nation into an intricate network of booze territories was that Remus could no longer be trusted. They knew he had turned state's witness several times, either seemingly on a whim or to settle a vendetta.

They could not trust a man like this, even if he had created the path for them to establish their own empires. "Remus the rat" rang out from the cells down in Atlanta. In the new environment, a rat that squealed once could never again be trusted. There were no loyalties.

Ironically, George's notoriety and national fame may have been the only thing that kept him from being assassinated. The murder case and insanity defense had turned Remus into a national celebrity. Furthermore, while he may have dabbled in underworld affairs after leaving the insane asylum, offering advice and assistance to dog track owners and other criminals, he left bootlegging to the new breed.

In contrast, George's one-time friend and business partner "Jew" John Marcus, who later became one of his fiercest enemies, remained a key figure in underworld circles in Cincinnati and Newport. As his notoriety intensified, he grew increasingly willing to settle disputes with gunplay. Jew John seemed destined for a harsh fall.

Remus may have faced a similar, deadly fate, if he were not willing to leave his dreams of a grand bourbon empire in the past.

On an unseasonably warm February day in 1931, Lorenzo Miller took a drive out to a small cottage on Line Road, just a few miles northeast of Hamilton, Ohio, which over the years had earned the infamous moniker "Little Chicago." The city seemed far enough outside Cincinnati and Chicago to offer safe haven for criminals and thugs, and was large enough to become a home for many criminals and bootleggers who operated there.

Lorenzo had heard stories about a raid that had taken place at the cottage the previous August. He wanted to investigate further, since he was considering buying the property. Even more intriguing, though, police had found a series of intricately hidden doors and secret passages. They had to break down a concrete wall, where they uncovered a still. Miller wanted to take another look, especially at the basement, which seemed cramped and dank on his first visit.

Eager to discover its mysteries, Lorenzo, his wife, and a handful of friends went to the abandoned house. He'd heard about a small compartment in the cellar that could only be reached by entering through a fruit cupboard. While the others waited, Miller found the secret passage and struck a match to see where it led.

As the glow lit the small space, Miller jumped backward.

On the floor before him, he saw a man's bound feet. He screamed and the entire group streamed out of the cottage. They called Tom McGreevy, the Butler County jailer, who dispatched Deputy Sheriffs Art Linkins and Charles B. Walke to the scene.

As other investigators arrived, they found a horrific mess, but they knew the victim—everyone knew him.

"His picture is in probably every police gallery in the country," one reporter speculated.

Jew John Marcus, one of the nation's roughest and most feared criminals, was found slumped on the floor in a sitting position, gagged with part of a silk shirt, while his hands and feet were bound with picture frame wire.

"Marcus had been dead for three weeks at least…His eyes were missing, his brains gone, and there was a hole in his skull, presumably made by field mice, which had chewed on his ears and nose," an observer at the scene noted.

His expensive silk hat lay strewn beside the body, a single bullet hole revealing that he had been shot at point-blank range above the right eye.

Tests later revealed that a .32 caliber Smith & Wesson revolver had been used in the murder. Officials interpreted Jew John's missing eyes as a gangland sign, reserved for a victim they assumed was a snitch. It was an ignoble end for the slick-dressing criminal, who authorities deemed "one of the toughest all-around racketeers in criminal life."

Federal agents and detectives from Cincinnati swarmed to Hamilton. Marcus had ties dating back to Remus's bourbon kingdom, while more recently he had been associated with both Al Capone in Chicago and the Egan's Rats gang in St. Louis. Robbery was not a motive. They found $60 in cash on the body, as well as an expensive gold watch and chain. Authorities estimated that his fashionable overcoat could have fetched upwards of $150. His identity was con-

firmed by Cincinnati Detective Chief Emmett Kirgan, who had testified in the
Remus case, and was the officer on duty the morning of the killing. Kirgan
recognized Jew John's trademark four gold teeth, despite the ghastly condition
of his decomposed body.

Cincinnati police, hearing rumors about Marcus's death, pieced together a
theory that he had been "taken for a ride" with his "sweetheart," Margie Henry,
a girl from Louisville. Henry went missing weeks earlier. Detectives assumed
that her lifeless body had been dumped in the Miami River or burned up in the
cottage incinerator.

This thesis rested on Marcus's feud with Bob Zwick, a notorious murderer
and criminal, known alternatively as "The Fox" for outsmarting federal agents
on his trail or "Ghost" for his ability to slip away from crime scenes before
police could catch him.

Zwick and Marcus each accused the other of hijacking their booze runs.
Allegedly, Jew John had stolen one of Zwick's "liquor trucks." Marcus accused
Zwick of hijacking him on a trek between Detroit and Cincinnati, with Jew
John and Margie driving away at eighty miles per hour in a hail of bullets.

Usually these kinds of feuds were kept private, but by the early 1930s, gangsters took their hostilities public. Marcus declared to reporters that he would
"get even with the man the cops can't catch," virtually challenging Zwick to
retaliate. The Hamilton hit would have sent a message that The Fox would defend his territory by getting rid of a chief competitor.

Hamilton investigators revealed that both Jew John and Bob Zwick had been
partners in a $68,000 distillery operation at South Monument Avenue, only a
couple blocks from the railroad. While signs on the exterior read "Ohio Valley
Rag Laundry," inside an immense distillery operation ran around the clock,
pumping thousands of gallons of illegal liquor into the national pipeline running
through Southern Ohio. When police raided after three months in operation,
they found 2,800 gallons of liquor and 40,000 gallons of mash being prepped.

An intricate network of tunnels and escape routes allowed several men to
evade capture during the raid. Rumors circulated that Remus ran the operation,
but others believed the Detroit-based Purple Gang or men from Capone's Chicago outfit managed it. The Marcus and Zwick connection, however, put another
black mark in their relationship and may have led to Jew John's assassination.

No one could crack the Marcus murder, but police got close when Lawrence
Shannon, who went by the alias "Larry Coates," got called in for questioning in
Miami Beach. Coates, from Newport, had been a smalltime "hustler" who spe-

cialized in stealing from other criminals, particularly bookies and gambling halls. He eventually graduated to murder and kidnapping.

The break occurred when Major Calvin Goddard, the nation's top ballistics expert, heard about Coates's arrest while on vacation in Florida. He contacted Butler County coroner Edward Cook and offered to test the bullets. Goddard concluded that the gun Coates had on him in Miami Beach matched the one used to kill Jew John Marcus.

Despite the evidence the ballistic tests revealed, a grand jury in Butler County refused to indict Coates. He remained a fugitive, reportedly hiding out in Chicago. Eventually, the thug made his way back to his former haunts, moving between Newport and Cincinnati. However, he had made too many enemies.

On July 28, 1931, Coates died in Cincinnati General Hospital from multiple head wounds. At 2 a.m., an unidentified car driven by a local gangster along Wooster Road on the east side pulled up next to his. Unknown assailants fired off a volley of bullets. Coates was hit five times. He later died, taking the mysterious details of the Marcus shooting with him to his grave. The two had been enemies since late 1929 when they were arrested after an altercation in a Cincinnati hotel. Coates pulled a pistol on Marcus, who wrestled it from him before a shot could be fired, and then beat the man senseless in retaliation. To teach Coates a lesson, Jew John reportedly stuffed bullets from the pistol into Coates's mouth.

Decades later, a Hamilton official who investigated the Coates murder concluded off-the-record that he knew the smalltime hoodlum did not kill Marcus. However, Coates's murder was probably a revenge hit by thugs loyal to Jew John.

Reporter Jim Blount, who sleuthed and wrote about the city's history for decades, revealed that in the 1970s that his sources claimed, "The man who killed Marcus died just a few years ago…He refused to identify the person."

Winning his release from the Lima facility gave George freedom, but he still had to worry about the government pursuing him on other fronts. First, the Labor Department hung the threat of deportation over his head, despite overwhelming evidence that Dodge and Imogene had originally planted the idea and pushed government officials to pursue the charge. When they had ransacked the Price Hill mansion, they had destroyed the paperwork that George had entrusted to Imogene, including documents that would have established his American citizenship.

Once he had been locked away, Labor Department leaders determined that serving time behind bars would be sufficient enough punishment. The government formally dropped the case on October 3, 1928, citing, "It would be too difficult for the government to prove that Remus, after all these years of residence in the United States…was not a citizen."

Plus, Labor officials were not even sure if Germany would take him back. It seemed that the United States was stuck with the former crime boss.

Remus's not-guilty verdict and his continued incarceration while the courts sorted out his sanity seemed a microcosm of Prohibition America. Enforcement had simply fallen apart. Public outrage, increasing violence, political corruption, and outright mismanagement led to ever-dwindling support.

The public loved the roaring 1920s and F. Scott Fitzgerald's "Jazz Age," but they hated the dry laws and enforcement practices. People also developed a love-hate relationship with criminals. Some cities, like Chicago, and rural burgs, like Hamilton, grew so lawless that they necessitated action.

In the waning days of the scandalous Remus trial, the *Cincinnati Post*, editorializing as "Cincinnatus" attempted to allay public censure for the newspaper's role in turning the bootleg baron into a national sensation. A front-page essay asked rhetorically:

**"Is there not enough righteousness
and beauty in the world that the public
must be fed this filth and ugliness?"**

Taking the high ground, the vaunted *Post* countered that the newspaper stood as a "true reflection of life" and that "Remus is a symptom of our national life. He is an interesting social and moral study."

In other words, the newspaper and other media sources simply filled the public demand for salacious news. From their lofty post above the Queen City, the editors warned: do not blame us for the ugliness of society. Look at this case as a reflection of us all. It must not be censored. We should not be censored.

What Cincinnatus hoped for, the editors professed, was that "Remus will retire into obscurity and never will be heard from again." After covering Remus off and on for most of the decade, the newspaper's call for the murderer and king of the bootleggers to simply disappear was more than a little disingenuous. Papers nationwide had run millions of words about George, Imogene, and Franklin, as well as photographs and drawings of every scene imaginable.

Indeed, Prohibition had turned ordinary citizens into criminals, and the media had turned criminals into Jazz Age icons. At the top of the heap stood those few, like Remus, who took advantage of the new illegal booze marketplace to gain untold power and riches. Increased media attention transformed them into folk heroes.

The question the public seemed unable to answer was whether or not Imogene's murder was premeditated. Taft attempted to make the point as clear as the water in the Imogene Baths, but George had convinced them that he'd pulled the trigger in a fit of mania.

On November 20, 1927, at Remus's trial, Mrs. August Bruck, the wife of a Remus henchman, had testified that she attended a Sinton Hotel meeting the night before the murder. The boss and several of his main lieutenants, including confidante and business manager Blanche Watson and the ever-faithful George Conners, were in the room. Bruck claimed that discussion of Imogene did not take place: she just wasn't on anyone's mind. Instead the bandits focused on some trips that were being planned. George was interested in getting into rumrunning in the Caribbean, according to witnesses. Even after serving out two jail sentences that took three years off his life, it seems that Remus still chased the idea of going "legit" via selling booze overseas.

In contrast to the staid conversation the night before the murder, Robert L. Dunning, head of the Department of Criminal Identification for the Cincinnati police, claimed Remus had been "courteous, intelligent, coherent, and without regret for what he had done." Actually, Remus showed no remorse whatsoever—except, perhaps, that he didn't catch Imogene and Franklin together.

He was levelheaded and following a plan, Dunning thought. Then, Remus told the investigator that he had been shadowing the lovers for about a year and a half "trying to catch them and kill them."

Charles E. Kiely and the team of alienists asked Remus when he first thought of murdering Imogene, a question they could ask him once he was on the stand during the insanity hearing, but the general public would not hear. George gave them three separate answers. The first, "Before he left the Atlanta prison and before the time he first began to suspect the relations of Dodge and his wife." The second, in the days just prior to the shooting, "when he heard she had employed gunmen to hang around the Sinton Hotel to kill him." Then, finally, "he said when she got into her taxicab laughing." The sweeping answer provided verification that Remus thought about murdering Imogene, but still did not give definitive proof that the shooting in Eden Park was according to plan.

Within hours of the murder, Remus met with reporters and answered questions at his cell. In the frenzy to uncover the "why he did it" angle, many of them overlooked compelling details that gave insight into the premeditation question, particularly given George's relative calmness and direct responses, despite having just ended his wife's life:

"How many times did you hit Mrs. Remus?" a reporter asked.

"I don't know exactly, three times I guess. I am not sure," George replied.

Later, Remus said that he "fired several shots...he thought that his pistol jammed."

At the county coroner's inquest, police Lieutenant Frank McNeal relayed that George confessed to shooting Imogene "three times" and that he "would have continued shooting had not his gun jammed."

Not being able to conclusively answer the question about how many times he shot her may perhaps cast some doubt on premeditation. Would someone as calculating as George—a person willing to drink poison to get a client that was clearly guilty off a murder rap—forget how many times he pulled the trigger?

The April 4, 1928, *St. Louis Star* quoted Remus on his plans for the future: "The first thing I will do on obtaining my freedom will be to return to my home in Cincinnati, where my mother is waiting for me, and then dig in and litigate my financial affairs," George explained.

The disgraced bootleg baron told reporters that his business had brought in revenues between $100 and $150 million in a two-year span in 1920 and 1921. He believed he had kept about $6 to $7 million of that, but sitting in the asylum in Lima, he claimed to have no idea exactly how much was left or where the money went. Most of his tangible assets—from the Price Hill mansion to the elegant Remus Building headquarters—were part of lawsuits dating back to the stint in Atlanta.

Finally released from custody, Remus used what skills he had left in his arsenal. He fired off a round of lawsuits in an attempt to reclaim a portion of his lost fortune, accusing Imogene of "squandering" much of his wealth.

"I will experience a new born feeling after my release from this hell hole of the earth," Remus reflected.

Then, he answered the burning question about his future and Dodge, explaining, "I will be forever through with the liquor business, you may be sure, and Franklin L. Dodge does not interest me in the least."

"The status of my affairs will be satisfactory and pleasing to me regardless of what it amounts to financially," claimed the bootleg baron. He professed the eternal "I've turned over a new leaf," saying, "The main thing is I will have again regained my precious liberty." He planned to spend time with his ailing mother and 23-year-old daughter Romola, "I shall always find great satisfaction and happiness in making their lives happy."

George became an object of ridicule in his new public persona. The *St. Louis Post-Dispatch* joked on its editorial page: "Business note: George Remus, dealer in wines and choice liquors, has returned from a long vacation to his old headquarters at Cincinnati."

The *Buffalo News*: "'It is wonderful,' says George Remus, apropos of his release from the insane asylum. The opinion is not unanimous."

The *St. Louis Star* slammed the sham proceedings, exclaiming that Remus's release "rung down the final curtain upon its farce of justice."

The paper wisely questioned Remus's state of mind, declaring, "It has yet to be determined whether Remus is not the dangerous psychopath, the menace to society it was charged he was when committed."

• • •

During the sanity hearings in late February 1928, the prosecutors also took a deep dive into his financial records. Led by Walter Sibbald, the attorneys had the same basic question that other observers wondered—what happened to all that money? If they could demonstrate that George had hidden it away, the feds would have a new avenue of attack to jail him as a kind of redemption for the jury's verdict in the murder trial. They were also fishing for information that they could use to nab other players in the illegal liquor marketplace.

Remus understood the prosecutor's tactic and avoided specifics whenever possible about his own income, all the while layering detail after detail on the timeframe when Imogene and Franklin depleted his wealth. When Sibbald asked for unambiguous figures for how much money he made in 1920, 1921, or 1922, George parried, "I cannot answer that. I can't approximate it."

Remus parried every attempt to pin him to specific income levels and frequently feigned that he forgot dates so that the prosecution could not catch him in a lie—getting him on a perjury charge—or go after his past business partners. The public was thirsty for the information as well, but mainly wanted to learn whether the "former bootlegger and wife slayer" was crazy enough to go after Franklin Dodge. They also dreamed of lost millions that would someday appear.

Dismantling the national bootleg network had taken time and a combination of recklessness and scheming by many parties who eagerly lusted after the leftover pieces, including the federal government. Both before and after he murdered Imogene, George remained guarded about his holdings and cash reserves, because he constantly feared tax officials in Washington would file charges against him.

Yet, Imogene's mismanagement had really lit the fuse that would blow up her husband's empire. Her addiction was cash. She often carted suitcases filled with money. The mountain of cash she had at her disposal gave her freedom, power, and luxury. She showered her family and friends with gifts. She and Franklin used the money on a two and a half year hedonistic spree that reduced her husband's holdings from millions of dollars in cash and assets to almost nothing.

In other cases, George's partners—with the backing of Imogene and Franklin—made moves that were catastrophic to his bottom line. At the Freiberg & Workum distillery operation in Lynchburg, Ohio, Remus had paid about $325,000 for 75 percent of the operation. Then, he invested another $50,000 to maintain the facility. Over time, he estimated that he had poured another $315,000 to $375,000 into the place.

"I felt it was the last smash of any of my substantial holdings," Remus lamented. With Imogene's approval and Franklin's backing, F&W was sold for just $285,000.

"It was just giving away a plant that would have netted a splendid income for me in afterlife." There were 14,000 barrels on site drawing rent and waiting to be sold.

"I had between $100,000 and $300,000 worth of judgment notes and promissory notes…many of them, the statute of limitations has run against," George testified at his February 1928 sanity hearings.

"I am taking those losses good naturedly as well."

Like F&W, many distilleries Remus purchased outright or as a silent partner required substantial amounts of money for upkeep, ranging from employee salaries to bribes for local officials. Firepower took money, too. As the bootlegging business grew increasingly vicious, George had to hire more and more thugs who could protect both operations and distribution.

In addition, once Remus was tainted by the bootlegging conviction, many criminals he worked with took advantage of his incarceration to conveniently forget about monies they owed him. The Jack Daniel's case might be the most egregious example.

"I did expect to receive that money, about $550,000, and I didn't get a dime out of it," he confessed during the sanity hearing.

Greed ruled the day for most underworld operators, preferring quick cash to long-term success. The heart of George's plan to build a nationwide bourbon network and corner the marketplace clashed with these get-rich-quick schemes. The conspirators in St. Louis wanted to milk the place, despite Remus's call for patience.

He hoped to use the Jack Daniel's whiskey stock as the centerpiece of a consolidated government-bonded warehouse that would include the 5,200 barrels he had at the Rugby distillery in Louisville and what remained of the Pogue bourbon in Maysville, Kentucky.

Instead, he explained, "those men got the physical property and they depleted it against my advice and opinion."

After he established a warehouse in the heart of bourbon country, he planned to do the same "west of the Mississippi River," where he deemed "the demand is very large from the viewpoint of liquor for medicinal purposes."

On one hand, Remus yearned to become a legitimate business leader, but too frequently his own greed forced him to keep dealing illegally. Remus's money and "interests," as he called them, "were all in the liquor line." George had chosen a primrose path to criminal mastermind. He had to live with that choice.

Liquidity forced George's hand in several instances. He needed fast cash and the ownership interests in the various distilleries constituted all he had to barter. For example, he sold his one-third rights in the Hill and Hill Distilling Company in Owensboro, Kentucky, for $21,000, though he estimated that it was worth $150,000 and had originally cost roughly $400,000. Although he was not in financial straits, George saw his overall wealth quickly dwindle in these lopsided fire sales.

In other cases, Remus was robbed or taken advantage of by business associates when they had the opportunity to intercede. Chicago mob boss John Torrio was a key figure in the Windy City's transformation to American crime center. Prohibition enabled him to turn an outfit that centered on prostitution and gambling into one of the most profitable and well-run bootlegging outfits in the nation. And, perhaps more importantly, Torrio unleashed a young enforcer from Brooklyn named Al Capone on the world, eventually turning over the business to the flashy, brutal youngster.

Unknown to George while he was in jail, Imogene had used the power of attorney to sell off property across the street from the Hermosa Avenue mansion. Remus had planned to build sixty to one hundred moderately priced homes there "for people in medium circumstances."

His wife struck a deal to sell the land for $37,500. Imogene's attorney on the real estate transaction was Joseph C. Breitenstein, a junior partner in the law firm Wertz and Breitenstein. Wertz was the former District Attorney for the Northern District of Ohio.

"Dodge, Wertz, and Breitenstein were friends," George declared in early 1928. "They entered into this conspiracy to defraud me out of that which was left."

Later, Imogene and Franklin realized that the lawyer was going to charge them the full amount for his legal fees, thus swindling them out of the land, money, and whiskey certificates. They went to court to reclaim the property.

"I knew that such conspiracy did exist," George revealed, "but I didn't know it as definitely or as I subsequently knew it, as I could not find the deceased no how."

Eventually, Torrio, who left Chicago and re-launched his career in New York City as a mentor to Lucky Luciano and Meyer Lansky, mysteriously gained the properties that Remus had planned to fund him into retirement. John's lifelong love, his wife Anna, was from the Covington area and had extended family in the Cincinnati region.

Torrio was a shadowy figure in the criminal world, alternatively serving as counselor and mob banker. In the early 1930s, he began moving aggressively, though quietly, into "legitimate" business, most notably real estate in Florida, Chicago, and Ohio. John and Anna lived in Cincinnati for a time from 1952 to 1954, but left when a mysterious government agency contacted them, forcing them to flee to New York to prevent family from being drawn into their past lives.

The federal government played a significant role in depleting Remus's riches. The majority of George's money vanished when Prohibition Bureau enforcement agents would raid a property he owned, and then shutter or confiscate the operations and goods. When these incursions took place, he would lose his initial investment and whatever liquor remained.

The feds seized the Fleischmann, Burks Spring, and Squibb facilities, George lamented, resulting in "many of hundreds of thousands of dollars I lost," after "the government confiscat[ed] those properties."

"Those were properties seized by the government…where I had reinvested my monies," George lamented. "I didn't see why I should pay income tax based upon those kind of inconsistencies."

Warehouse rental also set him back, sucking up funds that could have been used to extend or reestablish the network.

"We have to pay twenty five cents a month for every barrel stored," George said. "So it is a tremendous loss as well." While he was in prison, Blanche brought a bill from one warehouse that cost him $15,000.

To keep the Remus organization running while George served the sentence for the public nuisance charge at Death Valley, Blanche and George Conners sometimes had to sell whiskey certificates at a discount rate. In July 1926, for example, they fought with Imogene over ownership of certificates for 422 barrels of whiskey. While lawyers argued over who actually owned them, the offering price dropped from $20,000 to $12,000. Blanche finally sold them for the latter amount.

Remus did admit that he had not filed income tax returns for those years focused on building the bootleg operation. Once he was arrested and imprisoned, however, a handful of officers from the Treasury Department investigated his work and affixed an approximated income. They computed that Remus made deposits of about $25,000 to $78,000 per day during that span.

One intriguing possibility is that some of the lost millions are still hidden away—at the time of this writing—in safe deposit boxes at banks where Imogene and Franklin secretly placed them. More likely, however, her death led to the rent expiring on the boxes, which would have kicked the money to the state treasurer wherever it was located. Since the 1980s, some states, including Illinois, began cataloguing abandoned safe deposit box materials and attempted to deliver the items back to the owners' heirs.

Imogene had secret accounts and security boxes at banks around the nation, as well as in Canada. The institutions included the Roger Trust Savings Bank and Michigan Trust in Chicago, along with banks in New York, Buffalo, Cleveland, and Lansing. She and Franklin dealt in cash, cars, and jewels, preferring flashy to fiscally responsible. They lived reckless lives together.

When the lovers stripped the Dream Palace clean, they seemed to act out of vindictiveness and spite more than an attempt to gain real value out of Remus's exotic collection of historical artifacts and art. While George served the year-long sentence in Ohio, Franklin had the remaining art and valuables loaded into a truck and transported to Windsor, Canada, just across the river from Detroit.

Imogene and Franklin assumed, George explained, "I would be deported and I couldn't go on to Canada and recover it."

Remus's detectives, however, traced the goods through custom officers, so he knew that the artwork had been taken to Imogene's brother's gambling house, where the lovers set up residency during the summer of 1927.

Imogene treated her husband's long-term assets like poker chips, selling them off when she needed money with little thought about compounding growth over the long haul. She depleted George's extensive stock portfolio, including holdings in Sinclair Oil, Liberty National Bank, and Yellow Taxi. They also had real estate interests that she used to barter with banks, surety companies, and liquor wholesalers.

Imogene purchased at least seven automobiles while George was in prison, usually Pierce Arrow, Marmon, or Packard touring models. According to Remus, the cars cost between $3,800 and $5,000 each. She also gave away George's prized Packard, valued at $6,800, to Vance Hicks, her St. Louis attorney.

Imogene's bad decisions to sell off assets severely debilitated her husband after he left the prison system. Selling the Fleischmann operation at a loss of about $120,000 left a gaping wound in George's plan to reestablish himself. The profit from selling Fleischmann would have helped him alleviate the heavy tax bill dropped in his lap by federal officials. Paying down bank loans would also activate the whiskey certificates they held to secure the loans.

The complexity of the financial entanglements George created to build the bourbon empire was far too intricate for Franklin and Imogene to oversee. Instead, they pulled as much cash out as possible and bartered with land and currency to get their hands on the invaluable whiskey certificates.

Other family members close to Remus also stole from him when he was in prison. At one time Imogene's brother-in-law W. C. Campbell (husband of her sister Grace) was in the inner sanctum of the bourbon empire. George named him president of the Rugby Distilling Company in Louisville. The bootleg king's plan was to get the 1,500 barrels out of the plant quickly, but the enforcement agents in Kentucky would not accept bribes enabling him to siphon the alcohol. Campbell, afraid of the law, embezzled from the operation as soon as Remus went to prison.

His brother-in-law "ran out with all the moneys that were in the bank, with a Packard car, and with the stock book," George said later. Campbell then went into hiding.

* * *

Contrary to what journalists and some historians wrote about Remus in his later years, George was not destitute.

What emerged from his testimony during the February 1928 insanity hearings was that Remus owed his then-secretary, later third wife, Blanche Watson a considerable amount of money. For several years, the two had seemed to operate a series of money-laundering schemes that enabled them to keep a steady cash flow, and allowed her to pocket (or hide away) significant sums.

George admitted that he owed Blanche about $70,000 at the time. Just prior to entering Atlanta, Remus explained that he possessed about $450,000 "in notes and otherwise," including collateral against outstanding loans. He had the whiskey certificates and Blanche's willingness to front the cash he needed to secure the notes. Remus had funneled so much money through her operations that she had become wealthy. By mid-1921, Blanche was managing the Kenton Drug Company, one of George's wholesale outfits, and paying the Pogue Distillery $5,000 for bottling fees on 395 cases of bourbon. The transaction seemed legitimate on paper and Watson was sure to include that the payment was for liquor "which you hold permit." Yet, this bourbon almost certainly went into the bootleg market, not the Kenton Drug Company. In 1921, those cases equated to more than $40,000.

Unlike Imogene, Blanche was content to remain behind the scenes and out of the limelight, which made her incredibly valuable to Remus. Several years earlier, in 1925, Watson had taken over the deed for the mansion from Imogene while George was in prison. When the banks started fretting over his ability to repay several outstanding loans, Remus directed Blanche to sell off a number of properties he owned, including a farm and some land near the mansion. At the same time, Imogene was selling off assets, according to her husband, "it was all done, go ahead and get as much cash in hand as possible."

He claimed that the property Imogene had under her control totaled about $1.8 million, yet he could not raise a $50,000 bond to remain free as a government witness.

"It was a pitiful situation," George sighed.

. . .

Remus operated primarily outside the law, so keeping any form of records was strictly forbidden—and wrongheaded. Documentation exposed him to government oversight. At the height of his power and income generation prior to going to prison, when Remus had invoices to pay, he simply instructed Imogene or one of his men to visit one of their many vaults and pay the bills in cash.

"We didn't want those matters to show through the banks because the government always has access to those matters and they would assess the income tax on those matters," George explained. "Many of those matters we possibly paid two and three times the amount that someone else would pay on the theory that we had millions. I didn't care about those things—wasn't interested in those details much," he admitted.

19

Dodge's Demise

On a mission to get the elusive Franklin Dodge's perspective on the Remus trial's mudslinging directed his way, journalist Paul W. White found his man in prosecutor Charlie Taft's spacious office at the Hamilton County Courthouse. There, on the first day of December 1927, the journalist had discovered the "big, bull-necked man" nervously awaiting word from the courtroom, just one floor below. White gave the former Prohi a taste of what was being said about him by Remus.

"Lies, all lies," Franklin countered.

Increasingly irritated and finding it impossible to hide from the media spotlight, Dodge had decided to tell his side of the story to White, one of the prominent national correspondents covering the trial.

"I never was intimate with Mrs. Remus and no one can prove I was," Dodge boomed.

Remus had a keen way of producing sound bites that framed Dodge as an adulterer and criminal. George had just spent another day dragging the younger man through the muck. Like a prizefighter going for the knockout by landing body blow after body blow, George never let up on Franklin, attacking him with a litany of accusations and insinuations.

The former agent had to stay in Cincinnati during the proceedings, but the Queen City was the last place he wanted to be. The prosecution had not called the Michigan man to testify, so Franklin could not clear his name or counter any of the murderer's assertions in court. Desperate for *something* from Dodge, newspapers had pursued him nonstop until he agreed to sit for a photograph. Within days, hundreds of papers across the nation ran the image. At that moment, he might have been the most notorious man in America.

Finally cornering Dodge, White described him suffering acute "mental turmoil" created by the national news frenzy.

"The strain of the trial he is not permitted to attend is telling upon Dodge. Even within the past month lines that were not there before have appeared in his face," White reported.

Each day when he picked up the morning newspaper, Dodge saw his name filling columns and summaries of the trial. He heard people talking about Imogene's murder in the restaurants and bars he haunted. When Franklin attempted to go outside, reporters hounded him. He had been covering his face with his hat or jacket for months.

Here in private, in front of the reporter, Dodge tried to summarize his mental state, alternating between calmness and hostility for Remus. He allowed White to read a letter he had written to Willie Haar, one of the Savannah Four from Georgia whom Dodge had befriended during his investigations into Warden Sartain's corruption at the Atlanta Federal Pen. Haar had been called as a defense witness in the Remus trial to comment on George's mental state while he was in prison, as well as the relationship between George and Imogene. Dodge's letter, according to White, contained a multitude of "profane epithets concerning Remus."

Switching to attack mode, Franklin then told the reporter how amusing it was to hear that inmates in the Atlanta Federal Penitentiary referred to the bootlegger as a "rat." Having spent so much time investigating the criminal underbelly within the federal prison system and having locked up so many bootleg gangsters, Dodge clearly understood that using the term "rat" in a news article would devastate Remus when he saw it in the paper.

Franklin took more shots at George, using language that he knew Remus would find insulting. He told White that he considered George shooting Imogene a "cowardly act."

Despite Dodge's bravado, the stress of the trial besieged him. Throughout the proceedings he had wanted to fight back against the wave of publicity that accompanied George's allegations, but he could not jeopardize the potential outcome. Taft had to keep him from lashing out. If he were placed on the stand, his testimony would have to be viewed as authoritative and coherent.

Though he wanted Remus to burn, he also knew that the trial would change his life forever.

In the letter he let White read, Dodge explained to Haar that the publicity was like "having hell on earth for a long time." Its conclusion, Franklin knew, "will be like starting all over again."

Even when he had help from others—including Imogene's daughter—to prove his case, Dodge could not get people to believe him. For her part, Ruth staunchly refuted Remus's claims that Franklin and Imogene had ever been more than business associates. She sketched a portrait of her stepfather as vindictive and aggressive, with an unusual proclivity toward temperamental outbursts that frequently led to physical confrontations or erratic decision-making.

In Atlanta, Ruth claimed that his temper had landed him in solitary confinement. Even more dangerous, however, had been Remus's double-cross of members of the Egan's Rats gang in St. Louis. That betrayal had led to an assassination plot, the girl explained, not her mother or Franklin's desire to see him bumped off. Ruth's insight into her stepfather's life and career revealed how closely she watched and listened as a teenager. She had also been an almost constant travel companion for her mother while Remus was in jail.

Ruth said that Remus often used his influence and money to frame associates who he believed had double-crossed him. She accused him of attempting to do the same with her mother and Franklin.

"He no doubt spent thousands trying to get mother in a compromising position, but he failed," she had testified. "He should pay for so foully and cruelly assassinating my mother," the girl cried.

While Remus was pressuring Dodge verbally, maybe trying to draw out a confession from his adversary, he had also searched for physical evidence linking him to the bourbon empire money. He had sent Conners to Lansing to demand that bank officials reveal the contents of several safety deposit boxes at the American State Savings Bank, the bank that shared the Prudden Building with Franklin's father's law office.

When executives there had refused, George took the fight public, claiming that Franklin and Imogene held securities, jewelry, and whiskey certificates valued at $1.8 million.

"I do not care a snap of my finger for the money," George claimed. "It is my life for which I am fighting."

Merely the implication that Imogene and Franklin had been there together served George's purpose. His evidence was spotty, but several photographs allegedly showed Imogene on site. Remus had no idea if Dodge had been there, though the couple had supposedly been spotted there three weeks before the murder, removing several bundles.

Officials at American State Savings added mystery to Conners's whole investigation by neither confirming nor denying that they had ever rented to Imogene. Franklin also chose not to divulge any information. When asked by reporters, he openly questioned if Imogene had ever visited Lansing. Remus's chief aide, however, had interviewed a bank employee who said that Imogene was introduced to employees there by Wyllis Dodge, Franklin's younger brother.

The manipulative fallen Prohi narrative Remus had created about Franklin Dodge fell in line with how the public perceived the Prohibition Bureau. Polls showed the Mabel Willebrandt was personally popular, but even as her power increased and she cleaned up the agency, people generally still did not care for Prohibition or feds snooping around.

Making the intellectual leap that Franklin had gone from agent to rogue did not tax readers. George and his supporters had hammered away at the point.

"Dodge is liable to kill Remus," George Conners testified during the sanity hearings.

He labeled Franklin's instability "the greatest danger" to Remus if he were set free.

In an attempt to demonstrate his own impartiality, Conners told alienist Herman Hoppe, "I think I hate Dodge as much as any man in the world, but that doesn't say I would kill Dodge, although he has threatened my life."

What emerged from Remus's testimony at the insanity hearings is that Charlie Taft was probably wise in not bringing Dodge to the witness stand during the original trial. The intelligence George gathered revealed that the ex-fed had deep ties to organized crime, which Remus would have conveyed to Charles Elston during the cross-examination.

George's knowledge of the national bootlegging scene and insider's expertise of how outlaws got liquor onto the black market had made him more than just a criminal mastermind. He had served as an information broker, particularly when enforcement agents and investigators, led by Willebrandt, had turned to him while attempting to crack large cases.

The defense would've had a field day showing that Dodge had been duplicitous while working for Willebrandt and taking up with Imogene. Even if nothing more than her "business consultant," Franklin had crossed an ethical line.

"Why, most assuredly, the enemies that man has are by the score," George told Probate Judge Lueders, "He has betrayed every man he has ever been associated with."

In addition to his own snooping around for dirt on Dodge, George had found a ready conspirator in Thomas Wilcox, an investigator appointed by the attorney general to look into misconduct of Prohi agents. Remus claimed that Wilcox's findings had been reported to both President Calvin Coolidge and FBI Director J. Edgar Hoover.

"Wilcox stopped at the Metropole Hotel and we would take him out to the house," George explained about his role in piecing together evidence against Dodge. "He would tell me the evidence reasonably, what they had adduced."

"The government itself has made a very exhaustive investigation into the conduct of Franklin Dodge and has a great big file," Elston divulged.

Wilcox, George disclosed, urged Hoover to arrest Dodge for a long list of transgressions:

> Violation of the National Prohibition Act…assisting, aiding, and abetting in the pay of $15,000 so as to kill a governmental witness…not doing his legal duties during the course of his employment as a special governmental agent…and [violating] the White Slave Act.

Wilcox had even brought Remus to Detroit after the bootlegger left the Portsmouth jail, planning to use the information he gathered for "filing prosecutions against both of the characters, the deceased [Imogene] and Franklin Dodge."

In killing Imogene, George derailed the case that Wilcox and other agents from J. Edgar Hoover's office were compiling against Franklin. Hoover had aspirations of cementing his own place in the Washington power structure, and turning the Prohibition Bureau around was one of his primary concerns.

At one meeting with Remus, the investigator told George that they had irrefutable evidence that "Dodge has entered into a conspiracy to kill Remus while being a governmental agent in Indianapolis."

Important government officials were following Wilcox's investigation, particularly J. Edgar Hoover, who told Wilcox that Dodge's antics were having negative consequences, "making the Department of Justice the laughing stock."

According to Wilcox, Franklin Dodge became a liability for Hoover, Sargent, Willebrandt, and others. They worried that his meetings with several hitmen while still a federal agent would come to light. In St. Louis, he and Imogene allegedly hired Jim McDonough, a gangster who also went by the alias James Noonan, to kill Remus. Wilcox also reported that in October and November 1925 Franklin and Imogene "decided to call in a couple of gunmen who were then in St. Louis…to kill George Remus, and that she and Franklin Dodge would put up the money in payment for the killing."

The primary motive for killing her husband, Imogene explained, was "that unless this were done, that Remus would send them all to jail."

When Noonan claimed he wasn't a hired gun, Dodge interjected. The killer probably thought Franklin was attempting to set him up, since he had been a well-known Prohibition enforcement agent.

"Don't be afraid of me," Franklin reassured the thug. "I will help you do the job. I will decoy Remus and put him in the right spot to be knocked off." Then, he added that the reward would be "fifteen thousand dollars."

* * *

The federal government's waffling over what to do with Franklin Dodge had deepened, in part because of the spotlight on him as a result of Remus's ranting. George's position made sense—he required a bogeyman to employ the temporary maniacal insanity plea and save his own neck.

The other obstacle blocking the feds from taking definitive action against Dodge was his complex relationship with Mabel Walker Willebrandt.

Franklin's position with Willebrandt made him famous in Washington circles and nationwide as her "ace detective," a phrase used over and over again to describe his work. Mabel sent him to major hotspots where she needed his eyes, ears, and instincts. In the early years of Volstead enforcement there were few agents that she could rely on as unequivocally as Dodge.

Franklin responded by delivering time and again in major busts that brought Willebrandt an admiring public. She was not immune to the rumblings that Dodge would bend or break the law to get the information he needed. Mabel personally appointed John Snook as warden in Atlanta to clean up that national scandal. After observing Franklin's tactics, which bordered on criminal, Snook turned against Willebrandt. He became a one-man wrecking crew attempting to destroy the public image she had worked so diligently to craft over the course of a decade.

But it was more than just her ace detective's actions away from her that sullied Willebrandt's image. At one point during his testimony, George blurted out that the owner of the Hollenden Hotel in Cleveland had secretly visited him in his jail cell with alarming news. Dodge, he explained, "this same paramour" who bedded Imogene, "has said that he has been intimate with Mrs. Mabel Walker Willebrandt, in the same hotel" that he had been caught in with Imogene.

Franklin's lurid two-timing of his boss and his mistress was revealed in court during Remus's testimony during the insanity hearings in late 1927 and through the internal investigation launched by Attorney General John G. Sargent and led by Thomas Wilcox. Sexual impropriety within the organization had now been added to the list of Prohibition Bureau evils.

According to Remus, the investigation outcome and its potential for scandal caused concern at the very top of the Washington power structure.

"The President himself is exercised about this thing," the bootleg baron announced during the hearing in front of Judge Lueders, adding that Wilcox had informed him of its dire consequences.

Rather than allow this line of questioning to continue, thus risking that the details might make their way into public view, Judge Lueders changed topics, asking George a series of inconsequential questions about his official residence in Ohio.

Although Remus had this damning rumor about Mabel and Franklin in his hip pocket, he did not announce it to reporters. Or, if he did tell them about it in confidence, the newspapermen chose not to publish it. Given the shocking revelations, such an omission is difficult to consider. It is as if George were saving this piece of information for its most tactical use.

George did attempt to prove that Mabel Willebrandt was in on the conspiracy to have him assassinated. Former government officials did not let this accusation sit without a response.

"Mrs. Willebrandt wasn't in any conspiracy," A. Lee Beatty, the former Assistant US District Attorney in Cincinnati, testified.

For Beatty, the idea that Willebrandt was in cahoots with Franklin and Imogene was simply delusional—enough reason in and of itself to declare Remus insane.

Yet, when Elston asked him to furnish details regarding her role in George's many cases, Beatty admitted that Willebrandt ordered the Jack Daniel's bond to be raised from $5,000 to $50,000, assuring that Remus would spend additional time behind bars. Furthermore, Dodge worked as a special agent on the St. Louis case, which made the timing of the bond increase suspect. When Dr. Hoppe pressed further about Willebrandt's role, Beatty conceded that he did not suspect her as a conspirator, but Remus might have had information from a different source that corroborated this notion.

Beatty also explained that Willebrandt ordered him "not to prosecute" the one-year sentence against Remus's men on the public nuisance charge after they did their time at Atlanta: "not to take any further action in their cases." She changed her mind when it came to prosecuting Remus, leading to his additional year behind bars.

From her interviews with him, Mabel knew that incarceration was Remus's greatest fear. She had used this terror against him.

Franklin Dodge had initially denied ever meeting Imogene. Later, when irrefutable evidence materialized—his selling whiskey certificates to Matt Hinkel for accessing Pogue Distillery bourbon—he claimed that he knew Imogene, but that he served only as her business advisor. When witnesses confirmed that they had seen the two together at various luxury hotels, Franklin asserted that they were together, but never alone. The consistency of Dodge's story is its persistent alteration.

Ace detective. Undercover.

The authenticity of the relationship between Franklin and Imogene remains largely a mystery. Would they have married? Would he have milked her dry, then run off with another woman? The answers died with Imogene.

There is no doubt, however, about the link between Franklin and George. The two shared a deep and abiding hatred. Since they could not get their hands on one another after Imogene's murder or even find assassins to take the other out beforehand, they engaged in a war of words in the press.

Reporters eagerly threw fuel on the fire. They interviewed George and Franklin and wrote stories that enabled the two to repeatedly call the other's manhood into question. The fight had taken on renewed vigor when Fiorello La Guardia brought it to the floor of the House of Representatives. He used

Dodge as a straw man to implicate the entire Prohibition Bureau, Mabel Willebrandt, and the crooked agents working for her. Remus saw La Guardia's speech as support, but the congressman used the bootlegger to demonstrate that the Prohibition Bureau was a cesspool of corruption. George's story helped the diminutive leader make his point nationally with the convenient hook of Remus's lost millions.

Given the heightened animosity, it's astonishing that Remus and Dodge did not end up mowing each other down in a hail of bullets. Perhaps George imagined that murdering Imogene was the only way to truly get inside Franklin's head. Knowing that Remus ended her life would haunt Dodge for the rest of his life.

Remus never wavered in declaring Franklin his nemesis, even up to the precise moment he fired that handgun.

"One of the last things my wife did was to give Dodge $60,000," George revealed.

Conners, who had led or personally conducted many of the investigations into Imogene's life with Dodge, had full confidence in the veracity of his work.

"No, there weren't any delusions, they were all facts, testimony, and evidence that I got from other people," he told Judge Lueders.

Remus was his archrival, but Dodge's reckless conduct had earned him a slew of enemies as a federal agent. In Atlanta, where he had been most aggressive in uncovering information pertaining to Sartain's money schemes, prison officials could not wait for his lucky streak to end.

According to Remus, John Snook, who replaced Sartain as warden, claimed that he was "holding a cell open for that character" and would bunk him there with a lifer who had syphilis, or what George called "a contaminated disease."

Snook—and many others who had come into contact with Franklin Dodge—waited for his demise.

⁂

With Imogene dead and the heat from the Remus allegations cooking up headlines, Dodge attempted to disappear. He could not risk his own safety attempting to access the money he and Imogene had hidden. Even if he could get at it, as a nationally infamous figure he couldn't go into a bank where Imogene had been a customer and hope to be unnoticed. Franklin had few options, so he returned to Lansing to stay at the family mansion.

On June 21, 1928, the day after Remus was freed from the insane asylum, the United Press newswire put out a story based on rumors that Dodge was "considering an attractive offer with a nationally known manufacturing concern" that would take the former fed to London for "several years." The UP reporter received the information from the elder Dodge, the powerful local politician and attorney. No story would be complete without the younger Dodge's thoughts on Remus's release, but it was noted that Franklin Jr. "could not be located to comment on the order releasing Remus...He has refused to discuss the case in the past." There is no indication that Dodge ever went to London or that a job offer had been extended.

In 1929, on the day before Christmas, Frank L. Dodge, Sr. died at home in Lansing at the age of 76. His death left a power vacuum in Lansing politics and within the Dodge family. His father had been Franklin's staunch ally during the Remus investigations and served as a kind of spokesperson for his son when the press searched for a story. The front-page piece announcing the elder Dodge's death in the *Lansing State Journal* only mentioned Franklin Jr. in the surviving list of family members, indicating that both Dodge boys still lived in the city. It would fall to Franklin to care for the Turner-Dodge homestead and take care of his immediate family, which included his mother Abbie and two sisters.

Franklin may have yearned for anonymity, but he burst back into the headlines on November 8, 1930, when he was arrested in Lansing and held on $5,000 bond. The preceding May, Dodge had given false testimony in the trial of George Brown, a bootlegger he had investigated in 1923. Dodge wrote detailed, secret reports of the rumrunner's activities that came back to bite him.

In 1931, Dodge's misconduct after leaving the Department of Justice finally caught up with him. On January 3, headlines revealed that Franklin was being held in federal district court in Georgia, charged with seven counts of perjury.

"It is charged that Dodge, after working up cases which resulted in 146 indictments in Georgia, returned seven years later, after he had left the government service, and, as a defense witness for an alleged bootlegger, gave testimony which directly contradicted his own reports on the same case," reporters explained.

On October 26, 1931, Franklin received a sentence of thirty months in prison for perjury after pleading guilty in a federal courtroom in Augusta, Georgia, in front of Judge W. H. Barrett. The judge, noting Dodge's exemplary service to his nation during Prohibition, cut the maximum sentence in half.

Dodge was held in the sleepy southern town until officials in Washington determined where he would serve out his sentence, which ended up being a prison facility in Chillicothe, Ohio. In 1933, he was released from the federal penitentiary and returned to Michigan.

Perhaps not surprisingly due to his family's political ties in Lansing and his inability to stay out of the spotlight, Franklin jumped into the front-page headlines soon after he returned home. On August 1, 1933, Michigan Governor William A. Comstock announced major changes in his administration. State Auditor General John K. Slack appointed Dodge to "a key position in the democratic administration," replacing George R. Thompson, a Republican who had been budget director, holding the position for twenty-four years. The move raised concern in Michigan and was later questioned in a series of editorials by the state's most powerful newspapers.

Overseeing Michigan's investigatory unit concerned with disbursements, Dodge's annual salary was $2,000. His hometown paper, the *Lansing State Journal*, in a slashing editorial, asserted that Franklin's selection was part of the Comstock administration's "mess of ineptitude." The "Dodge appointment has set the public literally aghast," the paper claimed.

Undoubtedly, favors must have been exchanged by the Dodge family in return for the position. Slack, a rising star in Michigan state politics, had deep ties to the Dodges, even renting out the spacious family home on East North Street. According to one reporter, "Slack and his family occupy the Dodge estate here to which Franklin Dodge is an heir."

More criticism arose at the end of 1933, when Slack gave Franklin a $400 raise for auditing government expenses and saving the state "$500,000" annually. Slack said he had chosen Dodge for the woebegone position of auditing fellow employees because the man "hadn't a friend in the world." The complaints about Franklin rolled into Slack's office because workers "objected to questioning of minor expense items."

For a long stretch of his adult life, Franklin Dodge found himself in the public eye, exploding into the national headlines like a film star—sometimes a hero and often a villain.

His notoriety made a laughingstock of his undercover work for the Prohibition Bureau and Mabel Walker Willebrandt. That role necessitated stealth and a healthy dose of personal resolve to engage in situations where he could be exposed and murdered at any moment.

After the headlines of his government appointment trailed off, Franklin later left the Michigan budget post, taking a position—ironically—with the Michigan Liquor Control Commission, where he worked until he retired. Although son of one of the city's most well-connected families, he lived in a modest home and had a small place in Detroit. He died on November 26, 1968, in Lansing, at the age of seventy-seven.

Franklin Dodge stayed out of the spotlight for the last thirty-five years of his life. There is no evidence that he had or spent any of George Remus's lost millions.

20

Remus v. Prohibition

"He is an actor, and a bad actor at that. He stages anything that he
wants, he puts over anything that suits him, and he has all the
appropriate gestures and all the appropriate emotionality and
everything that goes with it." —DAVID WOLFSTEIN,
alienist, on George Remus

"Histrionic" is how Wolfstein labeled Remus in his testimony at the insanity
hearing. He was charged with determining Remus's sanity in the murder trial,
finding George sane in the first instance—which the bootlegger didn't want—
and then providing evidence in the sanity hearing that confirmed what Remus
and Elston needed to affirm. Wolfstein had plenty of evidence, having spent
more time examining Remus than any other person on the planet.

"He puts over anything that suits him."

Pure evil.

But while Remus may have been singularly violent and dangerous, his utter
disregard for Prohibition put him in accord with how much of American society felt about the dry laws. Within the government, the lack of resolve for enforcing Prohibition started at the top.

President Warren G. Harding had "little interest in the strict enforcement of
Prohibition," according to historians, because his own drinking during the dry
era was an open rumor. "He was troubled by the contradiction between his
public statements and his private habit."

"Troubled."

Harding's personal taste for a nip of the "good stuff," however, was not the challenge for dry America. Whether through indifference or blatant malfeasance, the president permitted his cronies to create a lawless environment.

The most persistent violator of the public's trust was Attorney General Harry M. Daugherty, who was supposed to be tasked with enforcing the law. He and his personal toady Jess Smith—along with a crew of underlings and hangers-on—had little trouble strong-arming bootleggers. The whiskey certificates Daugherty essentially controlled through the national and regional Prohibition Bureau offices were virtually priceless. The question that has bedeviled historians looking back on the era was how much the president knew.

Harding most likely realized something inappropriate was going on at Justice, even if the details were conveyed via the White House gossip mill. When these rumors became outright scandals involving members of his inner circle, the president traced some of the wrongdoing back to Jess.

Taking action to protect himself from the rumors and any potential crisis as a result of the allegations becoming public, Harding had Smith removed from the guest list for his much-publicized trip to the West Coast in Summer 1923. Daugherty had personally asked for Jess to be included, but Harding not only denied the plea, he also "ordered Daugherty to get Smith out of Washington and to keep him away."

The direct snub proved too much for Jess's delicate constitution. With the president's support spent, he worried that Harry could no longer protect him. Every passing stranger seemed a spy or undercover federal agent just waiting to take him in. He killed himself, but rather than throw off investigators, Jess's suicide gave them new impetus into look into Daugherty's alleged wrongdoing.

Historian Edward Behr, commenting on the feasibility of enforcing the Volstead Act, explained the stark realities that the drys and federal government faced, calling the legislation "hopelessly inadequate," because legislators and lawmen "grossly underestimated the willingness of the lawbreakers to risk conviction, the degree of human ingenuity displayed to get around its provisions, and the ease with which the lawbreakers would be able to subvert all those whose job it was to enforce it."

Continuing in the effort, Willebrandt used the Remus conviction as the focal point in hundreds of speeches she delivered to civic and women's groups. The primary thrust of her talks called for renewed public responsibility in enforcing the alcohol ban. She claimed only to refer to the Remus saga generally as "the type of law violation" that his "case illustrated." Remus was the bogey-man that Willebrandt needed, though it ultimately wasn't enough.

And George knew that the ever-crusading Willebrandt required his down-fall to temper the criticism that plagued the Prohibition Bureau. After all, Dodge's turn to criminality placed Willebrandt and her government agency deep in harm's way. Still, could Remus's vendetta against the former special agent strike a blow against Prohibition enforcement? George's outbursts against Dodge often seemed like the ranting of a lunatic. But when Fiorello La Guardia proclaimed the veracity of the bootleg king's accusations against Dodge, it turned the tables on the enforcement department and the Republican admin-istrations of Harding and his successor Calvin Coolidge.

Remus painted Willebrandt as being at the center of a vast conspiracy. In front of Judge Lueders, Charlie Taft, and other government officials, Remus questioned why Franklin and Imogene were never brought to task for their crimes while he rotted away for three years inside federal and state prisons.

"Where a man is an agent of the Department of Justice, how he can use that official badge to further his own selfish interests?" George wondered aloud.

The government, he claimed, never wanted to spend the money to prosecute the couple, even though they were under investigation and had four charges against them just waiting to be filed.

"The thing that is behind the thing is, apparently, Mrs. Mabel Walker Wil-lebrandt…on account of the relations there," George told the men who were to determine his sanity.

A small handful of federal investigators, including the young FBI Director J. Edgar Hoover, had Franklin and Imogene in their sights, but Mabel called them off, supposedly because Dodge might expose the truth about their sexual relationship.

No one, according to Remus, could risk the scandal, even Coolidge, who he surmised, "takes orders from her, that I know."

The suave, baby-faced thug George Conners seemed to have spoken for the people when he told a reporter in early 1926:

When you think it over, what was wrong about what Remus did? Remus took the whiskey out and sold it. It was his whiskey; he never stole a drop of it. We knew it was against the law. But there were plenty of people who wanted to buy it, and we dealt honestly with them. We never poisoned anybody.... It was against the law, but was it wrong?

For journalist Paul Anderson, who spent so much time covering Prohibition and its rule-breakers, Conners's thoughts echoed what he had seen and heard throughout his travels. The calculation worked:

"When reduced to a simple proposition his argument seems to be that Remus, the bootlegger, was no worse than the men entrusted with enforcing the law."

Remus frequently spoke about the hypocrisy of the dry laws and the disparity in how they were enforced. He called Volstead "unreasonable" and "foolish."

"Where once a man could ply the liquor trade as a respected citizen he now works in the dark, thrown in among drug traffickers, gunmen, and other criminals," George complained. "Meanwhile respect for laws breaks down slowly and surely and we are becoming a nation of men who laugh at the law—all law."

The public demonstrated its true feelings about the Eighteenth Amendment by disparaging the law at nearly every turn. Open hostility did not require taking up arms, but people found ways to voice their disapproval.

One such showing developed when the *St. Louis Post-Dispatch* published the Union Station's Track 7 train schedule on January 4, 1926. This was the train that would deliver the Jack Daniel's distillery criminals from Indianapolis to the federal penitentiary in Leavenworth, Kansas. Crowds of onlookers arrived hours in advance to catch a glimpse and show their solidarity. By the time the special Pennsylvania Railroad car arrived, some 4,000 people had braved the early January weather to cheer for them.

Some women openly wept as the train pulled in, others brought food, candy, and cigars for the men to have while in prison. One of the convicts, Tony Foley, a professional gambler and bootlegger, looked out at the crowd and announced: "We can't be so bad after all."

The public had been antagonistic seemingly from the beginning of Prohibition and provided a suitable climate for an evolution in the way people looked at criminals—ones like Remus, Al Capone, and Lucky Luciano, whom the media covered so extensively. Egged on by newspaper reporters eager to feed the mob myth to willing readers, the day's papers filled with stories of violent lives and spectacular deaths, all played out heroically in opposition to the Volstead Act. When the film *Little Caesar* premiered in 1931, the gangster persona had been established.

The movie, an adaptation of the novel of the same name by William R. Burnett, featured the character Caesar "Rico" Bandello, played by famed character actor Edward G. Robinson. Rico is a "wise guy" whose toughness and street smarts are unmatched. The mafia code of honor became a kind of costar and the public ate it up, essentially turning street thugs into celebrities and iconic figures. These were the kind of people they had read about in the newspapers and even seen in their neighborhoods. The *Little Caesar* tagline was loud and sensational, but with an underlying wink and nod to the audience: "The Power-Mad Monarch of the Murder Mobs!" The filmmakers knew people would cheer for their crime boss in his fight against unjust law enforcement.

The success of *Little Caesar* led to a quick succession of other gang films, including *The Public Enemy* (1931) and *Scarface* (1932). As one author puts it, "The mafia gangster was replacing the cowboy as the mythic figure of redemption and virtue."

Fighting for his life in front of a Cincinnati jury, Remus had provided a model for the cinema gangsters, repeatedly pointing to the difference between what he viewed as "legal wrong, but not a moral one."

He even claimed to be completely sober but not against others enjoying their drinks: "I brought joy into the lives of many though I never drank any of the damned stuff myself."

He reasoned that the public would side with him—and as the mobs of people showed up each day to watch his murder trial unfold, it became clear that he'd figured correctly.

Perhaps, had he not murdered Imogene, George Remus would have strangely fulfilled the American Dream. He had the hard-work part down pat: the successes he'd had as an attorney were based on laboring at an unyielding pace as a criminal and labor lawyer, often with a backload of cases in the hundreds. The massive amounts of corruption and criminality in Chicago kept him constantly toiling, even as he took on junior partners and expanded his practice overall.

When he entered bootlegging, he'd worked his way up, in a sense. Now he wasn't the manual labor, he was the corner-office decision-maker. In comparison with the life he'd led as an attorney, Remus called bootlegging "ping pong," simply watching the deals unfold. He took on tasks as a criminal that were similar to any other business executive, essentially maintaining a constant stream of sales calls and meetings with various liquor stakeholders, whether federal officials that he had to pay or local distillery operators.

Sure, selling booze was technically "criminal," but Remus did not view himself as a criminal mastermind. Rather, he was chief executive of a business entity, attempting—like many industry leaders in that era—to create a monopoly. In that regard, he did not want *some* of the bourbon market, he wanted it *all*. Unlike a corporate chieftain, however, Remus did not have access to the talent needed to keep his empire afloat. There would be too many weak links in the bootleg baron's chain of command and labor.

The product was illegal, after all. So Remus was attempting to set up a monopoly—which had in effect been outlawed since the 1890 Sherman Anti-Trust Act and Teddy Roosevelt's campaign against such practices—around an illegal product. His doubly illegal American Dream required an astronomical network of bribes and payoffs.

The fantasy just couldn't hold up under those conditions.

Near the end of his run as head of his own criminal outfit, after years in federal and state prisons, one of the decade's most celebrated murder trials, and fighting for his freedom in front of alienists and judges, Remus took on a morose attitude.

"As a businessman, I think I am a colossal fizzle," he told prosecutor Walter Sibbald.

Whether or not this statement authentically reflected Remus's mindset, he had to at least appear reticent for those listening who were going to determine his fate. George realized that if he were ever set free, the government would likely come after him for back taxes and other penalties. He set the stage by repeatedly talking about how he had no money left.

"I mean to say that I haven't a dollar of my own," he told the examiners in early 1928. "I think that type of person should have his mind examined," he said without a hint of irony.

"You think you are in the right place then," Sibbald asked sarcastically, pushing the issue as the alienists and judges looked on.

Money aside, for the rest of his days Remus would skirt the boundaries of legality, trying to craft a new life while tagged with the ex-bootleg king and wife-slayer labels. Even as he struggled to stay semi-hidden, he couldn't go anywhere without being spotted. In the Cincinnati region, his name came up any time detectives or enforcement agents suspected a new whiskey ring was being formed. The living ghost of George Remus hung over Cincinnati, Newport, Hamilton, and several other locales where he had significant operations.

The stock market crash in October 1929 threw the American economy in a tailspin that would last more than a decade. The turmoil paved the way for President Franklin D. Roosevelt to repeal the Eighteenth Amendment, which formally occurred on December 5, 1933. Dry laws seemed ridiculous in a nation where people were starving to death.

As the Great Depression gripped the country, people had already begun looking at the 1920s through nostalgic lenses. In early 1931, George got into a fistfight at a racetrack, which led the ever-litigious Remus to sue for assault and battery.

Editors at the *Cincinnati Post* described George as a "legendary figure" emerging "out of the past." In relative obscurity and purposely attempting to stay out of the headlines less than three years since gaining his freedom from the Lima insane asylum, Remus and his tale had already lapsed into folklore. In a city where his name still appeared in the tile at the entrance of the Remus Building on Third Street, the editors wrote lovingly of the "mythical silver doorknobs" at the Price Hill mansion (also still standing as a ghost of the past) and the "grandeur" of his unforgettable parties.

Although he loved the Dream Palace at 825 Hermosa, with its one-of-a-kind marble swimming pool, he needed liquidity. In July 1934, he sold the home and ten-acre lot to Alice Delehanty, a Coventry dilettante, who he had helped make rich by installing her as one of the leaders of the Kentucky Drug Company. She happened to be close friends and business associates with Blanche Watson. George and Blanche denied rumors that they were married in March 1930, but that was almost certainly to avoid any tax liens that might burden them from Remus's bootlegging days.

Three months later, Delehanty had the home and majestic pool bulldozed by the Cleveland Wrecking Company, selling the property to real estate brokers who would divvy the grounds up for a subdivision. Later, George opened a real estate business—Washington Construction Company. One of his projects focused on managing the construction of a forty-eight-apartment structure on the Dream Palace site, which he estimated would cost $2 million to develop. The work was never completed.

A 1934 story in the *Cincinnati Enquirer* claimed that Remus lived mainly in New York City, though it mentioned that he had recently spent time in Cincinnati to attend horse races at the Coney Island Park, a one-mile dirt track built on the banks of the Ohio River near the adjoining amusement park and boardwalk. Remus even returned to the Lima state hospital in January 1938 to act as an interpreter for Rebecca Lauffer, a German woman he had befriended during his time at the asylum.

Despite attempting to live a quiet life, Remus kept returning to the underworld. In November 1939, he sued the estate of Edward J. O'Hare, a racetrack operator and close associate of Al Capone, for $196,700. O'Hare got caught up in a power struggle with Capone and ended up murdered. According to Remus, O'Hare and others had stolen liquor from his St. Louis warehouse in 1923. George could not escape the dark side or the nonstop pursuit of the millions of dollars hidden away by his now-dead wife and her princely Don Juan. Like all the lawsuits he pursued, the case was dismissed. George never had proper paperwork for the deals he had made—most of them illegal or bordering on unlawful—so he could never prove ownership once the repeal of the dry laws took place.

Prohibition was a long, strange marvel that ebbed and flowed with the changing times politically, economically, and culturally. Remus had a central position in its vortex and during the dry years Prohibition continued to dominate his life. Looking back in 1934, only a year after Prohibition ended, historian Sidney B. Whipple sensed an "unmistakable current of dissatisfaction and resentment against conditions…born, in great part, of the Depression."

F. Scott Fitzgerald's Jazz Age had ended in the blink of an eye, and George Remus—like everyone else—either adjusted or failed to adjust to the new world of the Great Depression. The great American writer himself stood testament to the emptiness of the era, a drunken shell of his former self. His great hopes for *Tender Is the Night*, published in 1934, fell flat in the desperate Depression angst. The tale centered on a penetrating portrait of Dick Diver, a psychiatrist caught up in the shenanigans of moneyed expat life in France. It was as if the nation's readers asked: who had time to read about the rich when the world seemed as if it were falling apart?

Hungry and afraid, watching men stand for hours in soup and bread lines, people turned away from the perceived glamour of the underworld. They had already seen too much wretchedness.

· · ·

Historian Sidney Whipple had dubbed the criminal masterminds who had grown famous during Prohibition the "kings of the bootleg world." However, a new reality set in with the financial devastation of the Depression. With the economic collapse, the public began looking at gangsters in a different light—one that did not glamorize their lives: "The Capones and Remuses, the Maddens and the Waxey Gordons, had overreached…with every brutal murder that was added to the social cost of bootlegging, some of the romance was stripped away."

According to the Whipple, "America was becoming nauseated, with the nausea that comes from debauchery…the headache was beginning."

In an early pang of that post-Jazz Age headache, the *St. Louis Star* rebuked the public for rallying around the famous bootlegger and turning him into a celebrity during his murder trial: "George Remus, bootlegger and wife slayer, is made a hero."

The editorial wondered if "derelicts" in and out of jail were "justified in believing they might be better off if they broke the law and were made heroes?" Law enforcement, the paper implied, had little chance of success given these conditions.

There is an eternal thirst for salacious stories, and the media serves them up to eager audiences. Often a criminal's tale is down the hatch and gone like a shot. But with Remus, Americans asked the bartender to leave the bottle on the bar for an entire decade. His name blazed across the headlines for most of the Roaring Twenties.

> "America was going on the grandest, gaudiest spree in history…The whole golden boom was in the air—its splendid generosities, its outrageous corruptions and the tortuous death struggle of the old America in prohibition." —F. SCOTT FITZGERALD,
> "Early Success" (1937)

With a mix of savvy and insight, F. Scott Fitzgerald gave purpose to the 1920s, christening the era "the Jazz Age," a name that probably would have been applauded by teenage Ruth Remus more than her stepfather, who was a generation older than the famous writer. Although just twenty-six years old when he coined the phrase in 1922, Fitzgerald gazed deep into modern society and provided a panoramic view of its madness, mayhem, and intrigue. He chronicled the Roaring Twenties for a nation hungry for an understanding of what was happening. Scott also lived the age, drinking bathtub gin and dancing through the night with his beautiful flapper wife Zelda.

While Fitzgerald wrote, danced, and drank, Remus and his associates supplied the nation its liquor. The criminal kingpin would use the proceeds to create an opulent life for himself and his queen, yet it all came crumbling down around him. When the last saxophone hit its note and the piano twinkled for the final time, life went on for George's cronies.

Although never far removed from the public eye, Remus attempted to create a new life. His associates went on too, though their lives were short and filled with danger. Their stories matter:

ERNEST "BUCK" BRADY played a significant role in building Remus's empire and later gobbled up much of his former boss's territory from Hamilton, Ohio, to Newport, Kentucky. The notorious gangster was renowned for his toughness and handiwork with firearms.

Buck and George virtually ran the hardscrabble towns in the northern Kentucky wilderness by working the system. The difference is that Buck never shied away from violence to make his point, which enabled him to fit better into the new breed of American gangster that rose to power in the mid- to late-1920s and into the 1930s.

In 1931, a Newport jury acquitted Buck on a murder rap. In 1946, he was cleared of a malicious shooting charge in the attack on Red Masterson, a local gangster and former Remus associate, who managed the Merchants nightclub in Newport. Brady had fired a shotgun at Masterson after catching up to him on a side street and pulling up alongside his car. Buck sprayed the man's jaw, throat, and neck with buckshot, but did not kill him. Lucky for Red, the doorframe deflected the blast away from his head. After the acquittal, Brady headed to Florida to let the heat dissipate, an increasingly common route for criminals who had to get out of town fast. His long ties to Remus and Newport soon brought him out of semi-retirement.

In July 1948, Remus teamed with Brady on one of George's highest-profile episodes in decades. Unlike his more famous partner, Buck had cash from the thriving bootleg network he had run and the gambling businesses he managed in northern Kentucky. Brady put up $100,000 to purchase The Latin Quarter, a nineteenth-century slaughterhouse and meat packing plant that had been converted into one of Newport's hottest nightspots. The new owners bought out Thomas J. Callahan and a group of investors that ran the Licking Realty firm.

Remus became vice president of the new organization. Later, Buck renamed the joint "Buck Brady's Primrose Country Club." Only five minutes from downtown Cincinnati, but across the Ohio River in Kentucky, Brady turned up the heat at the joint, featuring three live shows a night. Newport had not only flourished on the basis of its illicit economy of gambling, prostitution, and alcohol during the 1920s, but by the 1940s it had become an even hotter magnet for the countless travelers, convention-goers, association meetings, and businessmen who streamed across the bridges from the Queen City. Buck ran his Primrose Country Club until it got too prosperous and attracted the attention of the Cleveland Syndicate, the mafia group that was quickly gobbling up independent operators in the area. They gave Brady no choice—sell or die.

Buck Brady lived another two decades, spending his last in Florida. In late September 1965, faced with a string of ailments and failing health, Buck went into the alleyway outside his apartment in Lauderdale by the Sea with a rifle. He turned the gun on himself and put a large-caliber bullet in his chest—a quick and ignoble end for one of a long line of violent 1920s criminals.

GEORGE CONNERS was Remus's staunchest ally, top aide, and best friend. Conners served time in Atlanta with George. Never deserting his boss, he remained by Remus's side throughout the bootleg baron's many ups and downs.

"He assisted Miss Blanche Watson in conserving whatever there was left of the wreck and since that time he has been consistently doing matters on my behalf," Remus said of his top lieutenant.

Conners traveled back and forth between at least eight large East Coast and Midwest cities "trying to conserve whatever was left."

Conners died on November 16, 1935, never fully recovering from a head injury he received in a freak car accident. Six months earlier, a mysterious car had come out of nowhere and pushed George's vehicle from the road. He careened sideways, eventually hitting a loading dock at Fischer Place and Harrison Avenue in Cincinnati's Westwood neighborhood.

Conners was taken to a doctor's office after the crash. The medical staff treated him for a concussion. The injury seemed minor at the time, yet Conners's health deteriorated. The brain trauma was more devastating than initially diagnosed, taking his life at forty-four years old. Rumors in the criminal underworld hinted that it was no accident at all, but rather an attempt to send Conners a message about his extensive gambling debts.

Remus's former henchman, dubbed "the Prince of Bootleggers" in the press, had been working as a salesman for the Red Top Brewing Company. Prior to that position, he had served as manager of the Cincinnati Fehr Beer Company. George and Alma Conners had three daughters: Rose, Mural, and Mary Elizabeth.

ROMOLA REMUS DUNLAP died in February 1987 in a Chicago hospital. She never again received the kind of attention sparked by her father's murdering of Imogene. What the papers in 1927 rarely mentioned, though, is that Romola had been a star herself in 1908.

Lillian Remus had taken her young daughter to the Selig Polyscope Studios to try out for the role of Dorothy in a film adaptation of Frank L. Baum's *Wizard of Oz*. Romola won the part and was paid $5 a day to play the iconic character. She left acting shortly after, concentrating on playing the organ, singing, and dancing.

Amazingly, in 1984, she appeared at a *Wizard of Oz* convention in toney Holland, Michigan. Although in her eighties, she regaled convention-goers by singing several songs, including "I Was a Flora Dora Baby."

An obituary in the *Los Angeles Times* reported that Romola taught music at her apartment on the North Side of Chicago, which she shared with "a cat, a turtle, a parakeet, and her clippings."

The piece did not mention her infamous father, but did note: "Her will asked that her age not be disclosed."

CHARLES ELSTON put his own reputation on the line for George and—literally—saved his life. The attorney not only won Remus's eventual freedom, but he also found a way to coexist with the bootlegger. Observing their interactions, one reporter remarked, "Elston hushed the wife-slayer and went on his own way. Elston seldom crosses the will of the bootleg monarch, but when he does Remus always yields."

Of all the infamous individuals associated with George Remus, from gangsters like Johnny Torrio and Al Capone, to whispered associations with Arnold "the Big Brain" Rothstein and Charles "Lucky" Luciano, relatively few emerged from their involvement with him unscathed. Many ended up murdered, their lifeless bodies dead and discarded. Remus had surrounded himself with hangers-on and sycophants, and tragedy followed in his wake.

Not for Charles Elston. He used the nationwide fame he gained in helping win Remus's freedom to become a statesman. He masterfully served the people of Cincinnati as a conservative Republican congressman from 1939 to 1952, including a stint on the House Armed Forces Committee during World War II, where he served with an up-and-coming Texas Democrat named Lyndon B. Johnson.

Later, Elston served on the House Atomic Energy Committee and held an appointment during the administration of Dwight D. Eisenhower. And he continued intermingling with the Taft family, not surprising given his intense commitment to conservative causes and their domination over the Republican Party in the state. One of his proudest achievements was the successful fight for the first federal water pollution bill in 1948, which he introduced with a number of legislators, including Senator Robert A. Taft. Elston's congressional seat was later held by Robert Taft, Jr., the nephew of his Remus murder trial nemesis Charlie Taft. In turn, his son, Robert Taft III would serve as governor of Ohio from 1999–2007.

JOHN GEHRUM took a great deal of heat from Conners and Remus for the Death Valley raid and was linked closely to Imogene after getting out of Big A. Regardless of these missteps, Gehrum remained Remus's close friend and business associate.

Despite the raid that started the chain of events that would topple the Remus bourbon kingdom, Gehrum resumed operations at Death Valley after he was released from the federal pen and continued bootlegging, though on a smaller scale than when Remus ran the show. He was arrested for Prohibition violations in December 1930 and August 1931. In the first instance Johnnie won dismissal, claiming that the fifty-five cases of bottled liquor and two burlap sacks with two dozen more were "near-beer," a low-alcohol substitute.

In the second case, a Prohi followed a truck onto the infamous farm and found that it carried thirty cases of Canadian whiskey and thirty cases of beer. When pinched, Gehrum gave the name "Brown" to authorities—Imogene's maiden name.

In the early 1930s, Gehrum, his wife Ada, and Remus bought ownership stakes in a dog-racing track in West Palm Beach, Florida. The deal fell apart and they sued in hopes of regaining some of the $32,000 they invested. A reporter at the *Palm Beach Post* implied that the investment was a scam, with Gehrum said to be "a wealthy resident of Cincinnati and owner of the U. S.

Soap Company." In March 1935, Judge Halstead L. Ritter dismissed the case, ruling that the plaintiffs never proved their position.

In early 1933, Gehrum exercised an option on the Butler County Fairgrounds in Hamilton to start racing horses. The track had originally opened in "Little Chicago" in 1927, allowing betting via a certificate system that circumvented traditional betting and laws forbidding the practice. In that last year of Prohibition, Hamilton had devolved to virtual lawlessness. The infamous John Dillinger had set up headquarters in the city.

One writer called Dillinger "a combination of Robin Hood and Jesse James," exclaiming, "His bold robberies during the Depression years of 1933 and 1934 would earn him status as a folk hero, not a criminal to be feared."

John E. Gehrum died on New Year's Eve 1968, at eighty-six years old. He still lived on Cincinnati's west side, surrounded by his large family.

BLANCHE WATSON REMUS is the most mysterious of all the individuals associated with the Bourbon King. Was she simply his secretary and business manager? Or, by some strange twist of fate, was she the mastermind behind the entire bourbon empire? Could she have been the "two Jews" Remus mentioned as his mentors? The paper trail is baffling.

We know many interesting things about Blanche that add to Remus's story—for example, she hid out during the murder trial and was never served a subpoena. Yet, she was always present at the insanity hearings, sitting directly behind George, as close as she could get.

Earlier, she seems to have helped Remus launder money, taking properties from him for ridiculously low figures, like a plot of land for one dollar, then turning around and reselling for legitimate market prices. Surely, George would have used the loss to cut away at his ever-present tax debt, the ticking time bomb always looming behind every thought. Would the government come after him for back taxes? Could it jail him?

Flying in the face of reports that Remus died destitute, Blanche owned racehorses in an era when horseracing was the sport of the wealthy. She had a successful career as an owner, spending a great deal of time in New Orleans and Baltimore.

In the mid- to late-1940s, Blanche and George faced legal difficulties when the Federal Trade Commission charged them with false advertising for selling compounds via the brand name "Giljan," particularly "Giljan Laxative Compound."

These types of fake remedies had been one of George's moneymaking schemes back in his Chicago pharmaceutical days. The FTC investigation into the product revealed that it had no actual medicinal value "in the treatment of stomach trouble" or "any beneficial effect" on any of the ills that it claimed to heal.

Blanche died in Chicago on March 26, 1974, living to ninety-three years old.

AUGUSTA IMOGENE HOLMES REMUS died on October 6, 1927.

George realized too late that Imogene had targeted him. Many of the clues surfaced in depositions or courtroom testimony during the murder trial and sanity hearings. In those moments—sworn to truth—Imogene's closest friends portrayed her as a person maniacally driven to achieve wealth and acclaim. She would go to any lengths to get recognition.

Months after Imogene's murder, while being held in the insane asylum, George believed that he had pieced together a fuller portrait of their marriage, as if time behind bars had given him the distance to finally acknowledge the truth. He told the alienists that Imogene herself had deliberately put the nail in the coffin of his first marriage.

She "had something to do with that manner of getting the matter into the public eye."

Remus had the notion that Imogene had created the 1919 incident with Evanston plumber Herbert Youngs over Ruth's lost watch as a way to force their affair into public view. The idea that Imogene had planned the whole thing haunted Remus. Had she paid the man in cash or otherwise bartered to get the assault into the public eye? She was press-savvy enough to know that the resulting scandal would destroy George's first marriage. She already knew the union with Lillian had been on shaky ground, due to his flashiness with women and exhaustive work habits.

Remus also later heard about Imogene's determination to get his money, learning of "her boast that she was going to have me."

Since Remus had grown into a prominent figure in the Windy City, reporters fed on the news, printing stories about the love triangle for weeks.

As George unraveled his life with Imogene in his mind and later in testimony at his insanity hearing, it became increasingly clear that Imogene had also demonstrated poor judgment. Although she knew Remus had an explosive temper, she most likely did not completely understand his deep psychological issues. Imogene pinned her hopes on a man with a worldview that blurred the line between good and evil. Maybe she just thought she could control him, like she did other men in her life. But George was not just able to separate the two, he was willing to act on the violence needed to rise to the top of the criminal underworld.

"He condones crime," alienist Kenneth L. Weber testified in early 1928. "Crime does not have an unpleasant feeling, he does not react unpleasantly to crime…He is insane."

If Imogene had considered that her husband possessed no negative feelings about crime, perhaps she would have taken her own safety more seriously or acted in a less cavalier manner with Franklin Dodge.

RUTH HOLMES (REMUS) WILLIAMS watched in horror as her adoptive father murdered her mother on that sunny fall day in 1927. She later played an important role in Charles Taft's attempt to bring Remus to justice, though ultimately just became another tragic figure in the spectacular downfall of the bootleg baron.

During the trial, Ruth unfortunately also lost her birth father, Albert W. Holmes, who died on December 14, 1927, at fifty-seven years old. During the trial, the teenager left for Milwaukee, staying with her aunt, Grace J. Campbell, who had spent a great deal of time with Imogene. Taking a cue from Imogene, however, Grace released a statement to the pestering press, who wanted details about the girl.

"There are some things in life far worse than death," Grace wrote in the release. "The struggle seems almost too much for the shoulders of so young a girl who feels she must fight on to restore the good name of her beloved mother, who this slayer, Remus, has so basely defiled for the last two years."

More than any other figure associated with George, Ruth shunned the spotlight. She shed the "Remus" name, and then lived a quiet life in Milwaukee. Sadly, she died during a hysterectomy surgery on April 23, 1947. Documentation reveals that there were complications related to the transfusion Ruth was mistakenly given.

CHARLES P. TAFT had gone into battle with George Remus, and like a cadre of people who fought the tenacious grappler, suffered a brutal defeat. Arguably, no one lost more in fighting him. His father, William Howard Taft, realized that his son had been outmatched by the astonishing theatrics of the little German hysteria-peddler. For a man who many observers believed might follow his famous father to the grand heights of the presidency, the defeat set in motion a much maligned and rather middling political career.

Taft, after presiding over the trial and the insanity hearings for the state, knew the culprit, but could do nothing but brood. He told all who would listen: "Remus was acquitted by the newspapers," who then "turned on him and sent him to the insane asylum." From his perspective, the entire jury system itself hung in the balance. He asked:

From the public standpoint, shall a defendant be allowed to try his case in the newspapers with material that is not admissible evidence in court and get himself acquitted in a wave of popular sentiment manifested by himself and his representatives?

In other words, Taft got stung by a strange convolution of sentimentality, cult of personality, duplicity, and flat-out wrongheadedness on the part of twelve jury members. The jurors had let their emotions dictate their decision-making abilities. But, the real point is that no one really cared. The scorecard: Remus 1, Taft 0.

Legal scholar T. Earl Sullenger agreed with Taft, but saw the issue from a broader perspective, concluding that "Reading of dime novels, sensational journals, newspaper reports, and so forth, often affects the administration of criminal justice indirectly." As a result of popular culture and media attention, jury members may judge a person a "heartless murderer" or "a man who has actually lived for a few thrilling moments, the untamed life which the juror has romantically envied in his reading." People are slaves to their culture, he explains, one's "imagination has been trained to create a glamorous background for the human before him."

Few characters in American jurisprudence were more charismatic or melodramatic than George Remus. In retrospect, one wonders if Taft ever had a chance.

An equally compelling set of issues about the Taft family and its fortune was raised when Remus testified in late February 1928. Walt Sibbald spent hours questioning Remus about his business ventures, trying to prod him into an outburst that might sway the panel of judges and alienists who would determine his case. Cagey as always, Remus turned the issue around and asked Sibbald if he wanted to know the truth about "Remus and his gang."

When the young assistant prosecutor said yes, George unleashed a mono-
logue that put the fabled Taft family hand-in-hand with Remus as he built and
maintained the bourbon empire. Not holding back, George revealed the links
and connections, from employing the law firm owned by Charles Phelps Taft
(William Howard's older half-brother and Charlie's uncle) to using Harry L.
Lynch, the investor who also managed Taft's money, to purchase real estate.

Remus never gave a full confession about his ties to the Taft family. He hinted
at the extent of the insider partnerships he had with them, particularly in real
estate, since that had been such a significant part of the Taft family fortune.
Charles Taft and his wife Anna Sinton were the richest family in Cincinnati at
the time and one of the wealthiest in the Midwest. Whether Remus just wanted
to reveal that the vaunted Tafts were tainted or that he could run to the press
with details will never be known, but the laundry list of intimate associations
put the bourbon king and the Tafts in close quarters, or as George concluded,
"the parties that assisted in the functioning of the Remus liquor business."

MABEL WALKER WILLEBRANDT rose from abject poverty to become arguably the most powerful woman in America in the 1920s. Born in a
dirt dugout dwelling on the rural plains of southwest Kansas, she overcame her
humble origins to achieve the American Dream. Mabel embodied the principles of the age: accomplishment through tenacity, intelligence, and hard work.
She reached this nearly unthinkable position by becoming the face of Prohibition enforcement, a vast contradiction, given the wholesale unpopularity of the
Eighteenth Amendment and those who imposed it on the exceedingly thirsty
public.

Much of her early success—a springboard to better things, really—centered
on jailing Remus and thwarting his efforts to reinvigorate his bootlegging career. Mabel exerted a considerable amount of energy in this endeavor. She took
great pride in her rise as a noted figure, as well as a popular one. Although
Remus was not the sole reason for her nationwide fame—which ranged from
consorting with presidents and dignitaries to being featured in countless newspaper and magazine stories—the bootleg king certainly played a costarring role
in her rise to celebrity status.

After she left the Prohibition Bureau in 1929, Mabel became a vocal com-
mentator about enforcement efforts, but rarely took blame for any shortcomings. In one article, Willebrandt discussed reasons why the agency could not

catch more "Remus type" criminals. She frankly laid the blame at the feet of the Prohi agents who worked for her, whom she labeled "untrained, incompetent, and sometimes dishonest." She also felt that the department suffered from a general lack of coordination.

Many upright officials wanted the Volstead Act enforced, but they could never really get control of the nation's large cities. Willebrandt, about the most incorruptible of the age, lumped the criminals together as the "dregs of society," including "bootleggers, the thugs, the potential murderers, the bribers, the grafters, and criminals of every description who live by preying on honest men and women."

Despite the countless missteps, however, Willebrandt employed the phrase "Remus type" as coded language for the accomplishments she assumed the Justice Department had achieved under her leadership.

What is assured is that Mabel needed to put George behind bars and keep him there as an example for other bootleggers and a constant reminder to the American people of her success. The Remus case enabled her to overcome criticism, such as being labeled a "protégé of Harry M. Daugherty" by Atlanta prison chief John Snook, who called her years in the Justice Department an "open sesame to misrule."

At the end of her long, rollercoaster reign over Prohibition enforcement, Mabel Walker Willebrandt said that there were simply too many people responsible for making it work, thus ensuring "constant buck-passing between them so fast that a person gets dizzy trying to secure improvements as though watching a toe-dancer whirl."

Willebrandt left government service in 1929, disappointed that President Herbert Hoover didn't appoint her attorney general after she had put so much of her personal reputation on the line in relentlessly campaigning for him. She opened a private law practice, ironically taking on winemaker California Fruit Industries as her first client. The company had uncovered a way to circumvent the Volstead Act, thriving in the home wine market.

Mabel's star status also gave her entry to Hollywood. She thrived in Los Angeles, working for clients in the aviation industry and for several film studios and executives. Willebrandt became friends with a wide variety of celebrities, from Amelia Earhart to Clark Gable.

In her later years, Willebrandt suffered from a number of health ailments, forcing her to shut down her law practice. She died in 1963.

EPILOGUE
Fall of the Bootleg Baron

GEORGE REMUS, WHISKY KING OF 20S DIES AT 79

The *Chicago Tribune*, which had launched George into the national spotlight in his early years, paid tribute to him when he died on January 20, 1952. Although just about every fact in the obituary was incorrect—including the spelling of "whiskey"—papers around the nation ran similar pieces, calling his career "spectacular" and reestablishing him as the "bootleg king."

Remus had been ill for the last couple of years after suffering a stroke on August 9, 1950, that kept him hospitalized for three months. He convalesced at 1810 Greenup Street in Covington, a small craftsman-style home next door to the house he and Blanche lived in and owned. What the newspapers failed to mention at the time was that, the day of the stroke, George had been admitted to Bethesda Hospital, the same facility that had attempted to save Imogene after the fatal gut wound nearly twenty-three years earlier.

By the early 1950s, Remus was an odd character for the public to figure out. Was this the criminal mastermind of the illegal whiskey trade or the wife-murderer who got off on a technicality? Few Americans looked back on Prohibition and saw it for the violence-filled era it had been, rather hoping to bury the dry laws in history's dustbin. The public in the late 1920s and 1930s had turned on gangsters, particularly after the Al Capone-sanctioned Valentine's Day Massacre in 1929 and a series of high-profile kidnappings in the early 1930s. Yet, in the 1950s, movies and television dramas had returned gangsters to mythic figures. Gangsters like Capone became celebrities, and cops-and-robber flicks starred Hollywood's most distinguished icons. Prohibition seemed inconsequential and something that the nation should remember selectively, celebrating the excitement of the Jazz Age.

* * *

When Remus died, the papers called his career "spectacular," but did not really provide many reasons for that inference. From a financial point of view, the idea is intriguing if Remus's wealth in the 1920s is compared to contemporary value, almost a century later. One of the most interesting facets of George Remus's bourbon empire was how quickly he built it and how large it became. The sheer size and magnitude is nearly breathtaking, particularly in terms of revenue.

Some assessments posit that the value of the Remus empire eclipsed $200 million. Utilizing the latest models to determine how to value commodity prices across time, that $200 million in 1924 would equate to about $2.9 billion (real price) to $46.7 billion (economic share) in 2018. This is an astronomical sum for an operation that held sway for just two and a half years. Even if the figures were one-tenth as much, they would still be prodigious.*

His personal income from bootlegging was also staggering, but could probably never be completely authenticated. In early 1928, Remus testified regarding what he liked to call his "period of liquor activities." Knowing full well that if he lied and was discovered that the prosecution would use that charge to jail him, George claimed that he cleared about "four or five million dollars."

At the height of his power, by 2018 standards, Remus's personal wealth would have ranged between $307 and $384 million (relative income). If he were able to achieve his most audacious plan—creating a legal corporation to sell bourbon—his personal fortune would have reached even greater amounts. This plan was solid but relied on the desperation of distillery owners who were sitting on mountains of essentially worthless product when Prohibition kicked off. While George and his operatives began gobbling up distilleries—frequently

---

* Assessing wealth and money over time is controversial and usually lags behind real time, since economic historians are using data from a variety of government sources. The most compelling model for comparing wealth over time is https://www.measuringworth.com, created by Samuel H. Williamson, cofounder and president of MeasuringWorth and Professor of Economics, Emeritus, Miami University.

skirting legality, or at least business ethics—Remus is rarely given credit for buttressing the industry during the darkest days of dry America.

While some bourbon historians might find Remus as the industry savior to be a shocking assertion, it bears consideration—he not only bought a large number of facilities, but in many cases kept people working at those locations, enabling them to feed their families and spend money in the local economy. What is difficult to imagine a century after Prohibition is the authority of the Eighteenth Amendment. Few believed that a constitutional amendment could ever be overturned, so they did not feel alcohol would be legal ever again.

Proposing that Remus were some kind of 1920s Robin Hood is not altogether accurate, but his stance on not cutting bourbon while it was under his care is noteworthy. As a matter of fact, the quickest way to greater profit would have been for Remus to order his men to dilute Kentucky bourbon three or four times over. His emphasis on "the good stuff" helped people—especially elite buyers—to equate bourbon with quality.

According to bourbon historian Michael R. Veach, when Prohibition ended the competition in the industry was fierce. A wave of consolidation left four large corporations that "controlled the majority of the trade in distilled spirits, domestic and imported." Remus's fingers are all over these organizations, from the strong brands owned by National Distillers (i.e., Old Crow and Old Overholt) to the importance of Squibb Distillery in the Schenley Distillery family. The reserves these companies owned and the power of the brands, maintained partially through Remus's actions, enabled the parent companies to create a national foothold that powered expansion in the 1940s and 1950s.

Consolidation in the industry proceeded—within reason—along the lines Remus had plotted. Organizations with capital and financing—playing the role the bourbon king did in the early 1920s—bought up smaller operations. Size enabled the large conglomerates to gather all the resources they needed to build, just as Remus's circle concept allowed him to create a national bourbon empire, if only for several years. He had drawn a blueprint for the future, but could not enact his dream, partially due to greed and largely because of the illegality of the product.

Adding to the challenge, of course, was the wholesale corruption of the medicinal marketplace, which turned many enforcement officials into double-cross specialists An industry that became illegal could not support Remus's vision, but then again, he reaped the rewards so quickly that it corrupted that dream. He was in the bootleg game for the money and excitement, and that's what he got. The ideal went away as he stuffed more money into his bank accounts and his suit pockets.

> "The bar is in full swing, and floating rounds of cocktails permeate the garden outside, until the air is alive with chatter and laughter, and casual innuendo and introductions forgotten on the spot, and enthusiastic meetings between women who never knew each other's names."
> —F. SCOTT FITZGERALD, *The Great Gatsby*

George Remus occupies center stage in one of America's great literary mysteries—who is the model for F. Scott Fitzgerald's fictional bootlegging character Jay Gatsby in *The Great Gatsby*? This question has interested readers for nearly a century, fueled by several popular film adaptations and the broad use of the novel in American high school and university classrooms since the 1960s. Generations have grown up counting F. Scott Fitzgerald's Jazz Age masterpiece as a candidate in the mythical debate over whether there has ever been a "Great American Novel." And generations have wondered about the identity or identities of the bootleggers who may have inspired Fitzgerald's debonair mobster title character.

There is no way to fully measure the popularity of *The Great Gatsby* or its influence on American culture. No other novel has led to continual revivals of an entire decade like Fitzgerald's masterpiece. In the twenty-first century, it is not uncommon to attend a Gatsby-inspired wedding or see an advertisement or commercial that would fall into the generic "Gatsby-esque" category.

We live with Gatsby every day.

The parties, the magnificent parties. And the pool. A string of pharmacies. Striving for respectability. Dandy dresser. Real books. Bootlegging.

All these endeavors, traits, and possessions sound like they were ripped from the life of George Remus...but they also could describe Arnold Rothstein or Max Gerlach, two other real-life criminals that have been linked to Jay Gatsby.

While many of Remus's exterior characteristics and mannerisms link him to Gatsby, the fictional character doesn't quite share Remus's pretentiousness nor his braggadocio surrounding his wealth. Gatsby buys many expensive trinkets, from the flashy touring sedans to the enormous mansion, but he doesn't boast out loud about them. Displaying wealth, but not talking about being rich, is a refined and distinct characteristic of Jay Gatsby.

As American literature scholar Thomas H. Pauly has stated, "Fitzgerald took great pains to endow his Gatsby with an attitude that sharply differentiated him from gangsters like the flamboyant Remus."

The Great Gatsby is set in the summer of 1922. The book was published in April 1925. Fitzgerald reworked the initial concept for the book from October 1922 until November 1923. He rewrote and revised for another six months, moving from Great Neck, New York, to France, so that he could concentrate on the draft and live a less expensive life with wife Zelda and their young daughter Scotty. In Europe, Fitzgerald got serious, writing *Gatsby* into the fall of 1924, before sending it off to Max Perkins, the famous Scribner's editor. Forever revising, the author kept improving the copy through early 1925.

"Sustained imagination of a sincere and yet radiant world," is how Fitzgerald encapsulated his ambition in a letter to Perkins in April 1924.

After he read a complete draft in November 1924, Perkins reported back to the author: "It is a marvelous fusion, into a unity of presentation, of the extraordinary incongruities of life today. And, as for sheer writing, it's astonishing."

But where did Fitzgerald find his inspiration? Preeminent literary scholar Matthew J. Bruccoli, in his copious research, posits that Gatsby was primarily drawn from Arnold Rothstein, while many of the character's quirks were modeled after the lesser-known "gentleman bootlegger" Max von Gerlach. The latter, one of Fitzgerald's Long Island neighbors, was mentioned in the late 1940s by Zelda Fitzgerald as the inspiration. Von Gerlach—like Remus—was a German immigrant, employed stilted formality in speaking, and feigned an aristocratic air. He is the one who introduced Fitzgerald to the British phrase "Old Sport," the term that audiences and readers so closely associate with Jay Gatsby.

Literary scholar Horst Kruse presents compelling research for linking von Gerlach and Fitzgerald, in both his biographical details and German background, dubbing von Gerlach, "the Real Jay Gatsby." The scholar contends that von Gerlach "did play a vital role" in helping Fitzgerald create Gatsby, but also sees the writer's ability to make him unique by drawing "on his own emotional life."

The case for Manhattan-based kingpin Arnold Rothstein is equally absorbing. One of the first criminal masterminds to figure out how to effectively bootleg liquor, "the Big Brain" turned his gambling and bankrolling exploits into the first dominant bootlegging empire, concentrating on selling "the good stuff," not rotgut, just as Remus would do. While Rothstein has frequently been considered the model for the Jewish mafioso Meyer Wolfsheim, AR was not a thug, poor communicator, or slovenly like the fictional character. In deed and appearance, Rothstein was Gatsby-like and mysterious.

From the beginning of Prohibition in October 1919 until the Fitzgeralds boarded an ocean liner to Paris on May 3, 1924, the *New York Times* wrote about Rothstein on some fifty-nine occasions. Many of these related to his relationship with Edward M. Fuller, the owner of a New York brokerage firm and resident of Great Neck. The firm went bankrupt due to insider manipulations and Fuller went to prison for a short time.

Fascinated with the Fuller case, Scott studied it and knew some of the individuals caught up in its deceit. Documentation revealed that Rothstein and Fuller had conducted a great deal of business together. Rumors abounded that some part of the Fuller demise could be traced back to losses from gambling on sports with Rothstein. Fitzgerald scrutinized the newspapers for details of Fuller and his life.

The *New York Times* wrote about George Remus seven times in the span leading up to the Fitzgeralds leaving for Europe. The *Daily News* only twice. Although the number for the paper pales in comparison to the ones with Rothstein, an article on January 16, 1924, about Remus's train ride to the Atlanta penitentiary did mention the pool, and may have caught Scott's attention.

"She [Imogene] said the mansion would be kept up and the water in the $100,000 Grecian bath located in the home would sparkle the same as ever," the paper noted.

Turning to the novel, one likes to remember the Gatsby pool that Fitzgerald describes as brilliant color and luminescence. Yet, there is only one early reference to the "marble swimming pool."

In Joseph Pulitzer's *The Evening World* on June 7, 1922—the time of the novel's setting—the paper ran an extended article on Remus, Imogene, and their magnificent mansion (see photo insert). The essay is full of errors about Remus's life, but it does paint a vivid scene of the infamous New Year's Eve party and Imogene's head-turning diving exhibition. There are Gatsby-esque flourishes, claiming for example, "The money from the sale of contraband liquor rolled in in millions." The pool is dubbed a "great marble bath," and the dedication compared to a "feast rivaling in magnificence…the debased Russian Emperors." Living in St. Paul at the time, Fitzgerald may have seen the article, given his deep interest in current affairs and the bright lights of the Big Apple.

There are no smoking guns in the Remus-as-Gatsby story. The depth of news coverage in the 1920s, however, makes the question fascinating, particularly given Fitzgerald's voracious reading habits, social commentary, and interest in journalism. There are numerous similarities, which make it seem the young novelist was at least informed by Remus and his escapades in the early 1920s.

Facets of the stories intertwine, most notably that Jay Gatsby is the shadowy owner of pharmacies that are fronts for bootlegging. Tom Buchanan, in the penultimate scene at the Plaza Hotel, defiantly exclaims that the mysterious Gatsby is nothing more than "a big bootlegger." Tom's derision is palpable. Remus faced similar contempt from wealthy Cincinnatians who were base enough to buy his illegal bourbon, but too well bred and elite to allow a common German immigrant into their exclusive circles. And, by the early 1920s, Remus had already earned the "king of the bootleggers" moniker.

Central to *The Great Gatsby* are the unrestrained, excessive parties Jay throws in hopes of drawing Daisy to him. These scenes contain some of Fitzgerald's most beautiful prose poetry. Like Jay Gatsby, George Remus claimed not to drink, nor did he particularly enjoy the grand bashes he hosted (though Imogene certainly relished being the center of attention). At the over-the-top parties, Remus might place a hidden $100 bill under each guest's place setting or give them diamonds and other expensive gifts, but he also retreated to his library to wait out the night in the company of nothing more than a good book. The abundance and spectacle at the heart of both fiction and reality seem a strong indicator that one fed off the other.

Searching tens of thousands of documents, including newspaper and magazine archives, the earliest definitive links between George and Gatsby are in a 1979 article on Big A in the *Atlanta Constitution* and a 1983 piece on Remus in the *Cincinnati Enquirer*. For many decades before these articles, however, the legend circulated that George drank in the Rathskeller Bar at the Seelbach Hilton Hotel in Louisville with Fitzgerald and Al Capone. Capone, for example, allegedly played cards in a private room on the second floor of the Seelbach that had a hidden door leading to a drainage tunnel under the city. Capone and others who couldn't afford to get caught drinking in the hotel purportedly used the tunnel as a means of escape if the police raided the joint.

While there is proof that all three men visited the Seelbach at different times, there's no definitive proof that they ever drank together at the grand hotel.

Is legendary, third-generation bartender Max Allen the person most responsible for the notion that Remus was "the" inspiration for Gatsby? Allegedly, one of the former owners of the Seelbach, actor and developer Roger

Davis, who lovingly brought the hotel back to life in 1982, possesses a photograph of Remus, Capone, and Fitzgerald at the Rathskeller Bar together. Many people claim to have seen the photo on a long ago visit to the Seelbach.

If that photograph, or something akin to it, exists...then one of America's most interesting literary mysteries might be solved.

> "It is said that a great part of what George Remus says may well be
> taken with accompanying grains of salt."

George Remus gained a new wave of notoriety when he became a central figure in the high-profile Ken Burns documentary *Prohibition*, which was released in 2011. The bourbon king was voiced by Academy Award-nominated actor Paul Giamatti.

The critically acclaimed television series *Boardwalk Empire* focused on Prohibition-era corruption in Atlantic City for five seasons from 2010 to 2014. Loosely based on the real-life criminal activities of Enoch "Nucky" Johnson (changed to Nucky Thompson in the show), *Boardwalk Empire* featured fictionalized portrayals of many key figures of the 1920s, including Rothstein, Meyer Lansky, Mabel Willebrandt, Lucky Luciano, Capone, and Remus.

Glenn Fleshler played Remus in a recurring role in seasons two through four. George served as a kind of comic relief, with other leading characters mocking and misunderstanding his use of third person when talking about himself as "Remus." And, at well over six feet tall, Fleshler is nearly a foot taller than the real-life Remus.

In one memorable scene—the last time we see Remus in the series—Prohis are seen chasing George around the Dream Palace, Keystone Kop-like, slipping and falling on the smooth marble floors. They chase him around a giant twelve-foot-high birdcage, the birds inside squawking loudly. Remus is—fittingly—in a long red velvet robe and bathing trunks. When they finally catch him, a large man who looks strikingly like Franklin Dodge makes the arrest. Then, Mabel Willebrandt walks in as they lead him out. The fictional George confesses that he has receipts from his bribes to Jess Smith. Ah, Hollywood.

Arguably the oddest Remus-related sightings today are made by the countless people who are convinced that Imogene's ghost can be seen in her long black dress and have heard weeping at the grand Spring House Gazebo in Cincinnati's Eden Park. Thousands of tourists visit Eden Park each year hoping to catch a glimpse of the slain moll.

Remus is also a brand name bourbon! GEORGE REMUS® Bourbon is produced just down the Ohio River from Cincinnati in Lawrenceburg, Indiana, at the 170-year-old MGP Distillery. The high-end whiskey is an enthusiast's delight, selling—when it can be found, because it is usually sold out—for either $45 (George Remus Straight Bourbon Whiskey) or $75 (Remus Repeal Reserve) per bottle.

.   .   .

Charlie Rentrop turned covering the Queen City into his life's mission. He launched a fifty-year career as a journalist at the *Cincinnati Post* in 1907. Some twenty-one years later, Rentrop was one of the paper's star reporters assigned to the Remus murder trial. Because of his affiliation with the *Post*, he got preferential treatment over the out-of-towners and wire reporters sent to Cincinnati for the dramatic proceedings. Over the course of the trial, Rentrop interviewed Remus many times. Some would say that the young reporter even formed a kind of friendship with the legendary bootleg king.

Rentrop was in the courtroom the day Harry Truesdale made his startling revelations—confessing publicly to accepting the hit directive from Jew John, Imogene, and Franklin. The young journalist witnessed Remus's hysterical reaction. Rentrop recalled seeing members of the jury and many spectators in tears.

The packed courtroom erupted into bedlam when Remus reacted and court officials rushed him out of the building. Like all the reporters who saw the fit and heard the shrieks, Rentrop rushed to George's cell. He saw Remus lying on his tiny cot.

Rentrop's memory of what Remus did next is one for the ages: "He opened one eye and asked: 'How am I doing, kid?'"

Timeline

• • • • •

1800s

November 13, 1876: George Remus born in Friedeberg, one of two walled cities in Neumark, a region within the Electorate of Brandenburg that had become part of Prussia in 1701.

June 15, 1882: The Remus family arrives in the United States on the *Fitlington*, a ship originating in Kristiansand, Norway.

September 15, 1884: Augusta Imogene Brown born in Milwaukee, Wisconsin.

May 23, 1889: Mabel Walker born in Kansas.

1890: Frank Remus (George's father) suffers from debilitating rheumatism, which leads to trouble finding work.

February 1890: Remus quits school to support the family financially. Gets a job at the drugstore owned by his uncle, George Karg. The store is in Chicago at 952 Milwaukee Avenue.

1895: Passes state exam to obtain pharmacist license. Lies on the application to make himself two years older so that he can be licensed at the minimum age of 21.

1897: George Karg finances Remus's purchase of the drugstore.

July 10, 1899: Marries Lillian Klauff.

1900s

April 7, 1900: George and Lillian welcome a daughter—Romola.

1902: Acquires another drugstore, launches a drug wholesaling business offering "Remus"-branded products, such as "Remus' Liver Pills" and others. George is also active in establishing several drug companies and speculates in Chicago real estate.

May 30, 1904: Receives law degree from Illinois College of Law.

1904: Establishes a law office in the Ashland Block Building (167 North Clark Street). His clients are primarily unions and business operations. Meets and begins a professional and friendly relationship with Clarence Darrow. The law firm later becomes Remus, LaBuy, and Gulano.

November 7, 1904: Marriage license issued to Albert W. Holmes and Imogene Brown in Milwaukee.

1907: Sets a winter swimming endurance record by staying in Lake Michigan for 5 hours, 40 minutes.

October 7, 1907: Imogene and Albert W. Holmes welcome a baby girl—Ruth.

1910s

Fall 1912: Defends Lillian Beatrice Ryall-Conway, who faced murder charges for conspiring with her husband Charles to murder Sophia Singer on October 29, 1912. She is sentenced to fourteen-years behind bars, rather than a death sentence.

Fall 1913/Spring 1914: Defends William Cheney Ellis, a wealthy Cincinnati merchant who murdered his wife Eleanor Hosea Ellis in a rage at Chicago's Sherman House Hotel on October 16, 1913.

March 6, 1914: Ellis convicted of murder and sentenced to fifteen years in jail. George saves him from a death sentence.

March 6, 1915: Outraged that George is rarely home at night and hearing rumors that he might be having an affair, Lillian files for divorce. George begs for forgiveness and she rescinds the lawsuit.

January 1, 1916: Frank Remus (father) dies in Chicago.

1916: Franklin L. Dodge, Jr. begins working for the Department of Justice.

Spring 1916: Mabel Walker Willebrandt graduates with a law degree from the University of Southern California.

Fall 1917: Imogene's divorce to Albert W. Holmes finalized.

December 26, 1918: George moves in with Imogene.

February 1919: George gets into a fistfight with Evanston plumber Herbert Youngs at the apartment he secretly shares with Imogene. Remus charged with assault and arrested. Lillian files for divorce after the newspapers pick up on the story and reveal details about his affair with Imogene.

March 7, 1919: Lillian is granted a divorce. The judge orders that Remus pay his first wife a lump sum of $50,000 and establish a $30,000 trust for Romola. He also must pay $25 a week in alimony.

October 28, 1919: Congress passes Volstead Act.

Late 1919: Relocates to Cincinnati, taking a suite of rooms in the luxury Sinton Hotel.

1920s

January 16, 1920: The Volstead Act becomes law.

May 12, 1920: Federal agents raid Remus' Chicago operation, charging him with forging whiskey certificates and violating the Volstead Act. The next day, a warrant is issued for Remus's arrest, and he is freed on a $10,000 bond.

May-June, 1920: Closes Chicago law office, liquidates assets in preparation for permanent move to Cincinnati.

June 25, 1920: George and Imogene are married in Newport, Kentucky.

July 31, 1920: Hearing scheduled in Chicago, Remus fails to appear.

August 1, 1920: Honeymoon in New York City at the Pennsylvania Hotel.

August 11, 1920: Fails to appear at a hearing for second time, the case is sent to a federal grand jury.

October 1920: William J. Mellin, a U.S. Treasury agent from New York, is sent to Cincinnati to wiretap the Remus hotel suite in Sinton Hotel.

November 1920: Remus purchases partial ownership in the Pogue Distillery in Maysville, Kentucky. Over the next year, he will purchase outright or partial interest at least twelve distilleries across Kentucky, Ohio, and other Midwest states (many in secret).

November 2, 1920: Warren G. Harding and Calvin Coolidge elected over James M. Cox and Franklin Delano Roosevelt. Harding appoints Harry M. Daugherty as U.S. Attorney General. Daugherty and the "Ohio Gang" establishes the Little Green House on K Street (1625 K Street) as its headquarters.

Late 1920: Remus's top lieutenant George Conners convinces him to purchase the Dater Farm, later known as "Death Valley," as the bourbon gang's primary distribution operation.

January 3, 1921: George adopts Imogene's thirteen-year old daughter Ruth, who becomes Ruth Remus.

January 8, 1921: Purchases a local retail pharmacy in Covington, Kentucky, and transforms it into the wholesale Kentucky Drug Company. Remus begins establishing a network of false-front drug operations across the East Coast and Midwest to funnel liquor into the black market.

February 1921: Remus buys the Edgewood Distillery in Cincinnati for about $230,000.

May 1921: Elijah Zoline sets up meeting with Jess Smith—Attorney General Daugherty's friend and aide—at the Commodore Hotel in New York.

September 27, 1921: Mabel Walker Willebrandt is appointed as Assistant Attorney General, the highest-ranking female in the federal government. Among her duties is enforcement of the Volstead Act.

October 1921: Harold Hughes stopped in Hammond, Indiana, for traffic violation. Police find that he is transporting a case of whiskey. Hughes tells police about Death Valley. A few nights later, Thomas Gallagher is stopped with a vehicle packed with liquor. Prohibition agents interrogate him, and he tells of nine wealthy men in Cincinnati who are delivering alcohol to sixty towns across the Midwest.

October 17, 1921: Purchases the Cincinnati-based Fleischmann distillery for $197,000.

October 23, 1921: Federal prohibition agents from Chicago and Indianapolis raid Death Valley. Remus arrested and indicted on 3,000 charges of violating the Volstead Act.

December 31, 1921/January 1, 1922: George and Imogene host a glittering, liquor-fueled New Year's Eve party that includes the dedication of the "Imogene Baths" marble swimming pool.

April 16, 1922: Remus, along with eighteen of his henchmen, is indicted for violation of the Volstead Act.

April 17, 1922: Remus in court in Indianapolis on charges of conspiracy in attempting to bribe Bert Morgan, federal prohibition director of the state, along with two of his underlings.

Spring 1921: Remus begins operations in Louisville, Kentucky, purchasing the Rugby Distillery. After operations there are stymied, he launches a move into St. Louis, Missouri. Remus buys part ownership in the Jack Daniels company, which has moved from Tennessee to St. Louis.

May 8, 1922: Remus and his men go on trial. They do not put up much of a fight, because Remus believes that his bribes to Jess Smith will keep them from being deemed guilty.

May 16, 1922: Judge John Peck of the U.S. Circuit Court sentences Remus to two years and $10,000 fine. His men are also fined and given jail terms, which they will serve in the Atlanta Federal Penitentiary.

May 22, 1922: The public nuisance trial opens in United States District Court. Remus is found guilty and sentenced to an additional year in jail in Ohio.

October 10, 1922: Remus initiates a confrontation with Cincinnati salesman Nicholas Shammas at the Claypool Hotel in Indianapolis. Shammas had traveled there with Imogene and a party of revelers. George assaulted Shammas, hitting him with the loaded walking cane he carried. Police charge Remus with assault with intent to kill.

May 30, 1923: Jess Smith commits suicide.

June 30, 1923: Remus's conviction is confirmed by United States Circuit Court of Appeals.

Summer 1923: Despite Remus's objections, the owners of the Jack Daniel's warehouse begin siphoning whiskey, ultimately stealing 893 gallons.

August 2, 1923: President Warren G. Harding dies.

August 20, 1923: Sheriff William Van Camp of Franklin County, Indiana, is shot and killed by two unnamed assailants. Folklore has it that Remus was one of the shooters.

September 20, 1923: A government gauger discovers that whiskey has been replaced with water at the Jack Daniel's warehouse. Prohibition agents shut down the operation.

January 7, 1924: Supreme Court refuses case petition for writ of certiorari.

January 24, 1924: Remus and his men leave aboard a special Cincinnati Southern train for Atlanta.

May 17, 1924: Remus testifies before the Brookhart-Wheeler US Senate committee investigating Attorney General Harry Daugherty for corruption. His testimony that he gave Smith some $250,000 to $300,000 in bribes makes national headlines.

May 1924: Mabel Walker Willebrandt denies Remus's travel to get the cancelled checks and documentation he described in the Senate testimony.

May 21, 1924: Imogene arrested at Price Hill mansion by Chief Deputy United States Marshal Lee Bollman for conspiracy (along with sixteen others) to violate Volstead Act in connection with plundering of the Jack Daniel Distillery Warehouse.

July 2, 1924: Imogene holds an auction at the Price Hill mansion in an effort to raise cash. George later claims that the auction was a rouse to thwart tax officials from pursuing him for unpaid back taxes.

September 1924: Daugherty publicizes Remus's repudiation of his claims of paying off Smith.

January 9, 1925: Imogene, working under the guidance of Franklin Dodge, sells whiskey certificates to Cleveland sports promoter Matt Hinkel at the Hollenden Hotel.

January 15, 1925: Dodge claims this is when he saw Imogene for the first time.

July 3, 1925: Franklin and Imogene allegedly have sex in the warden's office at the Atlanta prison.

July 18, 1925: Imogene sells the Fleishmann distillery for $80,000. She sends George $100 from the proceeds to his cell in Atlanta.

July 1925: Remus's American citizenship questioned.

August 11, 1925: Dodge resigns from the Department of Justice. He allegedly takes a position in the investigation department of the National Credit Men's Association in Cleveland.

August 31, 1925: Imogene files for divorce in Cincinnati, charging her husband with "extreme cruelty." Judge Robert LeBlond issues a temporary restraining order against George, barring him from the mansion.

September 2, 1925: Released from prison in Atlanta, immediately taken to Cincinnati to begin the year-long sentence related to the public nuisance charge. Simultaneously, Remus is served with a warrant for indictment in the Jack Daniels trial, set to take place in Indianapolis. And, he is formally served with divorce papers. Remus announces to the gathered newsmen that his repudiated testimony about the Smith bribes was coerced and that he had told the truth.

September 12, 1925: Taken by Deputy U.S. Marshal August Steinbach to jail in St. Louis. Remus cannot raise the $50,000 bond, but is granted freedom after agreeing to turn state's witness (primarily to testify against Imogene).

Fall 1925: Remus learns that a $15,000 hit has been placed on his head. He spends much of the next several months in hiding.

Early October 1925: Remus returns to the Hermosa Avenue mansion and finds it stripped. Has a mental episode in front of his attorney (and former judge) Benton S. Oppenheimer.

October 7, 1925: Remus files a countersuit against Imogene for misconduct and includes Franklin Dodge in the cross petition. Newspapers around the country run the story.

December 14, 1925: The Jack Daniel's trial begins in Indianapolis. Remus learns that Dodge and Imogene are trying to have him killed.

March 19, 1926: George hits Imogene with a new lawsuit, countering her claims and attempting to recover the valuables that he accused her and Franklin of hiding, including $600,000 in whisky certificates.

April 9, 1926: George is ordered to begin his one-year jail sentence. His lawyers continue the appeal process.

June 7, 1926: The United States Supreme Court "refused relief" in Remus's appeal of the one-year sentence based on the public nuisance conviction. However, George is granted freedom until July 1 by the district court to settle the many lawsuits in which he is either a litigant or witness.

July 1, 1926: Remus is taken into custody and begins his sentence at the Miami County Jail in Troy, Ohio.

August 1, 1926: Price Hill mansion caretaker William Mueller sees Franklin Dodge arrive at the Remus home in a Marmon roadster. Dodge attempts to hide his face, but Mueller identifies him.

August 21, 1926: Labor Department officials announce a warrant for arrest in a preliminary move to deport Remus.

November 5, 1926: Imogene faces contempt of court charge in domestic relations court for selling Remus's property after an injunction had been filed.

December 1926: Imogene and Franklin, according to caretaker William Mueller, stripped the mansion of everything except a "kitchen stove and a table." Mueller watches the couple drive away from the house.

March 27, 1927: Remus is transferred to the Scioto County Jail in Portsmouth, Ohio.

April 26, 1927: George is released at midnight. His top lieutenant, George Connors, drives him to Cincinnati.

May 11, 1927: Imogene is arrested for obtaining money under false pretenses. Franklin is also charged, but not arrested. A mysterious man named Frank Brahm claims that Imogene took $1,750 from him for whisky warehouse receipts.

May 23, 1927: Cincinnati police release Imogene from warrant sworn to in the Scioto County Court after Sheriff Elzey Canter of Scioto fails to appear in court with the original warrant or subsequent dismissal order.

September 22, 1927: Remus allegedly misses an opportunity to kill Franklin and Imogene in Chicago at the Dempsey-Tunney fight. Reports are that Remus arrived thirty-five seconds after they left.

October 6, 1927: Remus murders Imogene in Eden Park.

October 7, 1927: George pleads "not guilty" in Municipal Court in front of Judge William D. Alexander for the death of Imogene. He is held in the Hamilton County jail without bond.

October and November, 1927: Remus's co-counsel Charles Elston and aide George Conners travel the country getting depositions along with the prosecuting team in preparation for the murder trial.

November 14, 1927: The State of Ohio versus George Remus trial opens at the Hamilton County Jail presided over by Judge Chester Shook. Jury selection is the first order of business.

November 21, 1927: Opening arguments begin, followed by early eyewitnesses to the murder.

November 24, 1927: Remus celebrates the Thanksgiving holiday with the 150 inmates in the jailhouse with him.

November 25, 1927: Ruth Remus testifies.

November 26, 1927: The three court-appointed alienists file their report to Judge Shook. They determine that Remus is sane.

December 7, 1927: Harry Truesdale takes the stand and admits that he had been hired by Franklin and Imogene to kill George. In response, Remus suffered a loud outburst, which caused the court session to be cancelled while he recovered. Jurors were grief-stricken and several had tears in their eyes as they left the courtroom hearing Remus's wails.

December 14, 1927: Ruth Remus called to the stand to rebut testimony made by the defense witnesses.

December 17 and 19, 1927: Remus and Elston deliver their final arguments.

December 18, 1927: Charles Taft calls for Remus to receive the death penalty if convicted.

December 20, 1927: After a short deliberation and taking time for lunch, the jury finds Remus "not guilty of murder. . .on the sole ground of insanity."

December 28, 1927: Remus hearing begins in Probate Court under the direction of Judge William Lueders.

December 30, 1927: Judge Lueders finds that Remus is "insane and a dangerous person to be at large." The prisoner is committed to the Lima State Hospital for the Criminally Insane. Elston appeals the decision, but is denied.

January 6, 1928: Remus enters the asylum in Lima.

February 1, 1928: Remus files writ of habeas corpus in Allen County Court of Appeals.

March 20, 1928: The Allen County Court finds Remus not insane and orders that he is released from the Lima institution. The State of Ohio continues fighting the decision and appeals the case to the Ohio Supreme Court.

June 20, 1928: Remus is released from Lima after the Ohio Supreme Court votes four to three to confirm the decision of the lower court. George immediately returns to Cincinnati, where he is greeted by his associates, friends, and fans.

December 10, 1928: Marie Remus (mother) dies in Cincinnati.

May 28, 1929: After campaigning for Herbert Hoover and then not being chosen for attorney general, Mabel Walker Willebrandt resigns from the Prohibition Bureau.

August 30, 1929: Ruth sues to annul adoption and restore her name.

1930s

March 1930: George allegedly marries his longtime aide and business manager Blanche Watson.

November 8, 1930: Franklin Dodge arrested for perjury in Lansing and held on $5,000 bond. The preceding May, Dodge had given false testimony in the trial of George Brown, a bootlegger he had investigated in 1923.

October 28, 1931: After pleading guilty in a federal courtroom in Augusta, Georgia, in front of Judge W. H. Barrett, Dodge begins a thirty-month sentence at the federal penitentiary at Chillicothe, Ohio. The judge, noting Dodge's exemplary service to his nation during Prohibition, cut the maximum sentence in half.

August 1, 1933: John K. Stack, auditor general of Michigan, appoints Dodge as chief disbursement clerk. The move puts Dodge back in the spotlight and causes outrage across Michigan.

December 5, 1933: The 21st Amendment repealing Prohibition is ratified and announced in a proclamation by President Franklin D. Roosevelt.

October 1934: The Hermosa Avenue mansion is torn down after being sold.

November 16, 1935: George Conners dies suddenly from a head injury received in a mysterious car accident six months earlier. Folklore spins that the freak accident was part of an elaborate hit against Conners for gambling debts.

November 24, 1939: Remus files a claim in probate court against the estate of Al Capone associate Edward J. O'Hare for $196,000. When O'Hare attempted to wrest control of the organization from Capone, the gangster had him murdered.

1940s

May 23, 1940: Remus files suit in common pleas court against George R. Landen and Sidney H. Miller claiming one-third of interest in former Hill & Hill distillery in Owensboro, Kentucky, later part of National Distillers' Products Corporation of Virginia.

April 23, 1947: Ruth Holmes Williams dies after being given the wrong type of blood during a hysterectomy surgery in Milwaukee.

July 1948: Remus teams with gunman Buck Brady to purchase The Latin Quarter, a notorious speakeasy-turned gambling den in Newport. They later rename the joint "Buck Brady's Primrose Country Club." After the club becomes successful, the Cleveland Syndicate mafia assumes ownership, threatening Brady to turn the club over or die.

1950s

August 9, 1950: George suffers a stroke at his home in Covington, Kentucky. Some sources also imply that the ailment might have been a heart attack.

August to October 16, 1950: Remus is hospitalized during recovery.

January 20, 1952: George Remus dies at home with Blanche and Romola at his side.

1960s

April 6, 1963: Mabel Willebrandt dies in Riverside, California.

November 26, 1968: Franklin L. Dodge, Jr. dies in his hometown of Lansing, Michigan.

December 31, 1968: John Gehrum dies in Cincinnati.

1970s

March 26, 1974: Blanche Watson Remus dies.

1980s

June 24, 1983: Charles Taft dies.

February 17, 1987: Romola Remus Dunlap dies in Chicago. Later in life, she had received a resurgent fame when it was determined that she had been the first actress to play Dorothy from *The Wizard of Oz* as a child.

2010s

September 19, 2010 to October 26, 2014: The critically-acclaimed television series *Boardwalk Empire* (five seasons, fifty-six episodes) focuses on Prohibition-era corruption in Atlantic City. *Boardwalk Empire* features fictionalized portrayals of many key 1920s figures, including Arnold Rothstein, Meyer Lansky, Mabel Willebrandt, Lucky Luciano, and Al Capone. Actor Glenn Fleshler plays Remus.

October 2, 2011 to October 4, 2011: Eminent documentarian Ken Burns releases *Prohibition*, a three-episode, five and a half hour series. Remus is a central figure in the film. The Bourbon King is voiced by Academy Award-nominated actor Paul Giamatti.

Acknowledgments

. . . . .

I have been thinking about George Remus off and on for about fifteen years. He is the embodiment of the history that I find most interesting (and useful)—a complex character who exemplifies an era while also providing a means to better understanding of our current, contentious times. As America prepares for the centennial of Prohibition and the 1920s, there is so much to learn and consider from one hundred years ago. We see glimpses of the 1920s today in everything from corruption in Washington, DC to the obsession with celebrity and image. As my editor Keith Wallman says, "History may not repeat itself, but it certainly rhymes."

Keith has been a guiding spirit for *The Bourbon King* and his editorial wisdom and work has made it a better book. I deeply appreciate the entire Diversion Books team, including Scott Waxman, Shannon Donnelly, Melanie Madden, and Lissa Warren. I have learned so much in the group effort to produce this book.

As I researched, wrote, and worked on *The Bourbon King*, it was my pleasure to speak with, spend time with, and get to know an incredible group of people who help bring the past to light in many interesting ways. A legion of librarians, archivists, nonprofit leaders, and others helped me re-craft and reimagine Remus's legacy from sometimes spotty records. Sadly, it seems as if America tried to wash the Prohibition parts of its history away, so some incredible sources are simply gone. From my perspective, it is as if Americans love the glitz and glamour of the 1920s—the *Gatsby*-esque aspects—but generally hate Prohibition.

Anyone who writes history or biography understands how invaluable archivists and librarians are to our work. *The Bourbon King* is the culmination of the support and help I received from many, many professionals who have dedicated their lives to preserving our history and enabling it to be used for public education. My thanks to the staff at the Library of Congress, Miami University Libraries, Smith Library of Regional History, Cummins Local History Room at the Hamilton Lane Public Library, Lane Libraries, Public Library of Cincinnati and Hamilton County, Price Hill Historical Society, Delhi Historical Society, Turner-Dodge House & Heritage Center (Lansing Department of Parks and Recreation, City of Lansing, Michigan), Bardstown Historical Museum, Oscar Getz Museum of Whiskey History, Hamilton County Clerk of Courts, and Newspapers.com.

Endless thanks to Rachel Makarowski and Alia Levar Wegner of the Walter Havighurst Special Collections and University Archives at Miami University for priceless help in acquiring the full court transcripts of the Remus case and serving as such gracious hosts as I spent hour-after-hour in the reading room. The Remus trial transcripts—donated to Yale by Charlie Taft—were accessed due to the collegiality of Mike Widener, Rare Book Librarian & Lecturer in Legal Research at the Lillian Goldman Law Library, Yale Law School. My deep appreciation for granting access to this invaluable collection!

I would like to also thank Barbara Loyer at the Turner-Dodge House & Heritage Center for allowing access to Turner-Dodge family archives and images, as well as a tour of the house. Imagine walking the house where Franklin Dodge grew up and lived! Thanks to Brad Spurlock, Public Services Librarian for the Cummins Local History Room at the Hamilton Lane Public Library, for research assistance and insight. *The Bourbon King* also benefitted from research assistance from Mark Dahlquist and Jenny Presnell, both Humanities and Social Sciences Librarians at Miami University. Thank you to Joyce Meyer at the Price Hill Historical Society for research help and early encouragement, and to Mark Plageman, the Historical Society's Remus expert, for his work into the bootleg king and willingness to share his thoughts on Remus's place in American history. The book has also benefited from conversations about Remus and Ohio in the 1920s with Diane Gehrum, whose family has a deep history with the king of the bootleggers and Death Valley. A big thank you to Bill Remus, Emeritus Professor of Information Technology Management at the University of Hawaii for sharing his extensive genealogy into the Remus family history.

A special thanks to Peter and Bo Pogue and The Old Pogue Distillery in Maysville, Kentucky, for their friendship and assistance in all things Remus and bourbon. Peter and Bo graciously allowed the publication of priceless artifacts from their family collection and read an early draft of the manuscript. They are steeped in Remus and bourbon history and I am happy that they welcomed this book to more deeply explore the company's and industry's heritage.

The Bourbon King benefits from the insightful analysis I gained from Lawrence S. Kaplan, Phillip Sipiora, Thomas Heinrich, Jay Sandlin, and Richard Steigmann-Gall who read early drafts, provided thoughtful feedback, and endorsements. My friend Brian Jay Jones not only read the book, but has been a great comrade over the years. I have learned from his masterful writing and deeply appreciated his support of my own. Of course, they only improved the manuscript; any resulting errors are mine alone.

My family is incredibly supportive. Over the years, they have encouraged my work, which an essential facet of the writing life. Thanks to my parents, Jon and Linda Bowen, for everything they do to make our lives infinitely better. Thanks also to Josette Percival and Michel Valois for their support and thoughtfulness. Much love also to Carole and Laurent van Huffel and their sons: Nicholas, Ben, and Matthew.

Without a doubt, raising teenagers is much more difficult than writing a book. I love Kas and Sophie so much and hope that they live lives filled with compassion, love, and patience. I am blessed to have these two young women in my life.

Sometimes, even for a writer, you can't find the words to express your appreciation…but I'll try: My beautiful wife Suzette Percival is my everything. *The Bourbon King* would not exist without her. She envisioned this book from the start, served as an indefatigable researcher, and beta reader. Suzette's historical insight and willingness to dive deep into the archives helped me shape the story, in addition to the countless hours discussing and thinking through the tumultuous 1920s. I'm endlessly amazed at her intelligence, love of history, and willingness to put up with a messy, scattered writer. Suzette was with me through every moment of this book and, although my name is on the cover, hers is just as important.

Notes

• • • • • •

Abbreviations

AC	*Atlanta Constitution*		MT	*Munster (IN) Times*
BS	*Baltimore Sun*		NYDN	*New York Daily News*
BG	*Boston Globe*		NYH	*New York Herald*
BT	*Buffalo Times*		NYT	*New York Times*
CI	*Chicago Inter Ocean*		OI	*Owensboro (KY) Inquirer*
CT	*Chicago Tribune*		OT	*Oakland Tribune*
CE	*Cincinnati Enquirer*		PI	*Philadelphia Inquirer*
CP	*Cincinnati Post*		PDP	*Pittsburgh Daily Post*
CDS	*Corsicana (TX) Daily Sun*		SEP	*Saturday Evening Post*
DDN	*Dayton Daily News*		SHD	*Senate Investigation of the Honor-*
DH	*Dayton Herald*			*able Harry M. Daugherty*. Select
HDN	*Hamilton Daily News*			Committee, 68th Cong., 1st sess.
HEJ	*Hamilton Evening Journal*			11 Vols. Washington: GPO, 1924.
HSI	*Harrisburg Star-Independent*		ST	*Shreveport Times*
HH	*Huntington (IN) Herald*		SBT	*South Bend Tribune*
IG	*Indiana (PA) Gazette*		SPD	*St. Louis Post-Dispatch*
IN	*Indianapolis News*		SST	*St. Louis Star and Times*
IS	*Indianapolis Star*		SPJ	*Stevens Point (WI) Journal*
LSJ	*Lansing State Journal*		TT	*Tampa Tribune*
LC	Library of Congress		WP	*Washington Post*
LAT	*Los Angeles Times*		WT	*Washington Times*
LCJ	*Louisville Courier-Journal*		WEJ	*Wilmington Evening Journal*
MWW	Mabel Walker Willebrandt		Yale	*The State of Ohio vs. George*
	Papers			*Remus: Records and Arguments.*
MNJ	*Mansfield News-Journal*			7 Vols. Yale University Law
MEP	*Muncie (IN) Evening Press*			Library, Yale University.

Prologue: Awash in Red

x. the car salesman. (William Hulvershorn Testimony, Yale, Vol. 2, 575); x. I love you,"
George said, exhausted. (Earl L. Shaub, "Remus Says," TT, October 10, 1927)

PART ONE: BIRTH OF A BOOTLEGGER

Chapter 1: Napoleon of the Bar

4. lot of piffle." ("Remus Stakes," NYT, December 19, 1927); 6. frigid Lake Michigan. ("Lake
Baffles," CI, August 11, 1907); 6. first-class condition." ("Lake Baffles," CI, August 11, 1907);
6. in the water." ("Not Exhausted," CT, August 13, 1907); 7. lost to history. (William Remus,
"Descendants of Father of Friedrich Remus," The Remus Family of West Prussia: Volume II,
Part I, "West Prussia, Danzig, Saxony, Cloth maker villages near Posen, plus Volhynia and
Kiev," (remus.shidler.hawaii.edu/genes/home)); 7. in June 1882. (William Remus, "Descend-
ants of Father of Friedrich Remus," The Remus Family of West Prussia: Volume II, Part I,
"West Prussia, Danzig, Saxony, Cloth maker villages near Posen, plus Volhynia and Kiev."
(remus.shidler.hawaii.edu/genes/home)); 8. childbirth in 1884. (Ibid.); 8. of the family."
(Remus Testimony, Yale, Vol. 1, 161); 9. required toughness. (Remus Testimony, Yale, Vol.
6, 791); 9. sixty-seven years old. (Remus Testimony, Yale, Vol. 1, 161); 10. down the street.
(Remus Testimony, Yale, Vol. 6, 387–388); 11. successful young people. (Remus Testimony,
Yale, Vol. 1, 140); 11. advantage of that." (Remus Testimony, Yale, Vol. 1, 140); 12. 500 retail
druggists. (Remus Testimony, Yale, Vol. 6, 382); 12. wrong he had created. (Remus Testimony, Yale, Vol. 6, 411); 12. four walls," he said. (Remus Testimony, Yale, Vol. 6, 388; 411);
13. organized labor." (Remus Testimony, Yale, Vol. 6, 391); 14. a completer life." ("Strike
Inquiry," CT, February 14, 1903); 15. "law-abiding citizen." ("Remus Witness," BS, December
9, 1927); 15. crime" in Chicago. ("A 'Christmas' Verdict," Virginia Law Register New Series,
Vol. 13, 9 (January 1928): 566.); 15. in the courtroom. ("Remus Stakes," NYT, December 19,
1927); 16. 3229 Indiana Avenue. ("Tragic Death," HSI, October 29, 1912); 16. in a handkerchief. ("Tragic Death," HSI, October 29, 1912); 16. told the couple. ("Tragic Death," HSI,
October 29, 1912); 17. coldblooded murderer. ("Cramers Guilty," CT, March 8, 1913); 17.
and theatrics. ("Cramers Guilty," CT, March 8, 1913); 17. protect her husband. ("Cramers
Guilty," CT, March 8, 1913); 18. sick of it." ("Kills His Wife," CT, October 17, 1913); 18. the
man mumbled. ("Kills His Wife," CT, October 17, 1913); 19. a reporter noted. ("Ellis Gives,"
MNJ, February 27, 1914; "Ellis, On Stand," SPD, February 27, 1914); 19. and wrists." ("Ellis
Gives," MNJ, February 27, 1914; "Ellis, On Stand," SPD, February 27, 1914); 19. love for
him." ("Ellis Gives," MNJ, February 27, 1914); 19. hide the tears." ("'I Will Kill,'" CT, March
1, 1914); 20. could be revived." ("'I Will Kill,'" CT, March 1, 1914); 20. chair, swooning."
("Ellis Again," CI, March 4, 1914); 20. transitory insanity." ("Ellis Had," Daily Gate City
(Keokuk, Iowa), March 3, 1914); 20. right and wrong. ("'I Will Kill,'" CT, March 1, 1914); 20.
hour of need. ("Jury to Get," CI, March 5, 1914); 21. segment of orange." ("W.C. Ellis Guilty,"
CT, March 6, 1914); 21. to his children." ("'Damaged Goods,'" CT, May 16, 1921)

Chapter 2: Illicit Relations

22. suffered back home. ("Two Shoes," *Philadelphia Inquirer*, September 17, 1916); **23.** one pair of shoes." ("Two Shoes," PI, September 17, 1916); **23.** family suffered. ("Wife Sues," CT, September 13, 1916); **23.** shoes alternately." ("Two Shoes," PI, September 17, 1916; "'Other Woman,'" CT, September 13, 1916); **25.** had charisma. ("Amazing Human Study," *Springfield News-Leader* (Missouri), April 6, 1924); **25.** many nights away. ("News of the Day Concerning Chicago," Day Book (Chicago), March 6, 1915); **26.** instance," he professed. (Remus Testimony, Yale, Vol. 6, 764); **26.** of their relationship. (Remus Testimony, Yale, Vol. 1, 81); **27.** illicit relations," George confessed. (Remus Testimony, Yale, Vol. 6, 420); **27.** $285, which I paid." (Remus Testimony, Yale, Vol. 6, 464–465); **28.** to the glamour. (Remus Testimony, Yale, Vol. 6, 764); **28.** her," Remus claimed. (Remus Testimony, Yale, Vol. 6, 764); **29.** him the $15." ("$15 Reward," CT, February 4, 1919); **29.** threw him out." ("$15 Reward," CT, February 4, 1919); **29.** willing readers. ("Plumber Remus," CT, February 16, 1919); **29.** had taken place. (Remus Testimony, Yale, Vol. 6, 415); **30.** give him up." ("George Remus," BT, March 2, 1919); **30.** could have him. ("George Remus," BT, March 2, 1919); **30.** pearly teeth." ("George Remus," BT, March 2, 1919); **31.** absurd statements." ("George Remus," BT, March 2, 1919); **31.** one paper reported. ("Divorce Suit," BT, March 9, 1919); **31.** a [divorce] bill." (Remus Testimony, Yale, Vol. 6, 415); **31.** could uncover. ("Divorce Suit," BT, March 9, 1919); **31.** last three years." ("Mrs. Remus," CT, March 8, 1919); **31.** out of the office." ("Mrs. Remus," CT, March 8, 1919); **31.** many times." ("Mrs. Remus," CT, March 8, 1919); **31.** week in alimony. ("Divorce Suit," BT, March 9, 1919); **32.** acted," Remus said. ("Plumber Remus," CT, February 16, 1919); **32.** much interested." ("Plumber Remus," CT, February 16, 1919); **32.** "nodding pleasantly." ("Plumber Remus," CT, February 16, 1919); **32.** courtroom were not better." ("Plumber Remus," CT, February 16, 1919); **34.** keep him happy. ("Tells Wives," Washington Times (DC), March 20, 1919); **34.** that's all." ("Tells Wives," Washington Times (DC), March 20, 1919); **34.** Chicago's latest triangle." ("Tells Wives," WT, (DC), March 20, 1919); **34.** for his roll," ("Reveal Hidden Life Chapters of Mrs. Remus," CT, Oct. 28, 1927); **34.** she told Brockway. ("Reveal Hidden Life Chapters of Mrs. Remus," CT, Oct. 28, 1927; "Bank Account," CE, October 28, 1927); **35.** to make more." ("Bank Account," CE, October 28, 1927); **35.** told another friend. ("Colorful Career of Remus," LSJ, November 14, 1927); **35.** the early days." (J. H. Creighton, "Colorful Career," LSJ, November 14, 1927); **35.** on greater importance. (Remus Testimony, Yale, Vol. 6, 790-791); **37.** and politicians flourished." ("Over-the-Rhine Days," MNJ, November 5, 1925); **38.** happened to her." (Remus Testimony, Yale, Vol. 6, 764); **38.** Queen City locale. ("George Remus Weds," CT, July 22, 1920); **38.** for her husband. ("Remus, Wanted," CT, August 4, 1920); **39.** in the east." ("George Remus Weds," CT, July 22, 1920); **39.** violating national Prohibition. ("Remus Won't End," August 1, 1920); **39.** suppress the charge. (Wheeler statement, SHD, Volume III, 3232); **39.** pay it," Remus claimed. (Paul Anderson, "Disaster Came," SPD, January 10, 1926)

Chapter 3: Birth of a Bootlegger

40. "Stick 'em up high!" (Paul Y. Anderson, "First Attack," SPD, January 6, 1926); **42.** come out shooting. (Paul Y. Anderson, "First Attack," SPD, January 6, 1926); **43.** gift from his wife. (Remus Testimony, Yale, Vol. 6, 590); **45.** taking Prohibition seriously." (David Pietrusza, Judge and Jury: The Life and Times of Judge Kenesaw Mountain Landis. South Bend, IN: Diamond Communications, 1998, 204); **45.** here anymore." ("Brundage Says," CT, September 27, 1919); **46.** Chicago," George remembered. ("Parallel Seen," CP, October 11, 1927); **47.** taken seriously." (Michael D. Morgan, Over-the-Rhine: When Beer was King. Charleston: History Press, 2010); **47.** that city," George explained. ("Remus Bought Gem Store," CE, January 21, 1952); **47.** catch its breath." (Daugherty, SHD, Vol. 3, 2406); **48.** not the owner." (Daugherty, SHD, Vol. 3, 2406); **48.** Aurora, Illinois. (Remus Testimony, Yale, Vol. 6, 648); **48.** hip-pocket bootlegging." (Paul Y. Anderson, "Inside Story of the Amazing Career of George Remus," SPD, January 3, 1926); **49.** would be to get it out." (Paul Y. Anderson, "Inside Story of the Amazing Career of George Remus," SPD, January 3, 1926); **49.** and excitement." (Paul Y. Anderson, "Inside Story of the Amazing Career of George Remus," SPD, January 3, 1926); **49.** the thirsty nation. ("Parallel Seen," CP, October 11, 1927); **49.** quasi-criminal classes." (qtd. in Edward Behr, Prohibition: Thirteen Years that Changed America, New York: Arcade, 2011, 80); **50.** enforced," George explained. (Paul Y. Anderson, "Inside Story," SPD, January 3, 1926); **50.** good whiskey," George said. (Anderson, "Inside Story," SPD, January 3, 1926); **51.** nothing but the best." (Paul Y. Anderson, "Inside Story of the Amazing Career of George Remus," SPD, January 3, 1926); **51.** found the appropriate guides. ("Will Justice," NYDN, October 16, 1927); **52.** Yellowley's staff agents. ("U.S. Starts," Evening News (Wilkes-Barre, PA), October 22, 1921; "Dry Head," New York Herald, October 23, 1921); **52.** permits in the Eastern States." ("Dry Head," NYH, October 23, 1921); **52.** leaders at the top. ("Charge Big Liquor," BG, October 20, 1921; "Much Booze," Indianapolis Star, July 6, 1923); **53.** "medicinal purposes." (J. Anne Funderburg, Bootleggers and Beer Barons of the Prohibition Era. Jefferson, NC: McFarland, 2014); **53.** accustomed to in Chicago. (Paul Y. Anderson, "Inside Story of the Amazing Career of George Remus," SPD, January 3, 1926); **53.** Anti-Saloon League." (Paul Y. Anderson, "Inside Story of the Amazing Career of George Remus," SPD, January 3, 1926); **54.** command structure. (Herbert Asbury, The Great Illusion: An Informal History of Prohibition. Garden City, NY: Doubleday, 1950, 253); **54.** wholesale prices." (Remus Testimony, Yale, Vol. 1, 19–20); **54.** bootlegging prices." (Remus Testimony, Yale, Vol. 1, 19–20); **54.** always in demand." (Mary Chenoweth, "Remus Opens Way," LCJ, March 1, 1926); **55.** brothels dotted the city. (Robin Caraway, Newport: The Sin City Years. Charleston: Arcadia, 2009, 7); **55.** go out busted." (Hank Messick, Razzle Dazzle, Covington, KY: For The Love of Books, 1995, 57); **56.** has seldom seen." (Anderson, "High Tide of Prosperity," SPD, January 9, 1926; "Get-Rich-Quick," SPD, January 11, 1926); **56.** competitors "saps." (Paul Y. Anderson, "Death Valley," SPD, January 4, 1926); **57.** weeks," George said later. (Remus Testimony, Yale, Vol. 1, 24–26); **57.** crack your head." (Remus Testimony, Yale, Vol. 1, 24–26); **57.** with me." (Remus Testimony, Yale, Vol. 1, 24–26); **58.** country surroundings." (Remus Testimony, Yale, Vol. 6, 462); **58.** the blood to flow." ("Remus Plans," CP, October 10, 1927); **58.** to his will." ("Remus Plans," CP, October 10, 1927); **59.** frequent fits of temper." ("Remus Plans," CP, October 10, 1927)

PART TWO: KING OF THE BOOTLEGGERS

Chapter 4: The Bourbon Empire

64. 60 days thereafter." (Remus Testimony, Yale, Vol. 6, 445); **64.** and entirely." (Remus Testimony, Yale, Vol. 6, 445); **65.** volume of poison." ("44 Caught," PI, December 25, 1929); **65.** Gary to steel." (Paul Y. Anderson, "Inside Story of the Amazing Career of George Remus," SPD, January 3, 1926); **65.** and audacity." (Paul Y. Anderson, "Inside Story of the Amazing Career of George Remus," SPD, January 3, 1926); **66.** of employees." (Remus Testimony, Yale,

Vol. 6, 446); **66.** to about $400,000." (Remus Testimony, Yale, Vol. 6, 445); **67.** cost me $640,000." (Remus Testimony, Yale, Vol. 6, 445); **67.** liquor in there." (Remus Testimony, Yale, Vol. 1, 21); **67.** continually accumulate. (Remus Testimony, Yale, Vol. 1, 21); **68.** salary of $12,000. (Remus Testimony, Yale, Vol. 6, 446–447); **68.** at "$115,000." (Remus Testimony, Yale, Vol. 6, 447); **68.** strong-arm Buck Brady. (Chenoweth, "Vigilance of Kentucky," LCJ, March 8, 1926); **69.** out of the wreck." (Remus Testimony, Yale, Vol. 6, 448); **69.** break the law. (Remus Testimony, Yale, Vol. 6, 448); **69.** to the organization." (Remus Testimony, Yale, Vol. 6, 447); **69.** rolling in cash. (Remus Testimony, Yale, Vol. 6, 447); **70.** stocked Brady's car. (Chenoweth, "Vigilance of Kentucky," LCJ, March 8, 1926); **70.** illegal pieces. (Anderson, "Horde of Rum," SPD, January 7, 1926); **71.** Imogene's forged application. (Chenoweth, "Drug Firm Aids," LCJ, March 3, 1926); **71.** Covington or Cincinnati." (Chenoweth, "Drug Firm Aids," LCJ, March 3, 1926); **72.** off to the second one." (Paul Y. Anderson, "Death Valley," SPD, January 4, 1926); **72.** Dobrats Company liquor permit. (Mary Chenoweth, "Kentucky Drug Firm," LCJ, March 3, 1926); **72.** traced directly to him. (Remus Testimony, Yale, Vol. 6, 571); **74.** done it," Conners explained. (Paul Y. Anderson, "Inside Story of the Amazing Career of George Remus," SPD, January 3, 1926); **74.** containing armed guards." (Paul Y. Anderson, "Death Valley," SPD, January 4, 1926); **75.** at pursuing pirates." (Anderson, "Horde of Rum," SPD, January 7, 1926); **75.** Illinois, Cleveland." (Anderson, "How Remus," SPD, January 8, 1926); **76.** including St. Louis." (Paul Y. Anderson, "Huge Withdrawals," SPD, January 5, 1926); **76.** obtain the liquor." (SHD, Vol. 3, 2403); **76.** $300 a case for it." (Anderson, "High Tide of Prosperity," SPD, January 9, 1926); **76.** and put on new plates. (Anderson, "High Tide of Prosperity," SPD, January 9, 1926); **76.** expelled from the organization. (Paul Y. Anderson, "Huge Withdrawals," SPD, January 5, 1926); **77.** very strenuous life. (Paul Y. Anderson, "Death Valley," SPD, January 4, 1926); **77.** whiskey Remus stocked. (Remus Testimony, Yale, Vol. 6, 444); **77.** never permit that." (Remus Testimony, February 23, 1928, Yale, Vol. 6, 444); **78.** run the seedier aspects of his operations. (Coffey, Long Thirst, 88); **78.** the chief distributor." (Bootlegger King of '20s Sues for Distillery Stock," CT, May 24, 1940); **78.** customers none the wiser. (Coffey, Long Thirst, 88); **79.** more than $450,000. (Mary Chenoweth, "Kentucky Drug Firm," LCJ, March 3, 1926); **79.** the country," George explained. (Paul Y. Anderson, "Death Valley," SPD, January 4, 1926); **80.** to a Rockefeller." ("Bootleg King," PDP, July 9, 1922); **80.** captains of industry." (Paul Y. Anderson, "Inside Story," SPD, January 3, 1926)

Chapter 5: Underworld Boss of Death Valley

81. the vehicles sped off. (Paul Y. Anderson, "First Attack," SPD, January 6, 1926); **82.** "instant and terrific." (Paul Y. Anderson, "Inside Story," SPD, January 3, 1926); **82.** Conners told the journalist. (Paul Y. Anderson, "Inside Story," SPD, January 3, 1926); **82.** No policemen wanted." (Paul Y. Anderson, "First Attack," SPD, January 6, 1926; **82.** fifteen times without reloading." (Paul Y. Anderson, "Death Valley," SPD, January 4, 1926); **83.** face of the operation. (Anderson, "Horde of Rum," SPD, January 7, 1926); **83.** forty-four men were paid off. (William J. Mellin as told to Meyer Berger, "I was a wire Tapper," SEP, September 10, 1949); **84.** landowners in the Queen City. ("Mr. Taft's Cincinnati," The Bulletin, American Iron and Steel Association, July 1, 1908, 69); **84.** defend against pirates." (Paul Y. Anderson, "Death Valley," SPD, January 4, 1926); **84.** taste for strong drink. (Paul Y. Anderson, "Death Valley," SPD, January 4, 1926); **85.** in the barn loft." (Paul Y. Anderson, "Death Valley," SPD, January 4, 1926); **85.** Rugby Distilling Company in Louisville. (Remus Testimony, Yale, Vol. 6, 443–

444); **86.** of Death Valley Farm." (Paul Y. Anderson, "Death Valley," SPD, January 4, 1926); **87.** bootlegging on the side." (Paul Y. Anderson, "First Attack," SPD, January 6, 1926); **87.** knocked off," he exclaimed. (Paul Y. Anderson, "First Attack," SPD, January 6, 1926); **88.** illuminating everything below." (Paul Y. Anderson, "Death Valley," SPD, January 4, 1926); **88.** sawed-off guns, pistols, and rifles." ("Remus Was," SPD, January 8, 1928); **88.** shoot first. (Paul Y. Anderson, "Inside Story," SPD, January 3, 1926); **88.** death in Death Valley." ("Remus Was," SPD, January 8, 1928); **89.** Everybody knows Remus." ("Remus Appears," MT, October 31, 1921); **89.** explained further to Anderson. (Anderson, "Horde of Rum," SPD, January 7, 1926); **89.** stepdaughter Ruth would remember. ("Remus Plans," CP, October 10, 1927); **90.** their graves." (Remus Testimony, SHD, Vol. 3, 2400); **91.** trust another thief? (Anderson, "Horde of Rum," SPD, January 7, 1926); **91.** double-cross me," Remus explained. (Anderson, "Horde of Rum," SPD, January 7, 1926); **91.** train for New York." (Anderson, "Horde of Rum," SPD, January 7, 1926); **91.** could be consumed. (Thomas Barker, Gary W. Potter, and Jenna Meglen, Wicked Newport: Kentucky's Sin City. Charleston: History Press, 2008); **92.** skulls caved in." (Paul Y. Anderson, "Inside Story," SPD, January 3, 1926); **92.** murderous whiskey pirates." (Paul Y. Anderson, "Inside Story," SPD, January 3, 1926); **92.** runners and pirates." (Paul Y. Anderson, "Inside Story," SPD, January 3, 1926); **92.** do him most good." (Frederic William Wile, "Bootleg Corporation," *South Bend Tribune*, August 22, 1922); **93.** $2 million more if he wanted. ("Sentences," CE, May 25, 1922); **93.** flowed out upon the country." (Paul Y. Anderson, "Inside Story," SPD, January 3, 1926)

Chapter 6: Every Man Has His Price

97. hair until it was perfect. (Gaston B. Means, The Strange Death of President Harding, New York: Guild, 1930, 58, 86); **98.** views hush-hush. (Means, The Strange Death of President Harding, New York: Guild, 1930, 88, 90); **98.** took the cash. (Paul Anderson, "Attempt to Buy," SPD, January 8, 1926); **99.** Harding pardoned him. (Anderson, "Attempt to Buy," SPD, January 8, 1926); **99.** enough for me." (Anderson, "Attempt to Buy," SPD, January 8, 1926); **99.** possible and lucrative. (Charles K. Swafford, "Cincinnati Bootleg," PDP, April 24, 1927); **99.** never go to prison." (Anderson, "Attempt to Buy," SPD, January 8, 1926); **101.** of government agents." (Frederic William Wile, "Bootleg Corporation," SBT, August 22, 1922); **101.** "more openly than ever." (Anderson, "Sales of Contraband," SPD, January 9, 1926); **101.** Washington were our friends." (Remus Testimony, Yale, Vol. 1, 20); **101.** prosecute him." (Frederic William Wile, "Bootleg Corporation," SBT, August 22, 1922); **101.** started doing business." (Anderson, "Sales of Contraband," SPD, January 9, 1926); **101.** excess baggage to us." (Anderson, "Sales of Contraband," SPD, January 9, 1926); **102.** prices became almost standard. ("U.S. Moves to Deport Remus," CT, August 22, 1926); **102.** extorting the bootleggers. (Paul Y. Anderson, "Huge Withdrawals," SPD, January 5, 1926); **103.** distilleries that I was owner of." (Remus Testimony, Yale, Vol. 6, 424); **103.** private secretary of a cabinet officer." (Frederic William Wile, "Dare to Government," SBT, August 23, 1922); **103.** get a pardon." (Mary Chenoweth, "Remus Opens Way," LCJ, March 1, 1926); **104.** he explained sarcastically. ("Remus Bought Gem Store," CE, January 21, 1952); **104.** share in the graft." (Paul Y. Anderson, "Inside Story," SPD, January 3, 1926); **105.** might as well get yours." (Chenoweth, "Morgan Scorned," LCJ, March 11, 1926); **105.** presented to my office." (Frederic William Wile, "Dare to Government," SBT, August 23, 1922); **105.** all we want." ("Sentences," CE, May 25, 1922); **105.** the Remus organization." ("Sentences," CE, May 25, 1922); **105.** as the final answer." (Chenoweth, "Morgan Scorned," LCJ, March 11, 1926); **106.**

$100,000 if he would resign." ("Remus Was," SPD, January 8, 1928); **106.** he was offered $500,000. ("Remus Was," SPD, January 8, 1928); **106.** very comfortably without." ("Remus Was," SPD, January 8, 1928); **107.** in the criminal world. (Kerns Testimony, SHD, Volume II, 1483); **107.** "free from molestation." (Kerns Testimony, SHD, Volume II, 1482-1483); **107.** two quarts of bourbon a week. (Paul Y. Anderson, "Inside Story," SPD, January 3, 1926); **107.** skulls caved in. (Paul Y. Anderson, "Inside Story of the Amazing Career of George Remus," SPD, January 3, 1926)

Chapter 7: Epic Grandeur

110. which began at midnight." ("Bootleg King," PDP, July 9, 1922); **110.** diving and swimming." ("Bootleg King," PDP, July 9, 1922); **110.** everyone who will listen. (Remus Testimony, Yale, Vol. 6, 461); **111.** observer who studied George. (David I. Wolfstein Testimony, Yale, Vol. 1, 169); **111.** hundreds of whistles." ("Uneasy," CE, January 1, 1922); **111.** favorite bootleggers." ("Uneasy," CE, January 1, 1922); **111.** dances, and dinners." ("Uneasy," CE, January 1, 1922); **112.** George's illegal booze. (Remus Testimony, Yale, Vol. 6, 461); **112.** doesn't want to be seen." ("Will Justice," NYDN, October 16, 1927); **112.** *seemed a caress.*" ("Will Justice," NYDN, October 16, 1927); **113.** *her every movement.*" ("Will Justice," NYDN, October 16, 1927); **113.** *and Cleopatra.*" ("Will Justice," NYDN, October 16, 1927); **113.** count it," George said. (Remus Testimony, Yale, Vol. 6, 764); **113.** she saw fit to do." (Remus Testimony, Yale, Vol. 6, 764); **113.** $750,000 to $800,000. (Remus Testimony, Yale, Vol. 6, 457); **114.** rubrics—everything." ("Bootleg King," PDP, July 9, 1922); **114.** marble statuary," he said. (Remus Testimony, Yale, Vol. 6, 458); **114.** that I considered a gem." (Remus Testimony, Yale, Vol. 6, 458); **114.** his prized historical treasures. (Remus Testimony, Yale, Vol. 6, 465); **114.** pottery artists in the world. (Remus Testimony, Yale, Vol. 6, 457); **114.** The perfect name. ("Parallel Seen," CP, October 11, 1927); **115.** that was too much. ("Will Justice," NYDN, October 16, 1927); **116.** during the last few years." ("'Star Agent,'" CE, March 20, 1925); **118.** a full dress suit." (Remus Testimony, Yale, Vol. 6, 461)

PART THREE: PLUNDERING AN EMPIRE

Chapter 8: Ace Bags the King

123. on the outside." (Remus Testimony, Yale, Vol. 6, 522); **123.** husband in his business." ("Wife Aids," CP, November 3, 1921); **124.** penalty for that mistake." (Chenoweth, "Dry Raid Hurts," LCJ, March 7, 1926); **124.** clean up and be ready." (Chenoweth, "Dry Raid Hurts," LCJ, March 7, 1926); **124.** entrusted to him." (Paul Y. Anderson, "Death Valley," SPD, January 4, 1926); **125.** not come around here." ("Will Justice," NYDN, October 16, 1927); **125.** liquor off the premises. (Paul Y. Anderson, "Inside Story of the Amazing Career of George Remus," SPD, January 3, 1926); **125.** a trio of occasions." (Frederic William Wile, "Bootleg Corporation," SBT, August 22, 1922); **125.** care about enforcement. (Jack O'Donnell, "Can This Woman Make America Dry?" Collier's, August 9, 1924, MWW, Miscellany, LC); **126.** to its destination." ("Who's Who," SEP, September 27, 1924, MWW, Clippings, 1920-1935, LC); **127.** to the bow-wow." ("Gives Message," SST, April 23, 1925); **127.** is more than I can see." (Willebrandt letter to parents, March 22, 1922, MWW, Mabel Willebrandt Correspondence, Parents, 1922, LC); **127.** heart of the question. (Mary McCracken Jones, "Dauntless Mrs. Willebrandt," Woman's Viewpoint, October 1925, 15, MWW, Miscellany, LC); **127.** testimony," said one journalist. ("Heber Nations,'" SST, May 28, 1925); **128.** praise I have received." (Willebrandt letter to parents, June 19, 1923, MWW, Mabel Willebrandt Correspondence, Parents, 1923, LC); **128.** as many smaller fry." (Frederic William Wile, "Bootleg Corporation," SBT, August 22, 1922); **129.** the agency's ironclad position. (Jack O'Donnell, "Can This Woman Make America Dry?" Collier's, August 9, 1924, MWW, Miscellany, LC); **130.** "Tell everything," she urged. (Chenoweth, "Remus Chooses," LCJ, March 4, 1926); **130.** of the Remus gang." ("Ambition and Women," IG, October 14, 1927); **130.** suddenly and mysteriously." ("Dodge Labels," Herald-Press (St. Joseph, MI), October 8, 1927); **130.** his man," one reporter later noted. ("Remus Was," SPD, January 8, 1928); **131.** oust me as an organization." (Remus Testimony, Yale, Vol. 1, 22); **131.** prosecution or extradition. ("Fur Flies," LCJ, February 11, 1930); **131.** with enforcement agents. (Remus Testimony, Yale, Vol. 1, 11, 12); **132.** dugouts, and foxholes." (Edward G. Lengel, To Conquer Hell: The Meuse-Argonne, 1918, New York: Henry Holt, 2008, 153); **132.** bore him to safety." ("Read the," News-Messenger (Fremont, OH), October 28, 1924); **132.** bring George to justice. (Ruth Neely, "Women 'Fates' in Life of Remus, CP, October 8, 1927); **133.** she explained, remembering the scene. (Chenoweth, "Remus Chooses," LCJ, March 4, 1926); **133.** revelation more astounding. (Chenoweth, "Remus Chooses," LCJ, March 4, 1926); **133.** added credibility. (Chenoweth, "Remus Chooses," LCJ, March 4, 1926); **133.** keeping documentation. (Remus Testimony, Yale, Vol. 1, 23–24); **134.** face that huge loss. (Remus Testimony, Yale, Vol. 1, 20); **134.** had seen it in operation. (Chenoweth, "Guilty Verdict," LCJ, March 12, 1926); **134.** Federal buildings?" (Chenoweth, "Guilty Verdict," LCJ, March 12, 1926); **134.** No one made a sound. ("Whisky Ring," CE, May 17, 1922); **135.** hardly be heard." ("Whisky Ring," CE, May 17, 1922); **135.** various persons," a reporter noted. ("Sentences," CE, May 25, 1922); **135.** were no crime." ("Sentences," CE, May 25, 1922); **136.** consequences for them." ("His Whisky Transactions, MNJ, October 31, 1921)

Chapter 9: Business as Usual

138. accept my terms," Remus explained. (Chenoweth, "Remus Intended," LCJ, March 9, 1926); **138.** went to trial. (Chenoweth, "Remus Intended," LCJ, March 9, 1926); **138.** heat on Remus increased. (Remus Testimony, Yale, Vol. 6, 571); **139.** liquor out of Newport. (Thomas Barker, Gary W. Potter, and Jenna Meglen, Wicked Newport: Kentucky's Sin City. Charleston: History Press, 2008); **139.** the "Gentleman Grafter." (Thomas Barker, Gary W. Potter, and Jenna Meglen, Wicked Newport: Kentucky's Sin City. Charleston: History Press, 2008); **140.** Jew John told George. (Chenoweth, "Remus Intended," LCJ, March 9, 1926); **141.** about the heist. (Chenoweth, "Remus Intended," LCJ, March 9, 1926); **141.** with the whiskey." (Chenoweth, "Remus Intended," LCJ, March 9, 1926); **141.** George called Louisville. (Chenoweth, "Remus Intended," LCJ, March 9, 1926); **141.** I do not like to think of it." (Chenoweth, "Remus Intended," LCJ, March 9, 1926); **142.** watching over the transaction. (Anderson, "Get-Rich-Quick," SPD, January 11, 1926); **142.** the gauger is right." (Anderson, "Get-Rich-Quick," SPD, January 11, 1926); **143.** discovery would be negligible." (Anderson, "Get-Rich-Quick," SPD, January 11, 1926); **143.** Duncan Avenue side." ("Three Plead Guilty," SPD, December 14, 1925); **143.** garage," Remus's man said. ("Three Plead Guilty," SPD, December 14, 1925); **143.** through the hose." ("Three Plead Guilty," SPD, December 14, 1925); **144.** stop the pump." ("Three Plead Guilty," SPD, December 14, 1925); **144.** caught," he warned. ("Three Plead Guilty," SPD, December 14, 1925); **144.** at once and sell it quickly. (Anderson, "Get-Rich-Quick," SPD, January 11, 1926); **144.** all with their greed." (Anderson, "Get-Rich-Quick," SPD, January 11, 1926); **144.** filled the casks only with water. (Anderson, "Get-Rich-Quick," SPD, January 11, 1926); **145.** ten years for this job." (Anderson, "Get-Rich-Quick," SPD, January 11, 1926); **145.** started," Remus claimed. (Anderson, "Get-Rich-Quick," SPD, January 11, 1926); **145.** paid Colbeck off. (Anderson, "Get-Rich-Quick," SPD, January 11, 1926); **145.** gave me," George complained. (Anderson, "Get-Rich-Quick," SPD, January 11, 1926); **145.** such a position." (Anderson, "Get-Rich-Quick," SPD, January 11, 1926); **146.** to get arrest warrants. (Anderson, "Get-Rich-Quick," SPD, January 11, 1926); **146.** of an estimated $500,000. (Anderson, "Get-Rich-Quick," SPD, January 11, 1926); **147.** strong with the women." ("Remus Is," CE, December 29, 1927); **147.** for Indianapolis," Remus said. (Remus Testimony, Yale, Vol. 1, 79); **147.** that hour of the night." (Remus Testimony, Yale, Vol. 1, 79); **147.** alibi," Remus bellowed. (Remus Testimony, Yale, Vol. 1, 79); **147.** wife this way?" ("Remus Is," CE, December 29, 1927); **147.** cane wielded by Remus." ("Cane," CE, October 11, 1922); **148.** connections in the city. ("Cane," CE, October 11, 1922); **148.** that morning. ("Cane," CE, October 11, 1922); **148.** surrendered to local police. ("Noted Police Character," IS, October 14, 1922; "Remus is Once," *Times* (Munster, IN), October 16, 1922); **148.** pursue the charge. ("Charges Against," IN, July 20, 1923); **148.** had explained after the raid. (Chenoweth, "Jury's 'Guilty' Verdict," LCJ, March 12, 1926); **149.** me now," George demanded. (qtd. in Albert Rosenberg and Cindy Armstrong, The American Gladiators: Taft versus Remus Hemet, CA: Aimwell Press, 1995, 37); **149.** Remus's growing temper. (qtd. in Rosenberg and Armstrong, 37); **150.** I had no place to turn." (Mary Chenoweth, "Remus Opens Way," LCJ, March 1, 1926); **150.** failed, was gone." (Anderson, "Get-Rich-Quick," SPD, January 11, 1926); **151.** behind their operations." (Willebrandt memo (January 19, 1924), SHD, Vol. III, 3331–32); **151.** the National Prohibition Act. (Daugherty Investigation, SHD, Vol. III, 3333); **152.** had "no business." (Remus Testimony, Yale, Vol. 6, 517); **152.** access to 3,900 barrels. (Remus Testimony, Yale, Vol. 6, 517)

Chapter 10: Life in Hell

153. had cut himself. ("Remus Is," CE, December 29, 1927); **154.** because of the heat." ("Remus Is," CE, December 29, 1927); **155.** starvation, no money." (Remus Testimony, Yale, Vol. 6, 475); **155.** pen had broken him. (Remus Testimony, Yale, Vol. 6, 475); **155.** it is tremendous." (Remus Testimony, Yale, Vol. 6, 475); **155.** life while incarcerated. (Remus Testimony, Yale, Vol. 1, 28); **156.** prison," Remus explained. (Chenoweth, "Prison Term Convinced," LCJ, March 14, 1926); **156.** private records." (Chenoweth, "Prison Term Convinced," LCJ, March 14, 1926); **156.** entire two-year sentence. (Anderson, "Remus, Released," SPD, January 12, 1926); **158.** at the last moment. ("Special Car," CE, January 25, 1924); **158.** to plan a hijacking. ("Special Car," CE, January 25, 1924); **158.** the next week or two." ("Special Car," CE, January 25, 1924); **158.** during his confinement." ("Special Car," CE, January 25, 1924); **158.** forget the disgrace." (Chenoweth, "Prison Term Convinced," LCJ, March 14, 1926); **159.** opened or authorized. (Remus Testimony, Yale, Vol. 6, 459); **159.** while he was in prison. (Remus Testimony, Yale, Vol. 6, 459); **159.** directly to the prison. ("'Millionaire Legger,'" PDP, January 26, 1924); **160.** it during her husband's incarceration. ("'Millionaire Legger,'" PDP, January 26, 1924); **160.** finally overtook him. ("Silk Shirt," CE, January 26, 1924); **160.** intolerable," George explained. (Chenoweth, "Prison Term Convinced," LCJ, March 14, 1926); **161.** instructions," Remus explained. (Remus Testimony,

Yale, Vol. 6, 511); **161.** called "Cincinnati." ("Remus Was," SPD, January 8, 1928); **162.** "little bundle of sweetness." ("Testifies Remus," SPD, December 1, 1927); **162.** not obtain inside. ("Testifies Remus," SPD, December 1, 1927); **162.** and abused her." ("Testifies Remus," SPD, December 1, 1927); **163.** under the previous warden. ("Snook Would," BS, January 22, 1925); **163.** would land others in jail." ("Hager and Willebrandt," AC, February 1, 1930); **163.** "conferences" with Imogene. ("Hager, Willebrandt," AC, February 1, 1930); **163.** take away privileges. ("Hager and Willebrandt," AC, February 1, 1930); **164.** make the threat. ("Makes Broad Denial," AC, February 18, 1925); **164.** Mannie Kessler, and Remus. ("Makes Broad Denial," AC, February 18, 1925); **165.** before the Supreme Court. (Coffey, The Long Thirst, 158); **165.** the illegal liquor depot. (Thomas M. Coffey, The Long Thirst: Prohibition in America: 1920–1933 New York: Norton, 1975, 158); **166.** trembling earnestness." ("Rum's Gold," NYDN, May 17, 1924); **167.** informal manner requested." (Coffey, The Long Thirst, 158); **167.** certain of these parties." (Letter to President Coolidge, from J. A. Reed, Senator Missouri, January 15, 1924, SHD, Vol. III, 3333); **167.** during the Senate hearings. ("Senator Reed," SST, June 17, 1924); **167.** crooks or useless." ("Senator Reed," SST, June 17, 1924); **167.** faces of the senators." ("Senator Reed," SST, June 17, 1924); **168.** upcoming presidential campaign. (Remus Testimony, Yale, Vol. 6, 675); **168.** might be freed early. (Remus Testimony, Yale, Vol. 6, 675); **168.** satisfactorily arranged." (Remus Testimony, Yale, Vol. 6, 677); **168.** document to the media. (Remus Testimony, Yale, Vol. 6, 676); **168.** repudiated his testimony." ("Means Repudiates," BG, September 22, 1924); **168.** to destroy the nation. ("Means Repudiates," BG, September 22, 1924); **169.** corrupt "Daugherty gang." ("Wheeler Says," ST, August 29, 1924); **169.** Washington, and New York." ("Wheeler Says," ST, August 29, 1924); **169.** the bourbon empire. (Remus Testimony, Yale, Vol. 6, 680); **169.** out to Willebrandt. (Remus Testimony, Yale, Vol. 6, 680); **169.** my presence," he explained. (Remus Testimony, Yale, Vol. 6, 681); **169.** "everything that money will buy." (Remus Testimony, Yale, Vol. 6, 472); **170.** institution no more." (Remus Testimony, Yale, Vol. 6, 472); **170.** despite what George intoned. (Remus Testimony, Yale, Vol. 6, 505); **171.** not follow us." (Anderson, "Remus, Released from Atlanta," SPD, January 12, 1926); **171.** plotting my destruction." (Segal, "'Speech Written in Fire,'" CP, November 21, 1927)

Chapter 11: Freedom

172. I love you," Imogene cooed. (Snook Deposition, Yale, Vol. 5, 1959); **172.** handle his business." (Snook Deposition, Yale, Vol. 5, 1959); **173.** threatened to strike me." (Snook Deposition, Yale, Vol. 5, 1960); **173.** I have no reason to." (Snook Deposition, Yale, Vol. 5, 1960); **173.** "little honey bunch." (Snook Deposition, Yale, Vol. 5, 1960); **173.** surprised man," Snook remembered. (Snook Deposition, Yale, Vol. 5, 1963); **174.** I turned over to her." (Chenoweth, "Prison Term Convinced," LCJ, March 14, 1926); **174.** already begun. (Remus Testimony, Yale, Vol. 1, 82); **175.** woman in his room." (Remus Testimony, Yale, Vol. 1, 82); **175.** love for Dodge." (Remus Testimony, Yale, Vol. 1, 82); **175.** Can you beat that?" (Remus Testimony, Yale, Vol. 1, 82); **175.** send you there." ("Remus Plans," October 10, 1927); **175.** "This scum, Dodge!" (Anderson, "Remus, Released from Atlanta," SPD, January 12, 1926); **175.** listening to any rumors." (Snook Deposition, Yale, Vol. 5, 1975–1976); **175.** themselves," he kept repeating. (Anderson, "Remus, Released from Atlanta," SPD, January 12, 1926); **175.** funds in my enterprises." (Anderson, "Remus, Released from Atlanta," SPD, January 12, 1926); **176.** George cried out in agony. (Anderson, "Remus, Released from Atlanta," SPD, January 12, 1926); **176.** bars," he told a reporter. (Anderson, "Remus, Released from Atlanta,"

SPD, January 12, 1926); **176.** was going on." (Remus Testimony, Yale, Vol. 1, 30); **176.** I am always in her thoughts." (Alfred Segal, "Remus Finds Peace," CP, October 8, 1927); **176.** went about the country." (Alfred Segal, "Remus Finds Peace," CP, October 8, 1927); **176.** efficient officer," Remus claimed. (Remus Testimony, Yale, Vol. 6, 552); **177.** strike this plaintiff." ("Remus's Wife," CE, September 1, 1925); **177.** severe bodily harm." ("Remus Trial as Wife Killer," CE, January 22, 1952); **178.** there is in the world." ("Remus Declares," CE, September 3, 1925); **178.** spiritual anguish." ("Remus Declares," CE, September 3, 1925); **178.** of the federal government. ("Remus Declares," CE, September 3, 1925); **179.** give a reasonable bond." (Remus Testimony, Yale, Vol. 6, 683); **179.** authorities on George's back. (Remus Testimony, Yale, Vol. 6, 683); **180.** that kind of nonsense." (Remus Testimony, Yale, Vol. 6, 706); **180.** gains that I had made." (Remus Testimony, Yale, Vol. 6, 706); **180.** than another lawyer." ("Confession by Remus," SPD, September 14, 1925); **180.** 'Doesn't it strike you that way?'" ("Confession by Remus," SPD, September 14, 1925); **181.** break a window to get in." (Remus Testimony, Yale, Vol. 6, 707); **181.** that happening," Remus recalled. (Remus Testimony, Yale, Vol. 6, 707); **181.** and took them away." ("Slayer Says," CP, October 6, 1927); **181.** follow her to China." (Remus Testimony, Yale, Vol. 1, 144); **181.** "entertain the idea" of killing her. (Remus Testimony, Yale, Vol. 1, 144); **181.** Jack Daniel's whiskey heist. ("Wife Was," HH, October 6, 1927); **182.** with the jewelry," George said. (Remus Testimony, Yale, Vol. 6, 731); **182.** account for its value. (Remus Testimony, Yale, Vol. 6, 732); **183.** broken-hearted and disgusted." (Remus Testimony, Yale, Vol. 6, 446); **184.** killed at any moment." (Remus Testimony, Yale, Vol. 6, 707); **184.** Conners told his boss. (Remus Testimony, Yale, Vol. 6, 729); **186.** his ever-evolving myth. ("Remus Pleads," CP, October 7, 1927); **187.** two were gunmen." (Charles Rentrop, Jr., "Plot of Imogene and Dodge," CP, October 24, 1927); **187.** "no baggage" with them. (Charles Rentrop, Jr., "Plot of Imogene and Dodge," CP, October 24, 1927); **187.** to carry out the gruesome task. (Charles Rentrop, Jr., "Plot of Imogene and Dodge," CP, October 24, 1927); **187.** after she entered her plea. ("Three Plead Guilty," SPD, December 14, 1925); **187.** weapons before she return. ("Three Plead Guilty," SPD, December 14, 1925); **188.** "threatening" his client. ("Three Plead Guilty," SPD, December 14, 1925); **188.** $8,000 to kill me." (Alfred Segal, "Remus Finds Peace," CP, October 8, 1927); **188.** satisfaction of doing that." (Alfred Segal, "Remus Finds Peace," CP, October 8, 1927); **188.** a dual capacity," George explained. (Remus Testimony, Yale, Vol. 6, 705); **188.** serious proposition." (Remus Testimony, Yale, Vol. 6, 705); **188.** keep him in the room." (White, "Remus Assumes," CP, December 1, 1927); **188.** Dodge," the journalist explained. (White, "Remus Assumes," CP, December 1, 1927); **188.** not letting him get Dodge." (White, "Remus Assumes," CP, December 1, 1927); **189.** to assassinate Remus." ("Deposition in Remus' Defense," SPD, October 29, 1927)

Chapter 12: Heavy Lover

191. the night manager remembered. (Samuel Carlos Clapper Testimony, Yale, Vol. 7, Part 4, 229–244); **192.** shiny limousine. ("Reveal Hidden Life Chapters of Mrs. Remus," CT, Oct. 28, 1927); **192.** it was Imogene Remus. (Samuel Carlos Clapper Testimony, Yale, Vol. 7, Part 4, 229–244); **193.** as she was concerned." (Remus Testimony, Yale, Vol. 6, 705); **193.** Remus would recall. (Remus Testimony, Yale, Vol. 6, 705); **193.** country with Dodge." (Remus Testimony, Yale, Vol. 6, 619); **194.** assistance to Imogene. (Frederick H. Brennan, "'The Boys' Rally," SPD, December 1, 1927); **194.** wasted away in prison. (Paul W. White, "Recall Servant," MEP, November 30, 1927); **194.** safe haven there. (Shead, "Smudge Put On," IN, December 14, 1927); **194.** Imogene snapped. ("Wife of Remus," SPJ, November 29, 1927); **194.** little bundle." ("Wife of Remus," SPJ, November 29, 1927); **194.** between them. ("Testifies Remus," SPD, December 1, 1927); **195.** loved Mr. Dodge." ("Testifies Remus," SPD, December 1, 1927); **195.** Remus," Berger confessed. ("Testifies Remus," SPD, December 1, 1927); **195.** Dodge," Berger remembered. ("Testifies Remus," SPD, December 1, 1927); **195.** almost nude attire." ("Testifies Remus," SPD, December 1, 1927); **196.** door and get them." ("Testifies Remus," SPD, December 1, 1927); **198.** avert prying eyes. (Rentrop, Jr. "Mrs. Holmes with Dodge," CP, October 26, 1927; "Find Mrs. Remus and Dodge," CT, October 26, 1927); **198.** decorate the resort. (Remus Testimony, Yale, Vol. 6, 741); **198.** in that department. (Shead, "Smudge Put On," IN, December 14, 1927); **199.** daughter," the chief lieutenant offered. (Remus Testimony, Yale, Vol. 1, 98); **199.** was stripped." (Remus Testimony, Yale, Vol. 1, 98); **199.** on January 24, 1924. (Remus Testimony, Yale, Vol. 1, 75) at the Hollenden Hotel. ("Hinkel" is frequently misspelled "Hinkle" and "Henkel" in various accounts of Hinkel's activities; Remus Testimony, Yale, Vol. 6, 523; Remus Testimony, Yale, Vol. 6, 526); **199.** establishing Dodge's role. ("Misconduct," AC, October 8, 1925); **199.** belonging to him." ("Misconduct," AC, October 8, 1925); **199.** live off his fortune." ("Dodge, Who Caused Remus' Arrest," CT, November 29, 1930); **200.** was sequestered. (Remus Testimony, Yale, Vol. 6, 753); **200.** anger welling up inside. (Remus Testimony, Yale, Vol. 6, 753); **200.** worth about $600,000. ("Remus Starts Battle," DH, March 30, 1926); **200.** Wallenstein in New York. ("Remus Starts Battle," DH, March 30, 1926); **201.** I know it." (Remus Testimony, Yale, Vol. 6, 554); **201.** stay locked up. (Remus Testimony, Yale, Vol. 6, 431); **201.** government representative," Remus explained. ("Mind is Sound," CP, February 24, 1928); **201.** allowed to go free. ("Mind is Sound," CP, February 24, 1928)

Chapter 13: Plundering the Bourbon Empire

203. months and months." (Remus Testimony, Yale, Vol. 1, 85); **203.** to urge that stuff on." (Remus Testimony, Yale, Vol. 1, 86); **203.** treated me there." (Remus Testimony, Yale, Vol. 1, 87); **204.** "lying testimony." (Remus Testimony, Yale, Vol. 6, 548); **204.** than most judges." (Remus Testimony, Yale, Vol. 6, 548); **204.** catch you asleep." (Remus Testimony, Yale, Vol. 6, 548); **204.** three gunmen with him." (Remus Testimony, Yale, Vol. 1, 93); **204.** behind the bars." (Remus Testimony, Yale, Vol. 1, 93); **205.** to move or speak. (Remus Testimony, Yale, Vol. 1, 93); **205.** the adulterous practices." (Remus Testimony, Yale, Vol. 6, 714); **205.** that I had." (Remus Testimony, Yale, Vol. 6, 714); **205.** conversation rambles." (Charles K. Swafford, "Cincinnati Bootleg," PDP, April 24, 1927); **205.** affected his intellect." (Charles K. Swafford, "Cincinnati Bootleg," PDP, April 24, 1927); **206.** life than freedom." ("Freedom," CE, April 26, 1927); **206.** "What for?" ("Freedom," CE, April 26, 1927); **206.** down the phone. ("Bank Account," CE, October 28, 1927); **206.** never get one cent." ("Bank Account," CE, October 28, 1927); **207.** crazy," Imogene announced. ("Bank Account," CE, October 28, 1927); **207.** have him deported." ("Bank Account," CE, October 28, 1927); **207.** where I want him." ("Bank Account," CE, October 28, 1927); **207.** anything he might do." (Rentrop, Jr., "'I Love Dodge," CP, October 27, 1927); **207.** I love you, dear," Franklin said. (Rentrop, Jr., "'I Love Dodge," CP, October 27, 1927); **208.** confessed to her friends. ("Bank Account," CE, October 28, 1927); **208.** other special occasions. (Rentrop, Jr., "'I Love Dodge," CP, October 27, 1927); **208.** one day in April 1927. ("Reveal Hidden Life Chapters of Mrs. Remus," CT, Oct. 28, 1927); **208.** money," George sputtered. (Remus Testimony, Yale, February 27, 1928, Vol. 6, 714); **209.** confinement," George continued. (Remus Testimony, Yale, Vol. 1, 47); **209.** cuff buttons, etcetera." (Remus Testimony, Yale, Vol. 1, 47); **209.** utter destruction. (Segal, "Conners Asserts," CP, December 3, 1927); **209.** robbed," he exclaimed. (Paul W. White, "Remus Goes," CP, November 14, 1927); **209.** investigative reporter wrote. (Paul Y. Anderson, "Inside Story of the Amazing Career of George Remus," SPD, January 3, 1926); **209.** his forthright nature." (Paul Y. Anderson, "Inside Story of the Amazing Career of George Remus," SPD, January 3, 1926); **210.** or Dodge were mentioned." (Segal, "Remus, Fighting Chair," CP, November 28, 1927); **210.** exaggerated tone. (Segal, "Remus, Fighting Chair," CP, November 28, 1927); **210.** on that one subject." (Segal, "Remus, Fighting Chair," CP, November 28, 1927); **210.** took them away." ("Slayer Says," CP, October 6, 1927); **210.** my house," she barked. (Alfred Segal, "Conners Asserts," CP, December 3, 1927); **210.** want me here." (Alfred Segal, "Conners Asserts," CP, December 3, 1927); **211.** eyes bulged out." ("Testifies Remus," SPD, December 1, 1927); **211.** He was mad." (Qtd. in Rosenberg and Armstrong, 155); **211.** peeved," George recalled. (Remus Testimony, Yale, Vol. 6, 658); **211.** embarrassment," George admitted. (Remus Testimony, Yale, Vol. 6, 658); **212.** various buyers. ("Remus Brings," BS, April 2, 1926); **212.** behind my back." ("Remus Trial as Wife Killer," CE, January 22, 1952); **212.** every one so far." ("Remus Starts Battle," DH, March 30, 1926); **213.** Department of Justice ever had." ("Remus Starts Battle," DH, March 30, 1926); **213.** Dodge to surrender." ("Release," CE, May 12, 1927); **213.** of annoying her." ("Release," CE, May 12, 1927); **214.** with a handkerchief." ("Release," CE, May 12, 1927); **214.** you did not do," she exclaimed. ("Release," CE, May 12, 1927); **214.** competing hit contracts. (White, "Remus Assumes," CP, December 1, 1927); **214.** hurt Mr. Dodge." (White, "Remus Assumes," CP, December 1, 1927); **214.** him about Dodge. (Shead, "Smudge Put On," IN, December 14, 1927); **215.** perfect lady," he said. ("Remus Plotted," LSJ, October 7, 1927); **215.** not Imogene. ("Remus Plotted," LSJ, October 7, 1927); **215.** never been inappropriate. ("Remus Plotted," LSJ, October 7, 1927); **215.** little to show for it. ("Remus Plotted," LSJ, October 7, 1927); **215.** went to prison." ("Remus Plotted," LSJ, October 7, 1927); **215.** appear in person as well. (Remus Testimony, Yale, Vol. 1, 65); **216.** deteriorated his intellect. (Charles K. Swafford, "Cincinnati Bootleg," PDP, April 24, 1927); **216.** plot he knew about. (Remus Testimony, Yale, Vol. 6, 758); **216.** to knock me off." (Remus Testimony, Yale, Vol. 6, 758); **216.** "interchange courtesies." (Remus Testimony, Yale, Vol. 6, 759); **216.** in these conversations. (Remus Testimony, Yale, Vol. 6, 759); **216.** two barrels waiting for Remus. ("Deposition in Remus' Defense," SPD, October 29, 1927)

PART FOUR: A VERY DANGEROUS MAN

Chapter 14: A Shot Rings Out

220. think for a moment. (Remus Testimony, Yale, Vol. 6, 597); **220.** at any moment. (Remus Testimony, Yale, Vol. 1, 145; 148); **221.** joking as she left." (Remus Testimony, Yale, Vol. 1, 145; 148); **221.** screeching halt. (Remus Testimony, Yale, Vol. 1, 62); **222.** don't do it!" (Earl L. Shaub, "Remus Says," TT, October 10, 1927); **222.** blind with rage. (Earl L. Shaub, "Remus Says," TT, October 10, 1927); **222.** have the gun." (Earl L. Shaub, "Remus Says," TT, October 10, 1927); **222.** Remus answered flatly. ("Sobs Rack," CE, November 26, 1927); **222.** dazed condition." (Remus Testimony, Yale, Vol. 1, 69); **223.** know," Imogene moaned. ("Former Wife," CP, October 12, 1927; Alfred Segal, "Witnesses of Eden Park," CP, November 22, 1927; Martin Sommers, "Remus to Reveal," NYDN, November 28, 1927); **223.** for doing this?" ("Sobs Rack," CE, November 26, 1927); **223.** over me." ("Sobs Rack," CE, November 26,

1927); **224.** want to die!" (Martin Sommers, "Remus to Reveal," NYDN, November 28, 1927); **224.** of that sort." ("Parallel Seen," CP, October 11, 1927); **225.** say now?" they yelled. ("Slayer Says," CP, October 6, 1927); **225.** can I say?" George barked back. ("Slayer Says," CP, October 6, 1927); **225.** owes society." ("Slayer Says," CP, October 6, 1927); **225.** half years." (Ruth Neely, "Women 'Fates' in Life of Remus," CP, October 8, 1927); **225.** Remus business." (Ruth Neely, "Women 'Fates' in Life of Remus," CP, October 8, 1927); **225.** of outrage." (Ruth Neely, "Women 'Fates' in Life of Remus," CP, October 8, 1927); **225.** but sane. (F. H. Brennan, "Attempts to Identify," SPD, December 14, 1927); **225.** about five months. (F. H. Brennan, "Attempts to Identify," SPD, December 14, 1927); **226.** according to Swing. ("Remus Pleads," CP, October 7, 1927); **226.** defend himself!" ("Remus Pleads," CP, October 7, 1927); **226.** my fate," Remus declared. ("Remus Pleads," CP, October 7, 1927); **226.** wounded Mrs. Remus." ("Remus Pleads," CP, October 7, 1927); **227.** trying circumstances." ("Remus Plotted," LSJ, October 7, 1927); **227.** and his fortune. ("Slayer Says," CP, October 6, 1927); **227.** betrayal set in. ("Slayer Says," CP, October 6, 1927); **227.** what people say about me." ("Slayer Says," CP, October 6, 1927); **227.** in his voice. ("Slayer Says," CP, October 6, 1927); **227.** garage at home." ("Remus Pleads," LSJ, October 7, 1927); **227.** table, and chair." ("Remus Pleads," LSJ, October 7, 1927); **227.** owed society. ("Will Justice, NYDN, October 16, 1927); **228.** were now paying off. ("Remus Pleads," CP, October 7, 1927); **228.** sorry for him." ("Remus Pleads," CP, October 7, 1927); **228.** notoriety for her." ("Remus Pleads," CP, October 7, 1927); **228.** driven to it." ("Remus Pleads," CP, October 7, 1927); **228.** hurt a fly." ("Remus Pleads," CP, October 7, 1927); **228.** ex-wife told the papers. ("Remus Pleads," CP, October 7, 1927); **228.** home and office." ("Remus Pleads," CP, October 7, 1927); **228.** Imogene's older sister Grace. ("Remus Pleads," CP, October 7, 1927); **229.** battle for George's soul. (Alfred Segal, "Remus Finds Peace," CP, October 8, 1927); **229.** her adoptive father. ("Remus Plans," October 10, 1927); **229.** frequent fits of temper." ("Remus Plans," October 10, 1927); **229.** nose," she remembered. ("Remus Plans," October 10, 1927); **229.** without number." ("Remus Plans," October 10, 1927); **229.** as myself." ("Remus Plans," October 10, 1927); **230.** go to dust." ("Judge to Hear," CP, October 27, 1927); **230.** mock earnestness. ("First Wife," CP, October 12, 1927); **230.** his liberty." ("First Wife," CP, October 12, 1927); **230.** *Cincinnati Post*'s Alfred Segal. (Alfred Segal, "Remus Finds Peace," CP, October 8, 1927); **230.** in my place?" (Alfred Segal, "Remus Finds Peace," CP, October 8, 1927); **231.** been performed." (Remus Testimony, Yale, Vol. 1, 84); **231.** firing of that gun." (Remus Testimony, Yale, Vol. 6, 452–453); **231.** conniving lover? (Remus Testimony, Yale, Vol. 6, 455); **231.** was "charming." (Frederick H. Brennan, "'The Boys' Rally," SPD, December 1, 1927); **232.** "I am grateful." ("Remus Plans," October 10, 1927); **232.** seems to be planning." ("Find Mrs. Remus and Dodge," CT, October 26, 1927); **232.** to the court. ("Remus Stakes," NYT, December 19, 1927); **232.** stake," the newsman said. ("Remus Stakes," NYT, December 19, 1927); **232.** and coffee." (Martin Sommers, "Remus Discloses," AC, November 24, 1927); **232.** and his assistants." ("Remus' Driver," CP, November 9, 1927)

Chapter 15: Ready for the Battle—It's a Fight!

234. It's a fight!" (Segal, "Remus Goes on Trial," CP, November 14, 1927); **235.** for general reports. ("Remus Hides His Emotions," LSJ, November 14, 1927); **236.** gaining traction. ("Remus Hides His Emotions," LSJ, November 14, 1927); **236.** as "a five-room suite." (Frederick H. Brennan, "'The Boys' Rally," SPD, December 1, 1927); **236.** stash for visitors. (James L. Killgallen, "Bootlegger King," CDS, November 20, 1954); **236.** 2:30 in the morning."

(Remus Testimony, Yale, Vol. 6, 613); **237.** did his duty. (Frederick H. Brennan, "'The Boys' Rally," SPD, December 1, 1927); **237.** into a rage." ("Testifies Remus," SPD, December 1, 1927); **238.** his honor." ("Testifies Remus," SPD, December 1, 1927); **238.** and see stars." (Remus Testimony, Yale, Vol. 1, 85); **238.** Kiely concluded. ("Alienists' Report on Remus' Sanity," CP, November 26, 1927); **238.** national correspondent. (Paul W. White, "Remus Angered," CP, November 15, 1927); **238.** making wrong right." (Alfred Segal, "Remus Pose," CP, November 15, 1927); **239.** have him murdered." ("Testifies Remus," SPD, December 1, 1927); **239.** covering the trial. (Frederick H. Brennan, "'The Boys' Rally," SPD, December 1, 1927); **239.** packed courtroom. ("Remus Near Blows," NYT, November 19, 1927); **239.** troops for the war. (White, "Remus Says," CP, November 19, 1927); **239.** for an assault." (White, "Remus Says," CP, November 19, 1927); **240.** fit," reporters noted. (White, "Remus Says," CP, November 19, 1927); **240.** civic-minded leader. ("Remus Near Blows," NYT, November 19, 1927); **240.** myself," he threatened. ("Remus Near Blows," NYT, November 19, 1927); **240.** punch" him. ("Remus Near Blows," NYT, November 19, 1927); **240.** insinuate such a thing." ("Testifies Remus," SPD, December 1, 1927); **240.** a "hypocrite." ("Testifies Remus," SPD, December 1, 1927); **240.** Judge Shook to intervene. ("Testifies Remus," SPD, December 1, 1927); **241.** Justice," he bellowed. (Shead, "Remus Venom," *Indianapolis News*, December 13, 1927); **242.** several times. ("Find Mrs. Remus and Dodge," CT, October 26, 1927); **242.** about it," Frank responded. (Rentrop, Jr. "'Mrs. Holmes with Dodge," CP, October 26, 1927; Testimony Excerpts, LSJ, October 26, 1927, 11.); **243.** established definitely." (Rentrop, Jr., "'Testimony to Free," CP, October 28, 1927); **243.** would "free Remus." (Rentrop, Jr., "'Testimony to Free," CP, October 28, 1927); **243.** story" in cross-examination. (Rentrop, Jr., "'Testimony to Free," CP, October 28, 1927); **243.** Taft and his team. (Rentrop, Jr., "'Testimony to Free," CP, October 28, 1927); **243.** killing his wife." (Rentrop, Jr., "'Testimony to Free," CP, October 28, 1927); **243.** being investigated." (Rentrop, Jr., "'Testimony to Free," CP, October 28, 1927); **243.** and insinuation." (Rentrop, Jr., "'Testimony to Free," CP, October 28, 1927); **243.** over the phone. (Rentrop, Jr., "'Lies!'" CP, October 29, 1927); **244.** Remus developments." ("Remus Party," CP, October 31, 1927); **244.** framed against me." ("Remus Party," CP, October 31, 1927)

Chapter 16: Cutthroats and Assassins

245. when he took the stand. ("Remus Is," CE, December 29, 1927); **246.** George's murder trial. ("Remus Is," CE, December 29, 1927); **246.** men" watched over him. (Remus Testimony, Yale, Vol. 6, 748); **246.** seven months." ("Remus Is," CE, December 29, 1927); **248.** Conners told a reporter. ("Remus Feared," CP, October 6, 1927); **248.** program," the reporter noted. ("Remus Feared," CP, October 6, 1927); **248.** about that killing." ("Mind is Sound," CP, February 24, 1928); **249.** provoked," Remus stormed. (Remus Testimony, Yale, Vol. 6, 683); **249.** those people." (Remus Testimony, Yale, Vol. 6, 686); **249.** "reasonably certain death." (Remus Testimony, Yale, Vol. 6, 724); **249.** I would return." (Remus Testimony, Yale, Vol. 6, 557); **249.** conniving woman." (Remus Testimony, Yale, Vol. 6, 686); **249.** mutilate you." (Julia Brown Testimony, Tale, Vol. 7, 2791–2792); **249.** not kill me." (Remus Testimony, Yale, Vol. 6, 749); **250.** likely to get us." (Remus Testimony, Yale, Vol. 6, 688); **250.** call," George said. (Remus Testimony, Yale, Vol. 6, 689); **250.** too severe." (Remus Testimony, Yale, Vol. 6, 689); **250.** I befriended." (Remus Testimony, Yale, Vol. 6, 704); **250.** murdered Imogene. (Charles Rentrop, Jr. "State to Call Dodge," CP, October 22, 1927); **251.** affidavits of individuals." (Charles Rentrop, Jr. "State to Call Dodge," CP, October 22, 1927); **251.** with

Mrs. Remus." (Alfred Segal, "Remus Finds Peace," CP, October 8, 1927); **251.** for filing the lawsuit. (Alfred Segal, "Remus Finds Peace," CP, October 8, 1927); **251.** only "on business." (Alfred Segal, "Remus Finds Peace," CP, October 8, 1927). **251.** woman," he said. (Alfred Segal, "Remus Finds Peace," CP, October 8, 1927; **251.** "a perfect lady." (Alfred Segal, "Remus Finds Peace," CP, October 8, 1927); **252.** for my life." ("Tried to His Death," CT, October 8, 1927); **252.** safe for me." ("Remus Plotted," LSJ, October 7, 1927); **252.** "a well-known gun-man." ("Remus Plotted," LSJ, October 7, 1927); **252.** $8,000, saved it." ("Remus Plotted," LSJ, October 7, 1927); **252.** her husband." ("Remus Plotted," LSJ, October 7, 1927); **253.** a perfect lady." ("Remus Plotted," LSJ, October 7, 1927); **253.** from his path." ("Remus Plotted," LSJ, October 7, 1927); **253.** merit denial." ("Remus Plotted," LSJ, October 7, 1927); **253.** official business." ("Remus Plotted," LSJ, October 7, 1927); **253.** to prison. ("Remus Plotted," LSJ, October 7, 1927); **253.** not to know. ("Remus Plotted," LSJ, October 7, 1927); **254.** assassinate Remus." ("Deposition in Remus' Defense," SPD, October 29, 1927); **254.** threaten Remus. (Rentrop, Jr., "'Lies!'" CP, October 29, 1927); **254.** to kill me." (Remus Testimony, Yale, Vol. 6, 700); **254.** shot at Remus. (Remus Testimony, Yale, Vol. 6, 700); **254.** do the job. (Frederick H. Brennan, "'The Boys' Rally," SPD, December 1, 1927); **255.** during the murder trial. (Walter A. Shead, "Remus Ends," IN, December 9, 1927); **255.** requesting protection. (Walter A. Shead, "Remus Receives Rebuffs," IN, December 12, 1927); **255.** knock me over." (Remus Testimony, Yale, Vol. 6, 616); **255.** take my life." (Remus Testimony, Yale, Vol. 1, 60); **256.** leave the city." (Remus Testimony, Yale, Vol. 6, 775–776); **256.** gave him the gun. (Remus Testimony, Yale, Vol. 6, 701); **256.** level of protection. (Remus Testimony, Yale, Vol. 6, 701); **257.** dirty rat Dodge." (Martin Sommers, "Remus Discloses," AC, November 24, 1927); **257.** thousand bucks." (Martin Sommers, "Remus Discloses," AC, November 24, 1927); **258.** to-ward him. ("Hysteria Halts," CE, December 8, 1927); **258.** in the Hotel Sinton." ("Hysteria Halts," CE, December 8, 1927); **259.** was sobbing." ("Hysteria Halts," CE, December 8, 1927); **259.** out of the courtroom. ("Hysteria Halts," CE, December 8, 1927); **259.** will it never end?" ("Hysteria Halts," CE, December 8, 1927); **260.** half-hour," a reporter recalled. ("Hysteria Halts," CE, December 8, 1927); **260.** dramatic," one reporter noted. ("Hysteria Halts," CE, December 8, 1927); **260.** much money." ("Hysteria Halts," CE, December 8, 1927); **260.** work out the details. ("Hysteria Halts," CE, December 8, 1927); **260.** kill Mr. Remus." ("Hysteria Halts," CE, December 8, 1927); **261.** pay for expenses. ("Hysteria Halts," CE, December 8, 1927); **261.** kill him myself." ("Darrow Takes," WEJ, December 8, 1927); **261.** double-cross him." (Remus Testimony, Yale, Vol. 1, 52); **261.** and the sluggers." (Remus Testimony, Yale, Vol. 6, 614); **261.** Pennsylvania license plate. (Remus Testimony, Yale, Vol. 1, 51); **262.** al-leged assassin's testimony. ("Darrow Takes," WEJ, December 8, 1927)

Chapter 17: Let's Give Him a Nice Christmas

264. through the newspapers." (qtd. in Rosenberg and Armstrong, 110); **264.** of another man." (qtd. in Rosenberg and Armstrong, 110); **264.** with his prosecutors." (Segal, "Remus Fails," CP, November 16, 1927); **264.** making similar outbursts. (Segal, "Remus Attempts," November 30, 1927); **265.** giggled with him." (Shead, "Fare Tone Given," IN, December 16, 1927); **265.** own china shop." (Shead, "Remus Juror Bias," IN, December 15, 1927); **265.** hurrying the attorneys." (Shead, "Remus Juror Bias," IN, December 15, 1927); **265.** crazy," a woman nearby breathed. (Segal, "George Remus Gives," CP, November 30, 1927); **265.** every gasp and whisper. (Segal, "George Remus Gives," CP, November 30, 1927); **265.** en-thralled by the spectacle. (Segal, "George Remus Gives," CP, November 30, 1927); **265.** into the free world. (Frederick H. Brennan, "Remus' Board of Strategy," SPD, December 2, 1927); **266.** business transactions afloat. (Remus Testimony, Yale, Vol. 1, 96); **266.** tapped for this racket." (White, "Remus Says," CP, November 19, 1927; **267.** a different path. (Allene Sumner, "Mother Cooks in Mansion," CP, November 17, 1927); **268.** helpless in prison. (Alfred Segal, "Remus Finds Peace," CP, October 8, 1927; ("Remus Plans," CP, October 10, 1927); **268.** want disclosed." ("Taft Demands," MNJ, December 18, 1927); **268.** when he is dead!" ("Taft Demands," MNJ, December 18, 1927); **269.** stoical attitude." ("Sobs Rack," CE, November 26, 1927); **269.** in Remus's face." ("Sobs Rack," CE, November 26, 1927); **270.** before the murder." (Segal, "Remus, Fighting Chair," CP, November 28, 1927); **270.** to "justify this murder." (Segal, "Remus, Fighting Chair," CP, November 28, 1927); **270.** giggling to themselves." (Shead, "Remus Juror Bias," IN, December 15, 1927); **270.** and felt. (Shead, "Remus Juror Bias," IN, December 15, 1927); **271.** "atrocious killing," he said. ("Decision," CE, December 19, 1927); **271.** dare not produce it." (Shead, "Evidence Ended," IN, December 17, 1927); **271.** hang in the air. (Shead, "Evidence Ended," IN, December 17, 1927); **271.** on the stand?" (Shead, "Evidence Ended," IN, December 17, 1927); **272.** done to any man." (Shead, "Courtroom Tense," IN, December 19, 1927); **272.** assume he was guilty." (Shead, "Courtroom Tense," IN, December 19, 1927); **272.** it go unchallenged." (Shead, "Courtroom Tense," IN, December 19, 1927); **272.** "filthy louse." (Shead, "Courtroom Tense," IN, December 19, 1927); **272.** Remus, the defendant." (Shead, "Courtroom Tense," IN, December 19, 1927); **273.** in my breast." (Shead, "Courtroom Tense," IN, December 19, 1927); **273.** the empty chair." (Shead, "Courtroom Tense," IN, December 19, 1927); **273.** "leper among men." (Kenneth Doris, "Grand Gesture," CE, December 20, 1927); **273.** almost double." (Kenneth Doris, "Grand Gesture," CE, December 20, 1927); **274.** Merry Christmas to you." (Kenneth Doris, "Grand Gesture," CE, December 20, 1927); **274.** and "snitch." (Kenneth Doris, "Grand Gesture," CE, December 20, 1927); **274.** off the table. ("Insanity is His," DDN, December 20, 1927; **274.** no right to kill her. ("Insanity is His," DDN, December 20, 1927); **275.** Anonymous Juror, December 20, 1927 (Martin Sommers, "Remus 'Not Guilty – Crazy,'" NYDN, December 21, 1927); **275.** the gathered newsmen. (Shead, "Remus Must Stay," IN, December 21, 1927); **275.** the group's decision. (Shead, "Remus Must Stay," IN, December 21, 1927); **275.** jails," explained one juror. (Martin Sommers, "Remus 'Not Guilty – Crazy,'" NYDN, December 21, 1927); **276.** I'm so happy!" (Martin Sommers, "Remus 'Not Guilty – Crazy,'" NYDN, December 21, 1927); **276.** start," Hosford beamed. (Martin Sommers, "Remus 'Not Guilty – Crazy,'" NYDN, December 21, 1927); **276.** have one this year." (Martin Sommers, "Remus 'Not Guilty – Crazy,'" NYDN, December 21, 1927); **277.** the proof of guilt conclusive." ("The Remus Verdict," IN, December 21, 1927); **277.** the ultimate present. (James L. Killgallen, "Bootlegger King," CDS, November 20, 1954); **277.** long time, if ever." ("A 'Christmas' Verdict," Virginia Law Register New Series, Vol. 13, 9 (January 1928), 566.); **277.** such artistry." ("A 'Christmas' Verdict," Virginia Law Register New Series, Vol. 13, 9 (January 1928), 566.); **277.** in jury trials." ("A 'Christmas' Verdict," Virginia Law Register New Series, Vol. 13, 9 (January 1928), 566.); **277.** drama," claimed one reporter. (James L. Killgallen, "Bootlegger King," CDS, November 20, 1954); **277.** for the gangster." (Martin Sommers, "Remus 'Not Guilty – Crazy,'" NYDN, December 21, 1927); **277.** from its earliest days. (James L. Killgallen, "Bootlegger King," CDS, November 20, 1954); **277.** as he sees fit." ("Remus Hopes," St. Louis Star, April 4, 1928); **278.** strongly be condemned. ("Justice and the 'Mad' Murderers," NYDN, May 4, 1941); **278.** Remus's sanity for Lueders. (Remus Testimony, Yale, Vol. 1, 37); **278.** for the gander." (Remus Testimony, Yale, Vol. 1, 22); **278.** it is tremendous." (Remus Testimony, Yale, Vol. 1, 22); **279.** as a result of it." (Remus Testimony, Yale, Vol. 1, 22); **279.** "a wonderful daughter." (Remus Testimony, Yale, Vol. 1, 82); **279.** "Absolutely not!" (Remus Testimony, Yale,

Vol. 1, 82); **279.** to elicit reaction. ("Remus Doomed," OI, December 30, 1927); **279.** pathological degree," they concluded. ("Remus Doomed," OI, December 30, 1927); **280.** the alienists' report noted. ("Remus Doomed," OI, December 30, 1927); **280.** It is so humorous." ("Remus Insane," SPD, December 30, 1927); **280.** "The law rests with me." ("Remus Insane," SPD, December 30, 1927); **280.** "dumping ground of humanity." ("Mind is Sound," CP, February 24, 1928); **280.** him," said one newspaperman. ("Remus' Battle," CP, March 30, 1928); **280.** the crime himself. (Remus Testimony, Yale, Vol. 6, 604); **281.** of punishment." ("Remus is Freed," CP, June 20, 1928); **281.** to reporters after the announcement. ("Remus Goes Free," NYT, June 21, 1928); **281.** for the trip south. ("Remus Goes Free," NYT, June 21, 1928); **282.** been exercising." ("Remus Greeted," CP, June 21, 1928); **282.** was very light." ("Remus," CP, June 21, 1928); **282.** "obscure himself." ("Remus," CP, June 21, 1928); **282.** seemed satisfied." ("Remus," CP, June 21, 1928)

PART FIVE: LOST MILLIONS

Chapter 18: Rise of the Gangster

285. and studying Remus. (Remus Testimony, Yale, Vol. 1, 43); **285.** the slightest." (Remus Testimony, Yale, Vol. 1, 43); **286.** for Remus's riches. (Remus Testimony, Yale, Vol. 1, 43); **286.** or good enough. (Remus Testimony, Yale, Vol. 1, 44); **286.** sentence reduced." (Remus Testimony, Yale, Vol. 1, 124); **286.** is my business." (Remus Testimony, Yale, Vol. 1, 39); **286.** as prosecutor. (Remus Testimony, Yale, Vol. 1, 184); **286.** psychotic individual." (Remus Testimony, Yale, Vol. 1, 184); **287.** and crackdowns." (Thomas Repetto, American Mafia: A History of Its Rise to Power (New York: Henry Holt, 2004), 69.); **289.** country," one reporter speculated. ("Marcus, Slain," HDN, February 4, 1931); **289.** scene noted. ("Marcus, Slain," HDN, February 4, 1931; "Cincinnati Racketeer," HDN, February 4, 1931); **289.** criminal life." ("Jew John," CE, April 12, 1931; "Marcus, Slain," HDN, February 4, 1931; "Cincinnati Racketeer," HDN, February 4, 1931); **290.** a hail of bullets. ("Marcus, Slain," HDN, February 4, 1931); **290.** chief competitor. ("Marcus, Slain," HDN, February 4, 1931; "Marcus and Margie," HDN, February 4, 1931); **290.** to Jew John's assassination. (Jim Blount, Little Chicago, Volume 2, the Deadly Years, 1928-1942. Hamilton (OH): Quality Publishing, 1997, 42-43); **291.** kill Jew John Marcus. ("Coates' Gun," HEJ, April 11, 1931; "Jew John," CE, April 12, 1931); **291.** into Coates's mouth. (Jim Blount, Little Chicago, Volume 2, the Deadly Years, 1928-1942. Hamilton (OH): Quality Publishing, 1997, 47; "Jew John's," HDN, February 4, 1931; "Marcus, Slain," HDN, February 4, 1931; "Coates Dies, HEJ, July 29, 1931); **291.** identify the person." (Jim Blount, Little Chicago, Volume 2, the Deadly Years, 1928–1942. Hamilton (OH): Quality Publishing, 1997, 47); **292.** was not a citizen." ("U. S. Will Not," CP, October 3, 1928); **292.** *and ugliness?"* ("Cincinnatus," CP, November 29, 1927); **292.** moral study." ("Cincinnatus," CP, November 29, 1927); **293.** scene imaginable. ("Cincinnatus," CP, November 29, 1927); **293.** selling booze overseas. ("Testifies Remus," SPD, December 1, 1927); **293.** and Franklin together. (F. H. Brennan, "Attempts to Identify," SPD, December 14, 1927); **293.** and kill them." (F. H. Brennan, "Attempts to Identify," SPD, December 14, 1927); **294.** according to plan. (Remus Testimony, Yale, Vol. 1, 186); **294.** Remus?" a reporter asked. ("Former Wife," CP, October 12, 1927); **294.** I am not sure," George replied. ("Former Wife," CP, October 12, 1927); **294.** that his pistol jammed." ("Slayer Says," CP, October 6, 1927); **294.** not his gun jammed." ("Former Wife," CP, October 12, 1927); **294.** affairs," George explained. ("Remus Hopes," SST, April 4, 1928); **294.** of

the earth," Remus reflected. ("Remus Hopes," SST, April 4, 1928); **295.** me in the least."
("Remus Hopes," SST, April 4, 1928); **295.** their lives happy." ("Remus Hopes," SST, April 4,
1928); **295.** at Cincinnati." (Editorial, SPD, June 21, 1928); **295.** not unanimous." ("Press
Comment," WP, June 25, 1928); **295.** farce of justice." ("The Freeing," SST, June 21, 1928);
295. was when committed." ("The Freeing," SST, June 21, 1928); **295.** I can't approximate
it." (Remus Testimony, Yale, Vol. 6, 585); **296.** for just $285,000. (Remus Testimony, Yale,
Vol. 6, 637); **296.** and waiting to be sold. (Remus Testimony, Yale, Vol. 6, 637); **296.** February 1928 sanity hearings. (Remus Testimony, Yale, Vol. 6, 664); **296.** good naturedly as
well." (Remus Testimony, Yale, Vol. 6, 664); **297.** during the sanity hearing. (Remus Testimony, Yale, Vol. 6, 506); **297.** and opinion." (Remus Testimony, Yale, Vol. 6, 518; 519); **297.**
for medicinal purposes." (Remus Testimony, Yale, Vol. 6, 518; 519); **297.** live with that
choice. (Remus Testimony, Yale, Vol. 6, 519); **297.** lopsided fire sales. (Remus Testimony,
Yale, Vol. 6, 516); **298.** in medium circumstances." (Remus Testimony, Yale, Vol. 6, 527);
298. reclaim the property. (Remus Testimony, Yale, Vol. 6, 527); **298.** deceased no how."
(Remus Testimony, Yale, Vol. 6, 527; 530–531); **298.** confiscating those properties." (Remus
Testimony, Yale, Vol. 6, 587); **299.** those kind of inconsistencies." (Remus Testimony, Yale,
Vol. 6, 664); **299.** warehouse that cost him $15,000. (Remus Testimony, Yale, Vol. 6, 572);
299. the latter amount. (Remus Testimony, Yale, Vol. 6, 574); **299.** $78,000 per day during
that span. (Remus Testimony, Yale, Vol. 6, 586); **299.** reckless lives together. (Remus Testimony, Yale, Vol. 6, 509); **300.** Canada and recover it." (Remus Testimony, Yale, Vol. 6, 740);
300. went into hiding. (Remus Testimony, Yale, Vol. 6, 742); **301.** equated to more than
$40,000. (Blanche Watson to H. E. Pogue Distillery Company, Ludlow, Kentucky, July 7,
1921, Family Papers. Pogue Distillery. Maysville, Kentucky); **301.** cash in hand as possible."
(Remus Testimony, Yale, Vol. 6, 564); **301.** situation," George sighed. (Remus Testimony,
Yale, Vol. 6, 565); **302.** that we had millions." (Remus Testimony, Yale, Vol. 6, 665); **302.**
details much," he admitted. (Remus Testimony, Yale, Vol. 6, 665)

Chapter 19: Dodge's Demise

303. said about him by Remus. (Paul W. White, "Strain Tells On," CP, December 2, 1927);
304. his face," White reported. (Paul W. White, "Strain Tells On," CP, December 2, 1927);
304. concerning Remus." (Paul W. White, "Strain Tells On," CP, December 2, 1927); **304.** a
"cowardly act." (Paul W. White, "Strain Tells On," CP, December 2, 1927); **305.** starting all
over again." (Paul W. White, "Strain Tells On," CP, December 2, 1927); **305.** Remus was in
jail. ("Remus Plans," CP, October 10, 1927); **305.** assassinating my mother," the girl cried.
("Remus Plans," CP, October 10, 1927); **305.** I am fighting." ("Remus Seeking Court Order,"
CP, October 11, 1927); **306.** younger brother. ("Remus Seeking Court Order," CP, October
11, 1927); **306.** during the sanity hearings. (Remus Testimony, Yale, Vol. 1, 93); **306.** to
Remus if he were set free. (Remus Testimony, Yale, Vol. 1, 93); **306.** threatened my life."
(Remus Testimony, Yale, Vol. 1, 94); **307.** been associated with." (Remus Testimony, Yale,
Vol. 1, 204); **307.** they had adduced." (Remus Testimony, Yale, Vol. 6, 754); **307.** file," Elston
divulged. (Remus Testimony, Yale, Vol. 1, 207); **307.** the White Slave Act. (Remus Testi-
mony, Yale, Vol. 1, 208); **307.** Franklin Dodge." (Remus Testimony, Yale, Vol. 1, 208); **307.**
agent in Indianapolis." (Remus Testimony, Yale, Vol. 6, 625); **308.** the laughing stock."
(Remus Testimony, Yale, Vol. 6, 754); **308.** for the killing." (Wilcox Letter, Read into the
Record, Yale, Vol. 6, 761–762); **308.** them all to jail." (Wilcox Letter, Read into the Record,
Yale, Vol. 6, 761–762); **308.** "fifteen thousand dollars." (Wilcox Letter, Read into the Record,

Yale, Vol. 6, 762); **309.** caught in with Imogene. (Remus Testimony, Yale, Vol. 1, 37); **309.** its dire consequences. (Remus Testimony, Yale, Vol. 1, 37); **309.** residence in Ohio. (Remus Testimony, Yale, Vol. 1, 37); **309.** in Cincinnati, testified. (Remus Testimony, Yale, Vol. 1, 279); **310.** corroborated this notion. (Remus Testimony, Yale, Vol. 1, 284); **310.** behind bars. (Remus Testimony, Yale, Vol. 1, 285); **311.** Dodge $60,000," George revealed. ("Slayer Says," CP, October 6, 1927); **311.** he told Judge Lueders. (Remus Testimony, Yale, Vol. 1, 97); **311.** "a contaminated disease." (Remus Testimony, Yale, Vol. 1, 56); **312.** had been extended. ("Dodge to Take," *Daily Times* (New Philadelphia, OH), June 21, 1928); **312.** and two sisters. ("Frank L. Dodge," LSJ, December 24, 1929); **312.** back to bite him. ("Dodge, Who Caused Remus' Arrest," CT, November 29, 1930); **312.** case," reporters explained. ("Dodge, Ex-Dry," CT, January 4, 1931); **313.** and returned to Michigan. ("Dodge Gets 30 Months," NYT, October 27, 1931); **313.** powerful newspapers. ("Budget Chief," LSJ, August 1, 1933); **313.** aghast," the paper claimed. ("Appointment," LSJ, August 3, 1933); **313.** Dodge is an heir." ("Gov. Comstock Fires Chief of State's Budget," CT, August 1, 1933); **313.** expense items." ("Remus Foe," CE, December 31, 1933)

Chapter 20: Remus v. Prohibition

315. person on the planet. (Wolfstein Testimony, Yale, Vol. 1, 123); **315.** his private habit." (Eugene P. Trani and David L. Wilson, The Presidency of Warren G. Harding, Lawrence: UP of Kansas, 1977, 179); **316.** keep him away." (Eugene P. Trani and David L. Wilson, The Presidency of Warren G. Harding, Lawrence: UP of Kansas, 1977, 180); **316.** to enforce it." (Edward Behr, Prohibition: Thirteen Years that Changed America, New York: Arcade, 2011, 79); **317.** wasn't enough. (Ruth Neely, "Women 'Fates' in Life of Remus, CP, October 8, 1927); **317.** interests," George wondered aloud. (Remus Testimony, Yale, Vol. 1, 40–41); **317.** determine his sanity. (Remus Testimony, Yale, Vol. 1, 41); **317.** that I know." (Remus Testimony, Yale, Vol. 1, 41); **318.** but was it wrong? (Paul Y. Anderson, "Inside Story of the Amazing Career of George Remus," SPD, January 3, 1926); **318.** enforcing the law." (Paul Y. Anderson, "Huge Withdrawals," SPD, January 5, 1926); **318.** and "foolish." (Paul Y. Anderson, "Inside Story," SPD, January 3, 1926); **318.** law—all law." ("Confession by Remus," SPD, September 14, 1925); **318.** bad after all." (Tim O'Neil, "Crowd Cheers Politicians," SPD, January 6, 2013); **319.** and virtue." (Antonio Nicaso and Marcel Danesi, Made Men: Mafia Culture and the Power of Symbols, Rituals, and Myth. Lanham, MD: Rowman & Littlefield Publishers, 2013, 17); **319.** not a moral one." (Segal, "Speech Written in Fire,'" CP, November 21, 1927); **319.** damned stuff myself." (Segal, "Speech Written in Fire,'" CP, November 21, 1927); **320.** local distillery operators. (Remus Testimony, Yale, Vol. 1, 17); **320.** prosecutor Walter Sibbald. (Remus Testimony, Yale, Vol. 6, 577); **320.** without a hint of irony. (Remus Testimony, Yale, Vol. 6, 577); **320.** judges looked on. (Remus Testimony, Yale, Vol. 6, 577); **321.** unforgettable parties. ("Mr. Remus," CP, April 6, 1921); **321.** was never completed. ("New Subdivision," CP, October 21, 1949); **322.** great part, of the Depression." (Sidney B. Whipple, Noble Experiment: A Portrait of American under Prohibition. London: Mehuen, 1934); **323.** was stripped away." (Sidney B. Whipple, Noble Experiment: A Portrait of American under Prohibition. London: Mehuen, 1934); **323.** headache was beginning." (Sidney B. Whipple, Noble Experiment: A Portrait of American under Prohibition. London: Mehuen, 140); **323.** made a hero." ("Making a Comedy," SLS, November 26, 1927); **325.** of his top lieutenant. (Remus Testimony, Yale, Vol. 6, 712; 713); **325.** whatever was left." (Remus Testimony, Yale, Vol. 6, 712; 713); **326.** and Mary Elizabeth. ("Old Injury," CE, November 17,

1935); **326.** and her clippings." ("Romola Remus," LAT, February 21, 1987); **326.** not be disclosed." ("Romola Remus," LAT, February 21, 1987); **326.** Remus always yields." (Martin Sommers, "Remus Discloses," AC, November 24, 1927) **327.** low-alcohol substitute. ("'Innocent Beer,'" CP, December 4, 1930); **327.** Imogene's maiden name. ("United States," CE, August 4, 1931); **328.** U. S. Soap Company." ("Kennel Club," *Palm Beach Post*, February 14, 1933); **328.** never proved their position. ("Gehrums are," CE, March 13, 1935); **328.** to be feared." (Jim Blount, Little Chicago, Volume 2, the Deadly Years, 1928–1942. Hamilton (OH): Quality Publishing, 1997, 59); **329.** it claimed to heal. ("Cease and Desist Orders," Bureau of Investigation, Vol. 132: 2, 105, George Remus Collection, Price Hill Historical Society); **329.** into the public eye." (Remus Testimony, Yale, Vol. 1, 81); **329.** going to have me." (Remus Testimony, Yale, Vol. 1, 81); **329.** love triangle for weeks. (Remus Testimony, Yale, Vol. 1, 81); **330.** He is insane." (Remus Testimony, Yale, Vol. 6, 791, 792); **330.** last two years." ("Evidence Completed," *Sheboygan Press* (MI), December 17, 1927); **331.** his representatives? (Qtd. in T. Earl Sullenger, "Popular Attitudes toward the Administration of Criminal Justice," Journal of the American Institute of Criminal Law and Criminology, Vol. 20, 4 (February 1930): 517); **331.** human before him." (Sullenger, "Popular Attitudes toward the Administration of Criminal Justice," Journal of the American Institute of Criminal Law and Criminology, Vol. 20, 4 (February 1930): 517); **332.** purchase real estate. (Remus Testimony, Yale, Vol. 6, 649–655); **332.** liquor business." (Remus Testimony, Yale, Vol. 6, 653); **333.** men and women." (Willebrandt, "Inside of Prohibition," OT, August 26, 1929); **333.** her leadership. (Willebrandt, "Inside of Prohibition," OT, August 26, 1929); **333.** to misrule." ("Hager, Willebrandt," AC, February 1, 1930); **333.** a toe-dancer whirl." (Willebrandt, "Inside of Prohibition," OT, August 26, 1929)

Epilogue: Fall of the Bootleg Baron

336. "four or five million dollars." (Remus Testimony, Yale, Vol. 6, 450); **337.** and 1950s. (Michael R. Veach, Kentucky Bourbon Whiskey: An American Heritage, Lexington: University Press of Kentucky, 2013, 95–95); **339.** flamboyant Remus." (Thomas H. Pauly, "Gatsby as Gangster," Studies in American Fiction, 21 (1993): 229); **339.** in April 1924. (Fitzgerald to Perkins, April 16, 1924, reprinted in Matthew J. Bruccoli, F. Scott Fitzgerald's *The Great Gatsby*: A Literary Reference, New York, Carroll & Graf, 2000, 131); **339.** it's astonishing." (Perkins to Fitzgerald, reprinted in Matthew J. Bruccoli, F. Scott Fitzgerald's *The Great Gatsby*: A Literary Reference, New York, Carroll & Graf, 2000, 137); **339.** emotional life." (Horst Kruse, "The Real Jay Gatsby: Max von Gerlach, F. Scott Fitzgerald, and the Compositional History of The Great Gatsby," The F. Scott Fitzgerald Review 1 (2002): 75); **340.** ever," the paper noted. ("Bootlegger Enters," NYT, January 26, 1924); **341.** at the grand hotel. (Larry Johnson, The Seelbach Hilton: A Centennial Salute to Louisville's Grand Hotel, Louisville: Butler Books, 2018, 101, 102); **342.** visit to the Seelbach. (Larry Johnson, The Seelbach Hilton: A Centennial Salute to Louisville's Grand Hotel, Louisville: Butler Books, 2018, 59); **342.** *grains of salt.*" ("Remus Was," SPD, January 8, 1928); **343.** spectators in tears. ("Charlie Has," CP, September 13, 1957); **343.** I doing, kid?'" ("Charlie Has," CP, September 13, 1957)

Index

About the Author

Bob Batchelor is a critically acclaimed, bestselling cultural historian and biographer. He has published widely on American culture, history, and literature, including books on Stan Lee, Bob Dylan, *The Great Gatsby*, *Mad Men*, and John Updike. Bob earned his doctorate in English Literature from the University of South Florida. He teaches in the Media, Journalism & Film department at Miami University in Oxford, Ohio. Bob lives in Cincinnati, Ohio, with his wife, Suzette, and their two daughters.